The REWARDS of PATIENCE

Penfolds®

— SIXTH EDITION —

The REWARDS of PATIENCE

ANDREW CAILLARD

MASTER OF WINE

ALLEN&UNWIN

First edition 1986
This edition published in 2008

Copyright © Penfolds 2008

Allen & Unwin
83 Alexander Street
Crows Nest NSW 2065
Australia
Phone: (61 2) 8425 0100
Fax: (61 2) 9906 2218
Email: info@allenandunwin.com
Web: www.allenandunwin.com

National Library of Australia
Cataloguing-in-Publication entry:

Penfolds : the rewards of patience / Andrew Caillard.

6th ed.

ISBN 978 1 74175 596 1 (pbk.)
ISBN 978 1 74175 597 8 (special edition)

Penfolds Wines Pty Ltd.
Wine and wine making--South Australia.
Wine cellars--South Australia.

641.22099423

Internal design by Joanne Buckley
Photographs by Richard Humphrys, Adelaide
    and Penfolds' Image Library
Set in 10/13 pt Granjon
Printed in Australia by BPA Print Group, Burwood

10 9 8 7 6 5 4 3 2 1

Contents

Foreword

Penfolds: The Rewards of Patience is a unique book that follows our history, heritage and wines—vintage by vintage. The first edition, published in 1986, began an important tradition when the Penfolds winemaking team reviewed almost the entire body of work since we began making fine table wine. It was a modest book, but over the course of six editions it has grown in stature. We have invited many outside wine experts to these remarkably detailed tastings to help us understand progress made and to bring balanced and informed commentary. This sixth edition, published by Allen & Unwin, is another step up. It is a remarkably independent and authoritative book backed by thorough research, oral histories, vast personal experience and, of course, a library of Penfolds museum vintages.

The sixth edition panel members comprised international guests, Ch'ng Poh Tiong, the distinguished Singaporean wine critic; Joshua Greene, the influential publisher of the US magazine *Wine and Spirits*; and Neil Beckett, the scholarly editor of the UK's intellectual *World of Fine Wine*. Batting for the Australian side included Huon Hooke, authoritative wine journalist of the *Sydney Morning Herald*; James Halliday, the doyen of Australian wine writers, prolific author and columnist for *The Australian*; and Campbell Mattinson, one of Australia's most perceptive wine journalists and authors. Author Andrew Caillard, a Master of Wine and co-founder of Australia's leading wine auction house, Langton's Fine Wine Auctions, participated and chaired this profoundly historic tasting. It is doubtful that Penfolds can ever again replicate the extent of vintage reviews presented here.

As Chief Winemaker and the public face of Penfolds, I am mindful of the contribution of previous generations. Dr Ray Beckwith and Don Ditter both attended the tastings. John Bird, who straddles several decades of Penfolds vintages and continues to work as a Senior Red Winemaker, provided memorable anecdotes and useful context. Penfolds winemaking is teamwork and generational. The strength of Penfolds is that the wine comes first. We are custodians of a wonderful Australian tradition steeped in wine lore and the spirit of generosity.

I would therefore like to pay tribute to my winemaking team—especially Steve Lienert, Andrew Baldwin, Kym Schroeter and Tom Riley, and Oliver Crawford, former Senior White Winemaker—whose work has maintained and enhanced Penfolds' reputation across the globe. Paul Georgiadis, vigneron and Penfolds Grower Liaison Manager, has also brought considerable expertise. I would like to thank the Schubert Family for their continuing support and loyalty. Richard Humphrys, whose beautiful photographs are scattered throughout this book, is a nephew of Max Schubert.

As *Penfolds: The Rewards of Patience* reveals, Penfolds wines are better than ever before—yet they honour the ideas and philosophies of the past. It is this feeling of place and sense of purpose that culturally defines Penfolds. For many of us, Penfolds is a way of life. Our wines are made with the special care and attention you

would expect of master craftsmen, distinguished vineyards and great winemaking resources. Many Penfolds vintages build up complexity and richness with further bottle maturation. There is an extra ethereal and textural quality that comes with patience. This is the reward for buying and cellaring our wines.

I sincerely hope you enjoy the sixth edition of *Penfolds: The Rewards of Patience* and the Penfolds wine experience.

Peter Gago
Penfolds Chief Winemaker

Preface

The sixth edition of *Penfolds: The Rewards of Patience* comprises a wealth of information about Penfolds, its history and its wines. The tasting notes and commentary provide readers with a comprehensive overview of most Penfolds vintages. There are some gaps but these omitted wines are mostly old curios and experimental wines of minor interest.

The dotted-bar accompanying each tasting note gives the wine's 'drinking window'. This is the period over which the panel believes the wine will be drinking at its best. The bar bleeds away at the end because wine fades. It also shows that predictions are not necessarily definitive. Indeed there is a tendency for conservatism in Rewards of Patience tastings. As in previous reviews, panel members and winemakers were sometimes surprised by the evolution of vintages. Some wines have defied previous expectations, apparently either cheating the predictions of early death or evolving in rather unexpected ways. It is important, therefore, not to take the 'now' indication too literally. It means that the panel sees no likelihood of further improvement. The 'past' indication in the tasting notes suggests that the wine is either at or very near its end. In the case of older vintages of Grange, these wines remain valuable collectibles, but generally—and in all likelihood—these wines are past their best.

A star indicates exceptional vintages within each tasting bracket. Once again, a comparison of starred wines across five editions will reveal a number of upgrades and downgrades. Largely, however, there is a consistency of view that the 1955, 1962, 1963, 1971, 1976, 1983, 1986, 1990, 1991, 1996, 1998, 2002 and 2004 vintages are generally recognised as great Penfolds vintages.

In the text discussing the tastings, you will find taster's initials to remind the reader of the identities of the panel members. They are: Campbell Mattinson, Neil Beckett, Joshua Greene, Huon Hooke, Ch'ng Poh Tiong and James Halliday.

Periodically other comments are included from: Peter Gago—Penfolds Chief Winemaker, Don Ditter—former Penfolds Chief Winemaker, Dr Ray Beckwith—former Penfolds Research Chemist/Oenologist, Steve Lienert—Penfolds Senior Red Winemaker, Oliver Crawford—former Penfolds Senior White Winemaker, John Bird—former Penfolds Senior Winemaker and consultant, and myself, Andrew Caillard.

All the wines in this book come from Penfolds' own cellars and have been stored under optimum conditions. Cellaring conditions are important; temperature and humidity can accelerate or retard the ageing process. Readers should therefore understand that *Penfolds: The Rewards of Patience* is a collector's guide. The best way to enjoy the wines is to open the bottles and drink them!

The history and stories of Penfolds have also been further researched and updated. For this I am indebted to the recollections and trust of Penfolds winemakers and viticulturalists, past and present, the family of Max Schubert, media searches and my own library of old Australian wine journals and books. This includes editions of *The Wine Review* by Len Evans, *Classic Wines of Australia* by Max Lake and *Max Schubert—Winemaker* by Huon Hooke. Further, I have drawn substantially on the archives of Langton's, the wine auction house, and my own observations, interviews, Rewards of Patience tasting notes and comments and published articles of the last twenty years or so.

My sincere thanks to Bill and Collene Kalb who allowed me access to their extensive and unique collection of Penfolds memorabilia, photographer Richard Humphrys, Melissa da Silveira who commissioned and patiently navigated the sixth edition through to print, chief winemakers present and past, Peter Gago, John Duval and Don Ditter OAM, Allen & Unwin's editorial team, Diane Jardine, Angela Handley and Sue Hines, designer Joanne Buckley, and Stewart Langton and Tamara Grischy of Langton's. Also, I would like to especially thank my wife Bobby Caillard for her unswerving support from beginning to end.

Penfolds is a truly wonderful Australian wine house with a remarkable history and heritage. Max Schubert—the creator of Grange—always recognised that winemaking and wine business was a collaborative effort. While succeeding chief winemakers have taken responsibility for the style and quality of Penfolds wines, there are literally hundreds of people—including cellar hands, technical assistants, administrative and sales staff—who have given their working lives to Penfolds. It is a rollcall of exceptional and dedicated people who are inextricably involved in the Penfolds story. Without their contribution these utterly unique and beautiful wines would not resonate so profoundly.

I hope you enjoy this substantial and definitive guide to cellaring and enjoying Penfolds wines.

Andrew Caillard, MW

PART ONE

The
REWARDS
of
PATIENCE

CHAPTER ONE

The Story of Penfolds

The story of Penfolds is inextricably linked to South Australia's colonial settlement and Australia's subsequent journey to nationhood and the modern era. In 1844, eight years after the colony was established, Dr Christopher Rawson Penfold, a medical practitioner from near Brighton, England, and his wife, Mary, purchased 'the delightfully situated and truly valuable estate of Mackgill [named after Sir Maitland Mackgill], for the sum of £1200 ... comprising 500 acres of the choicest land'. The estate was farmed by Mary Penfold while her husband built up a busy medical practice. By all contemporary accounts it was Mary Penfold who was responsible for the management and early winemaking responsibilities of the fledgling wine estate. Initially the wines—made from grenache—were prescribed as tonic wines for anaemic patients. The famous Penfolds slogan '1844 to evermore' harks back to Penfolds' origins as a prescribed tonic. During the early years the Penfolds also grew barley, which was made into beer and sold at the nearby World's End Pub—where the wagon trains of the time terminated. Records survive today of Mary Penfold's wine output during the 1860s:

Wine in wood:

—No. 1 quarter cask white wine—mixture Sweet Water and Frontignac— made March 17/64.

—No. 2, 5 gallons red wine—mixture—made March 24/64.

—Wicker bottle—all Frontignac—made March 17/64.

—April 29th, racked off 10 gallons Muscat from that held—made by AG 1862.

—May 9th, 28 gals. Muscat—made April 30th—turned.

—May 9/1864 exposed to the air 3 days, then covered.

A catalogue of 1889 lists wines from the Grange and Magill vineyards such as: Mataro, Grenache, Constantia, Grange Port, Frontignac, Grange Tawny, Pedro Ximenes, Tokay, Madeira, Grange Sherry and Muscadine. The catalogue adds: 'We have also light Red and White dinner wines of Claret and Riesling types, suitable for use in clubs.'

By 1870 the Grange vineyard comprised over 60 acres with several different grape varieties including grenache, verdelho, mataro (mourvèdre), frontignac and pedro ximenez. The estate was producing both sweet and dry red and white table wines with a growing market in the eastern Australian colonies of Victoria and New South Wales. Indeed, Penfolds and Co.—the newly formed partnership of Mary Penfold, her highly ambitious but devoted son-in-law Thomas Hyland and her cellar manager Joseph Gillard—now claimed to be making over one-third of South Australia's wine production. Mary Penfold died in 1896, her remarkable contribution to Australia's wine industry largely overshadowed by her husband's position and popularity.

Out of affection, the Hyland grandchildren adopted the surname Penfold Hyland. Herbert Leslie Penfold Hyland took over the business in 1905 overseeing substantial expansion of Penfolds and enjoying all the trade benefits of the newly formed federation of Australia. His brother Frank, based in Sydney, oversaw considerable expansion of the business in New South Wales.

Fortified wine production dominated the industry throughout the first part of the 1900s and Penfolds gained a strong reputation for its fortified wines during the 1920s and '30s. Between the world wars the market for fine table wine in Australia was extremely limited. Penfolds did, however, produce an 'Italian Red' for Italian migrants working the cane fields of Queensland, but by the 1930s sparkling wine became fashionable. No old bottles of Penfolds table wines prior to 1945 have been sold on the secondary wine market over the last 40 years. A bottle (albeit without original contents) of Penfolds Muscadine circa 1900—with original Dr Penfold's Grange Vineyards label—lies at Penfolds cellar door at Magill. This perhaps reflects the way people drank wines in those days (in flagons) and the fact that they were never made to keep. However, the company began as a producer of sweet white, light table and tonic wines for both the domestic and export markets.

In 1943, Penfolds acquired the highly regarded and valuable Auldana Vineyard and winery—adjacent to the Magill vineyard. In 1945, Penfolds purchased the Kalimna Vineyard in the Barossa Valley—at the time the largest vineyard in South Australia. By the late 1940s Penfolds had acquired or planted vineyards in McLaren Vale, Griffith, the Hunter Valley and Minchinbury (now a western suburb of Sydney). The wine market was changing rapidly as soldiers retuned from the war and new immigrants from Italy, Greece and Eastern Europe settled in Australia. With this new multiculturalism came a new orientation towards dry table wine. Max Schubert, a young, inquisitive winemaker at Penfolds, returned to Europe after the war to investigate winemaking. The mission was to learn about sherry production but a side trip to Bordeaux led to the extraordinary development of Penfolds Grange and the production and refinement of dry and sparkling table wines.

At the same time, experimentation and research underpinned the winemaking regime at Penfolds. Ray Beckwith, the brilliant Penfolds research chemist, introduced the use of pH meters to control bacterial spoilage. Indeed, the entire 1950s embraced major advances in winemaking techniques from yeast technology to fermentation practices (particularly barrel fermentation in American oak) and oak maturation.

The years of innovation began a tradition of research and development at Penfolds. In 1951, Max Schubert began experimenting with the idea of making a long-lived red wine called Grange and in the mid-1950s John Davoren, a highly skilled and innovative senior Penfolds winemaker, came up with the elegantly styled St Henri Claret. During the 1960s Penfolds entered a bewildering number of experimental or one-off wines into Australian wine shows. The legendary Bin 60A— a blend of Coonawarra cabernet and Kalimna shiraz—is regarded by many as one of the greatest Australian wines ever made. Even today, old bottles with previously forgotten bin numbers or vintages turn up illustrating the sheer hive of activity at Penfolds during this period.

By the early 1960s, Max Schubert said he saw the creation of a dynasty of wines that may differ in character from year to year, but would all bear an unmistakable resemblance and relationship to each other. The backbone of Penfolds' emerging red wine portfolio—Bin 389, Bin 707, Bin 28 and Bin 128—were introduced during the 1960s, a time of considerable organisational change. Now a publicly listed company, Penfolds was already well known for its quality production focus. Over the following years, the Penfolds brand began to concentrate on red wine production and its vineyard and cellar assets in South Australia, culminating with the highly successful 'All You Need to Know about Red Wine' marketing campaign in the mid-1980s.

The Penfolds house wine style was immensely popular at every price level because it delivered quality and reliability. In 1976, Koonunga Hill 'Claret' (later called Koonunga Hill Shiraz-Cabernet) was introduced, gaining instant recognition from the consumer. It was also the year that Max Schubert retired—the baton of Penfolds' Chief Winemaker passed to veteran 'offsider' and senior Penfolds winemaker Don Ditter. The latter's contribution to and refinement of house style is palpable—especially considering the corporate upheavals of the time as company ownership and management changed. The remarkable reintroduction of Penfolds Bin 707 in 1976 illustrated Penfolds' commitment to a premium cabernet sauvignon. Within just a few years Bin 707 would be recognised as one of Australia's leading wines—illustrating that taking a step backwards by discontinuing the bin number after the 1969 vintage in favour of improving vineyard resources was a move forward for all Penfolds wines.

The launch of Magill Estate Shiraz (first vintage 1983) was an important addition to the Penfolds stable. The fruit from the Grange vineyard at Magill, mostly replanted to shiraz in the early 1950s, had been used for Grange, but it was felt that this remaining small patch of vines—barely 15 acres—should be put to a more meaningful use. The idea of a single vineyard shiraz from where Dr Christopher and Mary Penfold first planted their vineyard in 1844 would provide a link with the past. It would also mean that this important vineyard site would be protected from further suburban encroachment. The evolution of the Magill Estate wine style is fascinating because it has embraced both house style and the character of a single vineyard site without compromise.

In 1986, John Duval, 'understudy' of both Max Schubert and Don Ditter, took over as Penfolds' Chief Winemaker, ensuring a smooth transition of winemaking philosophy. Refinement of house style continued throughout the 1980s. John Duval's outstanding technical ability and instinctive nature are decisively illustrated in the profoundly opulent and beautifully balanced wines of the 1986 vintage—an important waypoint in the evolution of Penfolds wines. The 1990 and 1991 vintages, both remarkable Penfolds years, underscore his considerable talents as a team leader and chief winemaker.

The fortunes of Penfolds went arm-in-arm with the exponential successes in export markets. In 1988, Max Schubert, retired but still on the scene as a mentor, was named *Decanter* magazine's (UK) Man of the Year in recognition of his contribution to wine and the emerging importance of Penfolds in the world markets. This was followed by John Duval winning International Winemaker of the Year at the International Wine & Spirit Competition in the UK in 1989. In 1990, Penfolds was acquired by South Australian Brewing Holdings, marking a new chapter in its history.

The 1990s saw the introduction of an unprecedented number of new wine styles within the Penfolds portfolio. At the commercial entry-point level, Penfolds released Rawson's Retreat (both red and white) and enhanced the Koonunga Hill range with a Semillon Sauvignon Blanc and a Chardonnay. This was also a period of intense winemaking trials. The search for new wine expressions and experiences was reminiscent of the 1960s. The 'White Grange' project spawned the release of Penfolds Yattarna Chardonnay from the 1995 vintage. The barrage of media attention was extraordinary, illustrating Australia's national interest in the Penfolds brand. Red wine trials resulted in the release of Penfolds' first Barossa shiraz, RWT (Red Winemaking Trial), a wine which is matured in French oak. Penfolds continues to experiment—within the vineyard and the winery—to improve and enhance its wines at every quality level.

The 1990s also saw an extraordinary level of critical acclaim for both Penfolds wines and its winemakers. John Duval won the Red Winemaker of the Year at the International Wine Challenge in 1991. In August 1995, Robert Parker, the world's most influential wine critic, wrote in his self-published newsletter *The Wine Advocate* that Grange was 'a leading candidate for the richest, most concentrated dry table wine on planet earth'. By the end of that year, *Wine Spectator* had named the 1990 Grange its Wine of the Year.

In Australia, Penfolds also won considerable acclaim. Since 1991, Grange has held pride of place at the head of Langton's Classification of Australian Wine. The elite Bin 707, St Henri, Magill Estate and Bin 389 are also included in this internationally recognised benchmark listing of Australian wines. The introduction of Penfolds Red Wine Re-corking Clinics throughout Australia's major centres, and subsequently in New Zealand, the United Kingdom, Europe, the United States and Asia, is an ongoing project which emphasises the ageing qualities and secondary-market importance of the Penfolds brand. Over 90,000 bottles have been re-corked since the clinics began.

In 2001, Penfolds celebrated the 50th anniversary of Penfolds Grange at Magill, announcing plans to return some winemaking and maturation of Grange back to its original home. The following week, a rare bottle of 1951 Grange Hermitage in perfect condition sold at auction for a record A$52,211. It was also the year that the National Trust of South Australia, in a remarkable gesture, listed Penfolds Grange as a heritage icon. In 2002, grapes destined for Grange were crushed and vinified at Magill Estate for the first time since 1973. It was also the year that the baton of Chief Winemaker was passed on to veteran oenologist Peter Gago. Since 2002, Penfolds has reached into every major wine market of the world. The wines are widely celebrated for their diversity and quality across many price points. The strength of Penfolds is that wine comes first. Penfolds' range of table wines is utterly Australian, evoking a generosity of spirit and the beauty of the Australian landscape.

Penfolds Wines Pty.
VINTAGE 1955
BOTTLED
BIN 14
Grange
NET CONTENTS 26 FL.

CHAPTER TWO

'The Story of Grange'

by Max Schubert

Taken from a paper delivered at the first Australian National University
Wine Symposium in Canberra in September 1979

So much has been spoken and so much written about Grange Hermitage over the years that, as its originator, I welcome the opportunity of adding my own measure to the volume that has gone before, particularly as the spoken and written word has not always been laudatory, but often quite distinctly the reverse.

Grange Hermitage has always been a controversial and individual wine. It is my belief that if these two characteristics can be combined, then at least half the ingredients necessary for success have been achieved.

Grange Hermitage has been argued and debated around countless dinner tables. In its early years it was insulted and classified among the lowest of the low, yet through all this it has stood out as an individual wine with its own particular personality and has been consumed in copious quantity, whether it be with praise and pleasure or with dislike and condemnation.

It has been almost unbeatable in wine shows, whether it be in the young vintage classes or the old open classes, having accumulated since 1962 some 126 gold, 76 silver and 42 bronze medals, plus 28 trophies and seven championship awards. It has even won two Jimmy Watson trophies at the Royal Melbourne Wine Show, which is surprising as it is not the type of wine that usually wins Jimmy Watson awards—not because of its quality, but because of its revolutionary style.

It is a truly controversial wine, never without interest and always open to debate in one way or another. How, then, did an individual wine of this nature come into being?

It was during my initial visit to the major wine-growing areas of Europe in 1950 that the idea of producing an Australian red wine capable of staying alive for a minimum of twenty years and comparable with those produced in Bordeaux first entered my mind. I was fortunate to be taken under the wing of Monsieur Christian Cruse, one of the most respected and highly qualified wine men of the old school of France at that time and he afforded me, among other things, the rare opportunity of tasting and evaluating Bordeaux wines between 40 and 50 years old, which were still sound and possessed magnificent bouquet and flavour. They were of tremendous value from an educational point of view and imbued in me a desire to attempt to do something to lift the rather mediocre standard of Australian red wine in general at that time.

The method of production seemed fairly straightforward, but with several unorthodox features, and I felt that it would only be a matter of undertaking a complete survey of vineyards to find the correct varietal grape material. Then, with a modified approach to take account of differing conditions such as climate, soil, raw material and techniques generally, it would not be impossible to produce a wine which could stand on its own feet throughout the world and would be capable of improvement year by year for a minimum of twenty years. In other words, something different and lasting.

The grape material used in Bordeaux consisted of our basic varieties, namely cabernet sauvignon, cabernet franc, merlot and malbec, and these were used in varying percentages to make the Bordeaux wines. Only cabernet sauvignon and malbec were available in South Australia at the time, but a survey showed that they were in such short supply as to make them impracticable commercially—after all, the development of a new commercial wine, particularly of the high-grade range, depends on the quality and availability of the raw material, the maintenance of standards and continuity of supply.

I elected to use hermitage or shiraz only (which was in plentiful supply) knowing full well that if I was careful enough in the choice of area and vineyard and coupled that with the correct production procedure, I would be able to make the type and style of wine I wanted. If necessary, I could always use a small percentage of cabernet or malbec from our own Kalimna Vineyard in the Barossa Valley as a balancing factor to lift flavour and character. As it happened, this was not necessary, at least not in the early Granges.

It was finally decided that the raw material for the first experimental Grange Hermitage would be a mixture of shiraz grapes from two separate vineyards and areas consisting of Penfolds Grange vineyards at Magill in the foothills overlooking Adelaide and a private vineyard some distance south of Adelaide. I had already observed that both vineyards produced wines of distinctive varietal flavour and character with a great depth of colour and body weight, and felt that by producing them together the outstanding characteristics of both vineyards would result in an improved all-round wine eminently suitable for my purpose.

Accordingly, during the 1951 vintage the first Grange experimental wine was made incorporating five new untreated oak hogsheads which I had observed were used to such good effect in France and other European countries. The objective was to produce a big, full-bodied wine containing maximum extraction of all the components in the grape material used.

The procedure employed was first to ensure that the grape material was sound and that the acid and sugar content was in balance consistent with the style of wine as specified. Using the Baumé scale, this was to be not less than 11.5 degrees and not more than 12 degrees with a total acidity of not less than 6.5 grams per litre and not more than 7 grams per litre. With strict attention to detail and close surveillance, this was achieved.

The grapes were gathered and crushed and the must (consisting of skins, seeds and other solids comprising the fleshy part of the grape) and juice were pumped into a 12-tonne open concrete fermentation tank. During this operation the must received a dose of sulphur dioxide, to neutralise the wild yeasts, and an injection of pure yeast culture previously acclimatised to the level of sulphur dioxide used. The tank was filled to the exact level required. Boards, known as heading-down boards, were placed across the surface of the must in the open tank, with a narrow gap between each board. These were secured by two strong pieces of timber placed across the boards and locked in position underneath four lugs built into the upper tank walls. Fermentation began almost immediately and as carbon dioxide gas pressure developed, the juice was forced through the narrow gaps between the boards, keeping the skins and other solids completely immersed underneath the surface.

Although this was all fairly basic, it was important in achieving complete extraction during fermentation, particularly if viewed in conjunction with other procedures which followed. For instance, it was thought that in order to obtain full extraction, a much longer period of fermentation and skin contact would be required, necessitating strict fermentation control. This was to be achieved by controlling the temperature generated by the fermentation on the basis that the lower the temperature, the slower the rate of fermentation, since there would be a considerable reduction in the heat generated by the yeast in its frantic efforts to multiply and convert the grape sugars into alcohol. Of course, vice versa, by allowing the temperature to rise, an increase in fermentation rate would result. Temperature control was to be achieved by incorporating a heat exchanger in the process.

The actual fermentation rate in this case was governed by the predetermined length of fermentation, which was set at twelve days. This required a fermentation sugar conversion rate of approximately 1 Baumé degree per day. A further measure of control was achieved by using a graph system which showed the ideal fermentation line over a twelve-day period compared with the actual fermentation line, which was governed by daily temperature and Baumé readings of the fermenting juice. A glance at the graph immediately showed the degree of cooling or heating required to maintain an even daily rate of fermentation over the period stipulated.

I had previously determined that to assist in obtaining full extraction it would be necessary to separate the fermenting juice from the skins by completely draining the tank. This would cause all the solids, including the heading-down boards and cross pieces, to settle on the bottom of the tank. Then we would pump the juice back over the top so that it would percolate through the skins and other solids, thus extracting further essentials in colour, flavour and character. As the tank filled, the head boards would rise on the surface until they were again locked into position by the cross pieces. It was a comparatively simple matter to incorporate a heat exchanger in this process using salt brine as the coolant to achieve temperature control as indicated by the graph.

Fermentation proceeded slowly but evenly and the development of colour, body and character was extremely interesting. As the process approached its end, I decided that extraction from the solids was sufficient and that no useful purpose would be served by prolonging skin contact.

The fermenting wine was a beautiful rich, dark, ruby red already showing above-average body, bouquet and fruit flavour. In addition, a general slowing down of fermentation, which is normal during the latter stages, meant that temperature was no longer a problem and cooling could be dispensed with. In fact, a slight increase in temperature was desirable at this stage as an encouragement for the flagging yeast to complete the conversion of the remaining sugar into alcohol.

The wine was then separated from the solids for the last time, a portion was transferred to the five new untreated oak hogsheads, and the remainder to a 1000-gallon [4550-litre] well-seasoned, dry red cask. This was to be the control wine used to measure the success or failure of the new experimental hogshead wine. [This actually translates to a final bottling volume of three hogsheads.]

The solids that were left in the fermenting tank were removed and pressed and the pressings stored in small seasoned casks holding 30 gallons [approximately 140 litres]. This would be used later as a topping-up wine to keep the containers filled to the brim at all times. Topping-up is a preventative measure against bacterial infections and also makes good the removal of lees or deposits which accumulate on the bottom of containers during the self-clarification process following completion of fermentation. It was also intended to use the pressings as a balancing medium for the experimental wine before bottling if required.

The experimental hogsheads were stored in underground cellars where the temperature was constant at 15 degrees Celsius and fermentation was completed in twelve days as previously determined. Within a month, vast differences became apparent between the experimental hogsheads and the control cask. Whereas the control wine showed all the characteristics of a good, well-made wine cast in the orthodox mould, the experimental wine was strikingly different. The volume of bouquet, comprising raw oak mixed with natural varietal fruit, was tremendous. These characteristics were also very apparent on the palate. The overall flavour was much more intense than the control and for a big young wine, the balance was superb. To my mind, even at this early stage, there was no doubt that this wine would be different, with almost unlimited potential if handled correctly.

During the months that followed, treatment was confined to the removal of lees from all containers, including the control cask, and the addition of small amounts

of tannic acid. After twelve months both wines were crystal clear, with superb dark, full, rich colour and body—but there the similarity ended. The experimental wine was bigger in all respects. It was a big wine in bouquet, flavour and balance. The raw wood was not so apparent, but the fruit characteristics had become pronounced and defined with more than a faint suggestion of cranberry. It was almost as if the new wood had acted as a catalyst to release previously unsuspected flavours and aromas from the hermitage grape.

I was delighted with the result of the experiment so far. To my mind, the marriage of all components had taken place and it required only the sealing of all these wonderful characteristics into bottles for the marriage to be consummated.

After a total wood storage of eighteen months and without any further treatment, the wine was bottled and binned away in underground bins where the temperature was more or less consistent at 15 degrees Celsius.

Several hundred dozen of the control wine were also bottled and, while it developed into an exceptionally good wine in the orthodox manner, it never reached the heights of the first experimental Grange Hermitage. It did, however, set the guidelines for the production and marketing of a whole range of special red wines which have been sought after, vintage by vintage, to this day.

In the meantime, the 1952 vintage had come and gone with an increase in production of Grange Hermitage, using the same raw material and method of production with similar results. It was superb wine to my mind.

A variation occurred in 1953 in that, in addition to Hermitage, a straight cabernet sauvignon from our Kalimna Vineyard in the Barossa Valley was made experimentally, employing the same method of production as for Grange. The quantity made was five hogsheads, as in 1951. The decision to make an experimental cabernet at all, despite the shortage of this variety, was influenced by the fact that in 1953 the analytical balance of the grapes was similar to that laid down for Grange.

To obtain balanced cabernet, at least in my sphere of operations at that time, was rare and while the volume of flavour and character of the finished wine was usually magnificent, the imbalance of the fruit invariably manifested itself on the palate with a noticeable break in the middle and a thinnish, hard, astringent finish. However, this was not so with the 1953 vintage and I still rank this wine as one of the best Grange-style wines made.

As vintage followed vintage, the accumulation of bottled stock grew and the improvement shown in the earlier vintages was all that I had hoped for. Gone was any suggestion of raw wood; a complete wine was emerging with a full, buoyant, almost ethereal nose of great intensity and a palate which was full of rich flavour and character. The balance in every vintage, I thought, was near perfect. The time appeared to be ripe to remove the wraps and allow other people to see and evaluate this wondrous thing. Besides, my superiors at head office in Sydney were becoming increasingly aware of the large amount of money lying idle in their underground cellars at Magill.

Representative bottles from each vintage from 1951 to 1956 were called for and a wine tasting was arranged by the Managing Director. Those invited included well-known wine identities in Sydney, personal friends of the board and top management. The result was absolutely disastrous. Simply, no one liked Grange Hermitage.

It was unbelievable and, I must confess, that for the first time I had misgivings about my own assessment of Grange. However, I was determined to prove the Sydney people wrong and, with the help and support of Jeffrey Penfold Hyland who was then Assistant General Manager of our South Australian operations, numerous tastings were arranged in and around Adelaide and at Magill. We availed ourselves of every opportunity, donating various vintages to wine and food societies, Beefsteak and Burgundy Clubs and wherever wine drinkers congregated. However, the general reaction was little better than the earlier disaster in Sydney.

It may be illuminating at this time to record some of the assessments made by experts and critics alike in public and in my presence during the darkest hours of Grange Hermitage. Some of the remarks were downright rude and pained me no end: '*A concoction of wild fruits and sundry berries with crushed ants predominating.*'

This, by a well-known, respected wine man: '*Schubert, I congratulate you. A very good, dry port, which no one in their right mind will buy—let alone drink.*'

Then there was the smart person who wanted me to give him a couple of dozen. He was not going to pay for it because he did not think it was worth anything. Another very smart one wanted to buy it and use it as an aphrodisiac. His theory was that the wine was like bull's blood in all respects and would raise his blood count to twice the norm when the occasion demanded. A young doctor friend even thought he could use it as an anaesthetic on his girlfriend. I could go on, but I think that will give you an idea of Grange's initial reception by most people at that time.

There were, of course, some notable exceptions whose faith in Grange never wavered. They were people such as Jeffrey Penfold Hyland, without whose support Grange would have died a natural but not peaceful death, George Fairbrother, that doyen of wine judges, Tony Nelson, at that time Managing Director of Woodley Wines, Douglas Lamb, who needs no introduction from me, and Dr Max Lake who, I recall, either purchased for a song or consumed most of the 1953 experimental cabernet himself.

There were others who would not commit themselves, but preferred to wait and see. At least they did not condemn and were prepared to give the wine a chance. To all these I offer my gratitude.

The final blow came just before the 1957 vintage when I received written instructions from head office to stop production of Grange Hermitage. The main reasons given were that I was accumulating large stocks of wine which to all intents and purposes were unsaleable and that the adverse criticism directed at the wine was harmful to the company image as a whole. It appeared to be the end.

However, with Jeffrey Penfold Hyland's support, I disregarded the written instructions in part and continued to make Grange in reduced quantities. Finance was not available to purchase new hogsheads, but some benefit was gained by using hogsheads from previous vintages. This undercover production continued through to 1959 and the wines made, although good, lacked that one element which made the difference between a good wine and a great wine.

In all, it was ten years from the time the first experimental Grange was made before the wine gained general acceptance and the prejudices were overcome. As the earlier vintages matured in bottle and progressively became less aggressive and more refined, people generally began to take notice and, whereas previously it had been all condemnation, I was now at least receiving some praise for the wine. A little of this filtered through to my board of directors with the result that just before the 1960 vintage I was instructed to start making Grange Hermitage officially again, with ample funds available for this purpose. Since that time, Grange Hermitage has never looked back.

In 1962, after many years absence from Australian wine shows, the company decided again to take part in these competitions and Grange was first submitted as an entry in the Open Claret class in the Sydney show of that year. It was awarded a gold medal. This was the 1955 vintage which, in my humble opinion, was one of the best Granges ever produced. This wine won more than 50 gold medals until its retirement from the show arena in the late 1970s, not because it was defective in any way—in fact, in 1977 it was awarded the trophy for the best dry red in the Melbourne show—but because my board wished to give later vintages the opportunity of winning or adding to the number of gold medals already won.

In retrospect, the 1950s were exciting years of discovery, faith, doubt, humiliation and triumph. The 1960s were rewarding years of contentment in the knowledge that the continued making of Grange was in good hands.

I wish to pay tribute to the many winemakers, technicians, cellar managers, senior cellar hands and vineyard supervisors who, over the years, so ably assisted me in the making of Grange. Each one had a part to play in every vintage made and, even though I always retained absolute control of all stages of Grange production and indeed, company production generally, without their help, support, interest, and cooperation, it would have been almost impossible for me to cope, particularly in the later years before my retirement in 1975.

I would also like to express the hope that the production and the acceptance of Grange Hermitage as a great Australian wine have proved that we in Australia are capable of producing wines equal to the best in the world. But we must not be afraid to put into effect the strength of our own convictions, continue to use our imagination in winemaking generally, and be prepared to experiment in order to gain something extra, different and unique in the world of wine.

CHAPTER THREE

The Vineyards

The reputation, history and development of Penfolds wines is interwoven with the quality and individual character of company-owned and independently grown vineyards. At the very heart of Penfolds' winemaking philosophy is the requirement of the 'right fruit'. The purchase of the Kalimna Vineyard in 1945 and the subsequent acquisition of vineyard land during the 1960s in Coonawarra was a deliberate effort to take Penfolds forward into the brave new world of Australian fine wine.

With the loss of great old vineyards including Auldana, Modbury, Morphett Vale and most of Magill during the 1960s and '70s, Penfolds instigated a long-term strategy of establishing exceptional vineyard sites that would ensure the long-term quality and supply requirements of the Penfolds brand. Today, Penfolds owns a substantial network of vineyards in South Australia and has access to a wide range of sister company and independently grown fruit across the country.

Over the years, extraordinary progress has been made in vineyard management through refinement, innovation and inventiveness and Penfolds' viticulture and vineyard practices are highly regarded by the Australian wine industry. The management and control of vineyards is something of a cat and mouse game. Penfolds viticulturalists are constantly searching for new vineyard sites, improving established vineyards, providing the best possible technical advice and optimising the best results for its 350 independent growers.

Paul Georgiadis, Penfolds Grower Relations Manager in South Australia, says, 'A Penfolds vineyard is always an object of desire and a Grange vineyard is a tantalising prize. Independent growers have stayed with Penfolds for generations appreciating the long-term relationship with the winemakers and viticultural team. It's this collaborative effort and pride that underpins the success of the Penfolds brand.'

THE PENFOLDS VINEYARDS

Penfolds has a long history of vineyard ownership. In 1844 Dr Penfold was congratulated for purchasing a well-sited vineyard. *The South Australian Register* of 8 August 1844 reported the arrival of Dr Penfold in the colony, adding, 'he is the fortunate purchaser of the delightfully situated and truly valuable estate of Mackgill at the sum of £1200'. A century later, Penfolds had become a major landholder with substantial vineyard and winery holdings throughout New South Wales and South Australia, producing an array of light table and sparkling wines, ports and sherries. Today, however, Penfolds is predominantly a South Australian brand, sourcing fruit from its own vineyards and from independent growers. New South Wales, Victoria and Tasmania feature in cameo roles with a few vineyards contributing fruit to Yattarna and a number of Penfolds white wines including Bin 311 Chardonnay.

By the late 1890s, phylloxera arrived in the eastern states of Victoria and New South Wales, decimating entire vineyards and causing significant reduction in wine production. South Australia, which has always been free of this vine disease pest, almost doubled in vineyard size in just ten years during the 1890s from 12,314 acres to 20,860 acres. For the entire twentieth century and to the present day, South Australia has been the premier wine state of Australia.

Federation in 1901 brought new opportunities for Penfolds. In 1905, Frank Penfold Hyland purchased the Dalwood vineyards at Branxton—a famous Hunter Valley vineyard in New South Wales established by George Wyndham in 1827. This vineyard had a total area of 70 acres under vines of red hermitage, riesling, white shiraz, madeira, pineau and riesling. Wines from Magill and Dalwood were sent to Sydney for blending and bottling.

A period of growth followed with significant purchase of vineyards and construction of wineries. McLaren Vale was established in 1910 and the Nuriootpa winery was completed prior to the 1913 vintage. Although Minchinbury was purchased in 1913, the Great War intervened and kept expansion plans on hold. After the war, Minchinbury became famous for its sparkling wine and a light white wine called Trameah. Penfolds also established a winery in Griffith to process grapes for returned soldiers repatriated to the Murrumbidgee Irrigation Area by the New South Wales government. Frank Penfold Hyland offered an eight-year contract to growers at a minimum £8 a ton. The winery, which could crush around 250 tons a day, was ready for the 1921 vintage. Penfolds assisted around 300 settlers, providing plant material from its own nurseries and vineyards. Its association with the region lasted for decades.

In 1920, Penfolds built a winery and distillery in the Eden Valley. The improvement in road transport resulted in its early closure. However, it was used for the storage of flor sherry for many years. In 1920, Penfolds acquired the Sparkling Vale property in the Hunter Valley and installed Harold Davoren—the father of John Davoren, the creator of St Henri—as manager. Penfolds' wine business prospered throughout the 1930s with a strong emphasis on vineyards in New South Wales and South Australia. During the 1940s, Penfolds made some of its most important

AUSTRALIA

SOUTH AUSTRALIA

NEW SOUTH WALES

VICTORIA

TASMANIA

Orange • SYDNEY•

• Tumbarumba

• Henty • MELBOURNE

Derwent River
HOBART•

NEW SOUTH WALES,
VICTORIA & TASMANIA

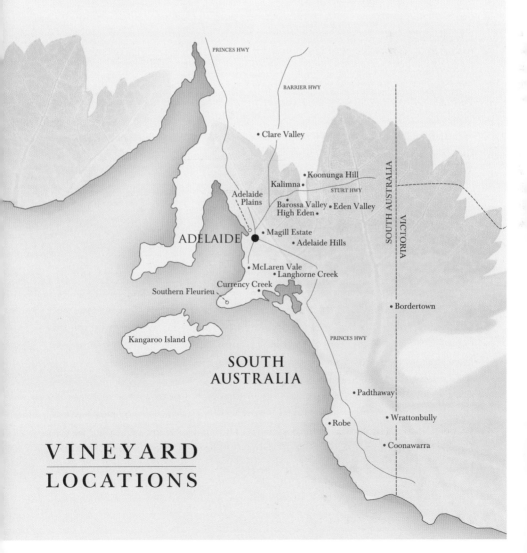

PRINCES HWY

BARRIER HWY

• Clare Valley

• Koonunga Hill
Kalimna •

STURT HWY

Adelaide
Plains

Barossa Valley • Eden Valley
High Eden •

ADELAIDE • Magill Estate

• Adelaide Hills

SOUTH AUSTRALIA

VICTORIA

• McLaren Vale
• Langhorne Creek

Currency Creek

Southern Fleurieu •

• Bordertown

Kangaroo Island

SOUTH
AUSTRALIA

PRINCES HWY

• Padthaway

• Robe

• Wrattonbully

• Coonawarra

VINEYARD
LOCATIONS

purchases, including more vineyard land in the Hunter Valley, Auldana cellars and vineyard adjacent to Magill, and the magnificent Kalimna Vineyard in the Barossa Valley. Both Nuriootpa and the Griffith wineries were also expanded to cope with the increasing intake of fruit. The sheer extent of Penfolds' vineyards was quite remarkable. By the 1940s, Penfolds was a major producer of fortified and sparkling wines. This heritage is of special significance. The emerging Penfolds red winemaking ethos of multi-district blending was a natural progression from the days of fortified and sparkling winemaking where house style played a critical role in capturing the loyalty of the consumer.

The acquisition of vineyards during the 1940s by Penfolds was effectively an each way bet on the future of post-war Australian wine culture. Frank and Jeffrey Penfold Hyland knew that the market would change—irrevocably—with the arrival of returned soldiers, refugees and immigrants. Initially providing fruit for its fortified wines, these vineyards would become an important source for Penfolds' emerging table-wine portfolio. Some of the early vineyards have now disappeared, mostly sold off because of intense urban pressure. These include the Auldana Vineyard— the original source of St Henri—and the Modbury Vineyard, further north in the Adelaide foothills. A small portion of the historic Grange Vineyard—now known as Magill Estate Vineyard—was saved and is now heritage-protected. A period of further consolidation followed during the 1960s and '70s, including the purchase of new vineyards in Coonawarra and the gradual sale of vineyards and winery assets in New South Wales. By the mid-1970s, Penfolds was once again predominantly a South Australian brand sourcing fruit from its own vineyards and from independent growers.

Some Penfolds vineyards have gone from strength to strength. Kalimna Vineyard is of special significance. It is an important historic Barossa Valley vineyard with many famous wines to its credit including the 1953 Penfolds Grange Cabernet and the 1962 Penfolds Bin 60A Coonawarra Cabernet Sauvignon, Kalimna Shiraz. Penfolds Bin 28 Kalimna Shiraz was originally a single-vineyard wine. Kalimna is also a regular contributor to Grange. In more recent times it has been dubbed the Grange 'Mother Vineyard'. The Koonunga Hill Vineyard, another Barossa vineyard, was established in 1973. It not only inspired Penfolds' Koonunga Hill label, but produces such high-quality fruit that it is considered a sister vineyard to Kalimna. Today Penfolds has significant vineyard holdings in the Barossa, but also draws fruit from a number of independent growers, many of whom are members of the elite Shiraz Growers Club and Grange Growers Club, because of the exceptional quality of their grapes.

Penfolds' investment in vineyards extends throughout South Australia's premium wine districts. Penfolds was an early investor in the region of Coonawarra, purchasing vineyards in the early 1960s. Penfolds Bin 128 Coonawarra Shiraz was initially a single-vineyard wine but now draws fruit from multi-vineyard sites. Penfolds also owns vineyards in McLaren Vale, Clare Valley and the emerging viticultural areas of Bordertown and Robe on South Australia's Limestone Coast. The sheer diversity and quality of regional provenance, vineyard sites and independently grown fruit provides Penfolds' winemakers with a rich palette of colour, aroma and texture—a superb resource which allows a remarkable consistency of style and quality across the Penfolds brand.

VINEYARD HOLDINGS

Adelaide environs

MAGILL ESTATE VINEYARD

Location:	Magill, Adelaide, 8 km east of CBD.
Vineyard:	Gentle, west-facing slopes ranging from 130 m to 180 m (430 ft–600 ft) at the base of the Adelaide Hills.
Soils:	Fertile red-brown soils.
Rainfall:	Average rainfall is 502 mm (20 in). About 221 mm falls during the growing season.
Irrigation:	All dry grown.
Viticulture:	Original shiraz vines were planted in 1951 with most recent plantings in 1985. Hand pruned and hand harvested. Yields on average usually less than 30 tonnes from entire estate.
Grape varieties:	Shiraz only.

The historic and heritage-protected Magill Estate Vineyard was established in 1844 by Dr Christopher Rawson and Mary Penfold—just eight years after the foundation of Adelaide. It was originally known as the Grange Vineyard, named after their new homestead 'The Grange', a cottage which still stands intact amongst the vines. In later years, this vineyard would inspire and supply fruit for Penfolds Grange—arguably Australia's greatest wine. The vineyard was first planted with grenache from cuttings taken from the South of France. At its peak in 1949 the vineyard, planted to several different grape varieties on rich chocolaty red-brown soils, covered 120 hectares of gentle north-west facing slopes. During the 1950s and '60s it was replanted with riesling, cabernet sauvignon, shiraz and mataro (mourvèdre), reflecting the waning demand for fortifieds and the increasing interest in table wines. Urban pressure (largely through commercially unsustainable land rates) and compulsory acquisition gradually forced the erosion of this vineyard to its present size of 5.24 hectares (12.94 acres). The Magill Estate Vineyard, one of the few city vineyards of the world, is now planted entirely to shiraz. Viticulture primarily follows organic principles. Largely because of superb drainage and predictable afternoon gully winds and sea breezes during the growing season, these contour-planted gnarled old vines, established over half a century ago, are extremely low yielding and bear fruit of exceptional concentration, flavour and balance. At vintage the fruit is hand-picked block by block—the very best parcels used for the limited release single-estate wine Penfolds Magill Estate Shiraz. On several occasions the vineyard has been able to produce parcels of very opulent powerful fruit, better suited to Penfolds Grange.

The Barossa

Penfolds draws fruit from a combined vineyard area of 618 hectares (1526.5 acres) in the Barossa region of South Australia. It owns several of its own vineyards, but also purchases fruit from independent growers. The Barossa, settled by Silesian and English immigrants in the mid-1800s, is about 70 kilometres north of Adelaide. In 1911, Penfolds established a winery at Nuriootpa which was completed for the 1913 vintage. It relied entirely on independently grown fruit in the Barossa, mainly for the production of fortified wines. The move towards table-wine production resulted in a vineyard acquisition and replanting program during the 1940s and '50s.

Colonel William Light, the South Australian colony's Surveyor-General, named the Barossa in 1837 after the site of an English victory over the French in the Spanish Peninsular War. Silesian and English immigrants settled it in the mid-1800s and wherever you go in the Barossa Valley, you can find the Germanic influence in the architecture and in the names of its communities and leading families.

The Barossa comprises two distinct sub-regions: Eden Valley at around 450 metres and the warmer Barossa Valley floor at 270 metres. The Barossa Valley is comprised of rich brown soils and alluvial sands with a climate similar to Margaret River and Bordeaux. Cool sea breezes from the Gulf of St Vincent and elevation modify temperatures. However, hot northerly winds can occasionally dominate, creating considerable vine stress. The region is also known for its relatively low rainfall. Many of the vineyards are dry-grown on single wire trellising. Water availability is a limiting factor in the spread of vineyards and supplementary irrigation is used extensively. The soils in the Eden Valley are derived from schistic and sedimentary rock. Soils are mostly red-clay and sandy, silty loams interspersed with schistic gravels. This region is widely known for its shiraz and riesling. The high altitude and cool climate of the region produce wines with great complexity and capacity for long-term cellaring.

KALIMNA VINEYARD

Location:	Northern Barossa, about 4 km north of Nuriootpa.
Vineyard:	Undulating slopes and flats with elevations to 340 m (1100 ft).
Soils:	Deep and sandy to sandy loams and heavy, red-brown clays.
Rainfall:	Average rainfall is 508 mm (20 in). About 201 mm during the growing season.
Irrigation:	Supplementary irrigation is used.
Viticulture	Original cabernet vines were planted around 1888. Succession of plantings and retrellising has followed since acquisition in 1945. Most blocks are mechanically pruned and harvested. Some blocks, particularly Block 42 which comprises century-old bush vines, are hand-picked. Yields at 1–4 tonnes/hectare (0.4–1.6 tons/acre).
Grape varieties:	Shiraz, cabernet sauvignon, mataro (mourvèdre) and 8 rows of sangiovese (planted in 1984).

In 1945, Penfolds purchased the highly significant Kalimna Vineyard. Originally planted to vines around 1888 by George Swan Fowler, prior to that the land was used as a source of firewood for D and J Fowler Ltd, the family's fruit preserving company. George Fowler named the vineyard Kalimna, which means 'pleasant view' in a local Aboriginal language. The vineyard lies on gently undulating slopes with elevations as high as 340 metres. Located at the northern end of the Barossa Valley about 4 kilometres north of Nuriootpa, the Kalimna vineyard represents an important part of Australian wine heritage.

In 1903, the Kalimna Vineyard covered 132 hectares (317 acres). Some of the unproductive land was sold off during the 1950s and '60s. During the 1970s, at the height of Australia's red wine boom, all of the white varieties were removed. Today, the 290-hectare property (700 acres) comprises 153 hectares (378 acres) under vine, mostly planted to shiraz and cabernet sauvignon. The average age of the vines is well over 50 years, illustrating the extraordinary provenance of this vineyard. A classic First Growth (premium fine wine) vineyard in Bordeaux, for instance, would be lucky to claim an average age of over 40 years. The Kalimna Vineyard is planted on rich brown soils and alluvial sands. The soil profiles, however, vary widely across the vineyard from deep and sandy soils on the slopes to sandy loams and heavy, red-brown clay soils on the flats. The vines are planted in blocks and trellising systems vary according to when each block was established or redeveloped. Varieties are carefully matched to soil profiles to achieve optimum performance.

Block 42, also known as the Golf Course Block, stands out as a very special piece of viticultural dirt. It is thought that these cabernet sauvignon vines, producing remarkably vibrant, beautifully balanced fruit, are the oldest in the world. Over the last 60 years, Block 42 has played an important role in the development of Penfolds reds. It contributed to the red table wine and Grange trials of the late 1940s and '50s—especially the rare 1948 Kalimna Cabernet and 1953 Penfolds Grange Cabernet. Although the vineyard provides unusually high-quality fruit in most vintages, limited yields meant that Block 42 could not be relied upon as a core source for Max Schubert's Grange. The development and continued success of Penfolds Bin 707 Cabernet Sauvignon, however, owes some part to the contribution of Block 42. Penfolds has released a 2004 and a 1996 Block 42 Kalimna Cabernet Sauvignon as Special Bin wines to highlight the exceptional provenance of this vineyard within a vineyard. These are wines with impressive concentration, balance and finesse.

The Kalimna Vineyard is one of the Barossa Valley's great shiraz vineyards and provides core fruit for Grange, RWT, St Henri and Bin 28. It also provides an essential element to many of Penfolds' Special Bin wines, especially illustrated by the renowned 1962 Penfolds Bin 60A—often cited by critics as one of the best Australian wines ever made. While it is romantic to think of old vines as a precursor of quality, the emphasis on vineyard management is to achieve well-balanced fruit. This goes beyond the shape and age of the vine. Penfolds' viticulturalists are constantly looking at ways of improving vine performance through vine selection and replanting, refinement of trellising systems and shoot positioning, optimising soil moisture and reducing pest and disease pressure.

KOONUNGA HILL VINEYARD

Location:	Northern Barossa, about 5 km north-east of Kalimna.
Vineyard:	64 hectares (158 acres) at an elevation of 280 m (930 ft).
Soils:	Red-brown earth over heavy clays.
Rainfall:	Average rainfall is around 508 mm (20 in). About 201 mm during the growing season.
Irrigation:	Supplementary drip irrigation is available for use.
Viticulture:	Planted in 1973. Vines are trained on trellises for mechanical pruning and harvesting.
Grape varieties:	Shiraz and cabernet sauvignon.

Named after a nearby landmark, the Koonunga Hill Vineyard was planted with shiraz and cabernet sauvignon in 1973 on the drier northern edge of the Barossa Valley. The vineyard inspired the name of Penfolds Koonunga Hill, originally released as an entry point to the Penfolds portfolio of wines. This low-yielding vineyard, however, has become a consistent producer of Grange and Bin 707 quality fruit. The vines, over 30 years old, are in their prime and produce core premium fruit for Penfolds St Henri, Bin 389 and Bin 28. Neutron probes are situated throughout the vineyard to measure soil moisture. If a particular block of vines is stressed, drip irrigation can be delivered to the exact location. In 1996, an adjacent property of equal size was purchased and planted to shiraz. These maturing vines are now quickly reaching an ultra-premium level of maturity and potential quality, illustrating that good vineyard management plays a vital role in delivering high-quality fruit at vintage time.

THE WALTONS VINEYARD

Location:	Central Barossa, about 3 km south of Tanunda.
Vineyard:	317 hectares (783.3 acres) of undulating Barossa heartland, 130 hectares (321.1 acres) planted.
Soils:	Sandy loams and red-brown soils.
Rainfall:	Average rainfall is around 508 mm (20 in). About 201 mm during the growing season.
Irrigation:	Supplementary drip irrigation is available for use.
Viticulture:	Planted in 1999. Vines are trained on high trellises for mechanical pruning and harvesting. Yields are about 3–4 tonnes/hectare (1.2–1.62 tons/acre).
Grape varieties:	Shiraz, cabernet sauvignon and mataro (mourvèdre).

The worldwide interest in Barossa wine has intensified over the last fifteen years, creating a scarcity of valuable premium grapes in the Barossa Valley. While the independent growers provide Penfolds with a vital element of supply, Penfolds recognises that it must also improve and develop its own vineyards.

The Waltons Vineyard, located on classic Barossa Valley heartland soils, is an important recent purchase and development. Over 130 hectares have already been planted—mostly to shiraz, cabernet and mataro. This is a contemporary vineyard, planned, planted and managed with extreme precision. The entire vineyard has been mapped and monitored to optimise vine performance and fruit quality.

'The Waltons Vineyard, located on classic Barossa Valley heartland soils, is an important recent purchase and development.'

One of the main issues is the use of water—a scarce resource. While many vineyards are dry-grown in the Barossa, the use of supplementary irrigation is an important insurance against drought and vine stress. Technology has allowed better water management in recent years. Electrodes placed throughout the vineyard are able to monitor soil moisture. This varies according to the depth and structure of the soil. Water can be directed to individual vineyard areas which need replenishing without wasting this highly valuable resource. Penfolds has great hopes for this vineyard. The oldest shiraz vines, planted in 1999, are already producing impressively concentrated and flavoursome shiraz—some of the best parcels used for Bin 28 and Bin 389. Such an achievement is a tribute to the skills of the vineyard managers.

MARANANGA VINEYARDS

Location:	Seppeltsfield Road, north-western Barossa, about 6 km north of Tanunda.
Vineyard:	110 hectares (272 acres) of varied blocks on gentle slopes.
Soils:	Sandy loams and red-brown soils.
Rainfall:	Average rainfall is around 508 mm (20 in). About 201 mm during the growing season.
Irrigation:	Supplementary drip irrigation is available for use.
Viticulture:	Orginally planted in 1852, but completely revamped in early 1990s. Some vines are trained on trellises for mechanical pruning and harvesting. Yields are about 5.5–6 tonnes/hectare (2.2–2.5 tons/acre).
Grape varieties:	Shiraz (25 ha/62 a), cabernet sauvignon (3 ha/7 a) and grenache (68 ha/168 a).

The leased Marananga Vineyards at Seppeltsfield in the north-western edge of the Barossa Valley is an important source of grenache for Penfolds Bin 138 and the Cellar Reserve Grenache. First planted in 1852, this vineyard, some of it still contoured, has been largely replanted. This is a high-quality vineyard providing fruit for Penfolds St Henri and the emerging Barossa classic Penfolds RWT.

STONEWELL VINEYARD

Location:	Stonewell Road, central Barossa, 4 km west of Nuriootpa.
Vineyard:	33 hectares (80 acres) on undulating slopes.
Soils:	Sandy loams and red-brown soils.
Rainfall:	Average rainfall is around 508 mm (20 in). About 201 mm during the growing season.
Irrigation:	Supplementary drip irrigation is available for use.
Viticulture:	First planted in the early 1970s, but a replanting program put in place when Penfolds purchased the vineyard in the early 1990s. Vines are trained on trellises for mechanical pruning and harvesting. Yields are about 5.5–6 tonnes/hectare (2.2–2.5 tons/acre).
Grape varieties:	Shiraz (23 ha/67 a), cabernet sauvignon (5 ha/12 a), grenache (0.8 ha/2 a), semillon (2 ha/5 a) and chardonnay (1.9 ha/4.7 a).

The Stonewell Road vineyard was purchased in the mid-1990s and is now producing quintessential Barossa shiraz—some of the crop also being used for Penfolds RWT and Penfolds St Henri.

Adelaide Hills

PARTALUNGA VINEYARD

Location:	Mount Pleasant, Adelaide Hills.
Vineyard:	82 hectares (201 acres) of contour-hugging vineyard.
Soils:	Shallow red clay soils and sandy-silty loams interspersed with schistic gravels. Many rocky outcrops.
Rainfall:	Average rainfall is around 760 mm (19 in). About 283 mm during the growing season.
Irrigation:	Supplementary drip irrigation is used.
Viticulture:	Planted in 1981. Vines are trained on high trellises for mechanical pruning and harvesting. Yields are shiraz—5 tonnes/hectare (2.2 tons/acre) chardonnay—7.5 tonnes/hectare (3.03 tons/acre).
Grape varieties:	Shiraz, chardonnay and pinot noir (Cellar Reserve).

The beautifully sited Partalunga Vineyard lies just within the boundary of the Adelaide Hills. With elevations of around 450 metres, this is a much cooler location than the Barossa floor. Water is also limited. The vines, planted on shallow slate and granitic soils, take longer to ripen but produce fruit of great finesse and elegance. It is a large vineyard covering approximately 82 hectares. Significant parcels of chardonnay were used for the Penfolds 'White Grange' Project. The elegantly structured qualities of shiraz are an extremely useful element when included in the St Henri blend.

Clare Valley

CLARE VALLEY ESTATE VINEYARD

Location:	Polish River Valley, about 5 km south-east of Clare.
Vineyard:	350 hectares (861 acres), 218 hectares (538 acres) planted, on the eastern slopes of the Clare Hills.
Soils:	Soils vary. Shallow brown earths over broken clay, slate subsoils on higher ground. Red-brown soils over clay and deep, black alluvial clay loams (with high level of organic matter) on lower elevations.
Rainfall:	Average rainfall is around 657 mm (26 in), most falling in autumn and winter.
Irrigation:	Supplementary drip irrigation is used.
Viticulture:	Planted in 1978. Vines are trained on high trellises for mechanical pruning and harvesting.
Grape varieties:	Cabernet sauvignon, shiraz, merlot, malbec, petit verdot, sangiovese, riesling, chardonnay, semillon, sauvignon blanc and gewurztraminer.

The Clare Valley Estate Vineyard is on the eastern slopes of the Clare Hills about 130 kilometres north of Adelaide. It is located in the famous Polish Hill River Valley, which was first settled by Polish migrants in the 1840s. The vineyard was purchased on the recommendation of Max Schubert who recognised the potential of this region as a premium grape supplier.

The Clare Valley is a corrugation of hills and gullies. While the climatic data suggests a hot region, Clare Valley Estate—like many other vineyards in the Clare—is elevated at between 430 and 470 metres. The Clare Hills protect the vines from strong south-easterly winds, although the vineyard does benefit from the moderating cool breezes that funnel up from the south. The vineyard now comprises a fruit salad of varieties, including cabernet sauvignon, shiraz, merlot, malbec, petit verdot, sangiovese, riesling, chardonnay, semillon, sauvignon blanc and gewurztraminer.

This huge vineyard of 350 hectares (218 hectares planted) is situated almost on the edge of a desert. Rainfall—which occurs mainly during autumn and winter—drops by an 'inch per mile' east of the Clare Hills! During summer the climate is generally hot, dry and continental with a high level of evaporation.

As a consequence of low disease pressure, 52.6 hectares of the vineyard is organically grown and certified by the National Association of Sustainable Agriculture, Australia (NASAA). While Penfolds has a philosophy of 'low-input' viticulture in all of its vineyards, the Clare climate does reduce the risk of disease. Hence it is possible to grow vines without the assistance of man-made herbicides, pesticides and fertilisers. The key is understanding the vines and working with mother nature.

Coonawarra

COONAWARRA VINEYARDS

Location:	Limestone Coast, far south-east of South Australia.
Vineyard:	Old Penfolds blocks including the revered Block 20 cabernet and Block 14 shiraz.
Soils:	Terra rossa—friable, vivid red clay loams over well-drained limestone subsoil.
Rainfall:	Average rainfall is around 593 mm (25.5 in). About 209 mm during the growing season.
Irrigation:	Supplementary drip irrigation is used.
Viticulture:	Vines trained on high single-wire trellises with overhead sprinkler system for use in combating frost. Yields are approximately 4–5 tonnes/hectare (1.6–2.0 tons/acre).
Grape varieties:	Cabernet sauvignon and shiraz.

Coonawarra is one of the most famous red wine regions in Australia. Its weathered limestone terra rossa soils, relatively cool climate and overall water availability make it a unique vineyard area. The region, however, is extremely flat and unprotected. Consequently, it can be exposed to the swinging influences of the cool Southern Ocean and hot, dry northerly winds. The unique confluence of cool maritime and warm continental climates are ideal for cabernet sauvignon. With the added benefit of natural aquifers and groundwater the vineyards can be tuned almost perfectly throughout the growing season. Drainage is excellent but spring frosts can be a problem and have been known to wipe out crops. Overhead sprinkling devices are sometimes deployed when temperatures drop in early spring—the danger period. The water effectively creates a warmer ambient temperature. Mechanical and machine harvesting is widely used in Coonawarra, although smaller producers prefer to tend their vines by hand. The region is best known for cabernet sauvignon and shiraz.

'Coonawarra's weathered limestone terra rossa soils, relatively cool climate and overall water availability make it a unique vineyard area.'

Penfolds Coonawarra Vineyards are located on over 100 hectares (250 acres) of prime terra rossa soil. The original vineyard, Sharam's Block, was purchased from Redmans in 1960. At the time, Coonawarra was barely known as a premium wine district, although Penfolds had been sourcing fruit from various vineyards in the region. Indeed, Max Schubert was largely sceptical about Coonawarra fruit, believing that it was difficult to achieve the optimum ripeness required for the Penfolds style. Initially he preferred Coonawarra shiraz to Coonawarra cabernet sauvignon, largely because it was more reliable. The success of Bin 60A was a turning point, although Penfolds has rarely released a 100 per cent Coonawarra Cabernet

Sauvignon. The Penfolds house style is largely based on warm climate fruit. Hence in cooler but well-regarded Coonawarra vintages such as 2000 or 2005, the cabernet sauvignon is not always suitable for Bin 707. Vineyard management, however, has progressed substantially over the last 40 years—the fruit supplying many of Penfolds' Bin range, including Bin 128, Bin 407, Bin 389 and Bin 707.

Three blocks within these vineyards are of particular note. Block 6, 19 and 20 are an important source of Penfolds Bin 707. These blocks are located on the eastern side of the Riddoch Highway which bisects the Coonawarra region—about 0.5 and 2 kilometres south of the Coonawarra township. Penfolds is also able to access fruit from independent growers and other vineyards in Coonawarra to supplement its own Coonawarra intake. Penfolds Coonawarra vineyards are now entirely planted to premium red wine varieties, in particular cabernet sauvignon and shiraz.

Robe

ROBE VINEYARD

Location:	Limestone Coast. The Robe region is centred on the small townships of Robe and Beachport.
Vineyard:	235 hectares (580.6 acres) under vine.
Soils:	Shallow (5 cm–45 cm) loamy sand over limestone with smaller areas of terra rossa over limestone and deep sandy loam.
Rainfall:	Average rainfall is around 667 mm (26.3 in). About 210 mm during the growing season.
Irrigation:	Supplementary drip irrigation and electronic probes are used.
Viticulture:	Vines are trained on a single-wire vertically positioned high trellis with overhead sprinkler system for use in combating frost. Yields are approximately 4–8.5 tonnes/hectare (1.6–3.4 tons/acre), depending on grape variety.
Grape varieties:	Shiraz, merlot, petit verdot, cabernet sauvignon, pinot noir, semillon, chardonnay and sauvignon blanc.

Penfolds Robe Vineyard, located close to the Southern Ocean and planted during the mid-1990s, is producing fruit of excellent definition and palate structure. Formerly a grazing property, it was originally used for breeding horses for the British Army.

The vines, which lie on the eastern slopes of the relatively low-lying Woakwine Ranges, are protected from prevailing winds. The climate is marginally warmer than Coonawarra—especially during spring. The growing season is long, cool and dry. The vineyard is well drained but also benefits from an artesian basin—a plentiful source of groundwater. The vines are all trained on high trellises and machine pruned and harvested.

The overall standard of fruit quality is extremely high. The cabernet sauvignon and shiraz are more refined than Coonawarra fruit, but both have masses of sweet fruit and depth. The vineyard now contributes various parcels to Bin 389, Bin 407, Bin 707 and St Henri, illustrating the sheer class of this vineyard site. The chardonnay and sauvignon blanc are of particularly high quality and are key components of the Thomas Hyland white wines.

> *'The sheer diversity and quality of regional provenance,*
> *vineyard sites and independently grown fruit provides Penfolds'*
> *winemakers with a rich palette of colour, aroma and texture.'*

Bordertown

Penfolds has developed vineyards in Bordertown, close to the South Australia–Victoria border. Although this district is a subset of the Limestone Coast geographical region, it has yet to be recognised as an official sub-region. This is a rich agricultural district well known for the production of cereals, wool, meat, seeds and vegetables. In more recent years, several wine companies and independent growers have planted new, often very large, vineyards in the region, taking advantage of the ideal warm climate and reasonable land prices.

The region was first settled in the early 1850s following the establishment of Alexander Tolmer's Gold Escort base camp on the banks of the Tatiara Creek and was located on the major supply route between the Victorian goldfields and Adelaide.

The district is warm and the most continental of the sub-regions within the Limestone Coast. The land is gently undulating, punctuated by large stands of eucalypt trees. Penfolds has been sourcing fruit from Bordertown for almost two decades.

Impressed by the sheer quality of the fruit—the cabernet has been selected for Bin 707—Penfolds recently purchased and planted its own 180-hectare vineyard. Planted to mainly cabernet sauvignon, but also merlot and shiraz, this vineyard produced commercial-quality fruit in 2002. Although it is still early days, Penfolds believes that the Bordertown vineyard will make a significant contribution to Penfolds reds in the forthcoming years.

BORDERTOWN VINEYARD

Location:	Approximately 265 km east of Adelaide and close to the state border of South Australia and Victoria.
Vineyard:	Planted on level ground elevated at 71–72 m (233 ft).
Soils:	Red-brown earth over limestone.
Rainfall:	Average rainfall is 520 mm (20.5 in). Majority falls during the growing season.
Irrigation:	Supplementary irrigation used.
Viticulture:	Single-wire trellis. Machine pruned with hand clean up. Overhead sprinklers used for frost control. Permanent grass sward between rows.
Grape varieties:	Chardonnay, cabernet sauvignon, merlot, shiraz.

THE GROWERS

Independent growers have been supplying Penfolds with wine grapes for over a century. While Penfolds owns substantial vineyard properties across South Australia, its relationship with growers—sometimes extending to several generations—is of key importance. Almost every Penfolds wine, except for its own single-vineyard releases, has a component of independently grown fruit.

The following table illustrates the winemaker expectations of regional fruit character of chardonnay and shiraz from Penfolds vineyard sites across Australia.

Australian chardonnay fruit profiles

VINEYARD	CHARACTERISTICS
Tumbarumba NSW	Lemon, mandarin, guava, mineral/flint
Orange NSW	Peach, lemon curd
Henty VIC	Citrus, grapefruit, lemon
Yarra Valley VIC (for comparison)	White peach, white nectarine, quince
Adelaide Hills SA	Grapefruit, white peach, apple
Padthaway SA	Melon, lemon, tropical
Coonawarra SA	Peach, tropical, pineapple
Margaret River WA (for comparison)	Pink grapefruit, pear essence, guava, summer orange blossom
Hunter Valley NSW (for comparison)	Nectarine, white peach, lemon
Tasmania	Lemon, grapefruit, mineral

Australian shiraz fruit profiles

VINEYARD	EARLY PICKING (SPICY)	OPTIMUM PICKING (BERRY)
Kalimna Vineyard SA	Cinnamon, cloves	Mulberry, raspberry and blackcurrant
Block 14 Coonawarra SA	Mint and finely ground pepper	Blackberry, leather-like and earthy
McLaren Vale SA	Raspberry, blueberry	Liqueured fruit/dark chocolate
Magill Estate, Adelaide SA	Cherry, green tobacco	Plum, licorice
Hunter Valley NSW (for comparison)	Herbal, menthol	Leather/earthy, pepper
Great Western VIC (for comparison)	Subtle raspberry with some pepper	Raspberry with hints of pepper Some earthy characters

Many of Max Schubert's early wines, including his experimental Granges, relied on outside vineyard resources. Ex-Penfolds Chief Winemaker John Duval's family, who were grape growers at Morphett Vale near Adelaide, regularly contributed fruit to Penfolds, including the early Granges.

Vineyard management

Penfolds has had a longstanding reputation for its exemplary vineyard management practices and works closely with its growers to ensure they also follow these methods. The pursuit of quality wine has always started in the vineyard. The early settlers of South Australia were equally concerned about getting the best from their vineyards. There are many recorded instances that illustrate the high expectations of nineteenth-century winegrowing from equipment catalogues, international wine shows, immigration records of European vine dressers and winemakers to old newspaper reports, letters and winery records. After World War II, the Australian wine industry geared up to meet the demands of a new era in fine winemaking.

Experimentation and research was not only confined to winemaking. During the early 1950s and '60s Penfolds embarked on a strong acquisition trail and invested greatly in vineyards in New South Wales and South Australia. Over the last 50 years, viticultural practices have been refined and improved. Penfolds has shared its accumulated knowledge with independent growers for decades. While Penfolds has always made the best possible wine from the best possible fruit, not a year goes by without further 'improvement of the breed'.

There was a general observation among the Rewards of Patience panel members that Penfolds' wines had increasingly become brighter with more pure fruit definition and richness of flavour as the decades progressed. During the 1950s and '60s, vineyard management was relatively ad hoc. There was erratic control over incoming fruit. Long distances between wine regions were also a problem. While winemakers knew where the best vineyards were located, the quality of the fruit was entirely dependent on growing conditions. In a top vintage, the fruit was generally ripe, but in more difficult years the quality of fruit was uneven, resulting in variable quality wines.

During the late 1970s, Don Ditter, former Penfolds Chief Winemaker, implemented better vineyard management and data collection systems. The long drought of the early 2000s, a renewed concern about water availability and the impact of global warming have resulted in further innovations and practices in the vineyard. Aerial mapping to analyse plant cell density/vigour and the use of portable soil moisture probes, which monitor water availability around the root zone, have become essential tools in water management. Biosecurity, especially disease and pest pressure, is a major issue. South Australia remains phylloxera-free over a century after it was first discovered in the eastern Australian states.

Paul Georgiadis, Penfolds Grower Relations Manager in South Australia, says: 'All our growers are encouraged to apply a philosophy of sustainable viticulture where minimal tillage and low-input applications to protect the vines from disease pressure are the norm. We try as much as possible to follow organic principles without being burdened with the cost of compliance. We have to maintain a balance between the vagaries of Mother Nature and the reality of grape growing. Our objective is to grow the best fruit possible regardless of vintage conditions. Even in difficult years we have always been able to provide the necessary fruit for Grange, St Henri and Bin 389.'

Minimal tillage, a system which involves minimal soil manipulation, is practised to maintain the health and structure of the soils, making them more resistant to compaction and structural degradation. The method also optimises soil moisture levels and natural water availability, thereby minimising the need for supplementary irrigation. It also encourages better vine root penetration and reduces soil erosion. The soils are only ever turned over once or twice a year. Paul Georgiadis prefers dappled light through the canopy to allow even ripening and colourisation of the fruit. Controlling vine vigour early during the growing season will create these dappled light conditions, maximising the sunlight into the vine without cooking the fruit. Shoot thinning and bunch thinning is standard practice, especially on vigorous and variable sites. This type of work requires skill and speed through the vineyard. Over the last ten years, Penfolds has used a team of skilled vineyard workers who have an almost legendary reputation for accuracy and reliability.

Traditional cultivation methods are still applied on heavier well-structured self-mulching soils. These techniques, more in keeping with European farming practices, are very much alive in the Barossa—especially among families with generations of successful grape growing in the region.

Grower liaison

Penfolds Grower Liaison Officers regularly visit grower vineyards to see progress through the growing season. Penfolds has a very clear idea of its fruit requirements. The process is about influencing change in the vineyard to achieve optimum ripeness and quality. Penfolds has nine Grower Liaison Officers servicing about 500 independent growers in South Australia, Victoria and New South Wales. They produce roughly 60,000 tonnes of grapes for Penfolds.

Vineyard assessment and monitoring is vitally important. Premium vineyards are visited regularly at pruning time, flowering and veraison. Penfolds viticulturalists, winemakers and growers walk each block together discussing its attributes and potential. During the growing season they look at growing tips, lateral growth and shoot length. They also observe periderm development, leaf condition and fruit exposure. Close to harvest, each vineyard block might be assessed several times by winemakers to scrutinise grape quality and flavour development, monitor chemical residues and potential disease, and predict harvest dates. Understanding the quality and variability of each vineyard block enables winemakers to match and batch fruit for specific Penfolds wines. Using hand-held personal digital assistant computers, grower liaison officers are able to schedule incoming fruit and provide winemakers with a quality grading.

Over a period of time, both growers and Penfolds are able to predict vineyard performance within the context of seasonal conditions. Growers are given grade level targets—an internal alpha-numerical rating system. Grade I—Icon, is likely to find its way into Penfolds' Grange and Yattarna. The fruit at this level must be sublime with superb colour, flavour and tannin ripeness. Paul Georgiadis maintains that you can spot a top vineyard by its appearance and by the look and taste of the fruit. 'We look beyond Baumé, pH and acidity. The fruit that scores the highest points are invariably grapes with concentration, richness, chewiness and plenty of sweetness and flavour length. The "spit test" is usually a very good indicator. If it's got the colour of dark purple ink, it's a winner.' Peter Gago says, 'Other quality variables include skin thickness and shrivel, seed colour and texture, lignification of stalks and rachis. We can usually predict the outcome of the vintage by the quality of the grapes prior to picking.'

Maximising quality

Penfolds' aim is to buy the best available fruit. In the past all growers were paid for their crop on a price per tonne basis. Today Penfolds rewards its growers for excellence. All growers are encouraged to optimise the quality potential of their crop. Members of the Premium Shiraz Growers Group, for instance, are paid on a per hectare basis—'rain, hail or sunshine'. Bonuses are also offered if the fruit exceeds expectations.

Penfolds pays special attention to pruning and the 'architecture of the vine'. This has always been an essential feature of grape growing because it relates directly to how the vine will grow and the fruit will ripen. The preferred method of spur or cane pruning will depend on the grape variety, character and capacity of vineyard site. As a rule, Barossa shiraz vines should be pruned to achieve around 3 kilograms of fruit per vine (or less) for consistent production of high-quality wine. Any more than this and vines run the risk of encountering water stress too early in the season. At budburst the smaller shoots can be thinned to encourage more even growth of stronger shoots.

At fruit set, when the berries are at pea size, viticulturalists can predict the size of the crop. If the vine is carrying too much fruit, the bunches can be removed by hand. At this stage viticulturalists need to assess whether permanent grass swards, encouraged to grow between the vine rows to manage soil moisture levels and to compete against vine vigour, should stay or be knocked down. At veraison, when the berries change colour and soften, there is an opportunity to reassess crop load and ripening. The less ripe or 'green' bunches can be removed at this stage. Prior to harvest, the fruit is further assessed and graded, usually with the grower, field winemaker and viticulturalist. At every stage of the growing season Penfolds works with its growers.

Top shelf

Penfolds' Top Shelf Project is a collaborative scheme to optimise vineyard performance. A typical example is a mature shiraz vineyard in the Barossa Valley. The cane-pruned low to moderate vigour vines are planted on red-brown earth over solid sandstone and ironstone. The vines are generally in equilibrium with balanced crop levels. However, the vines are anchored in relatively limited soil depths; in some years, because of water stress, they can suffer from leaf loss towards the end of the season. This can lead to variable fruit quality where some berries have achieved

Harry and Paul Georgiadis

sugar ripeness by raisining. A Penfolds Grower Liaison Officer, usually in consultation with the field team, will provide the grower with recommendations on how to improve the performance of his vineyard. This will include advice to reduce bud numbers in winter to ensure vines have the capacity to produce balanced canopies. Other recommendations may include the 'clean out of congested spurs to allow better fruit and canopy distribution'.

Between budburst and flowering the grower will be encouraged to implement shoot thinning and to retain grassed rows to control vigour. After flowering the grower is advised not to irrigate unless the vines are clearly under stress. However by January, after veraison, conditions have become quite dry. Recommendations regarding frequency and volume of watering are given to ensure vine health and balanced ripening. The result of this ongoing advisory work is improvement in overall consistency and quality of fruit. For the grower it means reliable annual income. In some cases, if the fruit is classified at a higher level, it can result in the payment of premium prices.

For some growers the ultimate prize is having fruit selected for Penfolds Grange. Generally these vineyards comprise low-yielding mature vines with an average age of more than 40 years. Some of the vines are a century old. The Gersch family vineyard in the Barossa Valley, a long-time supplier of fruit to Penfolds, is the youngest contributor on record. The vines started producing Grange-quality fruit after ten years. Paul Georgiadis points out: 'This is a beautifully managed block with the right clones and the right terroir. The vines have been encouraged to scavenge from the day they were planted, resulting in outstanding root penetration and naturally balanced canopies. The growers have collaborated brilliantly with our viticultural team. When they reach Grange- or Yattarna-quality fruit, they feel as though they have achieved top marks in a rigorous exam. While refinement and hard work in the vineyard can reap dividends for growers, vineyard site is the tangible yet enigmatic wildcard. The late Max Gersch once said, 'If we all knew the answer to making high-quality fruit, everyone would be growing grapes for Grange.' Peter Gago confirms this sentiment, 'There are many so-called ex-Grange vineyard claims out there. But don't be fooled, it is extremely difficult to produce fruit at this quality level. Over the last twenty years (1988–2007), fewer than 25 growers have succeeded in making the Grange cut. In fact, only ten growers have achieved this more than once!'

Paul Georgiadis was brought up on his family vineyard at Barmera in the Riverland in South Australia. In 1995, he and his father, Harry Georgiadis, purchased a 16-hectare property in the Dorrien sub-region of the Barossa, between Marananga and Tanunda. They have planted over 13 hectares of vines including shiraz, mataro and sangiovese. The vineyard lies on red-brown earths and red clay over ironstone and limestone at around 220 to 280 metres above sea level, just above the frost zone. The rows are orientated on a north-east south-west bearing to take maximum advantage of antipodean sunshine hours.

Paul takes a 'dry-grown' approach to viticulture with low input vineyard practices. 'We run our vineyard in the Penfolds way as we know it works. However, as a Penfolds Grower Relations Manager, I am also interested in trying new things to improve vineyard performance. We do have drip irrigation—but we only ever use this option when absolutely necessary. Our objective is to produce fruit with the best fruit profile and flavours possible.' This means keeping yields down to around 6 tonnes per hectare. After harvest the vineyard is planted with grasses to refresh the soils with nutrients. The vines are then spur pruned by hand during the winter months. In November, just before flowering, the vines are shoot thinned to 48 shoots per vine to ensure that the vines are correctly balanced.

Paul is one of the pioneers of the Italian grape variety sangiovese in the Barossa Valley. Captivated by the wines and heavily involved in establishing a sufficient crop for Penfolds, he felt that sangiovese seemed like an obvious choice to plant. The first years, however, were difficult. Georgiadis thought that he had made a big mistake; the vines were out of control. In 2000, he visited Tuscany, the original home of sangiovese, and observed vineyard practices. 'I realised that I was growing sangiovese like shiraz, however, it is a more fragile variety like pinot noir and can't be overly stressed out as it will defoliate very easily.

'During the growing season we now regularly practise shoot thinning and bunch thinning. We will remove any bunches over 200 grams and keep as many small-berried bunches as possible. Each vintage, this fruit is vinified for the Penfolds Cellar Reserve Sangiovese. I think the exciting quality of the wine reflects the great progresses we have made in viticulture as much as in the winemaking.'

While most of Penfolds' independent growers are located in the Barossa region, high-quality fruit is also sourced from growers in other regions. Adam Brown, a

Penfolds Grower Liaison Officer, says, 'A couple of Clare growers are at the very top level and are of strategic importance to St Henri [the fruit profile is too elegant for Grange]. These vineyards, like our own Clare Valley Estate, can be managed along organic principles. The region is very dry and the vineyards rarely endure long periods of humidity and disease pressure. Around Watervale and Sevenhill the soils are red clays over ironstone or limestone. These rusty red soils have marvellous water retention properties due to their good structure, ideal for such a dry warm wine region.'

McLaren Vale is milder than the Clare Valley. It does not have the extremes of frosty winters and searingly hot summers. The climate is typically Mediterranean with higher levels of humidity. The shiraz generally takes longer to ripen. Vigorous growth during the growing season is not uncommon, requiring hedging, shoot thinning and bunch thinning. Vineyards closer to the sea are often less vigorous because the afternoon onshore breezes can retard growth. The shiraz is generally larger berried than Barossa and Clare, with strong, rich flavours and excellent sugar ripeness. Cabernet sauvignon is more perfumed and classically structured than the chocolaty textured cabernets of the Barossa Valley.

Paul Georgiadis says, 'McLaren Vale produces highly consistent fruit, year in and year out.' Some McLaren Vale growers rarely produce fruit below B1 quality; that is a very premium standard when you consider the entire Penfolds intake.

Penfolds also sources fruit along the Adelaide Hills, Gumeracha and Moculta. The fruit is particularly exquisite with beautiful definition and minerally acidities. Vineyards planted on the red soils near One Tree Hill in the Northern Adelaide Foothills are also an exciting new development as they are located only a short distance away from Penfolds' original Modbury Vineyard. It is already providing grapes for Thomas Hyland Shiraz and Bin 28. Paul Georgiadis says, 'We have high hopes for this site. With a bit more age and vine equilibrium, we believe the fruit will eventually end up in wines like St Henri and Grange.'

Padthaway, Wrattonbully and Coonawarra are key sources of premium growers' cabernet sauvignon and shiraz. While Penfolds owns its own vineyards in southeast South Australia, independent growers are important suppliers of quality fruit. Paul Georgiadis says, 'Cabernet sauvignon from these regions is intensely varietal with concentrated and balanced flavours. It makes an important contribution to several wines in the Penfolds brand.'

The relationship between growers and Penfolds is an important one. Growers are given every opportunity to improve their knowledge and refine their vineyard management skills. Field days, regional workshops, overseas study trips, a range of planned feedback sessions and quality assurance programs are offered throughout the year. The use of field digital technology has allowed Penfolds to further improve the capture of information and feedback to growers. Membership of the Penfolds Grange Growers Club and Penfolds Yattarna Growers Club is the ultimate reward for growers who are able to achieve the most exquisite fruit quality. Aside from the financial rewards, they belong to an elite group of growers who are able to produce, on a regular basis, some of Australia's finest wine grapes. In 2007 Penfolds Growers were named Vignerons of the Year by the distinguished regional fraternity Barons of the Barossa.

CHAPTER FOUR

The Craft of Winemaking

Penfolds is steeped in a tradition of craft and science. It is a unique institution with a celebrated and enduring work philosophy of innovation and conviction. The wines are industry benchmarks with a strong thumbprint of house style and a reputation for quality and reliability. The strength of winemaking at Penfolds is that it is a way of life.

Some winemakers worked their way up through the ranks without formal training. Others have undertaken studies in applied science (oenology), but the average vintage experience of every winemaker at Penfolds is more than twenty years.

This tradition of excellence has led to the production of great Australian wines, recognised the world over, and people who have become pivotal figures of the wine industry.

'Penfolds' house style emerged from a fortified-wine producing culture and evolved as a winemaking philosophy— a way of making wine—which has had a profound effect on the entire Australian wine industry.'

THE PENFOLDS PEOPLE

Dr Ray Beckwith

Dr Ray Beckwith is one of the unsung pioneers of the modern Australian wine industry. His contribution to quality control and wine stability is of major significance. His influence was far reaching, yet his name is barely known. In 1932, he returned to Roseworthy Agricultural College with a cadetship in oenology, a paid position, after having graduated earlier in the year with an honours diploma in agriculture. His interest in the performance and efficiency of winemaking yeasts lead to an important association with Alan Hickinbotham, a pivotal figure in Australian wine science and whose work in pH and malolactic fermentation would have a profound generational effect on winemaking philosophy. The project involved the identification and analysis of a high-performance yeast of Portuguese origin, a yeast later designated A1, and used commercially by Penfolds in the production of millions of litres of fortified wines. After a brief stint with Thomas Hardy, working with Colin Haselgrove and Roger Warren, he was poached by Leslie Penfold Hyland who had read about Beckwith's findings and the potential economic benefits of pure yeast culture in an Australian brewing and wine journal. Ray Beckwith recalls:

> As Mr Hyland had asked for a decision and a convenient date to start work at Nuriootpa, I wrote and suggested December 13th 1934. He replied and sent a cheque for £4–10–0 for one week's holiday pay with the instruction to start at Nuriootpa on 2nd January 1935.

On joining Penfolds, Beckwith was immediately impressed by 'the row upon row of stacks of American oak hogsheads (300 litres), filled almost exclusively with port'—the drink of preference of the time. Submerged cap fermentation, still a classical method of vinification, was used extensively throughout Penfolds' cellars—even prior to the production of Grange. In later years, the drainings, the last free run but thick, unctuous, highly concentrated runnel of new wine from the cap of skins and pips, would be sent down to Max Schubert at Magill to beef up some of the premium and special bin reds. Beckwith observed, however, that 'the heat of fermentation was a major problem because too much heat resulted in the loss of quality and the prospect of bacterial spoilage'. Crude copper heat exchangers using bore water were brought in around this time (later these would be replaced by stainless steel). Presses, must pumps and crushers were driven by a shaft with pulley and belt drive, all powered by 60HP electric motors, which had only recently replaced a powerful steam engine still mounted on the front deck opposite the boiler house. In 1935, Penfolds did not own any vineyards in the Barossa—all the grapes were purchased from independent growers—many of whom still used 'German wagons and horses' to deliver their crop. Indeed the only company vehicle at Nuriootpa was a 'heavy masher dray pulled by a Clydesdale horse', Beckwith remembers. Wine, in hogsheads, left the winery by rail.

Beckwith immediately set about building a new laboratory and a yeast propogation tank made from an old gin still. Observation and innovation saw new ways of making wine at Penfolds. He introduced a highly analytical and practical winemaking regime—many practices now standard in the modern Australian wine industry. Bacterial spoilage of wine, however, was a major problem in the early 1930s. Initially, Ray Beckwith's role was to find ways to treat the wine through fining agents, ozone injection, pasteurisation and re-fermentation with fresh juice. The quest for stability led him down cul-de-sacs and new pathways. As one problem was solved, new problems arose. Out of frustration he introduced a philosophy of preventative winemaking which was to become a key to Penfolds reputation.

Ray Beckwith's interest in wine acidity lead to the important and far-reaching conclusion in 1936 that 'pH may be a useful tool in the control of bacterial growth'. Beckwith knew of John Fornachon's work with the disastrous sweet wine disease, identified as being caused by *Lacto bacillus*, which had damaged Australia's reputation in its key United Kingdom market. On reading Fornachon's report, Ray Beckwith now understood the influence of pH. He persuaded Leslie Penfold Hyland that Penfolds needed a pH meter with the Morton glass electrode—a highly expensive piece of equipment. He then experimented and applied new winemaking standards using the addition of tartaric acid, a natural constituent of wine, to lower pH. Ray Beckwith said, 'maybe it's overstating the case but bacterial spoilage could go through a winery like a bushfire. But with proper control, a winemaker could sleep easy at night.' Certainly this discovery was critically important in the development of all Penfolds dry red wines—notably Grange. Beckwith also noticed that on adjusting pH to his new standard, the 'colour brightened and with it a sheen'. Interestingly, many believe that Ray Beckwith's discovery—*the application of pH to the control of bacteria in wine*—was the first in the world.

Ian Hickinbotham, veteran winemaker, wine writer and ex-Penfolds manager, wrote in his autobiography *Australian Plonky*:

> Beckwith applied his unique knowledge to the making and husbandry of all wine types—with remarkable cost savings—when employed by Penfolds for the rest of his working life. In a nutshell, he saved the 25 per cent wine component that previously had to be destroyed by distillation due to bacterial spoilage. From that time, around 1940, Australia became a world leader in the making of table wine.

Beckwith remembers:

> After World War II, the engineers and metallurgists made a contribution
> [to fine wine production] with the provision of new and improved equipment
> such as refrigeration and heat exchanges, hermetic centrifuges, filters and
> sterile filtration equipment, pumps and bottling equipment and so on—all in
> stainless steel, thereby eliminating the earlier problem of metal contamination
> from brass and copper construction. Stainless steel tanks gradually came into
> common use, especially as the cost came down to practical levels. Insulation of
> these tanks against extreme temperatures improved their value.

Vigilance, care and attention to detail were important to Beckwith. He developed systems which are now standard throughout the industry. This went beyond the laboratory to practical winemaking solutions at every quality level. The list of innovations and inventions is extraordinary.

He designed and improvised new plant and equipment, and introduced new technology and quality control procedures. He was arguably the first person to introduce paper chromatography as a test for completion of malolactic fermentation. He designed quality standards in a time before consistency and standardisation became an industry norm. His early work with the mass production of flor sherry and solving the issues of contamination were critical to the success of Penfolds during the 1940s and '50s. Indeed, his work was so important that management told him 'he could go to the local horse races, but was not to talk to any other wine people on technical subjects!'

*'Vigilance, care and attention to detail were important
to Beckwith. He developed systems which are now standard
throughout the industry. This went beyond the laboratory
to practical winemaking solutions at every quality level.
The list of innovations and inventions is extraordinary.'*

Ray Beckwith was the quintessential winemaker's 'boffin'—a brilliant chemist and scientist. Clearly Max Schubert relied greatly on Beckwith's intuition and quiet determination. History will remember Max Schubert as the creator of Grange. However, without Ray Beckwith's contribution, the fame of Penfolds Grange may not have eventuated. Now approaching his century, Arthur Ray Beckwith's work has finally been recognised by the wine industry and the wider community. He is a winner of the prestigious Maurice O'Shea Award (2005), a recipient of an honorary doctorate from the University of Adelaide, and on 26 January 2008 he was awarded the Medal of the Order of Australia (OAM) 'for service to the Australian wine industry through contributions towards enhancing the quality and efficiency of the winemaking process'.

At a recent interview Ray Beckwith, as down to earth as ever, said, 'All these things have come only after the last few years. It's a good thing I didn't conk out earlier, otherwise I wouldn't have known!'

John Bird

John Bird is a Senior Red Winemaker who first joined Penfolds in 1960. In 2009 he will celebrate 50 vintages at Magill Estate. He is the last working Penfolds wine-maker of the Schubert era and a final tangible link with Penfolds' origins.

John Bird started work as a Laboratory Techni-cal Assistant at Magill Estate prior to the vintage in February 1960 on a wage of £5 a week. It did not start smoothly. He was told that he was 'a bit slow and casual' and warned that he was in danger of being relegated to the bottling department. Bird reacted by saying that he was 'a bit bored and needed more work'. He was promptly given a white lab coat in place of his grey general-purpose dust coat by Magill's chemist Karl Lambert. Penfolds Magill was a centre of wine-making innovation. The 1960 vintage represented a significant step up in Penfolds' table-wine production. John Bird, awestruck by the enormity of it all, found himself immersed in labora-tory work, winemaking, general cellar work, bottling and warehousing. This period of apprenticeship grounded Bird in Penfolds' philosophy and culture. He worked and learned his trade with longstanding senior winemakers Gordon Colquist, John Davoren and Newton Harris.

While the Penfolds management structure was strict (it was insisted that senior staff were called Mr, Mrs or Miss), the working atmosphere in the cellars was infor-mal—everyone called each other by their first names. Max Schubert and Jeffrey Penfold Hyland 'adored' their longstanding team of cellar hands and winemakers. John Bird noted at the time that around a third of the cellar and bottling staff were aged above 50 through to their early seventies, reflecting the values and loyalties associated with a family company.

As business went full steam ahead, Penfolds invested greatly in both staff and equipment. Karl Lambert, John Bird and a young Brian McGuigan from Dalwood in New South Wales were sponsored by Penfolds to gain further technical experi-ence at the Gawler and Nuriootpa Adult Education Centre. These series of lec-tures, mainly held during the winter off-season, were the preferred wine education option. The Roseworthy oenology course was still a relatively obscure and lengthy alternative and not greatly supported by the larger wine companies until the early 1970s. John Bird also learned 'vineyard husbandry', grape sampling and analysis. This important aspect of winemaking was relatively new, having been developed by Ray Beckwith during the 1950s with Max Schubert.

Penfolds' acquisition of Coonawarra vineyards during the 1960s resulted in new challenges. This isolated region was under-capitalised with rudimentary winemak-ing equipment and no three-phase power. When Penfolds began purchasing caber-net from the Redman family, it was John Bird who was given the task of training

Don Redman with sulphur dioxide analysis. It was vital that the must, tankered up to Magill (about 400 kilometres) from Coonawarra, would be in top condition on arrival. This method of crushing and transportation would continue until 1973.

Penfolds became a public company in 1963 and all employees over the age of 65 were forced to retire, including the legendary Alfred Scholz, the hugely respected manager of Nuriootpa winery. In 1964, Chris Hancock was transferred from the adjacent Auldana cellars to Magill as Senior Winemaker for two vintages under the newly appointed Technical Director Max Schubert. During the 1960s, John Bird was in the thick of wine production at Magill, working closely with various winemaking trials and experimental vintages. He assisted Max Schubert with the final blending of the famous 1962 Bin 60A Coonawarra Cabernet Sauvignon, Kalimna Shiraz and many other experimental wines including 'the curatorship of 1950s Grange bottlings'. The first vintages of Bin 28, Bin 128, Bin 389, Bin 707 and Max Schubert's beloved Grange were also assembled at Magill.

The sheer magnitude of activity and success during the 1960s was remarkable. Max Schubert was embroiled with the ramping-up of production across all of Penfolds' winemaking facilities. With a heavy travel schedule, he was increasingly reliant on the trust and care of his winemakers at Magill and Nuriootpa. It is during this period that a culture of shared winemaking philosophy developed. Faced with an ever-increasing level of wine stocks, Ray Beckwith introduced a revolutionary and methodical winemaking records system. Penfolds also made three prestigious Jimmy Watson Trophy-winning wines during this period: the 1963 Bin 64 Kalimna Cabernet, the 1965 Grange and the 1967 Grange.

The 1968 and 1969 were light vintages and left unblended. John Bird was appointed by Max Schubert as Magill's Senior Winemaker prior to the tough 1970 vintage. They worked closely together with the tasting, trial blending and planning of the 1968 and 1969 vintages. John Bird recalls, 'I don't think we have ever come across such difficult vintages. It took many trials before we knew what to do with the wines. This experience was invaluable.'

The early 1970s saw a reversal of fortunes for Penfolds and further reshuffling of winemakers and staff. Bird said, 'We were working on a white table wine which Max dubbed "Lady Grange". It was a late-picked style. Top management ordered the project to be stopped. The wines were blended and sold as Penfolds Autumn Riesling, much to our disappointment.' The 1972 was also considered to be a very good vintage but the winemaking team ran into problems with Grange. 'The wines were over-matured in barrel and then bottled under warm conditions leading to instability in storage.' Anders Josephson, an avid collector who possessed over $2 million of Grange in the early 1990s, said, 'I remember Max calling it his problem child. When he opened one of my bottles up and tasted the wine his face lightened up with delight; it was a good example.'

Max Schubert became seriously ill around 1973, resulting in the appointment of Don Ditter as National Production Manager. Ditter visited Magill regularly, overseeing the consolidation of production. He recalls John Bird as 'a very committed and thoughtful winemaker with a slight larrikin edge. We recognised that the volatility in the 1971 Grange was reaching unacceptable levels. He took it upon himself, with my approval, to adjust these levels down. I don't think we ever surpassed 1 gram per litre after that year.'

Production of white and fortified wines ceased at Magill after the 1973 vintage. Even the reds were crushed and fermented at Nuriootpa before being sent to John Bird, 'holding the fort at Magill', for maturation and final blending. In 1976, the Sydney-based Tooth's Brewing Company took over Penfolds, beginning a new golden period of wine production. Don Ditter was appointed Chief Winemaker. Max Schubert, still a director, was brought back into the winemaking fold as a wine consultant for the next seventeen years. John Bird observed, 'This was a great period for Penfolds. The previous management in Sydney had gradually sidelined the older school of technical staff in favour of younger hot shots. We found ourselves back in the box seat after it was realised that our experience was invaluable.'

Between 1981 and 1996, John Bird was Penfolds' Senior Red Winemaker which resulted in spending vintage time between Magill and Nuriootpa. Bird observed: 'Through the acquisition of Kaiserstuhl, Seaview and Lindemans we inherited some very talented winemakers including a very young Steve Lienert—who has since progressed to become a linchpin of the Penfolds winemaking team.' Bird was particularly interested in the development of Coonawarra cabernet. The reintroduction of Bin 707 was especially pleasing for Bird: 'I really enjoyed accepting the three consecutive trophies we won at the Sydney Wine Show. While Bin 707 has never been a 100 per cent Coonawarra wine, I have always been mindful of the quality of cabernet down there.'

Bird, like many of his colleagues at Magill, was devastated by the loss of vineyard land brought about by urban pressure. In 1984, Magill comprised only 12 acres of vines, a fraction of the huge sea of vines that covered the original property. The release of the 1983 Magill Estate Shiraz was an important milestone. Many people felt that the wine preserved the integrity of the place. The wine, however, actually struggled for some years. The original idea was to make a wine that was a foil to Grange rather than a wine made from the Grange Vineyard, as Magill was once known. A review of early Magill Estate vintages by John Duval and his winemaking team in 1989 resulted in the decision to make structural improvements to the wine style. During the outstanding 1990 vintage, John Bird instigated a plan to 'beef-up' Magill Estate Shiraz through later harvesting of fruit and further refinements in winemaking. John Duval said:

> This perhaps illustrates the level of overall trust and teamwork at Penfolds. John Bird has always had a deep affection for Magill and a desire to make a difference. His work with Magill Estate Shiraz honoured the original blueprint developed by Max Schubert and Don Ditter, but made the wine more contemporary in style. You will see such refinements made right across the Penfolds portfolio. While the Penfolds house style has always been important, Max Schubert always liked to think that the personality of his winemakers would be seen in the wines. I felt the same.

In 2001—marking its 50th anniversary—components of Grange were once again officially made at Magill. Although John Bird went into semi-retirement in 1996, he has continued to play a significant consultancy role in vinification, maturation and classification. In 2003, Chief Winemaker Peter Gago, keen to progress the idea of making a new crop of special releases, asked John Bird to make a visit down to Coonawarra in the hope of finding the 'right fruit' for such a project. Bird said, 'The 2004 Bin 60A is like a bookend to my winemaking career. I can remember Max Schubert pulling together blending options in the lab at Magill. And here I was almost exactly 40 years later on a scouting mission to look for the same type of fruit!'

John Bird celebrates 50 vintages at Penfolds in 2009. Peter Gago says, 'This is a remarkable milestone and a wonderful achievement. He has worked for all the great Penfolds winemakers and characters including Alfred Vesey, Jack Lang, Alfred Scholz, Max Schubert, John Davoren, Ray Beckwith, Don Ditter and John Duval. He is an integral part of the Penfolds story. His contribution to the evolution of house style, including the progression of Magill Estate and Grange, has been significant. There is something enduring and endearing about John Bird. It is hard to imagine vintage at Penfolds without him.'

THE PENFOLDS PHILOSOPHY

'We must not be afraid to put into effect the strength of our own convictions, continue to use our imagination in winemaking generally, and be prepared to experiment in order to gain something extra, different and unique in the world of wine.'

— MAX SCHUBERT

Is winemaking art, science or a craftsman's philosophy? At Penfolds, the role of the winemaker is to make the best possible wine within the constraints of each vintage. A deft hand, initiative, precision, a touch of guile and a sympathetic understanding of nature's colour and order are the tools in trade.

Penfolds' house style emerged from a fortified-wine-producing culture and evolved as a winemaking philosophy—a way of making wine—which has had a profound effect on the entire Australian wine industry. The development of red table wines during the 1950s was underpinned by an investment in new vineyards, winemaking equipment, skilled personnel and perhaps, most importantly, research and experimentation. Penfolds already had a reputation within the wine industry for its groundbreaking work during the 1930s and '40s in overcoming spoilage and wine stability problems—an industry-wide concern. It employed a full-time chemist, Ray Beckwith, to investigate and research every aspect of the winemaking process and to develop ways of improving all Penfolds wines. His contribution supported the extraordinary creative development during the 1950s of Penfolds Grange and St Henri by Max Schubert and John Davoren. It was again groundbreaking work

that would have an enormous impact on winemaking around the world. His preventative winemaking regime—originally kept under strict wraps—would eventually filter through the Australian wine industry and overseas. Ian Hickinbotham, a veteran Australian winemaker and industry observer, said, 'Let's be blunt—there would have been no Grange without Beckwith's brilliance. Possibly, Beckwith contributed more to Australian oenology than any other and he should be recognised in the same class as Louis Pasteur.'

During the 1950s, Penfolds was a centre of creativity and innovation. With highly intuitive and imaginative winemakers and benevolent, production-orientated owners—particularly Jeffrey Penfold Hyland—Penfolds made considerable technical and applied winemaking advances. The remarkable 'Story of Grange' by Max Schubert, reproduced in Chapter 2, gives an insightful view of the times. While he was ordered to stop production of Grange in 1957, Penfolds had already set an irrevocable course towards table-wine production.

The professional rivalry between Max Schubert and John Davoren resulted in a wide, rather than narrow, winemaking perspective. The development of Grange, however, had a major impact on Penfolds' winemaking culture. St Henri, a traditional style, inevitably played a cameo role, although its importance should not be underestimated. Penfolds' house style embraces the concept of multi-regional blending, optimum fruit quality, the use of fine-grained American (and increasingly French) oak, barrel fermentation and maturation.

Max Schubert, who was appointed production manager at Magill Estate in 1948, was an early proponent of regional definition. His fascination with fruit quality and its specific demands resulted in a comprehensive understanding of vineyard performance. He said, 'The development of a new commercial wine, particularly of the high-grade range, depends on the quality and availability of the raw material, the maintenance of standard and continuity of style.' He achieved this through identifying specific vineyard sites and developing relationships with growers. While developing Grange he observed that using shiraz from two specific vineyards would 'result in an improved all-round wine'. During the 1950s, Max Schubert searched widely for suitable fruit, particularly in the foothills around Adelaide, McLaren Vale and the Barossa Valley. Both Max Schubert and John Davoren were mindful of vinification and maturation practices in Bordeaux.

The development of both Grange and St Henri was modelled on claret styles. The availability of Bordeaux grape varieties in South Australia, however, was limited. Schubert soon favoured shiraz, largely because of the spectrum of ripe flavours, tannin structures and the relative ease of supply. He struggled initially with cabernet sauvignon, largely because of its scarcity and capricious nature in the South Australian climate. John Davoren was also similarly constrained. His first experimental St Henri vintages were based on cabernet and mataro. Shiraz, however, would play an increasingly important part in the style. Both winemakers, steeped in the historical importance of the 'noble grape variety', would use cabernet to add perfume and structure to their wines. The release of Bin 389 in 1960—a cabernet–shiraz blend now considered an Australian classic—reflects the winemaking attitude of the time: that cabernet sauvignon did not have the power or mid-palate intensity to be made as a single wine. Improved vineyard management, site selection and winemaking has resulted in the subsequent releases and success of Bin 707 and Bin 407 Cabernet Sauvignon.

The concept of multi-regional and vineyard blending, a feature of the Penfolds house style, is an amplification of the 'all-round wine'. Without the constraints of a single vineyard, winemakers could choose the best possible fruit with 'the outstanding characteristics of each vineyard'. This idea gathered pace during the 1960s, largely as a result of the success of Bin 389 and experimental cross-regional blends such as Penfolds Bin 60A. This method of fruit selection also contributed to a consistency of style. As the volume of production increased over the years, a method of classification was introduced to earmark particular fruit for individual bin numbers. This selection process has been further refined, allowing extraordinary blending options. The Rewards of Patience tasting showed that optimising fruit quality in blends does not compromise vintage character.

> *'At Penfolds the role of the winemaker is to make the*
> *best possible wine within the constraints of each vintage.'*

The felicitous choice of using American oak was one of availability. Max Schubert had noticed during his visit to Bordeaux in 1949 that some winemakers used new 'raw' oak during vinification and maturation. Actually, he had stumbled across a rare practice. Few clarets (red Bordeaux) at that time completed fermentation in barrel. However, it was true that top chateaux employed new oak during maturation; the percentage used depended on the quality of the vintage. His experiments with shiraz and American oak were profound. He discovered that if the wine completed fermentation in new American oak, the two components would generate a tremendous 'volume of bouquet and flavour'. Max Schubert remarked that, 'It was almost as if the new wood had acted as a catalyst to release previously unsuspected flavours from the Hermitage [sic] grape.'

The release of Bin 128 Coonawarra Shiraz in 1962 and Bin 28 Kalimna Shiraz in 1959 pre-empted the contemporary enthusiasm for regional definition by about 25 years. Max Schubert applied many of the techniques used in the research and development of Grange—using American oak and barrel fermentation—in these wines. All the same, the difference between the ripe opulent Bin 28 and elegant structured Bin 128—as shown in the Rewards of Patience tasting—illustrated strong regional differences.

James Halliday, the distinguished Australian wine critic and Rewards of Patience panel member once said, 'The so-called "Penfolds style" is so distinctive that to miss it meant either I or the wine was off-colour. The hallmarks are rich, sweet fruit which (within the constraints of the given vintage) is always at the riper end of the spectrum; oak influence which invariably manifests itself in the structure of the wines and, in the more expensive labels, to a marked degree in the flavour, with warm vanilla and spice, American oak to the fore; and in the invariably pronounced yet rounded tannins.'

While American oak has played a central role in the development of Penfolds red wines, French oak has been increasingly used in the evolution of new wines—particularly RWT and Yattarna. Don Ditter, who became Chief Winemaker in 1975, introduced French oak to the elegantly structured Bin 128 as a way of refining the style and emphasising its regional characteristics. RWT Barossa Shiraz, which is barrel fermented, is also particularly suited to the savoury nuances of French oak. Nowadays, Magill Estate Shiraz is matured in two-thirds French oak, and Bin 407 Cabernet Sauvignon in 50 per cent French oak.

Maturation in oak, which follows fermentation, is also a key to the Penfolds house style. Penfolds Grange, which is matured in American oak for a period of eighteen months, benefits greatly from the ageing process, where aromas and flavours derived from both fruit and oak evolve and tannins polymerise and soften. At the other end of the spectrum is Penfolds St Henri which benefits from the maturation effect—rather than from the influence of new oak. John Bird, however, has noted on several occasions a sibling likeness: 'There is some kind of similarity between St Henri and Grange between ten and fifteen years of age. There is no doubt about which stable they came from.'

Research and development continues to play an important part in the evolution of Penfolds. The Penfolds Flagship White Project—which resulted in the release of Penfolds Yattarna Chardonnay—echoes Max Schubert's sentiment of 'making something different and lasting'. Penfolds continues to experiment with new varieties, new vineyards and new winemaking techniques while improving on the tried and tested.

The Penfolds approach to winemaking has percolated through the Australian wine industry over the last 50 years. The use of American oak and barrel fermentation, for instance, is considered these days as a traditional Barossa winemaking practice! The techniques employed in the research and development of Penfolds wines are remarkable. Many of the discoveries and innovations have had a lasting impact on winemaking thinking. This is why 1951 Penfolds Grange is regarded as an historical curio and a treasure. The experimental Granges are a major body of achievement in the art and science of wine; perhaps the Australian wine industry's equivalent to the chronometer or powered flight.

Max Schubert and his team pioneered major advances in yeast technology and paper chromatography; the understanding and use of pH in controlling bacterial spoilage; the use of headed down/submerged cap fermentation and the technique of rack and return; cold fermentation practices; the use of American oak as a maturation vessel and, perhaps most critically, partial barrel fermentation. The Penfolds winemaking philosophy is the accumulation of more than half a century of knowledge and winemaking practice—initiated by Max Schubert and his 'navigator' Ray Beckwith. The Penfolds house style has a strong stamp of authenticity and provenance. While the wines have been refined over the years by chief winemakers Don Ditter, John Duval and Peter Gago, they are unmistakably Penfolds and distinctly Australian. In the end, however, the wines must speak for themselves—this is the essence of this sixth edition of *Penfolds: The Rewards of Patience*.

The issue of climate change has been gathering momentum in recent years. In Australia viticulturalists and winemakers have noticed that seasons are less predictable than they once were and a string of early vintages suggests that the growing season has accelerated. Many observers believe that climate change is an irrevocable reality and that the wine industry should prepare for an uncertain future. Scientists predict that by the end of the century the average mean January temperature in Australia will rise between 1 and 4 degrees Celsius. Other predictions include a rise in sea level, stronger winds, a higher risk of pests and diseases, and less water availability. Scientists have suggested that viticulturalists plant new vineyards at more southerly latitudes or at higher altitudes, grow heat-resistant grape varieties or adapt new techniques. Other observers believe that the Earth's temperatures are cyclic and that climate change is exaggerated. Dr Richard Smart, the eminent Australian viticulturalist, describes grape growing as agriculture's 'canary in the coal mine'.

The Australian wine industry has had a longstanding reputation for innovation and meeting new challenges. Whatever the truth, the climate change debate has already sparked initiatives and ideas to improve energy efficiency and carbon emissions across the entire Penfolds supply chain.

At the core of Penfolds' winemaking philosophy are the ideas of multi-district blending, individual vineyard selection, authenticity and guaranteed consistency of house style. Notwithstanding climate change, the hallmarks of great vineyard resources, advances in winemaking practices and excellence will always be a priority.

THE PENFOLDS WINEMAKERS

Max Schubert, Chief Winemaker 1948–75

Max Schubert, Penfolds Chief Winemaker and the creator of Grange, was one of the most important Australian winemaking figures of the twentieth century. His remarkable contribution to Penfolds wines is documented throughout this book and includes Schubert's own 'Story of Grange'—one of the most vivid and inspiring personal accounts of winemaking during the 1950s and '60s.

Max Schubert joined Penfolds in 1931 as a messenger boy. He learned his craft by working with some of the most experienced chemists and winemakers of the time. He never formally studied oenology, but his practical experience, natural inquisitiveness and team leadership led to remarkable innovations in winemaking, many of which percolated throughout the Australian wine industry. Huon Hooke, Schubert's biographer said, 'Max was a sensitive and highly intelligent but formally untrained man who learned by trial and error, by keen observation, by the seat of his pants. Hence he had his own explanations for some things and they may seem unorthodox.'

Schubert was appointed Penfolds National Production Manager (Chief Winemaker) from 1948 to 1975. His greatest achievement was Grange—a wine that would alter the course of Australian wine history and pave the way for future generations of winemakers. In his lifetime, Max received many awards including Member of the Order of Australia (AM) and the inaugural Maurice O'Shea Award for his contribution to the Australian wine industry. He was also named 1988 Man of the Year by the UK's *Decanter* magazine. James Halliday, Australian wine writer, noted, 'He was no more perfect than any of us, but he went as close to creating perfection in wine as anyone is ever likely to do.'

Don Ditter, Chief Winemaker 1975–86

Raised in South Australia's Barossa Valley, Don Ditter started work with Penfolds as a Laboratory Assistant at the Magill winery in Adelaide in December 1942.

From 1944 to 1945 he served in the RAAF and returned in 1946 to study winemaking at Roseworthy Agricultural College. After graduating in 1950 with first class honours, he was reassigned as an Assistant Winemaker at Penfolds Nuriootpa in the Barossa Valley. Without suitable technical people in New South Wales, he was lured to Sydney in 1953 to improve cellar operations and bottling at Penfolds' Queen Victoria Cellars in the central business district and at Alexandria in Sydney's inner west.

In 1963, Ditter was promoted to New South Wales Production Manager. In this position he was responsible for winemaking operations in Sydney, Minchinbury, Griffith and the Hunter Valley. As Chief Winemaker, the new title for national production manager, he oversaw the consolidation of Penfolds' winemaking to South Australia. This included a major overhaul of vineyard management, tracking of fruit, refinements in winemaking and bottling. A golden period followed with the release of Koonunga Hill and the re-release of Bin 707 and Ditter took the Grange style into the modern era.

Ditter retired in 1986 but remains a longstanding consultant with Penfolds. In 2008, Ditter received the Medal of the Order of Australia (OAM) for 'service to the Australian Wine Industry', particularly for his achievemnents as Chief Winemaker at Penfolds Wines'.

John Duval, Chief Winemaker 1986–2002

John Duval grew up on a mixed farm at Morphett Vale near Adelaide. His family were longstanding Penfolds growers. In fact, shiraz cuttings from the Duval's vineyard were used to plant blocks at Penfolds' Magill Estate Vineyard. After completing an Agricultural Science degree at Adelaide University and a postgraduate diploma in Oenology at Roseworthy College, Duval joined Penfolds in 1974 at Nuriootpa in the Barossa Valley. As an Assistant Winemaker he gained early experience working under managers John Davoren and Kevin Schroeter.

In 1989 he was named International Winemaker of the Year at the UK's 1989 International Wine & Spirit Competition. In 1991, and again in 2000, he was named Red Winemaker of the Year at the International Wine Challenge in London. John Duval oversaw many developments at Penfolds including the creation of Bin 407 Cabernet Sauvignon, Bin 138 Old Vine Barossa Valley Shiraz-Grenache-Mourvèdre and RWT Shiraz. The White Grange project, which would culminate in the release of the much vaunted Yattarna Chardonnay, also led to the spin-off Reserve Bin Chardonnay.

In 2002, John stepped down as Chief Winemaker after a 28-year distinguished career at Penfolds. He has since built up an international winemaking consultancy business and makes his own wine. However, he continues to act as a 'sounding board' to the red winemaking team.

Peter Gago, Chief Winemaker 2002–present

Peter Gago was born in Newcastle, England, and was raised from the age of six in Melbourne, Australia. After graduating with a Bachelor of Science degree from the University of Melbourne, he spent much of the 1980s teaching mathematics and chemistry.

At the age of 29 and at a career crossroads, Gago undertook a Bachelor of Applied Science in Oenology at Roseworthy Agricultural College graduating as dux of his course. In 1989 he joined Penfolds as a sparkling winemaker, eventually becoming Penfolds Red Wine Oenologist. In 2002, Peter Gago succeeded John Duval as Penfolds Chief Winemaker—the fourth person to hold the position since Max Schubert was first appointed in 1948.

Gago's imprint on the Penfolds house style reflects a strong sense of custodianship. 'I would not say that my style is particularly evident in the winemaking, although I'm a firm believer in no filtration or fining, natural yeasts, open-top fermenting and other non-invasive techniques. For me, it's about knowing when to interfere and when to stay out of the way.'

While Gago has won several awards, including the prestigious *Wine Enthusiast* magazine's Winemaker of the Year in 2005, he insists Penfolds is all about team effort. This strongly held view has brought an important perspective shift. In 2007 Penfolds' red winemaking team was nominated as Winemaker of the Year by the Australian *Gourmet Traveller Wine* magazine. The Barons of the Barossa further recognised Gago's team by awarding Penfolds' Grange winemakers Winemaker of the Year, also in 2007!

Peter Gago's peripatetic energy and drive has brought great enthusiasm for Penfolds wines across the globe. Under his bailiwick, Penfolds has released Bin 311 Chardonnay, Bin 8 Cabernet Shiraz, a multitude of great wines under the Cellar Reserve label and the widely applauded 2004 Bin 60A Cabernet Shiraz and 2004 Block 42 Cabernet Sauvignon. Grange, St Henri, Bin 707, Bin 389 and myriad other bins continue to grow in stature.

Gago's role as Chief Winemaker is wide-ranging and embraces the reality of a worldwide market. At vintage time, he is a hands-on winemaker, but during the off season he is in heavy demand as the face of Penfolds. In this capacity, Peter excels as a teacher and promoter of Penfolds and Australian fine wine. He is regularly asked to participate in international forums and is the co-author of three educational books on wine.

CHAPTER FIVE

Care and Enjoyment

Penfolds wines appeal to a wide market, from the deadly serious wine collector to the casual wine drinker. Not everyone is interested in building up a wine cellar; however, there are a few basic guidelines that can be followed to maximise your Penfolds wine experience.

CELLARING AND SERVICE

Penfolds believes that the cellaring and service of fine wine should be an enjoyable experience for everyone. While there is a marvellous tradition and culture that embraces fine wine, some of the ideas and practices may seem antiquated or intimidating, especially to newcomers. Here we demystify a few.

Storing your wine

While many Penfolds wines will benefit from further bottle ageing, not all wines within the range are made for long-term cellaring. Thomas Hyland, Organic and Koonunga Hill ranges are generally made as fresh, early drinking wines. Only very special unique vintages may have any cellaring potential. Generally these wines are relatively inexpensive (depending on taxes and duties) and most buyers will consume these wines soon after purchase. Older bottles lying on shelves for several years may not have their original freshness. White wines are especially vulnerable to fluctuations in heat. As with all wines, it is best to understand the provenance of a cellared bottle to maximise your enjoyment.

Most of Penfolds' Bin, Cellar Reserve, Luxury and Icon wines will benefit from cellaring. The optimum bottle maturation period will depend on whether the wine is red or white, its style and vintage. This book provides detailed tasting notes and commentary regarding the cellaring potential of each wine. It should be noted that reds generally have a longer and more reliable cellaring history and the changeover to screw cap closures has had an immediate impact on maintaining freshness and quality of wine especially whites.

Wine collectors have the option of cellaring their wine at home or in public storage. The commercialisation of wine storage cabinets (wine fridges) is an exciting development, especially in warmer climes. They have become a very economical and practical way of keeping wine, especially in high-density living areas. These cabinets are made to optimum cellaring specifications. Generally the ideal cellar temperature is a constant of 14 to 16 degrees Celsius with a relative humidity of 65 to 75 per cent. These conditions are difficult to achieve naturally all year round.

'The optimum bottle maturation period will depend on whether the wine is red or white, its style and vintage.'

Some collectors have had their cellars made to these specifications using refrigeration rather than air-conditioning but air-conditioned cellars are a preferred option by some collectors. Temperatures, however, cannot be brought down below 17 degrees Celsius and wines can suffer from the ambient long-term dryness causing corks to crumble in this environment and there are a number of incidents where air-conditioners have kicked into reverse cycle causing irrevocable heat damage. Notwithstanding these anecdotes, this option has worked extremely well in Australia—especially when buckets filled with water are placed nearby.

Public storage is a good option, especially if the purpose of maturation is wine investment, but it can be expensive. Aside from optimum cellaring conditions, insurance companies often prefer the detailed records and security advantage these storage companies provide.

Keep your wine in a cool secure place and avoid temperature variation. A constant temperature of 18 degrees Celsius is better than 14 to 26 degrees Celsius over a year. The cellaring conditions need to be dark and free from vibrations.

Always lie bottles on their side

Bottles should be stored on their sides to ensure the cork remains wet. Corks can dry out if a bottle is left standing up, which will lead to ingression of air and oxidation. Screw-capped bottles are more resilient, but it's best to have these bottles lying down as well so that if a bottle is damaged you will identify leaking earlier.

There is no need to turn the bottles. Believe it or not there are a dwindling number of collectors who have religiously followed this practice for years in the belief that it further protects the wine from leakage. It is always a good thing, however, to check bottles for any cork movement. It is not unusual to find 'leakers', even in the best cellars.

Opening your wine

The great thing about screw caps is that you don't have to bother with a corkscrew. This is very useful when you need to open a bottle of wine and you are miles away from town. Unfortunately the 'missing corkscrew' is also a general household phenomena. While a piece of string and a knot is the last resort, a half-decent corkscrew is an essential tool for opening bottles of wine. The Penfolds Red Wine Re-corking Clinics use the long-barrelled, standard table model Screwpull® corkscrew. This has a teflon-coated pliable wire screw and a rigid frame which guides the screw into the centre of the cork and pulls it out automatically. Penfolds has also developed a method of getting really old corks out of the bottle by using two of these wire corkscrews at the same time. You can spend huge amounts of money on beautiful corkscrews, but the simple 'waiter's friend' will do the job most of the time.

Serving your wine

White wines are best served at cool, refrigerated temperatures. However, if the wine is too cold you will find that it will deaden aromas and flavours. Red wine is best served at a comfortable room temperature of 18 to 24 degrees Celsius. In Australia and in other hot climates it is sometimes necessary to cool the wine down a touch if it is a hot day.

How to decant

Serving fine wine can be something of a ceremony and the world is divided into two types of fine wine people: those that like to decant and those that don't.

The purpose of decanting is to take wine off its fine film of sediment. Penfolds encourages the use of decanters because it creates a sense of occasion and suits its wines, especially old bottles of Grange, Bin 707, St Henri, Magill Estate and Bin 389.

Penfolds often uses the method of double-decanting, especially for large wine dinners. Many wine collectors also double-decant for the sake of ease and identification of bottles on the table during a meal.

It is always best to bring red wine out of the cellar a good six to eight hours (or a day or two) prior to service. Let the bottle stand to allow the wine sediment to settle. Unscrew the cap or pull out the cork and pour the wine carefully and steadily into a clean jug or another bottle. Some people like using a funnel. Keep observing the wine through the neck and shoulder of the bottle. The wine will be crystal clear until the very end when sediment will appear. At this point stop pouring. Some people will use a candle or a torch while decanting. However, it can be just as easy in a bright room or daylight. Rinse out the original bottle with water and then decant back.

You can decant white wine, but usually this is an issue of personal preference. Penfolds often decants Yattarna and old vintages of riesling as they believe the wines benefit from the aeration.

A warning about wine glasses

There are several wine glasses available on the market. The style and shape is very much a personal thing. Some glass manufacturers suggest that the shape is responsible for the quality and the intensity of the bouquet and the flow of the wine. Penfolds prefers simple but decent-sized stemmed clear-cut glasses. However, sometimes it is a question of what is available at the time.

The poor storage of glasses is a problem that is rarely written about. If wine glasses are not regularly used they can collect fine dust and attract ambient odours and taints. If the glass is not washed out thoroughly prior to filling, it can actually overpower the wine and create a completely wrong impression. Glasses stored in wooden or antique cabinets are particularly prone to this problem. Dishwashers can also leave a film of detergent and if the glasses are not properly dried they can pick up the odours very quickly. Penfolds recommends that you wash and polish glasses prior to use unless you are sure of how the glasses are stored.

Tasting your wine

The practice of smelling and tasting wine before dinner or at a restaurant is a very practical tradition. It gives you an opportunity to check the wine is sound and free of fault before serving. The incidence of cork taint is, thankfully, on the decline. If the wine smells musty or like wet hessian and tastes horrible it is probably corked or served in a poorly stored glass. If it smells flat or stale it is probably oxidised. Sometimes odours will blow off; however, if you are unsure, you should ask your sommelier to check the wine for you. If there's no one else around for second opinion ask yourself 'am I happy to drink this?' Penfolds does everything it can to make sure the wine arrives at your table in perfect condition and it is proud of its long track record and reputation as one of the world's greatest wine producers. Penfolds is confident its wines will provide rich and memorable experiences.

We recommend that you seek further cellaring and service advice from your local wine merchant. Or you can contact us at www.penfolds.com.

PENFOLDS RED WINE RE-CORKING CLINICS

The Penfolds Red Wine Re-corking Clinics, established in 1991, are a unique travelling forum which brings wine collectors in personal contact with the Penfolds red winemaking team. Over 90,000 bottles belonging to thousands of wine enthusiasts have been assessed and, if necessary, topped up and re-corked. This ongoing free health check of old Penfolds bottles has become a popular institution in Australia.

STEP-BY-STEP GUIDE TO THE PENFOLDS RED WINE RE-CORKING CLINIC

Visual check:	If the level of the wine has slipped below the shoulder of the bottle, it is a good candidate for topping up and re-corking—especially if the collector intends to keep cellaring the wine. Overall condition of the bottle, age of the wine and reputation of vintage are all factors.	Volume loss or ullage occurs because of absorption, leakage and evaporation. Time, cork failure and cellaring conditions can all contribute to varying ullage levels.
Opening	Penfolds has developed a system of opening old bottles to overcome the problem of crumbling or welded-in corks. This includes the use of two interlocking long Screwpull® corkscrews and other gadgets.	A tasting portion of 10–15 ml is poured into a tasting glass. The bottle is then gassed with nitrogen or carbon dioxide or a combination of both to prevent oxidation. It is then stoppered temporarily.

Assessment:	Penfolds winemakers assess the wine—benchmarked against accumulated knowledge of vintages and perfectly cellared museum examples.	The wine is checked for transparency and sheen, aroma, palate freshness and typicity. Any wines deviating from the window of acceptability are failed. Bottles that pass are topped up.
		Wines that fail assessment or are in unacceptable condition are not topped up. These bottles are sealed with a plain cork and not re-capsuled. This effectively weeds poor condition bottles out of circulation and the mainstream secondary market.
Topping up:	The bottle is topped up with a current vintage of the same Penfolds wine, for example, Grange is topped up with Grange. St Henri with St Henri.	The bottle is topped up with 10–15 ml (2% of volume) of new wine. Penfolds believes that the new wine will take on the character of the old. It is widely felt, through comparative tastings over a period of time, that this does not affect the integrity of the contents.
Re-corking:	The topped-up bottle is gassed and then re-corked using a reverse pressure (vacuum) re-corking machine creating negative pressure.	The new corks are stamped with Penfolds Red Wine Clinic and dated.
Re-capsuling:	A Penfolds Red Wine Clinic capsule is moulded onto the bottle with a capsuling machine.	A clinic back label—numbered, dated and signed by a Penfolds winemaker—is affixed to the bottle certifying condition and authenticity. The label is endorsed by specialist wine auctioneers Langton's Fine Wine Auctions and Christie's or, if appropriate, by recognised auction houses. All re-corked bottle numbers are stored in a data bank.

The clinics are a remarkable wine experience where collectors are able to learn about the ageing progress of their wines and share their stories. Over the course of a single year, winemakers will have tasted most back vintages of Grange, Bin 707, St Henri and Bin 389. While it was never initially planned, the clinics have become an important bellwether where Penfolds is able to monitor the development of vintages across all possible cellaring conditions. The program has been so successful that it has almost entirely weeded poorly cellared bottles out of circulation. It has also promoted confidence and positive sentiment in the secondary wine markets. The Penfolds clinics generally take place each year on a rotational basis in major Australian cities. Penfolds has also held clinics on a regular basis in New Zealand, the United Kingdom, the United States, Singapore and Hong Kong.

Penfolds Red Wine Re-corking Clinics were inspired by the practice of re-corking old bottles by United Kingdom wine merchants and Bordeaux chateaux. In fact, Max Schubert would re-cork old bottles of Grange and other wines for his friends. A number of these bottles have turned up at Australian wine auctions over the years. Penfolds has reinvented this ad-hoc practice into a serious after-sales service for Penfolds wine collectors, ensuring that after many years of cellaring the wine has not overdeveloped or oxidised, making it undrinkable.

Penfolds' experience with re-corking is unmatched by any other wine company in the world. It has developed an awareness of diverse cellaring conditions, giving winemakers an insightful understanding of the maturation process. Ideal cellaring conditions are not only a matter of a cool temperatures and optimum relative humidity, but overall constancy of temperature and environment. Bottles lying in warmer cellars may develop more quickly, but not necessarily to the detriment of the overall quality of the wine. Conversely storing wines in very cold cellars can retard the maturation process.

The issue of cellar provenance is becoming more important, especially as wine markets become increasingly global. Anecdotal evidence at the Penfolds clinics shows that even in warm climates like those of Singapore and Hong Kong, wines can be kept perfectly sound.

Clinics in these markets show that the overall pass rate for wines in need of re-corking was extremely high, reflecting a very strong awareness of optimum storage conditions among Asian fine-wine collectors. The proliferation of wine storage cabinets has clearly made a great impact on the sales and storage of fine wine in these markets.

Peter Gago commented that both Singapore and Hong Kong have challenging climates for the long-term storage of wine. 'While Penfolds red wines have a reputation for cellaring well under robust conditions, we were not expecting such an impressive pass rate. We have seen some really fresh, beautifully cellared old vintages of Penfolds Grange, Bin 707 and experimental bins including 1962 Bin 60A Cabernet Shiraz. Clearly consumers have hugely benefited from the commercialisation of home refrigerated wine cabinets and the increasing presence of fine-wine storage businesses.'

Provenance

Cellar provenance—past cellaring conditions and origin—is a double-edged sword wielded by both collectors and sellers. The issue of provenance plays on the minds of all collectors, oiling sentiment and propelling or holding back demand. In the art world, provenance—meaning place of origin—is a term used to confirm the authenticity of works of art or antiques through a sequence of documented previous ownership and research. A painting with strong provenance brings certainty to the market, whereas weak provenance suggests risk.

When wine fifteen years or older comes into a Penfolds clinic, the overall condition of the bottle will give clues: lead capsules corrode; aluminium capsules lose their sheen; labels fade through light, water damage or humidity; label damage can be caused by silverfish or acidity in paper; ullage levels can vary according to cellaring conditions or quality of cork (the 1976 Grange—a very great year—is renowned for its bad quality cork); the overall sheen and condition of a bottle including ingrained soil, marks and the clarity/turbidity/deposit of wine as seen through the neck or bottle. Judging by the overall pass rate, most wines assessed by the clinic had been stored in acceptable to optimum conditions. Anecdotal evidence shows that a vast majority of private collectors keep their wine in cool under-house areas, climate controlled cellars, wine cabinets or wine storage.

Counterfeit wine is a relatively insignificant issue but also relates to provenance. Fake bottles of Penfolds Grange were discovered some years ago. The spelling errors on the label ('poor' instead of 'pour') show that counterfeiters should learn how to spell! The Penfolds clinics, however, have probably played a role in discouraging fakes. The wine and bottles are all closely scrutinised by winemakers and veteran auction experts.

The issue of authenticity lies at the heart of almost every fine wine debate. Snobbery, fear of change and vested interest are deeply rooted in this concept. Real and imagined concerns have been used as 'weapons of doubt' for centuries in the pursuit of market dominance. Tradition and reputation, deserved or not, are completely central to the argument. The Penfolds clinics enjoy strong support among Australian wine collectors. The program has attracted interest and participation in traditional overseas markets. While there are some people who believe that topping up destroys the genuine authenticity and character of aged wine, the enduring success of the clinics and the overwhelming interest in re-corked bottles on the secondary wine market illustrate a general acceptance of clinics among wine collectors around the world. This is a fine example of showing how a market reacts to intellectual debate.

The Penfolds clinics—a free service—have brought great pleasure, a degree of certainty and confidence to wine buyers and collectors. Penfolds is a cornerstone of Australian wine collecting. It has a reputation for making wines that improve, mature and last. While Penfolds Grange is the ultimate cellaring wine, the Rewards of Patience tasting shows the remarkable staying power of its Luxury and Bin red wines. 'Cliniced' bottles are greatly valued by collectors. This is proven by their strong and equitable performance on the secondary wine market. Downward pressure only applies to bottles which are 'not in mint condition'. Uncertified bottles are rejected;

few poorly cellared Penfolds wines ever reach the consumer through the secondary wine market. Penfolds clinics are an essential addition to the Penfolds red wine experience. Penfolds invites all of its collectors, large and small, to visit a Penfolds Red Wine Re-corking clinic. It is one of the most engaging and interesting events on the fine-wine calendar, where collectors can see how their bottles are developing and also learn about the long-term cellaring, service and care of Penfolds red wines.

THE SECONDARY WINE MARKET

Following are the most frequently asked questions about Penfolds at auction.

Why is Penfolds Grange such an important secondary market wine?

Penfolds Grange is a cornerstone of the Australian secondary (auction) market with a reputation and track record that rivals some of the great classified growths of Bordeaux and Burgundy. From around the mid-1960s, Grange could be found in most Australian wine collectors' cellars. The 1955 vintage was listed by the American wine consumer advocate *Wine Spectator* as one of the greatest wines of the twentieth century. It has won such accolades numerous times and is the only wine to be heritage-listed by the South Australian National Trust. The highly influential *Langton's Classification of Australian Wine* acknowledges Penfolds Grange as Australia's leading secondary wine market wine. Volume of supply and demand makes it one of the most highly traded wines at auction anywhere in the world. It has over a half century of history and price data, making it the most researched and talked about Australian wine. The fame of Grange has reached far and wide. Aside from the marvellous tastings, the remarkable auction values and the controversies, it is really Grange's aesthetic quality that makes it such an extraordinary thing. It is one of the few wines in the world that is treated as a treasured piece of art—by all walks of life. If there's ever a wine that can be called an experience, it is Grange. That is why it is followed with great interest by all observers of the Australian fine wine market.

What are the best-performing investment/collectible Granges?

The Grange market increasingly falls into two categories: Rare Grange (1951–63) and Vintage Grange (1964–present).

Rare Grange—The early experimental Granges were largely given away, meaning, in principle, the beneficiaries have made some outstanding returns! Even the early commercialised vintages—sold into the market for a few dollars—represent good investments today. It is unlikely, however, that any buyer or recipient really looked at the investment value of Grange during the 1950s and '60s. These early supporters enjoyed Grange because it was an interesting wine. It was not until the 1980s that Grange really made its name as an investment-type wine.

The rarest Granges are years 1956, 1957 and 1958. The most valuable Granges are 1951 (the first experimental vintage) and 1952. Interestingly, the 1951 was kept back as museum stock for years. It wasn't until the mid- to late 1980s that collectors were able to secure bottles.

This is one of the reasons that the labels and general appearance of the bottles are often in better condition than other vintages of the 1950s. The value of the 1951 is intrinsically linked to its historic significance—it is the most important wine ever to be made in Australia as it set the direction of contemporary Australian winemaking. The market for rare Grange is not as liquid as vintage Grange and therefore exposed to both volatility and malaise. It is a highly specialised area of the secondary market. A complete collection of Grange—in pristine condition and signed by Max Schubert, the creator of Grange—once sold for just under A$250,000.

Vintage Grange—Vintage Grange plays a major role in the Australian secondary wine market. It is seen as a key indicator of the economy and indeed for many years forecasters Access Economics used the 1971 vintage as an economic yardstick. For many years this wine outperformed other alternative investments including race horses, taxi plates and rare coins. However, all wines have a life and 1971 has not really kept up with the overall interest rate for some years. At one stage in 2003, it enjoyed a 45-fold increase on release price.

The best-performing Vintage Granges in the current market are 1986, 1990, 1991, 1998 and 1999. The 2000, not a recognised vintage, is a millennium wine and still tracks above expectations. The 2002 is also highly regarded and should perform to a similar pattern to 1999. Thirtieth and fortieth anniversaries also drive prices up.

What economic and environmental conditions have affected Grange's value?

Grange only became a global secondary market wine during the 1990s. While it is now regularly sold by the major wine auction houses around the world, the Australian market is still overwhelmingly dominant. During the 1960s and '70s, prices tracked at fairly moderate increments. A strengthening fine-wine market, based on an ascendant boutique Australian wine scene, allowed prices to evolve rapidly during the late 1980s. In 1987, Penfolds released the 1982 at over A$50—something of a milestone and a quantum leap on the year before. These boom years, supported by wealth generated across the Pacific Rim, saw Grange cement its place as Australia's top secondary market wine. In 1991 (1986 vintage released) Grange headed the inaugural *Langton's Classification of Australian Wine*.

The 1990 sold into the primary markets at an enormous premium on the previous year. This hyped—through tight allocations and a perception of short supply—but great vintage made a huge impact on the overall fine wine market. Grange prices at auction moved up and at the same time pulled up the values of other highly rated wines.

Prices faltered in the early 1990s during the Australian recession, but Grange prices held on. By the end of the 1990s, market strength reappeared. By the end of 1999 the Australian cult wine scene came into prominence, effectively creating a sluggish market for Grange for 18 to 24 months. The crash of this scene in early 2001 and the release of the excellent 1996 alleviated the Grange market malaise. Indeed, the strength of renewed interest was stark proof that track record, enduring quality and reputation are key drivers when it comes to a wine's performance at auction.

Grange prices again spiked after the release of the celebrated 1998. A short period of short supply and high volume of bidding saw prices escalate. The speculative market, however, subsided during the early 2000s. The superb 1999 vintage—living in the shadow of the 1998—has performed slowly for years, but in recent times has moved up significantly as buyers recognise its potential. The small vintage 2000, a millennium wine and very tightly allocated, has performed beyond expectations.

The most recent vintages of Grange are generally still available on the primary markets. Auction values relate to overall availability and vintage reputation. Certainly pricing in the primary market has a direct link with secondary wine market movements. With the increasing world-wide interest in Grange, perceptions of short supply and increasing First Growth stature in the global secondary wine market, prices are likely to remain firm in the foreseeable future.

Has international recognition brought a greater status to Grange at auction?

The exposure of 1990 Grange as *Wine Spectator*'s Wine of the Year (the first 'outsider' wine) certainly propelled sentiment. The mid-1990s was a highly successful period for Penfolds with extraordinary media focus—no doubt adding some sparkle to the market. It was also a time of great vertical tastings and traders, such as Anders Josephson, emerged as important market influencers. The Asian market also came to prominence, particularly Singapore and Hong Kong. These buyers had a profound effect on the secondary wine market, changing the pattern of buying and the way of cataloguing fine wine. Anything that deviated from pristine condition, including minor scuffs on labels or capsules, was simply ignored. Once considered idiosyncratic, this expectation has become standard across all markets and is a contributing factor to the increasingly high quality of personal and public wine storage.

Leading US wine critic Robert Parker has had a strong influence on the Asian wine market. He has been a champion of single-vineyard shirazes and became a lightning rod for the cult wine scene. He has tasted all of the Granges and even gave the 1976 Grange 100 points. Parker's influence on the Grange market itself is marginal. The wine is steeped in folklore and has a life of its own. Australians are very proud of Grange—many of the buyers are ordinary people who may not even be aware of Robert Parker. On the other hand 99 points for the 1998 Grange no doubt generated interest. But Australian taxi drivers probably had more influence!

What part did Grange play in the rise and fall of the cult wine scene?

Grange is the only Australian wine in the market, with the possible exception of Henschke Hill of Grace, which can really claim icon status. It has certainly prepared much of the groundwork for ultra-fine Australian wine. But it should be seen as distinct from the recent phenomena of cult wine. Consistency, ageing potential and pedigree has earned it its own club of one.

How much does condition and provenance affect the price of Grange?

Penfolds, through its Red Wine Re-corking Clinic program, has made provenance a major issue at auction. Anything that deviates from pristine condition is now subject to downward price pressure.

The clinics effectively mean that wines with issues such as poor levels are purchased at a discount. Previous cellaring conditions are an issue, but not as great as some people would like to think. Indeed, I believe quite strongly that the wine trade in Australia (and the UK) uses the issue of provenance as a weapon of doubt—a way of casting influence with their clientele. My experience with the clinics has shown that wine bottles that appear in good condition are generally okay. Anything with level problems or leaking capsules or even damaged or mouldy labels, can all suggest questionable provenance/past cellaring conditions. These wines are always catalogued accordingly and generally achieve the prices they deserve.

A successfully cliniced bottle—topped up, re-capsuled and back-labelled with a clinic label and winemaker's signature—will generally provide extra confidence to buyers. In Australia the concept of topping up is well received. Increasingly, the Penfolds Red Wine Re-corking Clinic has become a part of the fine wine landscape in Australia. Generally, re-corked wines from the 1970s and '80s do not attract a premium. In theory, prices are restored to par value. Increasingly, the Penfolds clinics add an assurance value to mature bottles. Buyers seeking the best provenance possible are now paying premium prices for cliniced bottles in mint condition—especially for experimental wines and older vintages.

Does the winemaker's signature make a difference in price?

There is generally a premium paid for old bottles of Penfolds wines with the signature of Max Schubert—the creator of Grange. Indeed they add extra rarity value to Grange collections. It is difficult to tell exactly what the premium is because the rare Grange market is so specialised and prices vary widely—it can be 10 to 20 per cent extra within the life of an auction itself. Signatures of Don Ditter, John Duval and current Penfolds Chief Winemaker Peter Gago generally only obtain premiums at charity auctions! The same applies to most living artists.

If Grange is the 'world's most consistently performing fine wine', then why do vintage prices vary so much?

There was a time when the secondary market paid little attention to the vagaries of vintage. Australia almost always had benign years, the wines were relatively cheap and expectations were generally low. However, this has all changed hugely in the last 40 years. Recognition of vintages has become a very important feature of fine wine. While Grange is a multi-vineyard, often multi-regional, wine it still reflects the conditions of vintage. The overall winemaking philosophy allows for consistency of style and quality, but vintage conditions will bring a stamp of their own. There is no such thing as a bad Grange vintage—but they are all different to each other. The light and shade across vintages is as palpable as any other series of great wines. The market appreciates this and also the historic idiosyncracies of Grange. For instance, 1972 is considered a dud year—although it is a glorious wine. Grange was binned in both South Australia and New South Wales until the 1970s, so there is some form of bottle variation, although this is not necessarily qualitative or quantifiable as the clinics have never revealed a meaningful difference. Buyer sentiment is always driven by the perception of quality, reputation and short supply. There is possibly a market phenomenon which won't allow more than a few stellar vintages in a ten-year period.

What other Penfolds wines perform on the secondary wine market?

Penfolds—especially Grange—has always performed reliably well through the thick and thin of the secondary market. Collectors and wine enthusiasts have a strong affection for the wines. Through a long track record of performance, recorded histories of tastings and plenty of anecdotal stories and experiences, they know exactly what to expect. Even with changes in ownership, Penfolds has maintained a strong production-focused image where quality, consistency and heritage are seen as vitally important. It is a great reputation to have, especially in times of uncertainty. The following are Penfolds' key performing secondary market wines.

- Penfolds Bin 707 Cabernet Sauvignon, classified exceptional by Langton's, is a top performer at auction. While Penfolds has reshuffled its portfolio, the secondary wine market still sees this wine aligned with Grange. It is made the same way and has always been something of a consort. It must be remembered that Max Schubert always had cabernet sauvignon at the back of his mind during the Grange experimental years. Bin 707 tracks at about half the price of Grange so buyers see the wine as great value.
- RWT Shiraz belongs to the strong Barossa shiraz genre. It is a highly evocative style. While it is distinctly Penfolds, it does show beautiful regional character. It does not have the same track record as Bin 389, Bin 707 or St Henri, but does share similar market strength.
- St Henri Shiraz is a sentimental favourite among Australian auction buyers. It has always performed solidly, but never spectacularly. The wines are often considered as old fashioned but as the Rewards of Patience tasting shows, this is really perception rather than necessarily reality; one opinion against another. If anything, St Henri is undervalued considering the history of this wine. Further vintages from the 2000s are exciting wines.
- Bin 389 Cabernet Shiraz is regarded as an important auction wine. It regularly attracts a high volume of bidding and interest. Indeed, it is the quintessential

Penfolds wine and offers tremendous value and quality. It is arguably the most popular cellaring wine on the auction market. Older vintages achieve similar prices to St Henri.

- Bin 407 Cabernet Sauvignon, Bin 28 Kalimna and Bin 128 Coonawarra Shirazes are always well sought after and regularly feature at auction. They are renowned for their reliability and consistency, but they are not treasured in the same way as the Icon and Luxury wines. These are some of the very best value Australian fine wines.

- The new 2004 Block 42 Cabernet and 2004 Bin 60A Cabernet Shiraz have debuted at strong prices. This falls in line with all Penfolds' experimental wines. Collectors love them.

- Yattarna Chardonnay, after an initial flurry during the late 1990s, performs moderately. Indeed, white wines are generally not strong performers on the secondary wine market unless they are special vintages. The youngest vintages are the most sought after.

What are the most famous Penfolds vintages?

The Grange market actually plays an important part in the psychology of Penfolds vintages. The best-performing Penfolds vintages almost exactly follow recognised Grange vintages—1952, 1953, 1955, 1962, 1963, 1966, 1971, 1976, 1983, 1986, 1990, 1991, 1996, 1998, 1999, 2002 and 2004.

The most famous experimental Penfolds wines are:

1948 Block 42 Kalimna Cabernet
1962 Bin 60A Coonawarra Cabernet Kalimna Shiraz
1966 Bin 620 Coonawarra Cabernet Shiraz
1967 Bin 7 Coonawarra Cabernet Kalimna Shiraz
1980 Bin 80A Coonawarra Cabernet Kalimna Shiraz
1982 Bin 820 Coonawarra Cabernet Shiraz
1990 Bin 90A Coonawarra Cabernet Kalimna Shiraz
1990 Bin 920 Coonawarra Cabernet Shiraz
1996 Block 42 Cabernet Sauvignon
2004 Block 42 Cabernet Sauvignon
2004 Bin 60A Coonawarra Cabernet Barossa Valley Shiraz

Where can I get detailed price data on Penfolds auction prices?

The most extensive up-to-date Penfolds wine price data, vintage and sales reports can be found on Langton's website at www.langtons.com.au. Prices are in Australian dollars.

— PART TWO —

The

WINES

PENFOLDS LEGEND OF WINES

ICON WINES

Penfolds Grange and Yattarna are the icons of Penfolds, the pinnacle of its winemaking efforts.

LUXURY WINES

Penfolds Luxury wines all show a distinctive and consistently recognisable style, with added complexity from the vagaries of each vintage.

SPECIAL BIN WINES

Penfolds Special Bin wines are experimental in nature. Each bottling has represented a point of progress in the modern Australian wine industry.

CELLAR RESERVE WINES

The Penfolds Cellar Reserve wines show great experimentation and innovation in winemaking. They are never widely available but always worth seeking out.

BIN WINES

The heart of the Bin range is sourcing the best fruit, from the finest vineyards, to marry to the distinctive Penfolds style.

ORGANIC WINES

The Penfolds Organic wines represent low-input viticulture. The vineyard is not exposed to man-made fertilisers, herbicides or pesticides.

THOMAS HYLAND WINES

The Thomas Hyland wines, sourced from the Adelaide vineyard of that name, honour the legacy of Dr Penfold's son-in-law.

KOONUNGA HILL WINES

The outstanding quality and unique Penfolds style of Koonunga Hill wines have been upheld since the first vintage in 1976.

RAWSON'S RETREAT WINES

Every ounce of winemaking effort applied to Grange applies to Rawson's Retreat, Penfolds' entry-point wine.

FORTIFIED WINES

The Penfolds fortified wines represent the rich tradition of Penfolds' winemaking history.

THE PANELLISTS

The Rewards of Patience tastings have become something of an Australian wine tradition. The panel members are each invited to participate in this extensive museum tasting because of their expertise, experience and standing in the field of Australian and international wine criticism.

The tasting notes and discussion are constructed to reflect individual thoughts, perceptions and contrary points of view. The tasting notes are written to echo the overall consensus of opinion. The discussion is a construction of annotated conversations and individual tasting notes, highlighting personal perspectives and individual voices.

While panellists often agreed with each other, there were occasions when tasters had differing opinions. Together the tastings notes and discussion provide an authoritative, informative and unique insight into the Penfolds wine experience.

There are some tasting notes in italics. These additional reviews have been written by Andrew Caillard to fill in gaps where wines were not tasted by the panel. Most of these wines were tasted at Langton's, Sydney, in early 2008. There are a few older wines, mostly regarded as past, that were not tasted for the sixth edition. In rare instances, previous reviews—also in italics—from the fifth edition of *Penfolds: The Rewards of Patience* have been included for reference purposes.

INDEPENDENT PANELLISTS: Campbell Mattinson, Andrew Caillard, Neil Beckett, Joshua Greene, Huon Hooke, Ch'ng Poh Tiong and James Halliday.

PENFOLDS PANELLISTS: Peter Gago (Penfolds Chief Winemaker), Don Ditter (former Penfolds Chief Winemaker), Dr Ray Beckwith (former Penfolds Research Chemist/Oenologist), Steve Lienert (Penfolds Senior Red Winemaker), Oliver Crawford (former Penfolds Senior White Winemaker) and John Bird (former Penfolds Senior Winemaker and consultant).

From left to right above: Campbell Mattinson, Andrew Caillard, Neil Beckett, Joshua Greene, Huon Hooke, Ch'ng Poh Tiong and James Halliday.

CHAPTER SIX

Icon Wines

Penfolds icon wines are steeped in the ethos of a great winemaking culture, enduring philosophy and heritage.

Penfolds Bin 95 Grange Shiraz is an Australian national treasure. Its history is inextricably linked with the development of the modern Australian wine industry. Many of the winemaking techniques and philosophies associated with Grange were adopted by other winemakers around the country. Max Schubert, the creator of Grange, once said, 'Grange has always been a controversial and individual wine. It is my belief that if these two characteristics can be combined, then at least half of the ingredients of success have been achieved.'

It is with this type of spirit that Bin 144 Yattarna was born. A new generation of Penfolds winemakers embarked on a journey of research and experimentation. Yattarna, a South Australian Indigenous word meaning 'little by little, gradually', evokes the painstaking task of trial and error in making a completely new wine. Both Grange and Yattarna are utterly unique Australian icon wines which have set the standard of contemporary winemaking practice.

RED

Bin 95 Grange Shiraz

First Vintage:	1951 experimental, 1952 commercial.
Variety:	Shiraz and cabernet sauvignon (usually a small percentage).
Origin:	Almost always a multi-district blend, South Australia. Significant shiraz contributions from the Barossa Valley and McLaren Vale; cabernet sauvignon from Coonawarra, McLaren Vale, Padthaway, Robe and Bordertown.
Fermentation:	Stainless steel tanks with wax-lined/wooden header boards. All components complete fermentation in barrel.
Maturation:	18–20 months in new American oak hogsheads (300 litres).
Comments:	Named after Grange Cottage, built in 1845, at Magill Estate and itself named for Mary Penfold's family home in England. Labelled Grange Hermitage until the 1989 vintage, Grange since the 1990 vintage. Made at Magill until 1973, Nuriootpa, Barossa Valley until 2000 and partly returned to Magill for the 2002 vintage. Packaged in laser-etched bottles with identification numbers since the 1994 vintage. Limited availability in all Penfolds markets.

Penfolds Grange is an Australian icon—a National Trust heritage-listed wine—which captures both a 'sense of place' and the essence of Australian agricultural ingenuity and innovation. The story of Grange is steeped in the Australian ethos. Max Schubert is an Australian folk hero, a man who battled against the odds and then succeeded in creating one of the very great wines of the world.

Penfolds Grange is totally unique. It is a beautifully seductive, richly concentrated wine which evokes the spirit of the Australian landscape, its natural affinity with shiraz, and Penfolds' remarkable winemaking philosophy. Each vintage of Penfolds Grange—with its own vintage character—continually evolves and surprises. Today the style remains distinctive and individual. It is a wine of immense power, plush concentration and balance. The overall philosophy of style relies on a combination of ripe, concentrated fruit and fine-grained and specially selected American oak woven together by barrel fermentation and careful maturation. Great vintages will last longer than 50 years. Ordinary vintages will last for at least twenty. This is achieved through vintage triaging and classification—a system that ensures that only the best components find their way into the final Grange blend.

A complete review of Penfolds Grange over six decades is a rare event. In many respects, each progressive vintage reflects the advancement of the modern Australian wine industry. While there were other important pioneering winemakers, including

Maurice O'Shea, Colin Preece and Roger Warren, it is Max Schubert's legacy that is perhaps the most enduring and inspiring. His work was a collaborative effort. Like Sir Donald Bradman, Australia's legendary cricketer, Schubert was the star batsman in a team of outstanding players. His brilliance lay in the conviction of his own ideas, and in his inventiveness and leadership. When it was time to go he passed on the baton, allowing his beloved Grange to become entrenched in Australian wine lore with an identity of its own.

While many of the techniques employed in the research and development of Penfolds' red wines were kept under strict wraps for commercial advantage, Schubert's winemaking philosophies and innovations eventually percolated through the industry. Many of these methods are now standard winemaking practice. The fame of Grange has reached far and wide. Aside from the marvellous tastings, the extraordinary auction values and the controversies, it is really Grange's aesthetic quality that makes it such an extraordinary wine. It is one of the few wines of the world that is treated like a treasured artwork.

Max Schubert (1915–1994) was a pivotal figure in the modern Australian wine industry. Born at Moculta, near Angaston in South Australia, his family moved to Nuriootpa when he was five. It was here that he attended high school, working part-time at the local butcher's to afford his books and pay his way through school. Having completed his intermediate certificate, he joined Penfolds just shy of his sixteenth birthday. His first job was feeding the horses and cleaning out the stables. Shortly after, he was assigned to the laboratory. Schubert said, 'I was a fetch and carry boy, but I used to tell people I was a trainee laboratory assistant.' Penfolds was run like a military organisation in the early 1930s and working conditions were tough. Fortified wine production was the main focus although sherry was an emerging seller.

Working under the notoriously difficult Austrian wine chemist John Farsch, Schubert learned how to propagate and prepare winemaking yeasts, culture and seed flor yeasts into barrel, and identify problems including acetic acid, bacterial spoilage and metal contamination. Leslie Penfold Hyland, the Penfold family's entrepreneurial State Manager, noticed Schubert and relocated him to Magill where he worked with Alfred Vesey, one of the great blenders of his time, helping him prepare samples for wine shows. Don Ditter, who would replace Schubert as National Production Manager in 1973 said, 'Alf Vesey was one of the early Penfolds pioneers who attended to the style and quality of Penfolds brands commencing from the early days of operation in South Australia. Max would have learned a thing or two under Alf's wing.'

Schubert studied part-time at the Adelaide School of Mines to learn applied chemistry. At the time, Penfolds was losing about 25 per cent of its production to spoilage. Ray Beckwith, Penfolds' Research Chemist at Nuriootpa, made his groundbreaking discovery of pH control around this time. It solved Penfolds' spoilage problems and paved the way forward for the production of table wines (notwithstanding its high-strength Italian Dry Red, specially made for Italian immigrants working the sugar cane fields of Queensland).

Schubert's responsibilities steadily progressed, and he became Assistant Winemaker at Magill. In 1940 he left Penfolds to join the Australian Imperial Forces: 'I volunteered for service because I wanted to prove that I was 100 per cent Australian.' He served in the sixth division of the second AIF in the Middle East and was then redeployed to New Guinea in 1942 until 1945. He married Thelma Humphrys, who worked in Penfolds' accounts department at Magill, in 1944 while on leave. Schubert rejoined Penfolds in 1946 at the more junior level of Laboratory Assistant. Within twelve months he was promoted to the role of Chief Winemaker at Magill. In 1950, Max Schubert was sent to Europe to investigate advances in sherry and port production.

Schubert first arrived in London, where he was shocked to observe wine merchants bolstering Spanish sherry and cheap French and Italian reds with imported Australian wine. In Jerez he discovered barrel fermentation, an idea that gathered momentum when visiting Bordeaux. He discovered this unusual practice in the cellars of négociant firm Cruse et Fils Frères, Chateau Rausan-Segla and Chateau Pontet-Canet where, towards the end of vinification, the wine was racked into new oak barrels to complete fermentation. He also noticed the practice of tannin fining—a technique widely used in France to modify palate texture. He was fortunate to have been in Bordeaux twelve months after the great 1949 vintage and would never forget what great young Claret tasted like.

The septuagenarian principal, Christian Cruse, took Schubert around many of the great Bordeaux wine estates, including Chateau Margaux, Chateau Haut-Brion and Chateau Ausone. Such hospitality to a young Australian would have been rare in those days. However, Schubert's charm, inquisitiveness and credentials as an ex-soldier may have held him in good stead. The visit to Europe included Germany and firsthand observations of the latest innovations in white winemaking. While the purpose of the entire trip was to learn about advances in fortified technology—especially sherry—Schubert's chance visit to Bordeaux altered the course of Australian wine.

On his return to Australia, Max Schubert employed his newly acquired ideas and made an experimental wine from the 1951 vintage. Sandie Coff, his daughter, recalls, 'Dad told me he designed Grange in his head in the plane on his way back from Europe. It would be a truly Australian wine but able to rival the wonderful French wines he had seen.' Using shiraz fruit from Magill and Morphett Vale, he produced the first Grange Hermitage. Max Schubert called the wine Hermitage rather than Shiraz to 'pander to the snobs in New South Wales', an important market for Penfolds. Indeed, a visitor to Sydney, impressed by the number of Penfolds wine bars and advertising hoardings, once said that the city might as well be called Penfolds.

Ray Beckwith, Penfolds Research Chemist, said, 'Submerged cap fermentation (with the help of heading-down boards) was, and still is, in some quarters, the classical method of winemaking, particularly the reds. Max Schubert used this method with great success at Magill in the 1950s in producing his classical Grange Hermitage and other memorable wines. He did not use a centre pump, but he pumped or drained the fermenting juice from the fermenter completely and returned it via cooling equipment, thereby getting very good extraction of colour and tannin, which is such a feature of those special wines, plus good temperature control.'

Schubert favoured the use of drainings to bolster the colour and extract of his wines. At the tail end of vinification, the wines were racked into five new 300-litre American oak hogshead barrels to complete fermentation. The wine was then matured in new oak for a further eighteen months prior to bottling. These revolutionary techniques of the time have become practices central to Penfolds' winemaking philosophy of today. 'The Story of Grange' (Chapter 2), written over 30 years ago by its creator Max Schubert, makes compelling reading.

In Huon Hooke's biography *Max Schubert—Winemaker* (1994), Schubert lists his trademarks as a 'penchant for oak in every wine' and 'a little shiraz in everything I make'. The techniques employed in the research and development of Grange, however, are astonishing. Max Schubert and his team—particularly Ray Beckwith—pioneered major advances in yeast technology and paper chromatography; the understanding and application of pH in controlling bacterial spoilage; the use of headed-down/submerged cap fermentation and the technique of rack and return; cold fermentation practices; the use of American oak as a maturation vessel; and, perhaps most critically, from the point of view of style; the use of partial barrel fermentation.

One of the great strengths of the Penfolds Grange style is that it does not rely on the performance of a single vineyard. Max Schubert recognised that Grange should be based on a riper spectrum of fruit. He knew intuitively that fruit power, concentration and ripe tannins were key components of optimum fruit quality. He was well ahead of his time. His experimental work in the 1950s confirmed his view that cabernet was unreliable. He observed: 'The imbalance of the fruit invariably manifested itself on the palate with a noticeable break in the middle and a thinnish astringent finish.'

The 1951 is a historical curio and Australia's most expensive wine. It is now well past its best. In 2001 it achieved a record price of A$52,211 at auction. On the other hand, the early Granges in the tasting were holding up well. Joshua Greene wrote, 'Those early experimental wines—particularly the 1952, 1953 and 1955—are more than mere ghosts. They are present in the glass, feisty and still fresh. They haven't unravelled in old age, they haven't begun to separate into alcohol and tannin and acidity. Instead they glow as one complete entity. They seem to have stepped out of time.'

Don Ditter said, 'When Max started to put together Grange, he only imagined the wine would last at least twenty years. Instead they have aged for 50 years. I am amazed how they have stood up. Some have faded—especially the hidden Granges—but as a group these early 1950s wines are very impressive.' Neil Beckett observed, 'The 1950s were a real step back in time and very exciting to taste. They had astonishing aromas, flavours and glove leather textures. The 1953, 1955 and 1959 had a very aristocratic countenance, limpidity of flavour and finesse.'

The criticism fired at Max Schubert's early Granges reflected a conservatism prevalent throughout winemaking circles. Australian red wines at that time were relatively elegant wines with medium concentration and matured in old oak. Max Schubert remembered the jibes: 'A concoction of wild fruits and sundry berries with crushed ants predominating', or perhaps more famously, 'Schubert, I congratulate you. A very good dry port, which no one in their right mind will buy—let alone drink.'

With the benefit of hindsight it is perhaps unsurprising that Grange attracted so much criticism. Grange was a radical departure from the norm. Everything about the wine was substantial. The fruit was ripe and concentrated and the new American oak featured strongly. The barrel ferment characters and level of volatile acidity—features of the style—were also greatly misunderstood. To add insult to injury, the Grange project was also utilising a substantial amount of working capital in the form of unreleased and maturing wine. The infamous tasting of Grange by Penfolds board members (led by Gladys Penfold Hyland), Sydney wine identities, friends and top management, which resulted in the 1957 decision to cease Grange production, was a fait accompli and a disaster for Max Schubert.

Jeffrey Penfold Hyland, who was South Australian Manager of Penfolds and not one to buckle to authority (he had many run-ins with his father Leslie), was complicit in the making of the secret Granges. Schubert's biographer, Huon Hooke, says, 'The hidden Granges (1957, 1958 and 1959) were made, matured and bottled in strict secrecy and word never leaked out to the powers-that-be.' Without a budget, Max Schubert had to make do with abandoned bottles found lying in the cellars at Auldana and used American oak hogsheads, although the winemaking technique comprising partial barrel fermentation was continued. The maturation time in oak, however, was halved to just nine months. The 'hidden' Granges were stored away in the Magill drives built by Alfred Scholz. This whole affair could not have been carried off without the support of Murray Marchant and Gordon Colquist, Schubert's senior winemakers, who helped care for the wines during uncertain times. These early experimental wines, when eventually released, were affixed with Penfolds' famous postage stamp labels—specially typed up by Max Schubert's secretary. Some of the old type labels are actually carbon copies; such was the rudimentary approach to packaging in those days.

The 1957 and 1958 Granges—extremely rare these days—never had the complexity and power of earlier vintages. Many examples are well past their best. However James Halliday commented, 'The hidden Granges stand foursquare against 1952 to 1956. Without the new oak they are inevitably linear and less complex, but they are still remarkable old wines. One can only wonder at how good they would have been had Max Schubert had access to new oak.' The 1959 was subsequently released commercially after Penfolds management rescinded its earlier decision to stop making the wine. Max Schubert called it 'a full blessing from head office'.

A second tasting with the same board members was organised in 1960 by Doug Lamb, a consultant wine merchant, Penfolds director and supporter of Schubert. This time the 1951 and 1955 vintages—both with bottle age development—were greeted with enthusiasm (the 1955 went on to have a very successful wine show career). Grange was reinstated and gradually won acceptance among the cognoscenti. Len Evans, in his last published book, *How to Taste Wine*, remembered, 'Great Granges were often quite volatile and the 1955 caused a show incident. I was on a panel of three, two of whom, including me, gave the wine a gold [medal]. We recognised the acetic acid but also gloried in the flavour, depth and balance of the wine. The other judge gave it 13, a very low score, and wouldn't budge. The chairman, the late, great George Fairbrother, a man of infinite patience and great charm, took one sniff of it and said to the dissenter, "Well if you won't budge, I'm afraid I'll have to overrule you and give it a Chairman's gold." In the 25 to 30 shows I judged under his guidance he only did this with one other wine, the famous Stonyfell 1945 Vintage Port.' George Fairbrother, a doyen of Australian Wine Show judges, was clearly instrumental in garnering support for the style.

In 1960 Schubert was promoted to National Production Manager—the equivalent position to Penfolds Chief Winemaker. He was responsible for all the company's wineries and vineyards. This was a period of strategic expansion and consolidation for the company in both New South Wales and South Australia. While the purchase of New Dalwood in the Hunter Valley would be short lived, the acquisition of significant vineyard holdings on prime terra rossa soils in Coonawarra was an important step forward for Penfolds during the 1960s as the urbanisation of Adelaide would shortly engulf several longstanding vineyards, including Modbury, Morphett Vale, Auldana and Magill.

The expansion of Kalimna and the purchase of Coonawarra vineyards was all about protecting valuable grape supply and maintaining house style. Several of the old vineyard holdings used for port or sherry production were replanted to table wine varieties. This was an exciting period at Penfolds, when new ideas and practices were implemented at every level. John Bird recollects, 'Max Schubert adored his senior cellar staff. They had gone through thick and thin with him. As a new staff member, I was completely awestruck by the scale of table winemaking and the great working atmosphere.'

Max Schubert inaugurated the annual vintage Classification Tasting: a convocation of Penfolds winemakers that continues to this day. At this forum all wines of the vintage could be tasted and classified according to style and Penfolds wine type. New technology was also introduced, including temperature control, winery hygiene, inert pipes, stainless steel, Willmes air bag presses and general quality control.

During the 1960s, Penfolds Grange firmed up its position as Australia's most distinguished wine. Previously it had been a small-scale wine of 'only four or five barrels'. Vigneron and wine author Max Lake observed: 'There has been quite an amount of experimentation with various wines and blends till today it is obvious the style is consolidated into a consistently outstanding wine.' The 1960 and 1962 Granges were highly successful wines: 'They have superb, magnificent bouquet and balance running right through the start to finish.'

James Halliday noted: 'The 1960s started strongly. What a change they are from the hidden vintages—they have more perfume and lifted aromatics, silky and voluptuous red fruits. 1965 was a successful show Grange and one of Max's favourites, but despite its record it was never a headline Grange. The 1966 was a rich and satisfying wine. 1964, 1968 and 1969, however, were not as compelling.'

While Kalimna has been a longstanding source for Grange (since 1953), Coonawarra has occasionally contributed fruit to Grange since 1961. Schubert oversaw the commercialisation of several new Penfolds red wines, including the now-famous Bin 128 Coonawarra Shiraz, Bin 28 Kalimna Shiraz, Bin 389 Cabernet Shiraz and Bin

707 Cabernet Sauvignon. Several experimental wines were made during this period, including special one-off wines such as 1962 Bin 60A, 1966 Bin 620 and 1967 Bin 7 (see Special Bin Reds). However, it is the story of Grange that largely defines Max Schubert's career at Penfolds.

The 1960 to 1977 Penfolds Grange vintages were regularly entered into Australian wine shows with considerable success. Both the 1965 and 1967 vintages won the prestigious Jimmy Watson Trophy at the Melbourne Wine Show and it earned a considerable swag of gold, silver and bronze medals in Australian capital city wine shows. The 1962 won over 50 gold medals in its show career! Len Evans, the hugely influential wine show judge and legendary Australian industry leader, said in his publication *The Wine Buyer* in 1972: 'Most people who have been lucky enough to see the wines of the early 1950s and others like the '62 would agree that we have been treated to something quite extraordinary. And whatever comparisons made to the wines of Bordeaux I believe that the real Granges represent a new, great wine style of the world.'

Joshua Greene wrote in his review of the tasting: 'Ian Hickinbotham (an important pioneering winemaker at Wynns Coonawarra Estate), once said to me that Schubert used to encourage volatile acidity, leaving the bungs out of cask and then taking samples around to other winemakers. The 1971 is suffering a bit from VA [volatile acidity], but then it opened to a beautiful range of fruit and sleek tannins. What you lose in the initial mustiness, you gain in the wild mulberry, cranberry and boysenberry flavours. It almost seems a contradiction that a wine this volatile could be this fresh.' The panel agreed that 1971, 1976 and 1978 were the best vintages of the decade. James Halliday also pointed out the 'extra polish and assured footing of Grange—post 1976'.

Max Schubert retired as Chief Winemaker in 1975 but remained involved as a consultant 'winemaker emeritus' for another twenty vintages. He was recognised in his own lifetime with membership of the Order of Australia (AM) in 1984 and the inaugural McWilliam's-sponsored Maurice O'Shea Award in 1990. *Decanter* magazine designated him Man of the Year in 1988.

Schubert, who died in 1994, was a self-taught but practical winemaker with a natural inquisitiveness for winemaking theory. He had a whimsical and romantic view of winemaking too. He once said: 'I'd like to think that the wines with which I have been associated are descended from one ancestor vineyard established many years ago, marrying with another, and another, and even another if you like, thus creating and establishing a dynasty of wines. These may differ in character year by year, but all bear an unmistakable resemblance and relationship to each other ... This whole approach and concept has been of great assistance to me, not only in the technical sphere, but as a means of stimulating my imaginative powers as far as winemaking is concerned ... All winemakers should possess a good fertile imagination if they are to be successful in their craft.'

In 2000, the South Australian parliament created a new state electoral boundary, with the Barossa Valley at its centre, called Schubert, in memory of Max Schubert and his extraordinary contribution to the prestige of South Australia and its wine industry.

Don Ditter joined Penfolds as a laboratory assistant in 1942, and was appointed by Max Schubert as his successor in 1975. Ditter, who grew up in the Barossa, was interviewed and recommended by Ray Beckwith. He started at Magill and worked for John Farsch, who had a reputation for not being able to keep staff. 'He was so relieved to have help during vintage that he kept me on.' On turning eighteen, Ditter joined the Royal Australian Air Force but did not see active service: 'The war was ending and they didn't know what to do with us.'

In 1946 Ditter undertook wine studies at Roseworthy Agricultural College—now a part of the University of Adelaide. Les Eckert and Bill Jamieson were classmates. Ray Kidd, Doug Collett and Ray Ward, also important wine industry identities during the 1950s, '60s and '70s, were also students at the same time. During his last year at Roseworthy, Ditter was asked to join Penfolds and was paid a retainer. He graduated in 1950 with first class honours and returned to Penfolds, this time to Nuriootpa in the Barossa Valley, working with Ray Beckwith. Ditter said, 'Ray not only trained me about all applied technical aspects of wine, but he also taught me about diplomacy. Whenever I got worked up about an issue I used to sleep on it.' Alfred Scholz, who was manager of Nuriootpa, was an ex-miner (he built the wine maturation tunnel at Kalimna and the drives at Magill) with a notoriously fierce temper. He ran his winery with an iron rod. However, Ditter survived his internship with him at Nuriootpa.

In the early 1950s, Ditter worked for John Davoren, the creator of St Henri, but also a highly skilled maker of sparkling wine. In 1953 he was transferred to Sydney to take on the responsibility of winemaker of the two cellars in Sydney—located at Alexandria and the Queen Victoria Building in the central business district. At the time, Penfolds had several depots around Sydney. Ditter said 'a lot of the wine was unsound'. Ditter's diplomatic skills were essential. 'The cellars were full of old-timers adamant that nothing was going to change.' Bottling was postponed, for instance, if a thunderstorm was predicted. Within a few years Ditter had successfully put in place a modern winemaking regime, paving the way for a golden period of fine table wine production.

In 1958, a new state-of-the-art winemaking facility was built at Tempe near Sydney's international airport. In 1963 Ditter was promoted to New South Wales Production Manager. In this position he was responsible for winemaking operations in Sydney, the soon-to-close-down Minchinbury, Griffith and the Hunter Valley.

Max Schubert quickly identified Ditter as a kindred winemaking spirit with an eye for detail. They would travel extensively around New South Wales and Schubert commented that Ditter was 'a natural talent at blending'. Ditter was an exceptional winemaker whose main ambitions were 'to maintain the style and improve the quality and prestige of Penfolds'. In 1973 Ditter was appointed National Production Manager, in control of all winemaking operations. In 1975 the title of Chief Winemaker was added following the retirement of Max Schubert.

Don Ditter took the Grange style into the modern era. This included a major overhaul of vineyard management and tracking of fruit. With the advice of his red winemaking team—particularly John Bird and Chris Hancock—he refined a number of techniques including the controversial method of encouraging volatile acidity (VA): 'I insisted we keep the VA within legal limits to avoid being challenged by authorities. Further, it wouldn't have been good if our opposition had pointed it out!' A more flexible approach to maturation and bottling was also implemented. 'Maturation has always been an important aspect of Penfolds winemaking. Timing, however, is everything when it comes to getting the right balance of freshness, fruit and maturation characters. If the wine was a little worn, it can never be reclaimed.' Ditter also paid particular attention to the seasoning of American oak. Under Ditter's leadership, the Grange style was improved with fresher aromas, more richness and ripeness of fruit, and better oak selection. The vintages of 1976, 1978, 1983 and 1986 are probably his most admired.

The 1986 vintage—Ditter's last—is regarded by the secondary wine market as one of the greatest Grange vintages of all time. John Bird has said, 'Don Ditter will be best remembered for adding extra polish and finesse to Grange. While not always deeply involved in the nitty-gritty of the vintage cellar, he had a wonderful palate and really understood how to make the best of each vintage.' Further, Ditter steered Penfolds winemaking through the uncharted waters of further consolidation and company takeover. While the Penfold Hyland family lost control of Penfolds in 1976, the quality of the wines—especially Grange—remained on track. Joshua Greene believed the best of Ditter's vintages were the 1976 and 1978, 'but the cooler 1975 and 1984 also caught my attention. The 1982 was deliciously heady with sunny, sweet red raspberry flavours.'

By the early 1980s, Penfolds had stopped entering Grange into wine shows, largely because it is such a distinctive style that most wine judges could spot it easily in a blind tasting; there was nothing further to be gained. This was perhaps illustrated by the poor wine show results of the 1976 Grange—a wine which Max Schubert regarded as a classic Grange vintage. (Nonetheless, Penfolds has periodically entered Grange into various international wine competitions with considerable success. The 1971, for instance, created a sensation when it beat the best Rhône Valley wines at the Gault-Millau Wine Olympiad in Paris in 1979.) Further, Robert Parker, the highly influential American wine critic—also known as the 'Emperor of Wine'—awarded the 1976 Grange 100 points.

The winemaking talents of John Duval were spotted early by Don Ditter and Max Schubert. His family, Morphett Vale grape growers, were early suppliers to Penfolds. Indeed, many of the shiraz vines at Magill Estate are derived from cuttings from John Duval's family vineyard. John Duval, however, represented a new generation of winemaker: those with a very strong pure science and applied winemaking background. He joined the team at Nuriootpa and worked for John Davoren and for several years he played an understudy role with Kevin Schroeter, Don Ditter and Max Schubert.

Duval was appointed Penfolds Chief Winemaker at a remarkably young age. His contribution to the evolution of Grange has been critical. His stewardship saw some of the greatest developments and innovations in viticulture and winemaking. The 1990, 1991, 1996 and 1998 Granges are regarded by many as extraordinary wines with incredible power and finesse, while the 1999 Grange is fast establishing revisionist critical thought. Many believe that it will equal or eclipse 1998.

Campbell Mattinson found the 1980s and '90s reflected the enormous power of multi-regional blending and house style: 'Despite vintage variation in flavour profile this was a very strong line-up of wines.' Joshua Greene said: 'The highlight of Duval's career must be the 1996 vintage, among the top Grange vintages for its length of flavour and drive. If some of the classics from the 1950s and '60s glowed with the taste of "*fraise des bois*", fragile and delicate, here that flavour was amplified in its youth.'

Peter Gago was promoted to the role of Penfolds Chief Winemaker in 2002— only the fourth in 55 years. A graduate in mathematics and science from the University of Melbourne, Peter completed another degree, graduating as dux in oenology from Roseworthy College in 1989. Peter's outstanding winemaking and communication skills—he was a teacher for eight years—were quickly recognised by Penfolds. Soon after joining the team he became Penfolds Red Wine Oenologist—a hands-on role maintaining the quality and consistency of the existing Penfolds portfolio and developing new wines for an increasingly global market.

Gago's stewardship of Penfolds Grange is timely. He has been described as a 'perpetual-motion brilliant speaker, wine educator and winemaker'. In the old days, winemakers travelled to learn about new equipment and practices rather than attending speaking and dinner engagements. Peter Gago's commitments are especially demanding. One commentator remarked that the job of Penfolds Chief Winemaker is an honour only surpassed by being Captain of the Australian Cricket Team or the Prime Minister of Australia! Under Gago's leadership, Penfolds Grange has continued to attract worldwide interest and enormous respect. Indeed, Grange seems to have established a renewed and vigorous momentum. The accolades continue across myriad influential publications in almost every market.

Grange is still regarded as something very special. James Halliday has said: 'It is impossible not to single out Grange as by far the most inspiring vertical tasting, showing as it does the extraordinary ability these wines have to age, and a brand style every bit as consistent as that of a First Growth producer.' Peter Gago is the first to acknowledge and credit his red winemaking team—Steve Lienert, Andrew Baldwin and consultant and longstanding Penfolds winemaker John Bird: 'The production of Penfolds Grange has always been a collaborative effort. While it is a singular and distinctive style there are many contributors, including independent Grange growers, our own vineyard team, red winemakers and support staff.'

Neil Beckett said: 'The 2000s were magnificent wines with beautifully vivid fruit, graceful structure and timeless elegance.' The 2002 and 2004 were particular stand-out vintages. Ch'ng Poh Tiong said, '2002 was very fine, harmonious and feminine. I can imagine this Audrey Hepburn wine will mature in the same way as the 1954; it has ripe raspberry, violet, floral aromas and ripe, silky, elegant structure.' Campbell Mattinson observed, '2004 is a rage of violet, raspberry, plum fruits. The wine is beautifully structured and composed with integrated new vanillin oak. This is a fine, rippling, sturdy but supple wine.'

Half bottles of Penfolds Grange Hermitage 1952 were originally given away by Max Schubert as samples

IT IS IRONIC THAT THERE ARE SOME BOTTLES OF AUSTRALIAN WINE NOW THAT ARE WORTH MORE THAN AN OUNCE OF GOLD · COLLENE A. KALB 1999

The Grange winemaking philosophy hasn't really changed that much over 50 years. The style has been refined, reflecting progress in both vineyard and winemaking practices. Max Schubert originally aimed to make a wine of between 11.5 and 12 per cent alcohol. This has risen to around 13 to 13.5 per cent; tannin ripeness has become as crucial as fruit ripeness. The level of volatile acidity has been dropped and the quality of oak has improved. However, many of the original winemaking practices are still central to the style. Penfolds red winemaking team continues to identify the best and most exquisite fruit available, apply submerged cap/headed down vinification, and complete fermentation in new American hogsheads. These techniques have become standard practice across Australia.

Joshua Greene wrote in his publication *Wine and Spirits*: 'What was once an individual winemaking style has been adopted by any number of others, including some whose caricatures of Grange may tend to blur the distinctions that set it apart. Gago, charged with maintaining those distinctions, may be the most idiosyncratic Chief Winemaker at Penfolds since Schubert. He's sensitive to Schubert's legacy, and is now charged with sustaining it as the oldest wines begin to disappear.'

Since the early 1970s, Penfolds Grange has created a strong international image for Australian wine. Every time a person opens a bottle of fine mature Grange it strengthens the wine's reputation. Positive critical reviews have also helped. Hugh Johnson, the notable UK wine critic, once called it 'one of the only true First Growths of the Southern Hemisphere'. The highly influential US wine critic Robert Parker called Grange 'a leading candidate for the richest, most concentrated, dry red table wine on planet Earth'. *Wine Spectator* magazine has conferred two important honours: the 1955 Grange was named one of the top twelve wines of the twentieth century in 2000 and the 1990 vintage was named Wine of the Year in 1995. In 2002, grapes destined for Grange were once again crushed and fermented at Magill. A significant proportion of the blend is also matured in hogsheads in the Magill underground drives.

In 2007 Grange was ranked fifteenth most tradable wine in the world by Liv-Ex—the London-based Fine Wine Exchange: 'With relatively high production and price, and continued support from Robert Parker, and a series of great wines since 2000, its rise up the charts is understandable.' The *Wall Street Journal* even published a Dow Jones Grange Index. The accompanying text read, 'Wine lovers remember their first Grange the way they remember their first kiss!' Grange is the only wine to be heritage listed by the South Australian National Trust. It also heads up the highly influential and internationally recognised *Langton's Classification of Australian Wine*—in recognition of Grange's cornerstone presence in the secondary wine market. It continues to generate considerable collector interest and millions of dollars of auction revenue per year.

Stewart Langton, specialist wine auctioneer and founder of Langton's, said, 'Penfolds—especially Grange—has always performed reliably well through the thick and thin of the secondary market. Collectors and wine enthusiasts have a strong affection for the wines. Through a long track record of performance, recorded histories of tastings, and plenty of anecdotal stories and experiences, they know exactly what to expect. Even with changes in ownership, Penfolds has maintained a strong production-focused image where quality, consistency and heritage are seen as vitally important. It's a great reputation to have—especially in times of uncertainty.'

Until recently, Access Economics—an Australian economic think-tank—used the 1971 Grange as an indicator of wine investment performance. Certainly Grange prices ebb and flow according to economic conditions and reputation of vintage. Its sustained strong track record, however, illustrates Grange's solid reputation for longevity among collectors and wine enthusiasts. Indeed, Grange has weathered several economic cycles and trends within the ultra-fine secondary wine market.

Penfolds Grange, originally called Penfolds Grange Hermitage, is a very perfumed, concentrated wine which combines the intensely rich fruit and ripe tannins of shiraz with the fragrance and complementary nuances of American oak. Partial barrel fermentation, at the tail end of primary fermentation, weaves the two elements together, giving a 'meaty' complexity and roundness of flavours on the palate. This process has been described as 'getting the oak into the wine and the wine into the oak'. A portion of cabernet is used in some years to further enhance aromatics and palate structure. The 1999 and 2000 vintages, however, are both 100 per cent shiraz.

Penfolds Grange is released as a five-year-old wine. The time-lag is also a historical one, a legacy of its rejection in 1957 by Penfolds management in Sydney where Max Schubert was accused of 'accumulating stocks of wine which to all intent and purposes were unsaleable!' The early Granges were labelled under different but non-sequential bin numbers. While the line started as 1951 Bin 1, the bin numbers are seemingly ad-hoc. In 1970 Grange was standardised to Bin 95.

Penfolds Grange is considered by many as the ultimate Australian wine experience. At the Penfolds Red Wine Re-corking Clinics, now held throughout the world, collectors, wine enthusiasts and Grange owners bring their bottles—or even a single bottle—to be assessed by Penfolds winemakers. It has become something of an annual ceremony where stories and anecdotes are swapped while bottles are checked, topped up, re-corked and re-capsuled. It is an eclectic crowd, including millionaire wine collectors, doctors, labourers, taxi drivers and priests. Australians from all walks of life are immensely proud of the success of Grange.

Campbell Mattinson wrote, 'It's a beautiful thing—forget the arguments, the allocations, the speculation, the price—whenever I find a quiet moment and think about this thing called Grange, I can't help but think that without Grange the entire Australian wine industry would be entirely diminished.'

In the late 1940s, postwar Australia was embarking on a journey to modern nationhood. Max Schubert—himself a returned soldier—dreamed of making something different and unique in the world of wine. The development of Penfolds Grange reflects a national mood: a sense of purpose and an enthusiasm for progress. Australia is a young country and does not have the highly evolved traditions of the Old World. The future is its only reference point. The stature of Grange has been achieved—not through the hindsight of centuries of heritage and accumulated wealth, but through trial, error and persistence. Max Schubert described Penfolds Grange as 'buoyant—almost ethereal'. It is evocative of companionship, happiness and wonder—the essence of the Grange experience.

TASTING NOTES ~ BIN 95 GRANGE SHIRAZ

1951 NOW • • • PAST

Not tasted at the Rewards of Patience tasting—but several bottles opened during the 2002–03 Penfolds Red Wine Re-corking Clinics. The first experimental Grange and extremely rare, it is a valuable collector's item because of its historical significance and hand-blown bottles. The wine itself is past its peak although some bottles still have fruit sweetness and flavour length. Largely the wine has a dull tawny colour and skeletal palate structure with little flesh and fading tannins. 100% shiraz.
50% Magill Estate, 50% Morphett Vale (Adelaide environs). A hot, very dry growing season. 100 cases/ 3 hogsheads made. Released as Bin 1.

1952 ★ (cliniced bottle) NOW

First commercial vintage. Medium deep brick red. Intense mature complex roasted meat/demiglace/sandalwood/leather aromas. Lovely richly flavoured wine with sweet roasted meat/ demi-glace/dark chocolate/leather flavours and fine supple lacy/satin tannins. Finishes silky sweet and long. Great old bottles still holding up very well. Very rare. 100% shiraz.
Magill Estate/Morphett Vale blend. Average growing season with normal rainfall conditions. Around 100/150 cases made at less than A$1 a bottle at release. Some half bottle 'pints' were also produced. Released as Bin 4 and Bin 4A.

1953 ★ (cliniced bottle) NOW

Medium brick red. Fresh mocha/apricot/meaty/*Provençal herb/polished leather* aromas. A beautiful, velvet-textured wine with sweet-fruit/roasted meat/mocha/herb/leather flavours and loose-knit, slinky, dry tannins. Finishes long and sweet. A very famous old Australian wine still showing remarkable freshness and balance. Very rare. 87% shiraz, 13% cabernet sauvignon.
Magill Estate and Morphett Vale (Adelaide) and Kalimna Vineyard (Barossa Valley) blend. 260 cases made. Some half bottles (375 ml) were released. First vintage and then uninterrupted use of Kalimna fruit—hence the term Mother Vineyard. Released as Bin 2 (also Bins 10, 86C and 145).

1954 (cliniced bottle) NOW • • • PAST

Medium brick red. The wine is now in decline. It is showing some sandalwood/meaty/demiglace/fig/earthy aromas and flavours but it's shot with amontillado/salty characters. The palate is elegant and gracefully fading with some sweetness of fruit, dry, slightly gritty tannins and minerally/graphite/smoky finish. Very rare. 98% shiraz, 2% cabernet sauvignon.
Magill Estate (Adelaide) and Kalimna Vineyard (Barossa Valley) blend. Internal criticism of Grange led Max Schubert to lighten the style slightly. Only nine months in oak. Cool to mild growing season followed by a mild to warm vintage. Released as Bin 11 and Bin 12.

1955 ★ (cliniced bottle) NOW

Deep brick red. Coffee/mocha/gamy/grilled meat aromas with some camomile/leather notes. A fleshy, supple, smooth wine with mature meaty/gamy/mochas flavours and satin-textured tannins with a long fruit sweet finish. A famously great vintage, now quite rare. 90% shiraz, 10% cabernet sauvignon.
Magill Estate (Adelaide), Morphett Vale (Adelaide), Kalimna Vineyard (Barossa Valley), McLaren Vale blend. The most decorated Grange—winner of twelve trophies and 52 gold medals on the Australian wine show circuit. Spent only nine months in oak. A favourite of Max Schubert, partly because it

won a gold medal in the open claret class at the 1962 Sydney Wine Show—some members of the judging panel had previously been vocally critical of the style. Mild to warm growing conditions—interrupted by above average rainfall. A warm, dry vintage followed. Chosen by the US publication Wine Spectator *magazine as a Wine of the Millennium. Most common but later release (after show success) as Bin 95 (also Bins 13, 14, 53, 54 and 148A).*

1956   (cliniced bottle)   **NOW • • • PAST**

Medium brick red. Very developed crepuscular mocha/molasses/spice/vellum aromas. The palate is well concentrated with mature, sweet mocha/molasses/meaty flavours and muscular, dry firm tannins. The fruit is slipping away but it's just holding. Very rare. 96% shiraz, 4% cabernet sauvignon.

Magill Estate and Morphett Vale (Adelaide), and Kalimna Vineyard (Barossa Valley) blend. Only nine months in oak. A cool mild growing season. Released as Bin 14 and Bin 53.

1957   (cliniced bottle)   **NOW**

Deep brick red. Fresh dark chocolate/mint/herb aromas. A firmly structured wine with dark chocolate/earthy/minty flavours and cedary/leafy tannins. There is still plenty of fruit sweetness and mid-palate richness, but the finish is underpowered, grippy and dry. Very rare. 88% shiraz, 12% cabernet sauvignon.

Magill Estate and Morphett Vale (Adelaide), and McLaren Vale blend. A so-called hidden Grange because the wine was made without the knowledge of Penfolds management who had ordered Max Schubert to cease production. Matured in previous year's Grange barrels. A mild dry growing season. Released as Bin 50 and Bin 113.

1958   (cliniced bottle)   **NOW • • • PAST**

Deep brick red. Very complex and developed wine with rich dark chocolate/peat/malt whisky/herb garden aromas. The palate is savoury and dry with dark chocolate/sweet-fruit/burnt toast/earthy flavours and leafy tannins (a touch gritty). The fruit fades off towards the end leaving an austere, slightly acidic finish. This is well past its prime but it's holding firm. Very rare. 94% shiraz, 6% cabernet sauvignon.

Magill Estate and Morphett Vale (Adelaide), and Kalimna Vineyard (Barossa Valley), Barossa Valley, McLaren Vale blend. A 'hidden Grange'. Mild to warm growing season. Released as Bin 46 (also Bins 14, 47 and 49).

1959   **NOW**

Deep brick red. Dark cherry/bitter chocolate/demi-glace aromas with touches of marmalade. The wine is very firm with dark cherry/bitter chocolate/mocha/herb garden flavours and fine-grained chalky—almost stemmy—tannins. Finishes oily dry but it still has great flavour length. It's starting to lose freshness. Rare. 90% shiraz, 10% cabernet sauvignon.

Magill Estate (Adelaide), Morphett Vale (Adelaide), Kalimna Vineyard (Barossa Valley) blend. A 'hidden Grange'. Cool to mild growing season followed by a warm, dry vintage. Released as Bin 95 (also Bins 46 and 49).

1960 ★   **NOW**

Medium brick red. A beautiful wine with intense complex fresh dark chocolate/demi-glace/dried prune/apricot/herb garden aromas and flavours. The palate is well concentrated with lovely fruit richness and fine, lacy, supple tannins. Finishes silky, minerally and long. Rare. 92% shiraz, 8% cabernet sauvignon.

Magill Estate (Adelaide), Morphett Vale (Adelaide), Kalimna Vineyard (Barossa Valley) blend. A hot, dry growing season. Released as Bin 95 (also as Bin 49).

1961 NOW

Medium brick red. Fresh old wine with bitter dark chocolate/prune/almond/wet bitumen/roasted coffee aromas. A richly concentrated fleshy palate with bitter dark chocolate/dried plum/tea-leafy/leathery flavours and fine, slinky—almost cashmere-like—tannins. Finishes long and sweet. A classical old Grange. Rare. 88% shiraz, 12% cabernet sauvignon.

Magill Estate (Adelaide), Morphett Vale (Adelaide), Modbury Vineyard (Adelaide), Kalimna Vineyard (Barossa Valley), Coonawarra blend. A hot, dry growing season with hot vintage conditions. Released as Bin 95 (also as Bin 395).

1962 ★ NOW • • • 2018

Deep brick red. Vintage Grange with beautifully mature and fragrant chocolate/mocha/menthol/leather/cedar aromas. Mouth-filling, rich and exuberant wine with fresh, sweet mocha/demi-glace/ripe sweet-fruit flavours, underlying cedar/vanillin notes and fine-grained, chocolaty tannins. Finishes chalky firm and superbly long. Astonishingly still in its prime. A wonderful wine. Rare. 87% shiraz, 13% cabernet sauvignon.

Magill Estate (Adelaide), Kalimna Vineyard (Barossa Valley), Adelaide Hills blend. Barossa Valley fruit becomes ascendant component. Ideal warm, fairly dry growing season followed by a warm, dry vintage. Released as Bin 95 (also as Bins 59, 59A and 456).

1963 ★ NOW • • • 2018

Deep brick red. Utterly superb wine with intense perfumed meaty/demi-glace/rose-petal/apricot/camomile aromas. Rich chocolaty/meaty/apricot/demi-glace fruit, underlying wood-spiced notes and sweet, ripe, velvety tannins. A chalky firm but elongated flavourful finish. This is a perfectly composed, beautifully structured Grange. A very great wine. Will continue to hold for many years. Rare. 100% shiraz.

Kalimna Vineyard (Barossa Valley), Barossa Valley, Magill Estate (Adelaide), Morphett Vale (Adelaide), Modbury Vineyard (Adelaide) blend. A warm, dry growing season. Released as Bin 95 (also as Bin 65).

1964 NOW

Medium brick red. Fresh prune/molasses/leather/rustic aromas with touches of camphor. The wine is sinewy and dry with walnutty/leather/prune flavours and fine, leafy tannins. It still has some sweet fruit and good flavour length, but the palate is beginning to dry up. Rare. 90% shiraz, 10% cabernet sauvignon.

Magill Estate (Adelaide), Kalimna Vineyard (Barossa Valley), other Barossa Valley blend. A wet growing season followed by a fine, cool vintage. Released as Bin 95 (also as Bins 395, 66, 67 and 68).

1965 NOW • • • 2016

Medium deep brick red. Intense earthy/gamy/bitumen/cedar aromas with some spiced orange peel notes. An elegantly structured but substantial wine with earthy/dark chocolate/cedar/herb characters and fine, chocolaty tannins. Finishes leafy firm. Rare. 95% shiraz, 5% cabernet sauvignon.

Kalimna Vineyard (Barossa Valley), Barossa Valley, Magill Estate (Adelaide), Morphett Vale (Adelaide), McLaren Vale blend. Jimmy Watson Trophy Winner—a prestigious Melbourne Show award. A warm, dry growing season. Released as Bin 95 (also as Bins 69, 70 and 71).

1966 ★   NOW • • • 2015

Medium deep brick red. A very classical Grange with archetypal Penfolds wine structure. Beautiful opulent dark chocolate/meaty/prune/cedar aromas. The palate is ripe and perfectly balanced with smooth dark chocolate/prune/dark fruit/graphite flavours and loose-knit, slinky tannins. Finishes long and sweet. Rich, seamless and satisfying wine. Still has plenty of time ahead. Rare. 88% shiraz, 12% cabernet sauvignon.

Kalimna Vineyard (Barossa Valley), Barossa Valley, Magill Estate (Adelaide), Morphett Vale (Adelaide) blend. A dry growing season was followed by an ideal warm vintage. Released as Bin 95 (also as Bins 71 and 72).

1967   NOW • • • 2015

Medium deep brick red. Fresh plum/dried-fig/meaty/ground coffee/Provençal herb/liquorice aromas with traces of mint. An appealing contrast to the 1966. The palate is elegantly structured with plum/meaty/ground coffee flavours and fine, grainy, slightly leafy tannins. Finishes chalky firm but long and fruit sweet. Increasingly rare. 94% shiraz, 6% cabernet sauvignon.

Kalimna Vineyard (Barossa Valley), Barossa Valley, Clare Valley, Magill Estate (Adelaide) blend. A warm, dry growing season. Won the Jimmy Watson trophy at the Melbourne Show—for a second time. A generally dry growing season followed by a warm vintage. Released as Bin 95 (also Bin 74).

1968   NOW

Medium brick red. Fragrant herb garden/mocha/cedar/farmyard aromas with plenty of woodspice characters. The palate is still fresh with herb garden/cedar/rustic flavours and leafy, firm tannins. It finishes brambly dry at the finish. (At the clinics some bottles have revealed a mothball/napthalene character.) Drink up. Increasingly rare. 94% shiraz, 6% cabernet sauvignon.

Kalimna Vineyard (Barossa Valley), Barossa Valley, Magill Estate (Adelaide), Clare Valley, Adelaide Hills, Coonawarra Blend. A hot, dry vintage with only intermittent rains during the growing season. Released as Bin 95 (also as Bin 826).

1969   NOW

Medium brick red. Fresh dark chocolate/mocha/dark berry/leather/leafy aromas. The palate is dusty and dry with earthy/dark chocolate/polished leather flavours and astringent tannins. It is still holding but the fruit is dropping out now. Drink up. 95% shiraz, 5% cabernet sauvignon.

Kalimna Vineyard (Barossa Valley), Barossa Valley, Magill Estate (Adelaide), Clare Valley, Morphett Vale (Adelaide), Coonawarra blend. Mild, wet conditions prevailed during the growing season and vintage. Released as Bin 95 (also as Bin 826).

1970   NOW

Medium brick red. Intense complex black olive/herb garden/tobacco/polished leather aromas. The palate is savoury and sweet with black olive/polished leather/herb/spicy flavours and

dry tannins. Willowy rather than solid. Drink soon. 90% shiraz, 10% cabernet sauvignon. *Kalimna Vineyard (Barossa Valley), Barossa Valley, Magill Estate (Adelaide) blend. A dry, mild growing season and vintage. Standardisation of bin numbers starts—all vintages are now released as Bin 95.*

1971 ★ NOW • • • 2016

Medium deep brick red. A classic Penfolds year with an unusually low alcohol content of around 12.3%.* The wine is immensely complex and mature with lifted smoked meat/dark chocolate/mocha/liquorice/kelp aromas. A silky smooth, richly flavoured palate with dark chocolate/espresso coffee/tobacco/cedar fruit, underlying vanillin nuances and fine, lacy satin tannins. Finishes sinuous, long and bittersweet. This is a great Grange but bottles are increasingly variable, ranging from the frail to the fresh and sublime. 87% shiraz, 13% cabernet sauvignon.

Kalimna Vineyard (Barossa Valley), Barossa Valley, Magill Estate (Adelaide), Clare Valley, Coonawarra blend. 'If you had to point to a wine which fulfilled the ambitions of Grange it would have to be the 1971.'—Max Schubert, 1993. Topped the Gault-Millau Wine Olympiad in Paris in 1979, beating some of the best Rhône wines and creating a sensation. A great South Australian vintage; ideal, generally warm conditions throughout the growing season and vintage.

Alcohol originally stated 11.5% but records and analysis reveal 12.3%. 'A Grange that doesn't seem to tolerate poor storage or travel.'—Peter Gago

1972 NOW • • • 2015

Medium deep brick red. Lovely cedar/sweet-fruit/hazelnut/polished leather aromas and flavours with some plum/walnut notes. The palate is still fresh and elegant with plenty of fruit sweetness and fine, lacy cedary tannins. Finishes chewy firm. A controversial vintage, but this was a very good bottle. 90% shiraz, 10% cabernet sauvignon.

Kalimna Vineyard (Barossa Valley), Barossa Valley, Magill Estate (Adelaide), Modbury Vineyard (Adelaide), Coonawarra blend. A very good Grange vintage, but a batch was unintentionally oxidised during bottling, resulting in significant bottle variation. A mild, dry growing season and vintage.

1973 NOW • • • PAST

Deep brick red. Evolved meaty/prune/molasses aromas with some mint/menthol notes. Richly flavoured but quite a rustic wine with prune/meaty fruit and leafy/brambly tannins. Finishes sappy firm. 98% shiraz, 2% cabernet sauvignon.

Kalimna Vineyard (Barossa Valley), Barossa Valley, Magill Estate (Adelaide), Modbury Vineyard (Adelaide) blend. A dry growing season followed by a cool vintage. Last vintage made in open waxlined concrete fermenters (completed in barrel) at Magill Estate.

1974 NOW • • • PAST

Medium deep brick red. Intense prune/herbal/kelp aromas with touches of marmalade. The palate shows plenty of sweet/prune/herb garden flavours and underlying orange/clove notes. The tannins are slinky, dry and long. The fruit is fading now. 93% shiraz, 7% cabernet sauvignon.

Kalimna Vineyard (Barossa Valley), Barossa Valley, Magill Estate (Adelaide) blend. Winemaking transferred to Nuriootpa. Vinification in stainless steel tanks, completed in barrel. A very wet growing season made more difficult by the outbreak of downy mildew just prior to harvest.

Deep brick red. Intense aniseed/liquorice/dark berry/mocha aromas with some minty/graphite/rustic notes. The palate is chunky and concentrated with blackberry/mocha/graphite/minty/bitumen flavours underlying miso-soup notes and gravelly, dry tannins. Finishes savoury, grippy firm and long. Sound but unrefined. A 'dark horse' vintage. 90% shiraz, 10% cabernet sauvignon.
Kalimna Vineyard (Barossa Valley), Barossa Valley, Coonawarra blend. A cool summer was followed by a mild, dry vintage.

Deep brick red. An intense, plush powerful wine with rich dark chocolate/panforte/molasses/liquorice aromas and roasted/earthy/walnut notes. The palate is beautifully concentrated and buoyant with seductive dark chocolate/prune/molasses flavours and plenty of sweet-fruit characters. The tannins are sinewy and long, building up firm at the finish. A delicious well-balanced Grange with plenty of concentration and extract to last the distance. Regarded as a great Grange vintage, but bottles are increasingly variable. The best bottles have levels at base or into the neck or have passed successfully through Penfolds wine clinics. 89% shiraz, 11% cabernet sauvignon.
Kalimna Vineyard (Barossa Valley), Barossa Valley, Magill Estate (Adelaide), Modbury Vineyard (Adelaide). The 25th Anniversary of Grange. Max Schubert considered it 'More in the old style: a good vintage'. The first Australian wine to cross the A$20 barrier. An ideal warm, dry growing season.

Deep brick red. Fresh redcurrant/blackberry/cedar/herb garden/camphor aromas. Dried herb/blackberry/leather/meaty flavours, underlying savoury oak with powdery dry, slightly leafy tannins. The wine has peaked. Perhaps on its downward hill. Drink soon. 91% shiraz, 9% cabernet sauvignon.
Kalimna Vineyard (Barossa Valley), Barossa Valley, Magill Estate (Adelaide), Clare Valley blend. Cool, mild conditions prevailed during the growing season.

Deep brick red. Complex mocha/blackberry/demi-glace/meaty flavours with some minty notes. A lovely concentrated wine with plenty of sweet-fruit/mocha/blackberry/camomile/graphite flavours and powerful, chocolaty, fine tannins. Builds up dense and chalky at the finish, but the fruit follows through with excellent persistence. This is a very good Grange year. Probably drinking at its very best now. 90% shiraz, 10% cabernet sauvignon.
Kalimna Vineyard (Barossa Valley), Barossa Valley, Magill Estate (Adelaide), McLaren Vale, Clare Valley, Coonawarra blend. A warm, dry growing season followed by mild vintage conditions.

Deep brick red. Fresh blackberry/chocolate/prune/toffee aromas with some vanilla/menthol notes. A solid wine with rich black fruit/chocolate/panforte/earthy/menthol flavours and plentiful, fine-grained tannins. Finishes hard with some smoky/bitumen notes. Powerful with uncompromising tannin structure. 87% shiraz, 13% cabernet sauvignon.
Kalimna Vineyard (Barossa Valley), Barossa Valley, Clare Valley, Magill Estate (Adelaide), McLaren Vale Blend. An unusual wet but hot growing season. Magnums first released. Last vintage bottles used off-white foil capsules.

1980   NOW • • • 2020

Deep brick red. Fresh aniseed/earthy/meaty/cedar aromas with a hint of menthol. The palate is elegantly proportioned with rich, generous, dark berry/earthy/meaty/cedar/mint flavours and slinky/leafy tannins. It finishes sinewy and dry but long and flavourful. A very well-balanced Grange which could further improve. 96% shiraz, 4% cabernet sauvignon.

Kalimna Vineyard (Barossa Valley), Barossa Valley, Clare Valley, Magill Estate (Adelaide), McLaren Vale, Coonawarra blend. A fine, warm growing season followed by cool but late vintage.

1981   NOW • • • 2020

Deep brick red. Earthy/meaty/cedar/demi-glace aromas with some farmyard characters. The palate is generous and powerful with plenty of chocolate/meaty/cedar flavours and fine loose-knit but ample, chalky tannins. A firmly structured wine. Probably best to drink soon. 89% shiraz, 11% cabernet sauvignon.

Kalimna Vineyard (Barossa Valley), Barossa Valley, Magill Estate (Adelaide), Modbury Vineyard (Adelaide), Clare Valley, Coonawarra blend. A warm, hot, drought-affected summer followed by a warm dry vintage.

1982   NOW • • • 2010

Deep brick red. Perfumed red cherry/redcurrant/tea leaf/herb aromas. Rich, fleshy, smooth, plush wine with sweet cassis/red cherry/damson plum/mocha flavours and slinky fine chocolaty tannins. An idiosyncratic Grange at its peak of development. 94% shiraz, 6% cabernet sauvignon.

Kalimna Vineyard (Barossa Valley), Barossa Valley, Magill Estate (Adelaide), Modbury Vineyard (Adelaide), Clare Valley blend. A mild growing season followed by a hot vintage. Most 1982 Penfolds wines have a particular vintage character often described as exaggerated or oscillating fruit.

1983 ★   NOW • • • 2025

Deep crimson. An intense plush wine with plenty of volume and energy; herb garden/mocha/cedar aromas with smoky/graphite nuances. Ripe saturated plum/dark chocolate/mocha fruit, underlying savoury oak and rich, dense, close-knit, muscular tannins. Finishes firm with plenty of flavour length. A profoundly concentrated vintage with years of cellaring potential. 94% shiraz, 6% cabernet sauvignon.

Kalimna Vineyard (Barossa Valley), Barossa Valley, Magill Estate (Adelaide), Modbury Vineyard blend. A bizarre growing season marked by drought, the Ash Wednesday bushfires and March flooding. A very low-yielding vintage resulting in wine of immense concentration.

1984   NOW • • • 2015

Deep crimson. Evolved mocha/dark berry/cedar/menthol aromas. Long, expansive palate with richly concentrated mocha/dark berry fruit, underlying malt oak characters and chocolaty, firm tannins. Has considerable length at the finish. A classically structured Grange. Drinking beautifully now. 95% shiraz, 5% cabernet sauvignon.

Kalimna Vineyard (Barossa Valley), Barossa Valley, Magill Estate (Adelaide), McLaren Vale, Clare Valley, Coonawarra blend. A cool growing season followed by a cool, dry late vintage.

1985 NOW • • • **2015**

Deep crimson. Plum/ground coffee/dark chocolate/cedar/herb garden aromas with some walnut/ leather notes. The palate is richly concentrated with dark chocolate/plum/leather flavours and sinewy/savoury, dry tannins. Finishes firm and tight. A well-balanced wine with plenty of fruit power. 99% shiraz, 1% cabernet sauvignon.

Kalimna Vineyard (Barossa Valley), Barossa Valley, Clare Valley, Modbury Vineyard (Adelaide) blend. Cool to mild growing season and vintage punctuated by intermittent rains. Late rains delayed picking.

1986 ★ NOW • • • **2030+**

Deep crimson. Powerful intense mocha/cedar/liquorice aromas balanced with malty/smoky oak characters. A richly extravagant palate with complex mocha/dark chocolate/dark berry/herb fruit and dense, ripe tannins. Finishes chalky firm but superbly long and flavourful. A great Grange still on the ascendancy. 87% shiraz, 13% cabernet sauvignon.

Kalimna Vineyard (Barossa Valley), Barossa Valley, Clare Valley, McLaren Vale, Modbury Vineyard (Adelaide) blend. A mild, relatively dry growing season and vintage. An important and very successful vintage.

1987 NOW • • • **2020**

Medium crimson. Intense menthol/dark chocolate/mocha/meaty aromas. Sweet, fleshy mocha/ dark chocolate/minty flavours, underlying malty new oak and sinewy/sappy tannins. Finishes very firm and dry. 90% shiraz, 10% cabernet sauvignon.

Kalimna Vineyard (Barossa Valley), Barossa Valley, McLaren Vale blend. A cool vintage marked by October hailstorms and variable yields.

1988 NOW • • • **2025**

Medium crimson. Lovely mocha/redcurrant/brambly/roasted meat aromas with underlying vanilla/menthol notes. Well-concentrated, mouth-filling wine with mocha/demi-glace/brambly/ vanilla/flavours, a runnel of mint and savoury, dry, soupy tannins. Finishes lingering and grippy firm. Tastes evolved but will continue to develop. 94% shiraz, 6% cabernet sauvignon.

Kalimna Vineyard (Barossa Valley), Barossa Valley, Padthaway, McLaren Vale. Ideal growing season followed by a warm, dry vintage.

1989 NOW • • • **2015**

Medium crimson. Fresh aromatic redcurrant/musky/tea leaf aromas with some liquorice. Lovely early drinking Grange with redcurrant confit/blackcurrant pastille flavours, plenty of fruit sweetness, underlying vanillin oak and chocolaty, dense, dry tannins. 91% shiraz, 9% cabernet sauvignon.

Kalimna Vineyard (Barossa Valley), Barossa Valley, McLaren Vale blend. Extreme heat and heavy March rains followed an ideal warm growing season.

1990 ★ NOW • • • **2035**

Deep crimson. Powerful, ethereal, beautifully balanced wine with blackberry/plum/chocolate/ *sous bois*/spicy aromas. A rich, ripe, immensely concentrated wine with generous sweet blackberry/plum/dark cherry fruit, mocha oak, some earthy flavours and velvety smooth tannins. Finishes long and chocolaty. A superb Grange with tremendous energy, finesse and volume. 95% shiraz, 5% cabernet sauvignon.

Kalimna Vineyard (Barossa Valley), Barossa Valley, Clare Valley, Coonawarra blend. Voted Red Wine of the Year by Wine Spectator *magazine in December 1995. A very great Australian vintage with a perfect warm, dry growing season and harvest.*

1991 ★   NOW • • • 2035

Deep crimson. Substantial wine with dark chocolate/malty/liquorice/smoky/cedar aromas. Dense, multi-layered palate with abundant sweet fruit, saturated dark chocolate/plummy fruit, plentiful cedary/grainy tannins and ample toasted oak. Finishes with a chalky firm tannin slick. This is a bold and beautifully balanced Grange with immense concentration, refinement and extract. A long-haul wine which has slipped out of the shadow of the more famous 1990. A great vintage. 95% shiraz, 5% cabernet sauvignon.
Kalimna Vineyard (Barossa Valley), Barossa Valley, McLaren Vale blend. A warm, dry year with even ripening conditions. Vintage started early.

1992   NOW • • • 2018

Deep crimson. Ripe blackcurrant pastille/dark cherry/dark chocolate/*garrigue* aromas. The palate is well concentrated and balanced with pure blackberry/dark cherry flavours, savoury/malty oak and long, fine grainy/cedary tannins. Finishes bittersweet. An elegantly structured Grange with a good future. 90% shiraz, 10% cabernet sauvignon.
Kalimna Vineyard (Barossa Valley), Barossa Valley, Coonawarra, McLaren Vale blend. A cool to mild growing season marked by intermittent rains.

1993   NOW • • • 2015

Deep crimson. Fragrant cassis/prune aromas with silage/graphite/mint notes. Generously proportioned, juicy fresh but robust palate with redcurrant/prune/smoky/graphite flavours and sappy dry tannins. Finishes chalky/grippy firm. 86% shiraz, 14% cabernet sauvignon.
Kalimna Vineyard (Barossa Valley), Barossa Valley, Coonawarra blend. A very wet growing season was followed by warm, drier conditions resulting in a very late but sound quality vintage fruit. An Indian summer in Coonawarra delivered fully ripened fruit.

1994 ★   NOW • • • 2030

Medium-deep crimson. Lovely roasted coffee/black cherry/plum/mocha aromas with hint of fresh mint/herb. A beautifully balanced, powerful and expansive wine with deep-set blackberry/mocha/espresso coffee/bitter chocolate flavours, plenty of sweet fruit, leather/earthy/black olive nuances and fine, dense tannins. Finishes oaky dry but long and sweet. A gorgeous Grange. A classic vintage. 89% shiraz, 11% cabernet sauvignon.
Kalimna Vineyard (Barossa Valley), Barossa Valley, McLaren Vale, Coonawarra blend. A dry, mild, even-ripening vintage in the Barossa. Intermittent rains but mild conditions in McLaren Vale and a warm, dry autumn in Coonawarra delivered a very high-quality vintage which has gained considerable notice in recent years.

1995   NOW • • • 2020

Deep crimson. Intense blackcurrant/prune/liquorice/herb garden/mint aromas with fragrant savoury oak nuances. The palate is sinuous and long with cassis/prune/briary flavours, pronounced sweet gingerbread oak characters and dense, leafy, firm tannins. A difficult vintage. 94% shiraz, 6% cabernet sauvignon.

Kalimna Vineyard (Barossa Valley), Barossa Valley, Magill Estate (Adelaide) blend. A period of drought and September frosts reduced potential yields. Warm, dry conditions prevailed until late March/early April when a cooler weather pattern marked by drizzle set in.

1996 ★   2010 • • • 2040

Deep crimson. Beautifully balanced, utterly seductive wine with crimson plum/blackcurrant/ blueberry/dark chocolate/aniseed aromas and well-integrated savoury new oak. A supple generously flavoured palate with deep-set plum/dark chocolate/liquorice fruit, freshly grilled nut/malty oak and supple, fine-grained tannins. A substantial wine showing all the hallmarks of finesse, power and complexity. A great vintage. Best to hold. 94% shiraz, 6% cabernet sauvignon.

Kalimna Vineyard (Barossa Valley), Barossa Valley, McLaren Vale, Magill Estate (Adelaide) blend. After superb winter rainfall, soil moistures improved. This was followed by mild, dry weather conditions resulting in a vintage of exceptional quality.

1997   NOW • • • 2025

Deep opaque crimson. Liquorice/blueberry/dark chocolate/herb garden/polished leather aromas with some smoky oak characters. The palate is fruit sweet and concentrated with blueberry/dark chocolate/liquorice flavours and fine slinky/chalky-dry tannins. Malty oak characters pervade at the finish. A very good wine considering the vintage. A comparatively early drinking Grange. 96% shiraz, 4% cabernet sauvignon.

Kalimna Vineyard (Barossa Valley), Barossa Valley, McLaren Vale, Bordertown blend. Late spring rains followed a generally wet winter. Generally dry, cool conditions prevailed during October and November. A burst of hot weather arrived during summer but cooler temperatures and a week of rain during February slowed down ripening. A warm, dry period followed over vintage.

1998 ★   2010 • • • 2045

Deep crimson. A spectacular Grange showing extraordinary perfume, luxuriant fruit power and richness. Perfectly ripe, pure opulent blackberry/dark chocolate/apricot aromas with fresh cedar/ spicy oak. An expansive, densely packed wine laced with roasted coffee/dark chocolate/apricot/ meaty flavours and intertwined with beautifully seasoned toasty/cedar oak. Ripe, velvety smooth, mouth-filling tannins sweep and drive the fruit across the palate. The flavours seemingly last forever. So could the wine. A *Vin de Garde*. 97% shiraz, 3% cabernet sauvignon.

Kalimna Vineyard (Barossa Valley), Barossa Valley, Magill Estate (Adelaide), Padthaway blend. A mild, early growing season was followed by very hot, dry weather with virtually all dam water reserves exhausted. An exceptional vintage.

1999 ★   2010 • • • 2040

Deep crimson–purple. Dark, juicy blackberry/mulberry/Satsuma plum/espresso coffee aromas with malty/savoury oak. The palate is beautifully concentrated and condensed with deep-set blackberry/mulberry/apricot/herb garden/graphite fruit, mocha/vanilla oak and fine, rich, supple, dense tannins. Finishes chalky firm, but long, sweet and savoury. A great Grange, reflecting the impressive 1999 Barossa vintage. 100% shiraz.

Kalimna Vineyard (Barossa Valley), Barossa Valley, Magill Estate (Adelaide), McLaren Vale, Padtha-way blend. Dry winter conditions were followed by intermittent rains. Rain fell during November and December but just enough to maintain healthy vines. The Barossa and McLaren Vale experienced heavy rains in March and ripening slowed. Despite this, vineyards with good drainage produced fruit of exceptional quality. Padthaway escaped the burden of March rain and experienced a great vintage.

2000   NOW • • • 2018

Deep crimson. Intense redcurrant/raspberry/blueberry and brambly/minty aromas. The palate is fruit-driven with squashy redcurrant/raspberry fruit, demi-glace/leather nuances underlying fresh new American oak and fine grainy/sappy tannins. Finishes bittersweet but long and flavourful. An early drinking Grange. 100% Barossa Valley shiraz.

Kalimna Vineyard (Barossa Valley), Barossa Valley blend. After a dry, cool spring and a warm, sometimes hot summer, rains fell in late February/March resulting in a difficult year. A stop–start vintage.

2001   2012 • • • 2035

Deep crimson. Intense redcurrant/liqueur cherry/liquorice/cedar/mint aromas. A big, rich, super-ripe palate with deeply concentrated musky/dark cherry/redcurrant/blackcurrant pastille fruit, savoury oak and dense, soupy, fine tannins. Still fresh and exuberant but not overly powerful. A very fine Grange. 100% Barossa Valley shiraz.

50% Kalimna Vineyard (Barossa Valley), 50% Barossa Valley. Winter rains replenished soil moistures which sustained vineyards during a very hot, dry summer—marked sometimes by extreme heat. By late February/March cool, dry temperatures prevailed, stabilising Baumé levels.

2002 ★   2012 • • • 2045

Deep crimson–purple. A very powerful, beautifully poised Grange with inky/blackberry essence/blueberry/liquorice/aniseed aromas with plenty of malt/cedar oak. An immensely concentrated silky textured wine with saturated blackberry/meaty/cedar/mocha/spicy flavours and ripe, supple, dense tannins. Finishes long and sinuous. Still elemental, but lovely sustained palate structure, energy and volume of fruit. A great Grange. 98.5% shiraz, 1.5% cabernet sauvignon.

50% Kalimna Vineyard (Barossa Valley), 50% Barossa Valley. A long, cool winter with intermittent rains was followed by a cool, dry summer and a warm, dry autumn. A great vintage.

2003   2012 • • • 2030

Deep crimson–purple. Intense rhubarb/elderberry/vanillin/aniseed aromas with a hint of tobacco leaf. The palate is sweet and fleshy with generous elderberry/black cherry/liquorice flavours, malty American oak and fine, slinky, dry tannins. Finishes grippy firm. The wine has density, structure and flavour length. 96.5% shiraz, 3.5% cabernet sauvignon.

Barossa Valley, McLaren Vale, Langhorne Creek, Coonawarra and Magill fruit. A season of extremes. Drought conditions prevailed over spring and summer. The hot, dry weather was interrupted by heavy rainfall in February. A difficult vintage relying strongly on multi-district fruit selection.

2004 ★   2016 • • • 2050

Deep crimson–purple. Fresh, plush, buoyant blackberry/elderberry/blueberry/violet/aniseed aromas with some vanilla/savoury new oak nuances. A remarkably powerful yet composed wine with saturated blackberry/elderberry fruit, well-balanced vanilla/malt oak and beautifully weighted/structured tannins. Finishes chocolaty and long. A very intense, fragrant Grange with lovely fruit density, richness and tannin balance. A great Grange vintage. 96% shiraz, 4% cabernet sauvignon.

Barossa Valley (including substantial proportion of Kalimna shiraz), McLaren Vale and Magill fruit. An excellent year. Beneficial winter and spring rains were followed by cool to mild conditions over summer. Ripening accelerated through a warm Indian summer resulting in near-perfect fruit. A great Grange vintage.

2005 ★   2014 • • • 2045

Deep crimson–purple. Glossy cranberry/blueberry/rhubarb/herb garden aromas with plenty of nutmeg/malty seasoned, new American oak. A very elemental wine with smooth, ripe cranberry/blueberry/blackberry pastille flavours, plenty of fruit sweetness, roasted nut/malty characters and fine, dense, muscular tannins. It finishes chalky firm, but long and sweet. An impressive young wine with plenty of fruit power, line and length. Will need time to unfold. 95.9% shiraz, 4.1% cabernet sauvignon.

Barossa Valley (including substantial proportion of Kalimna shiraz), McLaren Vale and Coonawarra. A good, even vintage. Regular rainfall fell through winter into early spring establishing good soil moistures and dam levels. Mild conditions followed by a dry late summer and autumn led to optimum fruit ripeness.

2006 ★   2016 • • • 2050

Deep inky purple crimson. Intense brooding blackberry/dark chocolate/spice/roasted aromas with mocha/toasted malt oak. A very youthful, powerful and balanced wine with concentrated generous blackberry/dark mocha flavours, dense supple/chocolaty tannins and plenty of new malty/cedar oak. Finishes chalky firm with remarkable flavour length. A beguiling wine, built for the long haul. Reminiscent of the 1999 vintage. 98% shiraz, 2% cabernet sauvignon.

98% Barossa Valley shiraz (including significant contributions from the Kalimna and Koonunga Hill vineyards), 2% Magill Estate shiraz. A fine Grange vintage, but a short, difficult season. Good winter and spring rainfalls were followed by mild, warm conditions over summer. Some 50 mm of rain at the end of February and a warm burst of weather accelerated ripening. While it rained during vintage, the overall quality of the fruit was excellent.

DISCUSSION

1952–59: The experimental years

When Max Schubert started to experiment and make Grange he believed the wine should last at least twenty years. Instead they have matured and remained fresh for over 50 years. He would have been amazed at how the wines in this tasting have stood the test of time. Some of the vintages have faded, but as a group this was a very impressive and interesting line-up of wines. The 1953 and 1955 were beautiful old wines; I thought the 1952 came up really well. The hidden Granges (1957–59) were always much lighter in style; Max used one-, two- and three-year-old oak during these times. These wines never had the depth or character for long-term keeping, yet somehow—miraculously—they seem to have held on. (DD)

This was a real step back in time; the wines were very exciting to taste, showing astonishing richness and colour and wonderful integrity of aromas, flavours and texture. All the 1950s had a similar aromatic spectrum reminiscent of roasted meats, prune, gentle spice and glove leather.

Few wines showed any VA [Volatile Acidity]. The 1952 was mellow, mature and magnificent, but the 1953 was truly remarkable and sophisticated; fresh, focused and vibrant. The aromas and flavours were so subtle and interwoven it seems almost irreverent to unravel the wine through tasting notes. (NB)

There is a fascinating textural quality to the wines; they have one pure line of silk that weaves across the palate. 1952 showed quiet power in the glass. It's still showing astonishing freshness and a long arc of red fruit flavours. 1953 is a faded rose with complex ghosting of wood and fruit. It has the length of the 1952 and seems to strengthen in flavour towards the finish. 1954 is well past its prime but it's still a pleasure to taste. (JG)

This tasting was the ultimate in seriousness. The 1955 is the archetypal old, mature Grange style; lots of fruit, oak and tannins all elegantly pulled together. At first I was bothered by the oxidised characters in the 1952, but then I tasted through the ruins and thought this is fantastic! 1953 was dramatically long and in far better shape than I imagined. It had lots of ripe, mature tannins, sweet leather, mocha and port-soaked beef. The wine just soared in the glass. 1954 smelt porty and oxidised. (CM)

The fresher old wines reminded me of old-style Rioja wines with their dry wood/spiced fruit. My favourite of the 1950s was the 1952 with its perfumed sandalwood, joss stick characters. It has the impact of a temple: light, vibrant and spotlessly fresh. I found the 1954 charming and elegant; it had a mild Chinese tea colour, a bright, soft palate and the understated beauty reminiscent of Audrey Hepburn. (CPT)

I noticed the wines are now getting noticeably older and frailer. The 1953 is one of the greatest wines I have ever tasted. It's succulent, wonderfully harmonious, with silky texture and lovely symmetry. 1952 was initially impressive and then it became quite raisiny/pruney, but it is 55 years old and still drinking well. 1954 is lighter but still a lovely drink with soft, very round, gentle and mild characters. 1955 showed great harmony, balance and finesse. It had a very complex old nose of leather, beef stock and earth; a fleshy supple, smooth and satin palate. It's still sound, with great length and flavour. The 1956 was very deep and meaty with funky, rich, animal characters and rich, fleshy, layered molasses, roasted meat flavours. It's good but not great. 1957, 1958 and 1959—the hidden Granges—were simple wines; the fruit is fading and the flavours are beginning to crack up. The tannins are very drying, often taking over at the finish. At best they are just holding. (HH)

These first vintages were glorious old bottles. They are compelling examples of why in the future we could have 100-year-old bottles of Grange; the wines might still be frail but I can imagine them being gorgeous. 1952 could make it to 2052. It still has rich aromas and no sign of decay. The palate is as glorious as it promises with a satin and velvet brocade; vibrant fruit, length and harmony. You could write a book about this wine. 1953 was fractionally riper with spices, leather and sandalwood, but the tannins are alive and well. The acid balance is remarkable. 1954 is still beautiful but it's on a slow decline path. 1955 is very complex with a melange of dried fruit, spices and mocha; then a long, imperious finish with perfect acidity and fine tannins. The lack of VA across the bracket was remarkable (considering Schubert deliberately encouraged a tolerable level of volatile acidity in the overall wine style). (JH)

The wines don't look much different from when we looked at them in 2003. I was more than a little surprised at how well they all came up; especially the hidden Granges. The 1954 Grange was always a lighter wine. Max would never show that wine to the media! Yet it really has shown its worth in this line-up. (JB)

The 1952, 1953 and 1955 Granges reaffirm my belief in the class and longevity of these outstanding vintages. The 1953, always a personal favourite, continues to delight—alive, alluring, complete! (PG)

The 1952 to 1958 Granges were all previously assessed, topped up and re-corked at our Penfolds Red Wine Re-corking Clinics. Only a tiny amount of young Grange is added to the wine—around 10 millimetres. After 40 years, corks are beginning to lose their natural elasticity. Notwithstanding cellaring conditions, it is the time when old bottles are at increased risk of oxidation etc. The program is about preserving the integrity and freshness of good old bottles, while weeding out poorly cellared examples. We have cliniced over 90,000 bottles in the last two decades. Australian and international wine collectors have supported and have greatly benefited from the Penfolds Red Wine Re-corking Clinics. The overall condition of the wines in this bracket shows the effectiveness and success of this program. (PG)

1960–69: Acceptance to fame

This decade started strongly, but then dipped at the end reflecting difficult or moderate vintage conditions. The 1960 was massively different from the hidden vintages. It had the perfume and lifted aromatics, silky and voluptuous red fruits of classic Grange. 1961 smelled of black fruits and had more structure courtesy of fine, sustained tannins. (JH)

The early 1960s are really formidable wines; Schubert was skilled in producing the fireworks that define Grange today. The wines hit their stride in the 1960s. 1960 has powerful, fresh cedar, spice aromatics with broad, soft tannin and remarkable richness and juiciness on the palate. It just gets more ethereal. 1961 is also powerful with more apparent tannins and a lasting fruit brightness and succulence on the palate. 1962 was big, powerful and gruff with meaty shiraz, floral characters and the alcoholic warmth of the season. (JG)

I found this bracket even more exciting and more expressive. 1960 was astonishingly composed, elegant and spry—a Ray Beckwith of a wine; beautifully focused fragrant aromas and richly silken palate. It's ample, expansive, mouth-filling and lasting. 1961 was gloriously fresh and harmonious with voluptuous darkly glossy fruit and cashmere rather than silk tannins. But it finishes leathery dry. 1962 was captivating; a *liaisons dangereux*. It's very elegant, very refined and supple with amazing clarity, intensity and limpidity. (NB)

1960 was a nice old wine, perhaps starting to thin out a little. It's pleasant but not especially distinguished. 1961 is darker in colour with very earthy bass-notes. The fruit is fading, but there's still ripe sweetness on the palate. It finishes grainy. 1962 is a magical wine; the first sniff and I am in heaven. The wine showed tremendous complexity and fragrance; haunting flavours of great depth and style, harmony and persistence. This is a great wine, but the 1963—while less ethereal—had a majesty and presence that made it more of a sensuous experience. (HH)

1962 showed incredible brightness and persistency. It still showed blackcurrant/mint fruit on the nose and juicy prune fruit flavours on the palate. It's that combination of maturity and freshness that makes great wine. 1963 was restrained—almost dumb—but the palate is strongly flavoured with cinnamon/wood-spiced fruit, finishing slightly dry. I thought the 1964 and 1965 were off pace; the 1964 was fresh but short and the 1965 was too tart. (CPT)

1963 was clean, pure and full of aged goodness. It smelled of honeyed leather, herbs and cherry/kirsch; the flavours were long, lingering and lively. There were some tar and roses notes on the finish; a gorgeous wine. 1964 was shorter and stockier, but I thought it was in fine form with meaty, farmyardy, leather, spice and blood aromas and flavours. Those rustic characters seem to dry off the wine at the finish. Even so it has its appeal. I loved the 1965. It had power, juiciness, complexity and length. There was some rustic interest—for some perhaps a touch faulty—but the palate was throaty with a growl of tannins and full-fruited finish. It has a mountain of time ahead of it and no doubt will play out on its own terms. (CM)

1963 was pure hedonistic pleasure with supple, velvety fruits dancing around a circle of plum, prune, blackberry, black cherry and warm spices. 1964 isn't entirely convincing with its lighter colour and body; the sweet fruit, caramel and baked apple isn't tannin-supported as well as other vintages. It may be a phase (or a bottle); time will tell. 1965 was one of Max's dark horses; a favourite rather than a headline Grange. It has the structure missing from 1964 with mocha, vanilla, plum, blackberry aromas, good body and length. I thought this bottle was a fraction wayward. (JH)

1964 was very delicate with rose petal, red berry fruit and gentle persistent earthiness. It was a little woody at the finish, but I liked the silken texture and the gentle preservation of finely ripened memory of fresh redcurrant fruit. It's elegant rather than a power house. 1965 was still tight and powerful and still buttoned up with oak, but it had a blast of syrah gaminess, dark fruit power and potent alcohol. 1966 was back into power mode with black plum fruit and pyrazine/green edges. But it had strong red fruit/gamy flavours and savoury nuances. It shed some of that stemmy greenness with a bit of air. (JG)

1966 had great legs for a 41-year-old (this is after all the Year of the Horse in the Chinese Zodiac). It smells of cassis and mint. The palate has plenty of volume and is full of intense, dark, spicy rich fruits. I found the 1967 very engaging. It was light but balanced with a whiff of dried figs and liquorice, subtle red prune, wood-spiced fruit and soft, round acidity. I enjoyed the medium-bodied 1968 with its mint, cassis notes, spicy and still quite cedary fruit. There's still vigour and vitality, but it finishes dry; a very commanding and compelling food wine. (CPT)

1966 had a luminous quality; a beguiling, very seductive nose and gloriously rich, smooth, velvet-textured palate. It had great depth and intensity of flavour, excellent, seamless, gently spicy length. 1967 was flatter and a touch oxidised but it still had a pleasing Moroccan leather scent and very rich, dense, bitter-chocolate flavours. The wine had less finesse than others, but it was still potent. The moderately complex but powerfully structured 1968 had meaty, spicy aromas and flavours. It had plenty of sweet fruit and richness, but it lacked a degree of fleshiness and vigour of top vintages. It finishes dry and rather tannic. (NB)

1966 was right back on track with abundant plum, prune, blackberry fruit; perfectly balanced and integrated tannins, ditto oak. It was a very rich and satisfying wine. I liked the savoury edges of the 1967. It signalled a slightly cooler vintage and hence wine style. The wine was an appealing contrast to 1966 with its more spicy notes. The tannins were in no way rough or intrusive. 1968 had lots of ripe fruits, stewed plum, prune flavours and a dusting of chocolate. Rustic *brettanomyces* characters pervaded through the wine. (JH)

I found the 1968 very ancient, a bit harsh and thin. It had a very 'bretty' nose and the fruit is drying out. 1969 was also a bit rough and rustic with a dusty, earthy, peppery nose and drying out palate. It has a rasping, astringent tannin quality that takes over. It's still a much better drink than the 1968. 1970 smelled like an old leather arm chair, but the palate was lean and meagre. (HH)

The 1968, 1969 and 1970 were looking quite tired and very drying through the finish. There is a definite trough here. (CM) I would like to speak up for 1969. I liked the wine; it's a gentle vintage. The tannins are a little stiff, but there are plenty of red fruits, volume and flavour length. (JG)

1970–79: The cornerstone of every serious Australian wine cellar
This bracket did not have the spectacular peaks or highlights of the preceding decades but there were some very strong vintages. 1971 was a great year, but unfortunately we didn't see a truly great bottle. 1972 was surprisingly very good. 1976 was a big bastard with lots of flavour and structure. 1979—not regarded as a great vintage—was better than I remembered. (HH)

The 1970 was very mature and a little 'skunky'. It had some apricot, leather, lanolin aromas and flavours; there was a touch of volatility at the edges. 1971 was initially musty with some lanolin, mustard, vegetal notes. Then it opened up with a beautiful fresh range of fruit: wild mulberries, cranberry, boysenberry flavours. This was a remarkable wine. (JG)

1971 was always legendary for its volatility (and its relatively low alcohol of 12.3%). Max Schubert deliberately induced VA [volatile acidity]; that was part of the style. It had good, bright, clear colour, the typical highly lifted bouquet, predominantly red fruit characters and silky smooth tannins. The VA is very evident but this is a great—if not controversial wine. This example is looking a tad frail. Indeed evidence suggests there is increasingly more bottle variation. Drink soon. (JH)

1972 had quite good intensity of prune, mocha, wood-spiced fruit. 1973 was not so expressive on the nose but it had fresh minty, liquorice, spicy fruit. 1974 showed plenty of fresh blackcurrants, mocha, milk chocolate, cinnamon aromas and flavours. The colours of these wines were more mid-black/mid-brown—with a tawny rim—compared with the 1960s. (CPT)

1972 was a very good bottle; it drinks very well with meaty, gamy, rich chocolate aromas and hints of raisin. The palate is very savoury with lots of tannin; deep, structured and slightly chewy. (HH)

1972 is a notoriously variable wine; bottling staff apparently knocked off for the weekend in the middle of bottling this wine, leaving the unbottled Grange lying in a large ullaged storage tank until the Monday. Curiously though, the 1972s have always shown well at the Rewards of

Patience tastings. Perhaps most of the wines were bottled on the Friday after all. The best bottles are very good wines. (DD)

1972 certainly has a lot of appeal with its fresh rosewater, dark leather, musky fruit and beefy tannins. 1973 was astringent, super tight and all dried up at the finish. It's past its peak now. 1974 has an ounce more flesh but it's a touch green with bitter herb, olive, leather, violet aromas and flavours. (CM)

1973 was sweet and pretty but the fruit is tiring out. It's not holding together as perfectly as others. 1974 is more generous, soft and juicy with peppermint, smoky, raisin fruit but the volatility pokes out. 1975 was a beautiful mature wine, still with a long life ahead. It was black and spicy with layers and layers of aromas and flavours; date, fig and panforte fruit and sweet, long tannins all tightly woven together. (JG)

1973 had a deep mahogany colour and lifted nose with chocolate, prune aromas and flavours. It's still harmonious and succulent but the tannins are drying/muscling in. 1974 was a little murky with meaty aromas and dense, refined, textured tannins; the fruit is fading away. 1975 was supple, very glossy, rich and smooth with harmony and integrity of flavour and texture. It becomes slightly lean at the finish although it has good lingering length. (NB)

There are plenty of red and black fruit flavours on the fore-palate but it then gets quite dry and hard. Disruptive tannins are more evident now than in earlier years. The fruit will go before the tannins. (JH)

1976 is an elegant, fabulously refined wine with prune, sandalwood aromas, plenty of richness, succulence and flowing velvet texture. 1977, by comparison, is relatively light, slightly hard and lean with leather, dried spice, fruit characters and drying tannins. 1978 had great composure and harmony with a gently expansive bouquet and a supple, relatively mellow spectrum of flavours. (NB)

1976 was a rich, satisfying powerful wine with abundant black and red fruits which are ripe rather than jammy or dead-fruited. The tannins are present but in balance. 1977 is lively with red fruits, spices and touches of mint/leaf. It hasn't exalted itself in this tasting. The tannins are slightly green. Those sweet and sour characters will attenuate over time; drink soon. 1978 is a rich, round, mouth-filling wine with black fruits, bitter dark chocolate fruit. The batting opens with assurance; the only question is whether the quite powerful tannins will cause a late order batting collapse. It does hang in the balance. 1979 is powerful with black, spicy, savoury fruits and solid tannin foundation. It's probably not showing its best as it moves away from primary youth to secondary maturity. (JH)

1979 is flush with vanilla, musk, eucalypt, coffee and toffee; in that order. It seems to have some cabernet sauvignon characters including herbs and mint and strong, uncompromising tannins. In all this is a pretty serious Grange, but are the tannins pulling away from the fruit? (CM)

1980–89: Recognised as Australia's 'only true First Growth'
The following two decades show the enormous power of multi-regional blending. There are a remarkable number of strong characterful vintages; all marked by vintage variation and differing favour profiles. (CM)

1980 is a very lively and balanced 27 year old. It has cassis, eucalypt, minty fruit. It's ripe, persistent and elegant with ripe, crisp tannins and plenty of freshness on the finish. I found the 1981 hollow and dry. 1982 smelled of blackcurrants and wood with prune, liquorice characters. (CPT)

1980 was restrained with bitter chocolate, graphite, coal aromas. It's rich and succulent but lacks a degree of subtlety and complexity in comparison to other older Granges. 1981 is increasingly expressive in the glass with black fruits, spice, vanillin, earthy, sandalwood aromas and tangerine top notes. It has lovely refinement of texture and is effortlessly expansive on the mid-palate with saturated, sustained chocolaty flavours. 1982 is very elegant and fragrant with chocolate, kirsch, prune, tea aromas and refined silken textured palate. The wine blossomed in the glass, it was more aromatic, floral and impressively smooth. (NB)

1981 is definitely ready now. It was possibly better a few years ago with mature gentle red fruits, blueberries and rich prune fruit. I found the palate a touch metallic. I know the 1982 is not generally liked by Australian wine critics, but I found the wine succulent, delicious and heady with ripe, juicy, sweet and lasting raspberry fruit. The tannins duck and weave through the fruit, but it has excellent flavour length. 1983 was showing more maturity and some bitterness. It really needs meat to assuage the tannins. It's still got a good long run ahead, but the fruit could fade before too long. (JG)

1982 is a smart old wine with lovely chocolate, raspberry, red fruit flavours and texture; a rich, fleshy, smooth and plush palate. It doesn't show the negatives of the 1982s but the fruit idiosyncracy is still there. 1983 smells of mocha, honeycomb, Violet Crumble and tastes chewy and thick. It's not a vintage of finesse but it has very ripe fruit and lots of tannins. 1984 has more red fruits on the nose with mocha, chocolate, liquorice nuances. The palate is deep and structured, tight and statuesque; the mark of a classic Grange. It could go on for another few decades. (HH)

1983 is as robust as ever with uncompromising powerful but balanced structure. It's a love it or hate it style of wine. 1984 is much fresher with crisp, red and black fruits, considerable length and refined acidity. Oak and tannins are only bit players here. 1985 is a lovely wine; supple and rich with great texture and structure. It has the full array of red and black fruits, perfect tannin/oak balance and integration; a long lingering finish. (JH)

1983 is in mighty form; glorious, aged fruit characters rumble in synch with powerful, monumental tannins. The good run continues with the 1984. At first I found it quite lifted and toffeed, but then it opened up with redcurrant minty flavours and well-balanced tannins. 1985 was also powerful, balanced and complete with wood smoke, toffee, coffee, plum, soy aromas and pure, clean, velvety textures. (CPT)

1985 was very fresh and focused with floral, chocolate, kirsch aromas and plenty of volume, decent dense well-knit flavours and textures, but it's not quite in the same league as the top vintages. 1986 has a very exciting, invigorating, complex nose with an almost prickly intensity. It's very rich and weighty with impressive fruit depth, light and shade across the palate. 1987 has a very powerful peppery nose; right up both nostrils. It has astonishing length of flavour; it's unbridled wildness in need of bottle-taming. (NB)

1986 is superb. It's still ascending with rich rum and raisin aromas and very ripe, grainy tannins. The wine finishes quite dry but the wine responded to airing. 1987 was a rich, sumptuous wine with rich, chocolaty, meaty, demi-glace aromas, lots of fruit and deep, plush flavours. It's more forward developed than 1986 or 1985, but it's good. 1988 is slightly lighter and more youthful in colour with roasted meat, pan-scraping aromas and very grippy tannins. It tastes quite evolved, but it's got plenty of life ahead. (HH)

'The 1980s vintages show a remarkable number of strong characterful wines; all marked by vintage variation and differing flavour profiles.'

The 1986 is smoky and black-fruited with saturated jammy flavours and plenty of new oak. It's the type of wine that inspires such overwrought prose; flowing robes of satiny fruit flavours. 1987 was still youthful with barbequed meaty, roasted blueberry, iodine characters. 1988 was a gentler vintage with smoky/cherry/mushroom aromas and silken texture. The tannins build up very firm and tight. (JG)

1987 is a medium-plus-bodied wine with cassis/eucalypt/peppermint aromas, ripe fruit, an equal measure of rich, ripe tannins and lots of freshness. 1988 smells of cassis again but isn't as harmonious as 1987. I was impressed by 1989, with its prune, blackcurrant, fig aromas and soft, almost velvet-textured palate. It was rounder, sweeter and more wood-spiced compared with 1987 and 1988. (CPT)

1988 has a perfect limpid red crimson colour. The wine bounces back into familiar Grange territory with lovely mouth-filling, perfectly ripened, black and red fruits and superfine but persistent tannins. It's showing exceptionally well; no crime in drinking it now though. 1989 is slightly darker in colour with more brooding dark fruits and good overall structure and texture. (JH)

Apart from the gentle run of mint, I think the 1988 is a very fine Grange. It has a sweet hit of blackberry fruits through the palate prettied up with rose-like nuances and plentiful tannins. 1989 is sweet and raisiny with liquorice allsorts, musky aromas and soft delicious palate. It finishes a touch bitter but this is utterly hedonistic. (CM)

1989 is an unusual Grange with sweet, leafy, jammy aromas and fruit sweet, mocha, chocolaty flavours. It doesn't have the firm lasting structure of Grange; this is something of a fruit bomb. (HH)

Grange has a more assured footing—post 1986; the wines have greater polish and more refinement in structure. Like all other First Growth-type wines—like Chateau Mouton Rothschild—Grange can't escape the bad years or the personality of the vintage. (JH)

1990–99: International superstar
The 1990 and 1991 vintages inaugurated the modern Penfolds Grange style. These were the first Granges I tasted on release. I have always admired the 1990 for its freshness, dynamic, bright fruit and lovely textural pleasure. However, I have always preferred the 1991. It is a beautiful wine with a bold pure shiraz intensity and fireworks that sets Grange apart in a great vintage. 1992 smells of toasted wheat, cherry liqueur and some woody/spirit nuances. The palate is fruit sweet but the tannins are a touch drying. It gets better with air. (JG)

1990 was unexpectedly powerful and youthful with deep, rich blackberry, plum fruit, a touch of *sous bois* and firm tannins. The components are completely balanced. The wine is undoubtedly in the process of changing from young to mature, a process that will take years. 1991 is a substantial energetic wine with abundant sweet fruit and equally plentiful tannins; oak sweetening plays a positive role. This is definitely a teenager but with a great future. 1992 is charming and seductive with silky red fruits and fine tannins running through a bell-clear palate. The wine has considerable length and aftertaste. (JH)

1990 was rich, fleshy, deep and stately with peppery, bracken, spice aromas and smooth, refined textures. 1991 was a particularly distinguished bottle with deeply concentrated plummy fruit and rich tannic structure. The toasted char oak shows through, but the wine is beautifully balanced. I have never thought much of the 1992, but it performs very well against the more famous 1990 and 1991. It smells of blackberries and chaff and tastes sweet and ripe with good structure; it's very elegant and tidy on the palate with delicious flavour and balance. This is a very under-rated wine. (HH)

1991 was well composed but penetrating on the nose. It was dense, refined, intensely flavoured but still unyielding. I found the 1992 much more successful than the 1990 and 1991. It had an intense, spicy, tangy, black-fruited nose reminiscent of a top young Hermitage. It was richly silky with very vivid fruit, dripping succulent, suave tannins and excellent length. 1993 was comparatively lean and faltering in style. (NB)

1992 was succulent and soft with medium-bodied blackcurrant fruits and slightly dry tannins. 1993 was lovely and harmonious with fresh tannins and plenty of cassis/mint/herbaceous fruit. 1994 was deep and darkly coloured with chocolate/dark plum aromas, rich, ripe, juicy fruit and underlying but well-layered oak. (CPT)

> *'Penfolds Grange is inextricably linked to the foundation of the contemporary Australian wine industry. As the market for ultra-fine Australian wine evolves, embracing new ideas and enthusiasms, Grange remains the rock on which Australian fine wine was built.'*
> —LANGTON'S FINE WINE AUCTIONS

I enjoyed the 1993 as well. It had fresh aromatics; inviting leafy, ash, tomatoes, violets and black-currants. It seems to be quite cabernet in style with an atypical Grange flavour profile. The tannins are sappy and stalky but there's excellent juiciness and freshness. 1994 could be a classic Grange. It's big, sweet and welcoming with crushed ant, coffee, blackberry aromas and complex earthy, leathery appeal. (CM)

1994 has tremendous density with powerful tannins and plenty of fruit stamina. There's loads of treacle, spice, meaty flavours and traces of blueberry, black fruits. 1995 is extravagantly perfumed with smoky, gingerbread, black fruits and juicy, earthy, mocha flavours. 1996 is one of the all-time great Granges with tremendous length of flavour and drive; potent bright blueberry, strawberry, dark spice fruit, subtle succulent flavours and sleek, new oak. This is a wine that has the completeness and staying power of the 1991; it looks to have the longest potential to age. (JG)

1995 is not entirely convincing. It has some spicy, savoury, briary characters but it does not have the line or length of the better Granges. 1996, on the other hand, was a picture-perfect display of finesse and power, elegance and complexity. It's not a blockbuster but it is perfectly balanced and incredibly long in the mouth. The tannins and oak are there, but they just hover discreetly in the background. 1997 has an array of sweet fruits, with contrasting hints of blackberry confit and mint/leaf. The tannins are well balanced; the wine only suffers because it sits between two spectacular vintages. (JH)

1996 is another stately but characterful wine with ripe, deep, lush, berry aromas and hints of bitumen and black olive. The wine is complex and vigorous, firm and tight. This is a long-term Grange with at least 30 years ahead of it. 1997 was somewhat jammy and loose-knit, but soft and smooth. It lacks the power and gravitas of good vintages, but it's still pleasant to drink. 1998 is not really a classic, tightly structured Grange; it's ample and broad with big roasted, ultra-ripe poached fruit aromas and flavours, underlying toasty oak and big, ballsy dense tannins. It doesn't have the tightness or finesse of 1996 but it's very warm and very ripe. (HH)

1997 was a little closed but it had a supple fruit quality and crisp tannins. 1998 was ripe and juicy with persistent primary raspberry, cherry fruit and effortless tannins. This is so youthful for a nine-year-old wine; a great Grange. (CPT)

1998 was superb wine with balanced, brambly fruit and lovely, glossy mocha richness. It's smooth and supple with silken, lacy tannins; the wine just glows and glows. 1999 is brambly again. It's dense and fresh, but the flavours are still to unpack. Everything seems to be in place; it just needs more time. (NB)

I have seen the 1998 a few times but this was the best showing so far; colossal fruit, colossal tannin and colossal integration. It's big, black and beautiful but it needs plenty of time to settle down. 1999 has lovely power, softness and savoury flavours. It's sweet-fruited with ground coffee aromas. You can really notice the new oak in these younger wines. The acids and tannins are yet to fully integrate, but even so there is a lot to be impressed by here. (CM)

1999 was a totally delicious wine; as pure an expression of Barossa shiraz in a perfect vintage as is possible to imagine. It's drinking beautifully now with satsuma plum, blackberry fruit and silky tannins. Or you can allow the wine to mature and develop for another 30 years. (JH)

2000–present day: A wine to try before you die

The 2000s were magnificent wines with beautifully vivid fruit, graceful structure and timeless elegance. 2000 was very creditable for a very difficult and uneven vintage. It had lovely blueberry fruit and softly chewy, round, velvety tannins. 2001 had a magnificent blueberry nose but also more complex, completely enveloping spicy, well-integrated oak. The palate is deceptively effort-less, so well balanced are the fruit, oak and tannins. (NB)

As should be the case this is definitely the best Penfolds red from 2000. It's lively and fresh with spicy, minty red fruits which enliven the palate. The wine doesn't have great structure but it's a real achievement nonetheless. 2001 was very rich and sumptuous with plenty of black and red fruits and soft, fine tannins; a rainbow of flavours and colours. 2002 was like a Merlin engine throbbing away silently. It had beautiful focus and balance; none of the over-intense characters of lesser 2002s. It's all spice and silk with a marvellous finish. (JH)

> *'Even though Australia has become a major player on the world's wine scene over the past decade, no other wine has come close to approaching the quality and fame of Grange.'*
> —WALL STREET JOURNAL, 2007

2000 smelled like a young vintage port with raspberry, floral aromas, vivacious fruit and ripe tannins. 2001 was richer, more extracted and tannic with floral violet characters. 2002 was very fine, harmonious and feminine. I can imagine this Audrey Hepburn wine will mature in the same way as the 1954; it has ripe raspberry, violet, floral aromas and ripe, silky, elegant structure. (CPT)

I found 2001 borderline 'porty'. It's big, rich and super ripe with sweet kirsch, plum, aniseed flavours. It's very sweet-fruited; this is not classic Grange. 2002 is not so big, but tight and elegant with cherry, spicy plum fruit and fine, tight structure. I suspect it will age like the 1962. 2003 is very scented with plenty of florals and super-ripe berries. The palate is fleshy and well concentrated with supple spiced fruit, grainy tannins and superb overall balance. (HH)

2002 had lovely tension with juicy blueberry, coffee, mocha, plum fruit and supple tannins. There's nothing abrasive about the wine. 2003 is comparatively light for Grange, but still substantial with plenty of blueberry fruit, mocha oak; the new oak has still yet to settle down. 2004 is a smart, potent, dense wine with great freshness and fully mature tannins. 2005 is completely primary and unresolved yet still shows beautiful power and lasting fruit flavours. (JG)

2003 is a great result for a difficult vintage. There's lots of flesh and fruit through its core. 2004 is a rage of violet, raspberry, plum fruits. The wine is beautifully structured and composed with integrated new vanillin oak. This is a fine, rippling, sturdy but supple wine. 2005 looks very impressive for a wine so young. It's rich, tight, musky and luxurious with lovely soft tannin. (CM)

As expected, 2004 is incredibly plush, rich and complex, but with beautifully weighted and structured tannins; they take the wine beyond the other fruit bombs such as the 1998! 2005 is even tighter and more compact than the 2004, yet the fruit line is glossy and smooth. The tannins and acidity act as a brake, giving overall tightness. It will be fascinating to see how this wine develops. (JH)

2004 has a stunning early appeal with great floral, anise, violet aromas and fresh powerful structure. It's a deliciously fruity wine and not overly tannic. 2005 is a class act too; nutmeg, spicy oak shows drive over violet/floral fruit, but it's superb oak. The wine is very elegant and balanced. (HH)

WHITE

Bin 144 Yattarna Chardonnay

First Vintage:	1995.
Variety:	Chardonnay.
Origin:	Multi-district blend—primarily Adelaide Hills but contributions from Tumbarumba, NSW; Henty, Victoria; and Derwent Valley, Tasmania.
Fermentation:	100% barrel fermented in varying percentages of new and older French oak barriques depending on vintage.
Maturation:	10–14 months in French oak.
Comments:	Packaged in laser-etched bottles. Released entirely under screw cap since the 2004 vintage.

The release of Penfolds Bin 144 Yattarna Chardonnay marked a new chapter in the Penfolds story. The inaugural 1995 vintage was the most talked about and eagerly anticipated white wine in Australian history. At the presentation of the Tucker-Seabrook Perpetual Trophy at the 1997 Royal Sydney Wine Show, the Chairman of Judges, the late Len Evans, described the wine as 'a revelation' and 'a step forward for Australian chardonnay'.

The 1995 Yattarna was perhaps the most famous culmination of wine research and experimentation since the launch of Grange some four decades earlier. Indeed, the work behind the scenes, which began in 1992, was dubbed by wine writers as the 'White Grange' project. Unconstrained winemakers were allowed to venture across state borders to find important and distinguished vineyard sites capable of yielding the rare and exquisite fruit quality desired for a truly great Australian chardonnay.

Yattarna derives from an Indigenous word meaning 'little by little' or 'gradually'. This utterly unmistakable Australian name, which evokes organic momentum and vintage-by-vintage effort, captures the essence and culture of Penfolds' winemaking philosophy. At first, John Duval said consistency of quality from vintage to vintage would be a key factor in consolidating Yattarna's reputation. He said at the time: 'My aim is to create a style which shows restraint and fineness of structure when released at three years of age, and will continue to develop richness and greater complexity as it ages in bottle. As with all Penfolds wines our success relies on the rigorous fruit selection, care and attention to detail in the winery and use of the finest quality oak.'

With an incredible portfolio of vineyard resources around Australia, Penfolds gradually—through trial and error—identified suitable places where the best fruit could be grown. The Adelaide Hills district was an obvious starting point. This historic winegrowing region of the mid- to late 1800s had slumped out of fashion by the early 1920s. Brian Croser, Geoff Weaver and other contemporary winemaking

pioneers revitalised the district during the 1980s and quickly established a strong reputation for Adelaide Hills chardonnay. Indeed, Penfolds, inspired by this success, ventured into the region during the early 1990s and now sources from both its own vineyards and independent growers. A number of trial bin Adelaide Hills chardonnays and semillons were released from the ongoing research and development of cool-climate Reserve bin wine styles. Impressed by the results, winemakers have earmarked Adelaide Hills fruit as a key component for Yattarna Chardonnay in almost all vintages so far.

Initially, Yattarna included a proportion of fruit from McLaren Vale to provide richness to the middle palate. The style impressed wine show judges and critics, but the wine has evolved more quickly than expected. Winemakers have had to perform a balancing act to make a wine that is delicious to drink when young, but has the structure and refinement to mature and improve in the cellar. Profoundly elegant fruit with perfume, naturally high but linear acidity and plenty of flavour length is the type of requirement winemakers require in sparkling wine production. However, richness, volume and flavour are essential for a great drinking wine.

The desire to make something singularly exquisite and lasting has taken winemakers along the underbelly of the south-eastern Australian mainland and across the Bass Strait into the island state of Tasmania. Tumbarumba, Henty, Adelaide Hills, Fleurieu and the Derwent Valley have all played a role in the evolution of style. Yattarna follows in some respects a champagne philosophy. The wine is ultimately about respecting the character of individual sites where each component plays an essential part in the final blend. 'Minerality, texture, layering and longevity' are the key characteristics of the style.

Winemakers are looking for specific ripe fruit characteristics: well-concentrated grapes which possess apple/white peach/melon flavour profile and natural/mineral acidity. Whole bunch pressing and barrel fermentation, including use of wild yeasts, malolactic fermentation and yeast stirring (*bâtonnage*), bring important elements to the Yattarna style. The first Yattarna vintages saw 100 per cent new oak maturation. While it added a strong savoury component, winemakers believed that it over-seasoned the wine, masking overall fruit quality and broadening the palate. Penfolds has since moved towards tightly grained, lightly toasted oak using coopered barrels from Dargaud and Jaegle, Seguin Moreau and Louis Latour in France.

Oliver Crawford has further fine-tuned the style by varying the proportion of new oak. The oak regime is entirely dependent on the character of each vintage. The 2004 Yattarna was all fermented and matured in older oak. Generally, however, the aim is roughly about 50 per cent new French oak and further oak maturation for approximately twelve months prior to bottling.

Yattarna has achieved considerable acceptance as one of Australia's best chardonnays. In 2006 Oliver Crawford was nominated as Winemaker of the Year by *Australian Gourmet Traveller Wine* magazine in recognition of his work.

James Halliday said, 'As a group, all the wines carried the Yattarna cachet extremely well. They are of an exceptionally high standard.' Ch'ng Poh Tiong observed that the style had developed 'a clear thumbprint'. Joshua Greene was also impressed, describing the wines as having 'all the fireworks, power and balance on a vast scale'. Huon Hooke was complimentary about the overall style and structure of Yattarna: 'They have a symmetry and voice reminiscent of a great painting.'

Yattarna is now sealed with screw cap—a move which was met with plenty of approval from the panel. James Halliday said, 'With screw cap the wine will keep for much longer. The fruit may drop out with age but this will be well compensated by a Burgundian-type complexity and richness.'

TASTING NOTES ~ BIN 144 YATTARNA CHARDONNAY

1995   PAST

Medium deep gold. This wine has developed considerably now; butterscotch/crème-brûlée/toffee aromas with some ripe peach notes. The palate is overdeveloped, rich and broad with crème brûlée, oxidised flavours and malt oak notes. It's well past its prime. No point keeping. Adelaide Hills, McLaren Vale blend.

1996   PAST

Medium yellow gold. Intense butterscotch/honeydew melon/vanillin aromas with some caramel notes. The palate is rich and concentrated with butterscotch/crème brûlée/toasty/dried fruit flavours, creamy richness and fine mineral acidity. The fruit is overdeveloped. It's drinkable but well past its prime.

1997   NOW • • • PAST

Medium deep gold. Pear/citrus peel/vanilla/butterscotch aromas. The wine is fully mature with pear/cumquat/apricot/grilled nut/toasty flavours, underlying savoury oak and hard acidity. Surprisingly fresh bottle. Drink up.

1998   NOW • • • PAST

Medium deep gold. Matchstick/lanolin/pear/white peach aromas with some vanilla/toasty oak notes. The palate is creamy with rich sweet pear/peach/melon/grilled nut flavours, vanilla/toasty oak and linear tight acidity. The wine is still quite fresh and complex but drink soon.

1999   NOW

Medium straw gold. Intense pear skin/tropical fruit/lemon curd/biscuit aromas and plenty of malty oak. Sweet pear skin/tropical fruit/honey flavours with overlapping new oak and cutting/minerally acidity. It's fully mature now. Drink up.

2000   NOW • • • 2010

Pale straw gold. Smoky/lanolin/pear skin/herb garden/honey aromas with some vanilla. Well-concentrated creamy pear/melon/vanilla flavours, underlying toasty/cedar oak and long, bright acidity. The wine is still showing plenty of freshness and life.

2001   NOW • • • 2010

Medium straw gold. Rich, complex butterscotch/pear skin/nectarine aromas with some savoury notes. Lovely and complex wine with pear/nectarine flavours and underlying new oak. Finishes minerally and long. Manages to combine complexity and elegance. Best to drink soon. 83% Tumbarumba, 17% Adelaide Hills. 60% new oak.

2002 ★   NOW • • • 2011

Medium straw gold. Lanolin/pear/rockmelon/tropical fruit aromas with some yeasty complexity. A sweet, concentrated wine with pear/lanolin/rockmelon flavours, underlying savoury oak and minerally long acidity. A very stylish, classy and satisfying wine. 76% Adelaide Hills, 24% Tumbarumba. 55% new oak.

2003   NOW • • • 2012

Pale straw gold. Fresh, elegant pear skin/camomile aromas with plenty of toasty/savoury new oak. The palate is very refined with lemon curd/white peach/toasty flavours and fine minerally long acidity. Builds up chalky/sappy firm. 100% Adelaide Hills. 69% new oak.

2004 ★   NOW • • • 2014

Pale gold. Intense and beautifully complex lemon curd/rockmelon aromas with touches of butterscotch/herb garden. A fresh, elegantly structured wine with lemon curd/melon/flavours and lean high-pitched acidity. Finishes minerally and crisp. Will build up richness with age. Yattarna now released under screw cap. 92% Henty, 8% Adelaide Hills. 0% new oak.

2005   NOW • • • 2012

Pale gold. Fresh and fragrant wine with apple/nectarine/melon aromas and toasty/lanolin nuances. A beautifully balanced wine with lemon curd/nectarine/grilled nut flavours, leesy complexity and underlying vanillin/savoury oak. Lovely, long, silky finish. Outstanding vintage. 100% Adelaide Hills. 55% new oak.

2006 ★   2009 • • • 2015

Pale gold. Flinty pear/melon/lemon curd/white peach aromas. The palate is fresh and concentrated with deep-set lemon curd/lime/pear/white peach flavours and fine pronounced tangy acidity. A sinuous wine with tremendous velocity and extreme flavour length. Has excellent potential. 37% Derwent Valley, 36% Adelaide Hills, 27% Henty.

DISCUSSION

As a group all the wines [from 2001] carried the Yattarna cachet extremely well. They are of an exceptionally high standard. These are exemplary Penfolds white wines of great interest. The **2001** needs drinking now. Despite its bottle age and warm vintage provenance it manages to combine complexity and elegance. Here is a striking example of where cork has both added to and taken away from the wine. There is a toasty, developed, gossamer feel to the wine and yet it has advanced in age. (JH)

This tasting not only showed increasing refinement of the Yattarna style, but also a stark lesson about cork and screw cap. 2001 was almost like a control experiment and gave me a sense of direction. I appreciated the wine greatly. It has a different kind of mineral development and toasty maturity. (JG) This was from memory a very hot vintage. It has a chrysanthemum tea colour, ripe tropical/passionfruit/pineapple aromas and vanilla/flinty notes. The palate has an engaging roundness and sweetness of fruit on the finish. (CPT)

2002 is fully developed with plenty of sweet tropical fruit and moderate complexity. It's still lovely to drink with delicious flavour and style. This is a distinctly Australian chardonnay. (HH) The wine has a lower proportion of oak, but seems to show more oak character through the wine. However, I found greater texture and tension on the mid-palate. It's quite a compact wine and perhaps lacks succulence. (NB)

2003 is a very elegant wine and very much in the Yattarna style of today. This is a fine and disciplined wine reflecting whole-bunch pressed characters and unobtrusive malolactic complexity. The wine surprised me because it gave me more than I thought it would. (JH) The wine is pale in colour, but is rich and round with plenty of new oak, and mineral/leesy characters. (JG) This was drier and a touch more chalky than previous wines. The wine was showing plenty of toasty/cashew nut characters and some sappy notes. It's not bad for the year, but it should be enjoyed soon. (HH)

2004 is a brilliant wine. It's subtle and elegant with sweet pear/lemon candy characters, and complexity develops with air. The oak and fruit interacts extraordinarily. (JG) This is a superfine, fresh and beautifully poised wine. It has so much movement in the mouth with a long, crisp, haunting aftertaste. It's more Chablis-like than any of the other vintages in this line-up and really foils against 2005. (JH) It's a very gentle, soft wine with lovely refinement, energy and texture. The acidity is so well integrated into the wine that it is barely a feature. (NB) It's more restrained than the previous wines but is smooth and clean with lovely refinement and subtlety. It's ageing gracefully and slowly. A very long and satisfying drink. (HH)

2005 is medium-bodied but perhaps more expressive than previous vintages. It's a bit oaky but it has a soft toastiness. (CPT) The oak does poke out and it's especially apparent after 2004, which has seen no new oak. However, the wine is remarkably pale and bright in colour with lovely apple/nectarine/melon aromas and well-balanced palate. (JH) I agree, the oak does come through as well, but the wine does have an exhilarating freshness and vigour. (NB)

2006 is a beautiful young wine. It has real velocity and extreme length with a delicious nectarine/white peach fruit profile. I scored it really highly and could give it more with a touch more age. Penfolds must have a good malolactic bug because the wines have a lovely creaminess without enhancing or shifting the character of the fruit. (JH) It is a very impressive wine with lovely complexity on the nose. It has a beautiful molten quality with ample, expansive mouth-filling flavours. I sense this is a new departure for Penfolds and what I see is very exciting. (NB)

You can certainly see through these wines how the various cool-climate regional components interact in them. The Derwent River Chardonnay has an extra floral lift and very fine crisp acid balance. The 2006 vintage illustrates the very exciting potential of Tasmania as a source of cool-climate chardonnay. (OC)

CHAPTER SEVEN

Luxury Wines

Penfolds' Luxury wines reflect the essence and prestige of house winemaking philosophy and provenance. These are classic wines in their own right. Bin 707 Cabernet Sauvignon and St Henri have a remarkable heritage and a fascinating evolution, reflecting the extraordinary energy and vision of Penfolds' winemakers of the 1950s and '60s. These are instantly recognisable names among wine collectors, with a strong, distinctive, individual style and a wonderful track record of cellaring performance.

Magill Estate is an elegant, modern, classic, single-vineyard wine based on a historic vineyard first planted in 1844 by Dr Penfold. It is one of the great city wines of the world, with the promise of greater things to come. RWT Shiraz, on the other hand, is a modern, generous, buoyant wine reminiscent of the warm-hearted and beautiful Barossa landscape. Bin A Chardonnay embraces a tradition of experimentation and development at Penfolds. This wine was the precursor to Yattarna. The Aged Release Riesling illustrates the seductive and complex qualities of an important Australian varietal style. All of these wines reflect the compelling evolution of Penfolds' winemaking philosophy and individual winemaking skills.

REDS

Bin 707 Cabernet Sauvignon

First Vintage:	1964.
Variety:	Cabernet sauvignon.
Origin:	Coonawarra and Padthaway.
Fermentation:	Stainless steel tanks with wax-lined/wooden header boards. All components complete fermentation in barrel.
Maturation:	18 months in new American oak hogsheads (300 litres).
Comments:	Bin 707 was not made from 1970 to 1975, nor in 1981, 1995, 2000 or 2003. Bin 707 was named by a marketing executive who had previously worked for the Australian airline Qantas. Available in all Penfolds markets. Packaged in laser-etched bottles from the 1997 vintage on. Released under screw cap in some markets since the 2005 vintage.

'These wines are of pure concentration;
true wonders of the wine world.'
—CAMPBELL MATTINSON, PANELLIST

1964 Bin 707 Cabernet Sauvignon was Penfolds' first commercial release of a single cabernet-based wine. After a stop–start beginning, it is regarded today as one of Australia's most important cabernets; a distinct Penfolds house style and a foil to the great regional cabernets of Coonawarra and Margaret River. Jeremy Oliver, a leading Australian wine critic, describes Bin 707 as 'Penfolds' most eloquent expression of cabernet sauvignon' and 'one of eighteen "Grand Cru"-type wines which define the limits of contemporary Australian wine'. It is also rated 'Exceptional', alongside Grange, in *Langton's Classification of Australian Wine*.

When Max Schubert returned to Australia from his extensive tour of Europe in 1949, his thoughts were never far from cabernet. He had visited many of the great chateaux of Bordeaux and had been very impressed by the wines. Christian Cruse, head of the distinguished négociant firm Cruse et Fils Frères, was particularly influential. Schubert was able to observe winemaking practices at Cruse's properties, including partial fermentation and maturation in new oak. Having seen similar practices in Spain, he was inspired to use these techniques at Penfolds. Indeed, Penfolds' Kalimna Vineyard, acquired in 1945, comprised some of the world's oldest surviving genetic cabernet material. Block 42 was planted around 1888. These original, direct-producing cabernet sauvignon vines, still going strong, have been isolated from the ravages of the vine pest phylloxera, which destroyed many great vineyards during the 1890s.

In 1948, Max Schubert, who had been recently appointed Senior Winemaker, made a one-off, single-vineyard cabernet sauvignon. Max Lake, author of the seminal work *Classic Wines of Australia*, wrote in 1966: 'It is becoming magnificent and can only be compared to the big cabernet wines of Europe.' Two bottles of this 1948 Kalimna Cabernet Sauvignon surfaced at an auction in Sydney in 1987, unearthed with other rare Australian vintages from Max Lake's cellar at Greenwich. The wine, probably blended and bottled on Schubert's return, was never released commercially. This may explain its scarcity. It has never been seen since a memorable Royal Sydney Wine Show dinner in 1994. One of the auction bottles, which had been given to John Duval by the successful auction purchaser (a Queensland wine merchant), was tasted by several wine judges, including Rewards of Patience panel members James Halliday, Huon Hooke and Andrew Caillard. Despite the evolution of winemaking practice and time, the wine, with duck-egg coloured capsule, was unmistakably Penfolds; it had classic, mature, sweet-fruit characters, chocolaty tannins and superb flavour length.

Schubert, who was based at Magill, regularly experimented with cabernet, at one stage hoping that it would form the backbone of Grange. The experimental 1952 and 1953 Grange Cabernets were also made largely from Block 42 fruit. Schubert revisited Kalimna cabernet every year but the trials were inconsistent. The fruit was used mostly for blending material, including early vintages of Grange. By the early 1960s, Schubert revisited the question of a Penfolds Cabernet Sauvignon. 1960 Bin 630 Kalimna Cabernet Adelaide Foothills Mataro, 1961 Bin 58 Cabernet, 1963 Bin 64 Cabernet and 1963 Bin 511 Kalimna Cabernet Ouillade were all precursors to Bin 707.

The release of 1964 Bin 707 began a false dawn of only six successive vintages. While the Block 42 vines were over 80 years old, the fruit quality was too inconsistent to justify an ongoing single-vineyard cabernet. Nonetheless, the 1964 was well received by critics of the day. Doug Crittenden, whose family wine business in Melbourne is celebrating 50 years, purchased parcels of the same wine and bottled it in Melbourne as Crittenden's Celebration Reserve 1964 Kalimna Cabernet Sauvignon. Len Evans, the distinguished Australian wine show judge, said in note number 18 of *The Wine Buyer* (1968), 'It is one of the best red wines I have tasted for some time, being light and balanced, yet it will undoubtedly improve for some years and should develop into a wine that will long be remembered.' All of these wines were open fermented under wax-lined header boards. However, invariably, they were matured in seasoned rather than new oak. Penfolds sourced other Barossa material from 1967 but, after the disappointing 1969 vintage, the line was abandoned.

The inconsistency of quality fruit supply and a niggling, but practical, concern about house style and the spectrum of cool-climate cabernet fruit aromas, flavours and structure were constant themes during the 1960s and early '70s. While the variety showed enormous promise, Coonawarra was in the process of rediscovery and Margaret River was a viticultural backlot. By the release of the 1976 vintage, the first to use Coonawarra fruit, such concerns had been largely sorted out. Within a few years, Penfolds Bin 707 was already achieving strong support and recognition as a benchmark Australian cabernet. Don Ditter, Penfolds Chief Winemaker of the time, said, 'The original Bin 707 was a marvellous wine; it comprised almost entirely Block 42 cabernet. The first releases had the richness and ripeness expected of warm- to hot-climate fruit. A gradual move to Coonawarra during the 1980s changed it to a more elegant cool-climate wine. During the mid-1990s, it seems to have reverted back to its original style, a distinctive Penfolds wine divorced from other Australian cabernets.'

The overall winemaking philosophy and barrel maturation of Bin 707 is almost identical to Grange; both are direct descendants and beneficiaries of Max Schubert's experimental wines of the 1950s and '60s. The wine is vinified in open, stainless steel fermenters with wax-lined wooden and stainless steel header boards to optimise extraction of colour and flavour. All components are partially barrel fermented in new seasoned American oak hogsheads for a period of eighteen months.

The modern Bin 707 represents the Penfolds house red wine style at its most rich and powerful. The cabernet fruit is largely drawn from South Australian vineyards in Coonawarra, Padthaway and Barossa Valley (including the famed Block 42 vineyard). Everything about Bin 707 is large scale. Winemakers seek fully ripe fruit with strong flavours derived from partial barrel fermentation and maturation in new American oak hogsheads for a period of eighteen months. This explanation of style shows why Penfolds will not make Bin 707 in difficult or more elegant years where the fruit profile is underpowered, sinewy or out of character. The years 1981, 1995, 2000 and 2003 were not made. Some observers will note that both 2000 and 2003 were generally good vintages in Coonawarra. However, the style still relies on the contribution of warmer-climate fruit—particularly Block 42 and Barossa cabernet sauvignon—for overall richness and density.

The way bin numbers were chosen can always yield surprises. Rowan Waddy, an ex Qantas executive and member of Australia's Z Force during World War II, christened Bin 707 after the Boeing 707, the aircraft that brought Australia closer to the rest of the world during the 1960s. A Bin 747 was also released but was discontinued in 1975. It should be pointed out, however, that brand marketing was in its infancy and that few would have predicted that Penfolds Bin numbers would carry so much cachet in the future.

Bin 707 is an immensely concentrated style with dark berry/dark chocolate fruit balanced by well-seasoned new oak, plenty of fruit sweetness and strong, but not overwhelming, tannins. This is a medium- to long-term cellaring style of wine. If you can wait the distance, Bin 707 builds up into a wonderfully complex and interesting wine.

Joshua Greene said that 'Bin 707 shows the virtue of blending. While the older wines were quite muscular and broad-shouldered, the style has steadily improved. The real changes begin around 1996 and 1998. The wines have more substance and balance.' James Halliday agreed: 'The last decade of vintages has seen more home runs. The wines show massive fruit sweetness and the tannin quality is riper and more integrated.'

The development of Penfolds Bin 707 Cabernet Sauvignon mirrors the advances in winemaking and viticulture. It has always been a beacon of progress and uncompromising excellence; each release has always received strong critical support as a benchmark of the time. From the reintroduction of the 1976 vintage, Bin 707 has been given the full Grange-type treatment. Over the last decade, however, Bin 707 has become a stridently confident style; in Peter Gago's words, 'the wines are now reaching a similar level of quality and the potential longevity expected of a great Penfolds cabernet sauvignon'.

TASTING NOTES ~ BIN 707 CABERNET SAUVIGNON

1964 ★ NOW

Brick red. Mature cedar/meaty/mushroom/leather aromas with some old mint/sandalwood notes. The palate is still fresh with sweet meaty/cedar/earthy/minty flavours and slinky, fine tannins. Finishes chalky firm but long and sweet. Almost entirely sourced from the Kalimna Vineyard's Block 42, established around 1888.

1965 PAST

Brick red. Over-developed dark chocolate/coffee ground/leather/maderised aromas. Sweet meaty/dark chocolate/dried meat/earthy/herb flavours and chocolaty fine tannins. Fruit fades towards the finish. Drink up.

1966 ★ NOW

Brick red. Delicious old wine with beautifully focused and mature liquorice/dark chocolate/ gamy/mocha aromas. Deep, rich, firm palate with plenty of dark chocolate/mocha/spice/meaty flavours and firm, slinky, dry tannins. Finishes long and cedary.

1967 NOW • • • PAST

Brick red. Lovely herb garden/rose petal/ground coffee aromas with some cigarbox notes. Herb garden/brambly/mocha flavours and loose-knit, chalky tannins. A smooth, sound wine with elegant weight and structure. It's very old and fragile now.

1968 PAST

Brick red/brown. Maderised marmalade/roasted coffee/treacle aromas. The palate has lost freshness and sweetness of fruit. It's old, leathery and dried out with muscular, hard tannins. Has well and truly faded now.

1969 PAST

Brick red. Leathery and dry with faded old parchment aromas and leafy/bitter tannins. (AC)

1976 ★ NOW

Brick red. Intense liquorice/dark chocolate/briary/malt aromas with some graphite notes. There is plenty of freshness and fruit sweetness on the palate with liquorice/dark chocolate/lead pencil/ demi-glace flavours and fine, rich, grainy tannins. Finishes chalky dry, but smooth and long.

1977   **NOW**

Medium red brick. Lovely herb garden/plum/dark berry/brambly aromas with some cedar notes. Plum/redcurrant/molasses/espresso/herb flavours and grainy loose-knit tannins. Builds up slinky firm. Has really outperformed expectations. Expect bottle variation.

1978   **NOW • • • PAST**

Brick red. Dark chocolate/cassis/herb/minty aromas. Generous, juicy wine with blackcurrant/demi-glace/herb garden/capsicum flavours and fine, supple, lacy tannins. It finishes strikingly chalky dry. Beginning to lose its fruit sweetness now.

1979   **NOW • • • PAST**

Brick red. Smoky/earthy/burnished cedar aromas. Chocolaty/prune/earthy/bitumen flavours and firm savoury/grippy tannins. The wine loses energy through the mid-palate and then finishes lean and dry.

1980   **NOW • • • PAST**

Brick red. A very solid wine with blackcurrant/cedar/herb garden/leather aromas with some minty/tar notes. The palate is savoury with blackcurrant/cedar/leathery flavours and substantial, dry, firm, stringy tannins. It finishes very brambly and austere. The fruit is overwhelmed by tannin. It's not getting any better.

1982   (cliniced bottle)   **NOW • • • PAST**

Brick red. This wine has fared well beyond expectations. It was originally feted at release and then hammered by critics for its contrived cherry/tomato leaf aromas and flavours. It has developed really well and shows attractive cassis/tea leaf/rosehip aromas and some malty/chocolate. It's succulent and smooth with blackcurrant/rosehip/mocha flavours and fine, supple, silky tannins. Not a classic vintage but enjoyable all the same. Drink up.

1983   **NOW**

Brick red. Intense inky/smoky/earthy/dark chocolate/jammy aromas and touches of cedar/herb. It's richly concentrated and big-boned with deep-set dark chocolate/raisin/gamy/cedar flavours and rustic, firm, assertive tannins. It still has plenty of fruit sweetness, but ripe/under-ripe characters are beginning to pervade the wine. A famous bushfire/drought year. Probably best to drink soon.

1984   **NOW**

Brick red. Rosehip/plum/chocolate/meaty/rustic aromas. The palate is juicy and buoyant with plum/dark chocolate/meaty flavours and silky, fine tannins. It finishes chalky and dry but the fruit sweetness drives through. It's a generous, balanced wine.

1985   **NOW**

Brick red. Intense blackberry/saddle leather/wet bitumen/minty aromas. The palate is well evolved with complex saddle leather/blackcurrant/herb garden fruits and sinewy, grippy, hard tannins. Drink up.

1986 ★ NOW • • • 2015

Brick red. Lovely complex cedar/blackcurrant/meaty/demi-glace/dried herb aromas. It's deeply concentrated with plenty of blackcurrant/meaty flavours, underlying mocha/malt oak and chocolaty, ripe tannins. It finishes fresh and sweet; long and flavourful. A great Bin 707. Perfect drinking now, but will hold.

1987 NOW

Brick red. A cool vintage wine with herb garden/cedar/cassis/leafy aromas. An underpowered wine with light cassis/leafy/cedar flavours and grainy, fine tannins. Finishes savoury and dry but loses persistency. Drink up.

1988 NOW • • • 2018

Brick red. Perfumed and mocha/cassis/camomile/herb aromas. Rich soupy gamy/cassis/mocha/dried herb flavours and pronounced chocolaty tannins. Finishes chalky and dry. Has evolved well. Can still go on for a while.

1989 NOW • • • 2014

Brick red. Bitter chocolate/rum and raisin/tomato leaf aromas with strong malty oak notes. A very chunky palate with plenty of fruit sweetness, cassis/raisin/molasses/chocolaty fruit, sappy dense tannins and lashings of oak. It's not particularly graceful but it's laden with flavour. Drink while the going is good.

1990 ★ NOW • • • 2020

Deep crimson. Lovely cassis/redcurrant/leafy aromas with some walnut/malty notes. A very rich, concentrated, tannic wine with dense blackcurrant/prune fruit and chocolaty, ripe, supple tannins. Finishes long and sweet. Balanced and integrated. Beautiful, powerful wine. Drinking brilliantly now but worth keeping.

1991 ★ NOW • • • 2020

Deep crimson–purple. Intense aniseed/chocolate/ground coffee aromas with some demi-glace notes. A classically structured cabernet with lovely blackcurrant/cedar/espresso flavours, underlying vanilla/toasty oak and fine, grainy tannins. Sophisticated and sensuous.

1992 NOW • • • 2015

Medium deep crimson. Perfumed cassis/herb garden/camphor/spearmint aromas. Concentrated, fresh palate with deep blackcurrant/herbal/menthol flavours and pronounced biting/aggressive tannins. It finishes very brambly and dry. The tannins are beginning to drive over the fruit. It will hold for years, but improved complexity is doubtful.

1993 NOW • • • 2012

Deep crimson. Another cool-vintage year. Early developed wine with complex dark cherry/leafy/silage/demi-glace/malty aromas. The palate is dense, broad and firm with rich beef stock/dark cherry/leafy flavours and astringent/stemmy dry tannins. Best to drink while the sweet-fruit flavours persist.

1994   NOW • • • 2025

Deep crimson. Fresh blackcurrant essence/dark plum aromas with some cedar/malt notes. Delicious, complex wine with plum/blackcurrant/inky/tobacco flavours, underlying new toasty/smoky oak and plush mouth-coating grippy/graphite tannins. A big, structured, glossy wine with plenty of volume and energy. A dark horse. Could be regarded as a star vintage in the future. Wait a while?

1996 ★   NOW • • • 2025

Deep crimson. Lovely fresh classical wine with pure cassis/cedar/herb garden aromas. Powerful complex wine with intense sweet cassis/dark chocolate fruit, vanilla/malt oak and fine-grained cedary tannins. Finishes firm but long and sweet. A superb Bin 707.

1997   NOW • • • 2015

Deep crimson. Fragrant cedar/herb/mocha aromas. A very savoury style reflecting the cooler vintage; cedar/herb/mocha/raspberry/minty flavours and fine, leafy, dry tannins. Fruit fades towards the finish. Best to drink soon.

1998 ★   2012 • • • 2030

Deep red. Gorgeous, intense dark chocolate/blackcurrant/inky/cedar aromas with plenty of liquorice notes. Velvety, rich, dark chocolate/cassis/mocha/cedar flavours, malty new oak and dense, plush, chocolaty tannins. A fabulously concentrated wine with wonderful purity and sweetness of fruit. Has the power and flavour length to go the full distance. A great Penfolds year; a classic Bin 707. Best to wait.

1999   NOW • • • 2020

Deep red. Bright aniseed/liquorice/chocolaty/cedar/herb garden/slight mint aromas. The palate is loose-knit with blackcurrant confit/chocolaty flavours and silky, long, savoury tannins. Builds up firm and leafy but it has good fruit sweetness and flavour length.

2001   NOW • • • 2020

Deep red. A very forward, fruit-driven wine with fresh redcurrant/raspberry/mulberry/cedar aromas. Well-concentrated, sweet-fruited wine with plenty of redcurrant/mulberry/slightly jammy fruit and thick, dense, chewy tannins. This is a big, fleshy wine with loads of fruit and prominent tannin structure.

2002 ★   2012 • • • 2035

Deep red–purple. Beautifully focused and ethereal wine with pure, ripe blackcurrant/dark chocolate/mocha aromas. The palate is everlasting and powerfully concentrated with impeccable reach of flavours: buoyant dark chocolate/cassis/espresso coffee fruit, integrated, perfectly seasoned oak and dense, supple, ripe, mouth-filling tannins. It finishes cabernet firm, long and sweet. A great vintage.

2004 ★   2012 • • • 2035

Inky purple. Fresh elemental wine with concentrated pure cassis/mulberry aromas and under lying savoury/vanillin oak. A fresh, buoyant, very youthful wine with densely packed mulberry/

cassis fruit, mocha/vanillin oak and bolstering chocolaty mouth-coating tannins. A very generous, well-balanced, fruit-driven wine. A classic Penfolds year.

2005   2015 • • • 2035

Inky purple. Fragrant almost floral/blueberry/blackcurrant/violet aromas and new savoury/toasty oak. The palate is richly concentrated and luscious with ripe—almost unfathomable—rhubarb/blueberry/elderberry flavours and thick, plush, ripe tannins. Finishes grippy, sweet and long. Needs time to evolve.

2006 ★   2012 • • • 2035

Inky purple. Lovely blackcurrant/espresso/mocha aromas with toasted malt/spice oak. Beautifully balanced but elemental wine with deep-set, generous blackcurrant/espresso flavours, fine-grained/muscular tannins and well-seasoned toasted malt/cedar oak. Finishes firm, with plenty of flavour length. A classic Bin 707 vintage.

DISCUSSION

The tasting started with a bang and finished with a bang. Some of the very old wines were just hanging in there but for both sentimental reasons and deference to their age and provenance, I marked them up. Whereas the fruit had survived and the tannins had departed in the old Bin 389 vintages, the reverse was a feature of the Bin 707s. The 1964 and 1965, however, were lovely old wines, both nearing their end, but still fresh with earthy, cedar flavours. (JH) The old vintages were quite muscular and lean, but by the mid-1980s the wines stepped up with extraordinary concentration, power and ultra-ripe fruit. (HH)

1964 was a very mellow, complex aged wine with stacks of lovely aged flavours. (HH) It was a very fresh, round, enjoyable wine with sandalwood, leather, wood spice, coffee, chocolate fruit characters and plenty of sweet fruit. (CPT) It had a lovely, composed, refined, mature nose with cedar, sandalwood and vanilla aromas. The palate had a mature sweetness of fruit, fine-grained leather texture and full, gentle, valedictory warmth at the finish. It's delicious now, but it will hold for a few more years at least. (NB)

1965 is very old now with earthy, animal, coffee ground characters. The palate is still pleasant but the wine is fading now. (HH) It is quite rustic with blue cheese, leather, old hide, feral characters. It still has flesh and firm tannins. (CM)

1966 has impressive persistence of fruit and legs for a 41 year old. It still has blackcurrant, sweet sandalwood and liquorice fruit characters. (CPT) I wish I was born in 1966. It had widespread tannin, power and delicacy. (CM) It's unbelievably dense and rich, almost like a dry port. It has very inky liquorice, black olive, bitumen aromas with sweet honeycomb notes. It's very deep, firm and intense with huge extract. (HH)

1967 was faintly medicinal with gentle warmth and dried orange peel aromas. The palate was intricate, richly textured and ample with impressive integrity and length. (NB) It had plenty of cedar, briar, earth, bramble aromas but the tannins were somewhat a one-way argument. (JH)

1968 is a light, spicy, delicate wine. It's soft and funky, but not obviously cabernet. It's already beginning to fade. (JG) It had an old-style Rioja-type nose and tasted austere with dried prune, old wood flavours. (CPT) It's an earthy, dusty old wine; the fruit has faded and the tannins are left high and dry. (HH) The Bin 707 style has changed over the years. When we started making Bin 707 the wines were matured in older oak. (JB)

Bin 707 was not made between 1970 and 1975.

1976 was still quite lively and fresh with blackcurrants and traces of mint. It had fine tannins and good overall balance. (JH) The wine was rich, layered and complex with crème brûlée, beef stock, old vanilla aromas and flavours. It's a superb old wine that persists on and on. (HH)

1977 was broad-shouldered with good fruit presence and persistent firm cabernet grip. There was a lovely satin richness across the palate. (JG) The wine was good and sound with aniseed, dark leather, coffee, toast and molasses-type fruit and strong length. (CM)

1978 is compact, but it lacks harmony and richness now. (NB) It was the first wine to show primary cabernet fruit with cassis, rose petal aromas. The palate was deep, layered and generously flavoured, with assertive cabernet structure. (HH)

1979 showed ripe black fruits and some earth, bitter chocolate overtones. It finishes very savoury. (JH) It had a juicy, structured appeal with fresh, polished, sweet-toast aromatics. It lacks mid-palate stuffing. (CM)

1980 was bright and refreshing with sweet redcurrant fruit and mature, rounded palate. (JG) It has some meaty/minty characters as well, but the tannins were grippy and tight. It has more succulence than 1979 but it's thinning out now. (NB)

1982 has a very vegetal cabernet nose with some shaded fruit notes. The palate had plenty of sweet fruit and very fine, supple, silky tannins. It was succulent and smooth. It's a very atypical Bin 707 but it's delicious all the same. (HH)

1983 is somewhat tough. The tannins have outlived the fruit. (JH) It has a smoky appeal but it has strong ripe and under-ripe—sweet and sour—type aromas and flavours. (CM) It's a big, structured wine with plenty of grunt but not a lot of elegance. Those jammy, port, raisin characters do not match the rustic, assertive tannins. (HH)

1984 is a generous wine with plenty of varietal blackcurrant fruit and balanced tannins. (JH) It was a solid, juicy, enticing wine that flows on the palate despite the muscular structure. It's drinking very well now. (CM)

1985 is fresh but slightly green with mint, cassis, herbaceous aromas and flavours. (CPT) The wine was mellow and mature with dusty, earthy, smoky char characters and very gripping hard tannins. It comes across as unbalanced. (HH)

1986 has assertive cabernet personality with plenty of capsicum, herbaceous, mint, cassis aromas and rich, ripe tannin structure. (CPT) This was a mixture of power and finesse with supple blackcurrant fruit, fine, persistent tannins and balanced oak. (JH) It had some sweet and sour aromatics but plenty of herb, leather and malty oak notes. It was spicy almost, with great tannin balance and length. (CM)

1987 was quite herbaceous with some fruit richness. The tannins were fine-grained but they dominated the finish. (NB) It's medium-bodied with sweet chocolate/cassis/cedar fruit but the palate is very dry. (CPT)

1988 is still powering on. It is a smooth, savoury, elegant wine with aged cassis flavours and tight tannins. (HH) There's a heavy weight to the wine with dark fruits and dark tannins. (JG)

1989 has some appealing bitter chocolate characters and persistent—relatively ripe—tannins. (JH) It's a looser-knit style with supple structure and nice purity of flavour. It lacks the fruit weight of other vintages but it's still harmonious in a minor key. (NB)

1990 is rich and ripe, strongly shot with cassis, chocolate, sultanas and musk. It has a gorgeous spread of tannins across the palate. This is a beauty! (CM) It was rich and full with lovely cassis, redcurrant, blackcurrant fruit, supple tannins and balanced, integrated oak. (JH)

1991 showed some dusty, capsicum and crushed leaf top notes. The wine smelled riper and better as it sat in the glass. It was full-bodied and soft, fleshy and sensuous, round and supple, smooth and luxurious. (HH) This was a super Bin 707. It suffers a little in comparison to the gigantic 1990, but it's still a very successful wine with elegant coffee, blackcurrant, toasted fruits and strong chocolaty tannins. (CM)

1992 was balanced but it lacked intensity. It showed some mint, eucalypt characters and spicy, herbaceous, capsicum fruit. The tannins were fresh and the acidity was crisp. (CPT) It has a lovely minty, leafy nose, but the palate is all seeds and skins. It finishes dry and puckering. (NB) It has a mix of ripe and less ripe flavours; its ageing potential is a worry. (JH)

1993 has flowing bangs of tannin and attractive varietal cassis, leafy characters, but you need to drink this before the tannins completely take over. (CM) The wine has green, leafy, herbal aromas yet super-ripe fruit. It's fat, soft and round but there are stacks of firm, grippy tannins. (HH)

1994 was a big structured wine with beautiful tobacco/cassis fragrance, blackcurrant, tobacco, cloves, mint flavours and mouth-coating tannins. (CM) It had bold, rich blackcurrant fruit and glossy, round flavours. The tannins are polished and there is no hint of under-ripeness. (JH)

1996 is a very long-term wine. It is a massive wine and quite difficult to drink now. It has rich, smoky, developed fruit and toasty oak. The palate is dense and fleshy with enormous chewy tannins. (HH) This is a lovely vintage with bright, shining blackcurrant, plum fruit, prominent oak and silken texture. It really hits the mark. (JG)

1997 is savoury and slightly peppery. It's drier and tighter than 1996. (NB) It smells good and tastes good with plenty of raisins, blackcurrant, mint and toast flavours. However it doesn't have the stuffing or the length for the long term. (CM)

1998 is very squashy and ultra-ripe with rich blackberry/blackcurrant fruit. The palate is almost syrupy but dense, ample, thick tannins bring freshness and balance. This is so concentrated that you could stand a spoon in it. (HH) It's a very high-quality wine. It's more closed than the 1996 but is still brooding, rich and savoury with well-integrated oak. It's very compact and elegant. (NB) It's sensually opulent and round with gorgeous cassis, blackcurrant fruit and velvety richness. Once again it shows how the best vintages produce the greatest wines rather than the winemakers! (JH)

1999 has a powerful, black, smoky, dense, fig scent. It's luscious but there is nothing elegant about the wine. The tannins are weighty and strong and fill every pore of the mouth. It has a cherry-liqueur fruit sweetness that crosses the palate. (JB)

2001 has plenty of blackcurrant aromas and very well-handled oak. It's a very agreeable wine. (CPT) It has big, bruised raspberry, mulberry fruit and some celery, herbal notes. The palate is big, fleshy and concentrated with blackberry jam flavours and thick, chewy tannins. This is a huge wine with lots of flavour and appeal. (HH)

2002 is as deep, intense, layered and focused as anyone could wish. The tannins are ripe and the wine has not been over-extracted. (JH) This is an amazing wine with impeccable structure and reach of flavour. It has plenty of black olive, blackcurrant, cedar, toast, plum fruit and seriously boned tannins. (CM) This is a knockout Bin 707 with saturated colours, youthful elegant fruit and potent ripe tannins. (JG)

2004 is an exceptional wine with inky purple colour, glorious blackcurrant fruit and mouth-feel; all bolstered up by ripe tannins and integrated oak. It's so generous. (JH) It's very deep with concentrated cassis aromas. The oak takes a back seat. The palate is full of chocolaty/mocha flavours and dense, mouth-coating, thick tannins. There are some reduced demi-glace/simmered stock characters. This is an elegant, fruit-driven wine. (HH)

2005 is still a baby with ripe, juicy raspberry fruit, vanilla oak and equally ripe, fine, tannins. This is a really well-balanced wine with a very long future ahead. (CPT) This is a very vivid, tightly wound wine. It's dense, well extracted and so concentrated it verges on bitter at the finish. It's very young and yet to show its full personality. (NB) 2005 is amazingly luscious and viscous; ripe cassis fruit sweeps across the mouth like a tidal wave. The tannins and oak are nowhere to be seen. The last decade of vintages has seen more home runs. The wines show massive fruit sweetness and the tannin quality is riper and more integrated. It will be fascinating to see how these contemporary vintages age. It's unlikely they will develop like the older wines where the tannins are left like shags on a rock. What has changed? (JH)

We stopped using continuous presses in 1994 in favour of bag presses. The pressings are not quite so extractive and sappy. Generally there has been a huge focus on tannin management over the last decade. It starts in the vineyard right through vinification and blending. It has been a long road, but we think the wines are looking better than ever. Bin 707 has always been given the Grange-type treatment; the wines are now reaching a similar level of quality and the potential longevity expected of a great Penfolds cabernet sauvignon. (PG)

RWT Barossa Valley Shiraz

First Vintage:	1997.
Variety:	Shiraz.
Origin:	Barossa Valley, South Australia.
Fermentation:	Stainless steel tanks with wax-lined/wooden header boards. Fermentation completed in barrel.
Maturation:	12–15 months in (generally 50–70% new) French oak hogsheads (300 litres).
Comments:	Packaged in laser-etched bottles. Released under screw cap in some markets since the 2004 vintage.

'A distinctly individual wine with the stamp of
Barossa terroir and the strong house style of Penfolds.'
—HUON HOOKE, PANELLIST

Penfolds RWT Barossa Valley Shiraz was released after several years of red wine-making trials and a pent-up demand for a 100 per cent Penfolds Barossa shiraz. During the 1990s the Barossa emerged as one of Australia's most exciting wine regions with an extraordinary and unmatched heritage of old vine shiraz material going back to the 1840s. Max Schubert, who grew up and worked in the Barossa, was well aware of the potential of Barossa shiraz. He experimented extensively with this variety during the 1950s and '60s. Early vintages of Grange included Barossa shiraz. The first vintages of Bin 28 Kalimna Shiraz were 100 per cent single-vineyard Barossa wines. Bin 389 and St Henri also draw fruit from the region.

During the 1970s and '80s, Penfolds relied increasingly on multi-regional blending and house style philosophy. The return to single-vineyard and single-region wines is a reflection of the growth and development of the contemporary Australian fine wine scene. Regional definition, individual winemaking philosophy and connection with landscape have captured the imagination of wine drinkers all over the world.

The Barossa Valley has emerged as one of the world's great wine regions with great characters, a fascinating story and beautiful and compelling shirazes. While Penfolds Grange is seen as a Barossa-type wine—based on the Kalimna Vineyard—it does draw fruit from other regions. Only on rare occasions is it a 100 per cent Barossa wine. A 1973 Bin 170 Shiraz was the last pure Penfolds Barossa shiraz until the 1997. The release of RWT Barossa Valley Shiraz was, therefore, an obvious step

forward. The Barossa Valley is an undulating landscape with the Barossa ranges along its eastern and north-eastern edge and rolling farmland along the western boundary. It was first settled by English and Silesian immigrants during the early 1840s. The region has been making shiraz wines for over 160 years. While table wine was made for local consumption, most of the harvest was used for the production of fortified wine. In 1911, Penfolds established a winery at Nuriootpa, sourcing fruit from independent growers for the production of port-style wines. At the end of World War II, Penfolds moved towards table wine production, resulting in a vineyard acquisition and replanting program.

In 1945, Penfolds purchased the Kalimna Vineyard, originally planted to vines around 1888 by George Swan Fowler. During the 1950s and '60s the bin range and philosophy of house style was developed and based on multi-vineyard and multi-regional blending. It planted and acquired new vineyards around the Barossa in the 1970s and '80s, including Koonunga Hill, Stonewell Road and Waltons. Penfolds also developed longstanding relationships with independent growers throughout the region. During the early 1990s, more attention was given to the character of sub-regional Barossa shiraz and the quality of individual parcels of fruit. The development of RWT Shiraz is inextricably linked to the evolution of precision viticulture and a general awareness of vineyard character. Penfolds has enjoyed long-term, cross-generational relationships with several Barossa grape-growing families.

The two disciplines of viticulture and winemaking are increasingly intertwined as growers and winemakers work together in search of optimum balance, ripeness and flavour development. Identification of the best vineyard sites around the Barossa Valley, securing a regular supply of independently grown fruit and establishing a clear idea of winemaking philosophy were the key elements in Penfolds' red winemaking trials, which began in 1995. Vineyards with a track record of producing the best shiraz grapes in the region are constantly targeted by competitors. An ex-Grange or RWT vineyard brings certain guarantees of quality and strong marketing/provenance cachet. Grower relationships, which extend to vineyard improvement programs, and loyalty and quality premiums, are especially important. Penfolds has a dedicated field team of grower liaison officers that work and advise independent growers on how to grow Penfolds-standard fruit at optimum ripeness and flavour development.

When a new Penfolds Barossa shiraz was first mooted, it was necessary to start an extensive red winemaking trial from the ground up. It needed to be distinctly Barossa in character yet foil the other great shirazes in Penfolds' portfolio. The wine had to be different from the elegant and muscular Magill Estate Shiraz, the maturation style of St Henri, and the opulent and powerful Grange. Winemakers preferred the perfumed, richly textured and seductive shirazes grown in a broad arc across the west and north-west Barossa Valley. These 20- to 100-year-old vineyards are found in the dry, hot northern districts around Kalimna, Moppa and Ebenezer. This is open, sweeping country of alluvial plains, with red loam and red-brown clay soils dissected by gullies and rivulets. Stands of eucalypt trees and scrub protect the vines from desiccating winds. Other top vineyards are located in the central west district around Stonewell, Marananga and Seppeltsfield in a rolling landscape—a rumpled patchwork of vineyards, many planted several generations ago. The shiraz is particularly perfumed, with fine textures and plenty of fruit richness.

Paul Georgiadis, Penfolds Grower Liaison Manager, talks about the pride and passion of Penfolds growers: 'When they make the grade for this type of fruit it's like getting top marks in an exam.' Each parcel of fruit that comes into the winery is like a jigsaw piece. Ultimately winemakers are looking for a classical plum/blueberry essence fruit profile with voluptuous intensity, ripe tannins and juicy flavours. After vinification this will translate into what Huon Hooke describes as 'a distinctly individual wine with the stamp of Barossa terroir and the strong house style of Penfolds'.

At vintage time the fruit is batch vinified and then classified according to intensity, texture and concentration. The components of RWT are each vinified in headed-down, open stainless steel fermenters. Towards dryness, the wine is racked into new, tightly grained French oak to complete fermentation. This Penfolds technique is exactly the same treatment given to Grange, but RWT differs because of its regional fruit selection and the use of French rather than American oak. It was Penfolds' groundbreaking work with Grange that began a Barossa tradition and love of American oak with shiraz. By the 1990s, however, there was an increasing movement of Barossa winemakers towards toning down the characters of American oak in Barossa shiraz.

Barrel fermentation and maturation of shiraz in new French oak is of great importance to the RWT style; the subtle underlying spice/savoury oak characters season and bring further complexity to the wine. The wine is matured in new and seasoned French oak for a period of twelve to fifteen months. RWT Barossa Shiraz is an opulent, powerful wine with sumptuous fruit sweetness and seductive texture. Joshua Greene noted, 'these are wines that completely absorb and harness the oak to drive and sustain flavour development'.

Winemaker Peter Gago said, 'The RWT style has further evolved since first vintage. We have pulled back from 100 per cent new oak to around 50 per cent to 70 per cent and changed the mix of French coopered barrels. Our winemakers are very focused on the voice and vintage character of the fruit. While this is not a fruit-driven style, the wine is all about the richness and beauty of Barossa shiraz. The oak plays a supporting role to the fruit. Hence the proportion of new oak each vintage is dependent on the overall volume and intensity of the wine.'

Panellist Neil Beckett described the RWT style as 'a glossy, rich, smooth wine with seductive, mouth-filling flavours and seamless texture. The wines have developed more succulence and better oak integration since 2002. The overall harmony and power of the wines all promise excellent cellaring potential.'

Huon Hooke summed up the bracket as 'very impressive. The best years—2002, 2004, 2005 and 2006—were absolute blinders, showing understated power and lovely balance of fruit, oak, tannins and alcohol. In hindsight, the 1997 was still an experimental-type vintage. It is the 1998 vintage that sets the standard and orientates the overall style.'

Panellist Campbell Mattinson described the most recent vintages of RWT as 'Grange killers. The 2004, 2005 and 2006 vintages are effortlessly beautiful wines with superb integration of oak and a perfect storm of tannins. These are all future greats.'

RWT Barossa Valley Shiraz has quickly developed a strong reputation in the primary and secondary wine markets as a classic cellaring Barossa shiraz style. While these wines are best enjoyed with five to fifteen years of bottle age, the top vintages should hold or develop for a lot longer. If properly cellared, these bottles could last up to 40 or 50 years. It's that type of wine. RWT is already establishing a strong track record of support as collectors recognise the cellaring potential and consistent quality of RWT vintages. The 1999 was served at the Nobel Prize award ceremony in Stockholm. More recently the 2003 won the coveted George Mackay Trophy for Australia's best exported wine. The 2000 RWT was in *Wine Spectator*'s Top Ten Wines of the Year in 2003.

TASTING NOTES ~ RWT BAROSSA VALLEY SHIRAZ

1997   NOW • • • 2015

Medium deep crimson. Intense black fruits/plum/tobacco leaf/cedar aromas. The palate is medium-bodied with ripe, succulent dark chocolate/blackberry fruit, earthy/walnut notes and fine but firm tannins. It finishes fresh and long. A refined vintage that is drinking best now.

1998 ★   NOW • • • 2020

Deep crimson. Fresh, opulent blackberry/blueberry/plum/chocolate/malt aromas with some cedar/spice/leather notes. A beautifully concentrated, harmonious wine with blackberry/blueberry/chocolate/spice flavours, ripe loose-knit, granular tannins, integrated new vanillin/malt oak and plenty of flavour length. Perfect fruit/tannin/French oak balance.

1999 ★   NOW • • • 2020

Deep crimson. Intense liquorice/aniseed/blueberry/apricots/camomile aromas. A layered concentrated palate with lovely energy, fruit sweetness and vibrancy; generous blackberry/blueberry/dark chocolate flavours, pronounced grainy tannins and underlying savoury oak. An outstanding Barossa vintage.

2000   NOW • • • 2012

Medium crimson. Mulberry/redcurrant/brambly aromas with some earthy/silage notes. Medium-bodied, sweet mulberry/redcurrant/cherry flavours, fine loose-knit lacy tannins and savoury oak. Finishes a touch underpowered. Ready to drink now. Will hold but not a great vintage.

2001   NOW • • • 2020

Deep crimson. Intense blackberry/plum/briary/mint/dried-spice aromas. The palate is well concentrated with rich dark chocolate/plum/spice flavours, plush dense chocolaty tannins, savoury new vanilla oak and some leather/demi-glace notes. A very rich tannic wine with plenty of stuffing to last the distance.

2002 ★ NOW • • • 2025

Medium deep crimson. Lovely liquorice/blackberry/dark mocha/espresso coffee aromas. Rich, ripe blueberry/blackberry/bitter chocolate/roasted coffee flavours, dense grainy tannins and underlying savoury oak. Finishes firm but long and sweet. A wine with tremendous intensity and volume of fruit. A great RWT vintage.

2003 NOW • • • 2015

Medium deep crimson. Dried plum/blackberry confit/roasted aromas/underbrush aromas. The palate is not as powerful or as rich as previous vintages and is showing some developed leather/roasted meat flavours. The tannins are chalky and dry, but there is a good core of fruit sweetness and plenty of flavour length. A brusque, firm style, but showing typical Barossa vintage character.

2004 ★ 2009 • • • 2025

Deep crimson. A beautiful, classical vintage. Ethereal violet/blackcurrant/blueberry/chocolate aromas with some herb garden/floral notes. A buoyant, expansive, mouth-filling wine with richly concentrated chocolaty/plum/blueberry flavours, chalky fine tannins and underlying cedar oak. Finishes long and sweet. An utterly seductive and brilliantly balanced wine.

2005 2010 • • • 2020

Deep crimson. Fresh, fragrant raspberry/mulberry/camomile/dark chocolate/musky/mint aromas and flavours. The palate is well integrated with succulent, supple sweet fruit, ample lacy dry tannins and mocha oak. Seamless, flowing wine for both early drinking and medium-term cellaring.

2006 ★ 2012 • • • 2030

Deep crimson. A very young exuberant wine with classic blackberry/liquorice/bitter chocolate aromas and plenty of new savoury/vanilla oak characters. The palate is richly concentrated and buoyant with deep-set liquorice/blackberry/blueberry fruit, chocolaty dense tannins and savoury/ginger oak. Finishes long and sweet. Beautifully balanced wine with fantastic fruit/tannin/oak integration. Reminiscent of 1999. A great RWT.

DISCUSSION

RWT is a distinctly individual wine with the stamp of Barossa terroir and the strong house style of Penfolds. There is no excessive ripeness. Looking back at the **1997** once again I feel that it was an experimental-type wine. It's the 1998 that sets the standard and orientates the overall style. (HH) The wine had plenty of black fruits, including plums and wet tobacco leaf characters. While it is medium-bodied, it had ripe, succulent fruit, fine tannins and freshness on the finish. (CPT) The wine has evolved with meaty, savoury notes. It is surprisingly fleshy on the palate with very grippy tannins which swamp the fruit. (NB) The wine is ready for drinking now. It's still fragrant with cedary, earthy aromas, touches of spice and fine tannins. But it has developed quite quickly. (JH)

1998 is big, blue oak and big, blue fruit. It has some spice/cedar notes and early signs of leather and touches of tar. Then comes a swagger of gorgeous tannins. The tannin alone will power it through a long cellaring life. (CM) It's an elegant wine in every respect with perfect fruit/tannin/French oak balance and integration. The fruit profile was very much in the plum/cherry/blackberry spectrum. (JH) There's nothing heavy or ponderous. It's a dark, powerful wine with richly seductive fruit and dense, energised palate; the smell and taste of a great wine. (JG)

1999 is layered and savoury and full of character. The aromas are complex with meaty/beef stock notes and threads of aniseed, dried bananas, dry spices and nutmeg. It's rich and tannic, solid and firmly gripping. Does it have a hint of farmyard character? (HH) The wine was attractive with intense black fruits but I felt the overall fruit concentration wasn't enough to support the overall structure. (NB) I found it a profound, beautifully proportioned wine. It shows just how good Barossa shiraz was in 1999. It had wonderful melting tannins, cascades of fruit and quality oak. (JH)

2000 was a very fresh, ripe wine with blackcurrant, plum, red prune and pepper notes. The wine is medium-bodied and elegant with ripe, round tannins and a freshness that seals all that fruit. (CPT). It's not a great Barossa vintage but strict selection of fruit has made a wine that certainly doesn't disgrace the label! It's quite savoury and lean; no surprise. Drink up! (JH) It's lighter bodied than other RWT vintages with some shaded fruit characters and earthy/asparagus hints. The fruit tapers off to a lean, short, rather astringent finish. It's perfectly decent to drink, but it's not worth cellaring further. (HH)

2001 smells like a young vintage port with violet/dried fig aromas. The palate is rich and ripe with muscular long tannins; an impressive wine. (CPT) It had touches of seaweed characters—which I also saw in the 2000. However it has lots of smashed plums, mint and signs of leathery development blowing through. It has terrific tannin structure. This is a fine, mature, lengthy, sophisticated wine. (CM) It's a big, rich, tannic, highly structured wine of big body and density, grip yet balance. There is no excess of alcohol. This is a dark-horse-type wine with a long-term future, but how long? Twenty years? (HH)

2002 is as expected: dense, concentrated and slightly introverted with black fruits, bitter chocolates and liquorice. The tannins are firm but not dry. This is a superb wine—all in balance and the oak eaten up by the wine! (JH) It's a voluminous, big chocolaty wine with a mass of fruit and tannins racing up from behind. The components are all excellent. (CM) It has blue- and blackberry scents and elegant tannins. It has that buttoned-down feel of a great Penfolds red. It's tailored and seamless. (JG)

2003 is highly successful for the vintage. It has thick blackberry/black leather aromas and lots of sandy/gritty tannins. The wine is all structure and power. (CM) The wine has plenty of black cherry/smoky aromas. The palate is plush with glossy, rich, smooth fruit, great succulence and appetising acidity. (NB)

2004 is an impressive wine with vivid, ripe, black fruits. It has a dense, very cushioned feel with ample, expansive, mouth-filling, juicy flavours. (NB) The wine is very impressive with raspberry/floral/violet aromas and juicy, succulent, velvet-soft fruit; all delivered by Rolls-Royce-type tannins. (CPT) It has a really superb floral/aromatic nose with dark fruits/violets and cherries. The palate is lovely and smooth with supple, sweet fruit and lashings of tannins. The wine's very young and underdeveloped but it's delicious. It has a big future. (HH)

2005 is even more alluring than the 2004 if that is possible. It's packed with black and red fruits, anise and violets, spices and Provençal herbs. It's a superb wine with great length and wonderful structure. (HH) It's an utterly delicious wine with fragrant aromas of black cherry/plum/blackberry and seductive mouth-feel and fruit flavours. This will be well and truly open and revealing by time of release. It will live but patience is not needed! (JH) It's a super-classy wine with beautiful integration of oak and fruit. It's total seduction but not tarty! Plums/toast/violets/blueberries pervade and flow effortlessly across the palate. Great tannins again! RWT has really hit its straps. (CM).

2006 is harmonious and promising and smells of black fruits and incense. It's rich—almost syrupy—but is still incredibly elemental and needs time to settle down. It should come together really well. (NB) It's so lifted and bright! It has beautiful fresh aromatics and perfect preservation of fresh fruits: strawberries, wild raspberries and blueberries. The oak underscores the fruit adding a touch more oak tannin richness and flavour. It's that pure, sleek, fruit quality that makes this wine so beautiful and sumptuous. (JG)

The best years—2002, 2004, 2005 and 2006—were absolute blinders, showing understated power and lovely balance of fruit, oak, tannins and alcohol. (HH) The most recent vintages of RWT are Grange killers. The 2004, 2005 and 2006 vintages are effortlessly beautiful wines with superb integration of oak and a perfect storm of tannins. These are all future greats. (CM)

Magill Estate Shiraz

First Vintage:	1983.
Variety:	Shiraz.
Origin:	Single-vineyard 'monopole' wine using selected parcels of fruit from Blocks One, Two and Three of the 5.2-hectare (13-acre)Magill Estate, Adelaide, South Australia.
Fermentation:	Wax-lined, open concrete fermenters with wooden header boards. After basket pressing, components complete fermentation in barrel.
Maturation:	12–15 months in new French (65%) and American (35%) oak hogsheads.
Comments:	Approximately 1500–3000 cases. Packaged in laser-etched bottles.

The historic and heritage-protected Penfolds Magill Estate 'monopole' is one of the few single vineyards in the world located within city boundaries. It was here that Dr Christopher and Mary Penfold settled in 1844, just eight years after the founding of Adelaide. The vineyard itself today only comprises 5.2 hectares but remains a highly evocative piece of South Australian history. The original cottage, built in 1845, still remains among the vines. Penfolds' turn-of-the-century bluestone cellar complex is an important landmark: the cellar door located in what was once

Penfolds' Still House (distillery) and the critically acclaimed contemporary Magill Estate Restaurant are both important drawcards for all wine lovers.

Max Schubert, Penfolds Chief Winemaker from 1948 to 1975, worked at Magill Estate and lived nearby. This is where the experimental and early Granges were first made. When the South Australian Heritage Council recognised Grange as a heritage icon of South Australia, it was decided to partly return winemaking of Grange back to Magill Estate for the 2002 vintage.

Dr Penfold and his wife Mary originally planted the Magill vineyard with grenache cuttings brought out from France and England. By 1903 over 49 hectares of vines covered the property rising to around 78 hectares in 1949 (the adjoining property Auldana comprised 43 hectares). The fruit—including the workhorse variety shiraz—was overwhelmingly used for fortified wine production or 'iron-rich' tonic wines exported to England during the early 1900s. It is unlikely that any wine from this era now survives, although a bottle of circa 1900 'Dr Penfold Grange' was purportedly found and tasted some years ago. The vineyard was completely replanted from the early 1950s to 1966 with varieties including riesling, cabernet sauvignon, mataro and shiraz, reflecting a major postwar shift in consumer demand to table wine.

During the 1950s, Magill became a centre of winemaking experimentation using both grapes from the estate and fruit from surrounding vineyards. There are many bottlings: the early Grange vintages and single one-off releases including the celebrated 1956 Bin 136/Bin S56 Magill Burgundy. In 1975 the South Australian Land Commission acquired 65 hectares (160.5 acres) of vine area under compulsory conditions. This created uproar within the community and attempts were made to reverse the decision but to no avail. Ironically, media coverage of this debacle brought further fame to Penfolds Grange—Magill was also known as the Grange Vineyard and the controversy made Grange a household name across Australia.

> *'Lovely medium-bodied perfumed wines,*
> *soft of nature and yet structured and substantial.'*
> —CAMPBELL MATTINSON, PANELLIST

Magill Estate Shiraz is Penfolds' only single-estate wine. It belongs to a rare genre of urban vineyard wines; Chateau Haut-Brion and Chateau Pape Clément in Bordeaux are other examples. Although the wine was only first made in 1983, the vineyard has been in production since around 1847. (It was planted in 1844.) Located approximately 8 kilometres east of the centre of Adelaide in the sheltered haunches of the Mount Lofty Ranges, it was regarded as one of the choicest sites in early colonial South Australia. The mostly dry-grown vineyard, established on a two-wire trellis system, is elevated at around 130 to 150 metres and planted on relatively fertile red-brown earth over limestone—ideal for the production of shiraz. The vines are hand-pruned to mostly the cane and spur method. The vineyard comprises three blocks replanted in 1951 (2.85 ha), 1967 (1.87 ha) and 1985 (0.52 ha). All of the vines are planted on their own roots. None of the original Magill vines used for the production of the early Granges survive.

The Penfolds winemaking team were greatly affected by the loss of their prized vineyard land. It was a major blow to see a great and important colonial vineyard resource levelled to the ground. While the remaining 5.2-hectare vineyard and substantial bluestone winery complex are now heritage listed, Don Ditter, Penfolds Chief Winemaker of the time, said, 'We needed to find a continuous and meaningful use for the vineyard to protect the last remaining vines from further threat. The release of Magill Estate Shiraz was our way of justifying its existence.'

Don Ditter consulted with Max Schubert—who still retained an office at Magill. It was agreed that the wine needed to be a completely different but contrasting—rather than competing—style to Grange: 'Our ambitions were to make an elegant wine based on a different fruit profile and maturation regime. It was meant to be lasting and reflect the character of vineyard site rather than something that could go on for 100 years.' Curiously the specifications required the fruit to be picked at around 11.5 to 12 Baumé—almost identical to the early experimental Granges but well below the potential alcohol levels of contemporary vintages.

Over 23 different trial wines were made, 'to work out a method of attack'. Don Ditter said, 'We had to design the wine according to the character and constraints of the vineyard. At this level you don't just let it all happen. For something enduring and consistent you have to think about how the wine will look when it's young and then how it might develop.'

The first Magill Estate vintages (1983–89) represent a work in progress rather than a clear vineyard style. The older wines are holding, but some vintages have not lasted the distance. It has been commented that the early-picked, low-alcohol strategy of the 1980s had not paid long-term dividends. Don Ditter suggests that the first few vintages were probably left too long before bottling. Substantial vineyard investment and winemaking trials have followed, resulting in a distinctive sublunary wine that evokes the light and shade of vineyard character and yet honours the heritage of this historic vineyard. From 1990 the wines start showing much brighter fruit definition and more expansive palate structure. Penfolds winemakers are particularly interested in flavour development and tannin ripeness resulting in wines with supple structures and more fruit richness.

Penfolds Magill Estate is batch-vinified in open wax-lined concrete tanks at low temperatures. Towards the very end of fermentation the wine is drained and gently basket pressed. Fermentation is completed, then matured in a combination of two-thirds new French and one-third new American oak for a period of around twelve to fifteen months. John Bird, retired Penfolds Senior Red Winemaker and a longstanding consultant, says, 'Magill Estate is a genuine single-vineyard monopole wine. It is equivalent to a *Grand Vin*. We now more fully understand the nuances of vineyard site and the overall fruit profiles. One part of the vineyard will bring perfume and structure, another concentration and ripeness, and another complexity and finesse. The best wine is made through selection, classification tastings and trial blending.'

Neil Beckett was impressed by the 'authentic character and smooth seductive fruit'. Campbell Mattinson described Magill Estate Shiraz as 'lovely, medium-bodied, perfumed wines, soft of nature and yet structured and substantial'.

Magill Estate Shiraz is a medium- to long-term cellaring wine that builds up further complexity over time. In an exceptional vintage, like 1996, 1998, 2002 and 2004, optimum cellaring potential is around 15 to 25 years. In a lesser vintage the wines develop more quickly and should be consumed earlier—a concept that applies to all great single-vineyard wines.

TASTING NOTES ~ MAGILL ESTATE SHIRAZ

1983–1989   NOW • • • PAST

The first vintages, while commercially released, are quite variable in style reflecting an evolution in winemaking philosophy and an increasing interest in the terroir of the last remaining vineyard blocks at Magill. Initially the style relied on elegantly balanced shiraz fruit on the cusp of ripeness, with classical, fine-grained tannins and underlying new savoury oak. The wines are now well past their prime. The years 1983, 1984 and 1985 have dried out and are too austere to really enjoy. 1986 is just holding and is one of the best from this era, but it still has lost freshness and richness of flavour. 1987 is now past—the tannins have taken over. 1988 and 1989 are drinking quite well with developed tobacco/earthy fruit and firm tannin structures; however, they are not keepers.

1990   NOW

Medium red. Complex dark cherry/cassis/cedar/wet bitumen/barnyard aromas. Elegantly proportioned wine with developed dark cherry/tar/earthy flavours and loose-knit cedary, dry/muscular tannins. Finishes firm and savoury.

1991 ★   NOW • • • 2016

Medium deep red. Fully mature blackberry/walnut/earthy/sweet-fruit aromas with touches of leather/sandalwood. Richer, more concentrated wine than 1990 with evolved black fruits/leather/sandalwood/panforte/earthy flavours, plenty of sweet fruit and dense savoury/gravelly tannins. Will still hold.

1992   NOW

Medium red. Developed blueberry/redcurrant/panforte/earthy aromas with hint of mint. Old-fashioned maturation style with earthy/panforte/sweet-fruit flavours, some herb/sappy notes and sinewy, long tannins. Drink up.

1993   NOW

Medium red. Fresh redcurrant/plum/cedar/sandalwood aromas with touches of capsicum/dried herb. Redcurrant/capsicum/earthy flavours, malt/vanilla oak and fine-grained—slightly sappy tannins. Approaching full maturity now.

1994 ★   NOW • • • 2020

Medium deep red. A classic Magill Estate with complex earth/cigar box/redcurrant/cassis/aniseed aromas. Beautifully structured and seductive palate with earthy/cedar/cassis flavours, a lovely core of sweet fruit and fine, smooth, chocolaty tannins. Firms up at the finish.

1995 NOW • • • 2018

Medium deep red. Intense rich cherry/plum/blackberry aromas with graphite/savoury notes. The palate is well concentrated and balanced with plum/blackberry/dark cherry fruit and fine-grained savoury tannin. Finishes firm but long and flavourful. An impressive wine for the vintage.

1996 ★ NOW • • • 2025

Medium deep red. Fragrant black cherry/cedar/herb garden aromas with some lead pencil/leather notes. Smooth, balanced, beautifully poised wine with plenty of sweet-fruit/black cherry/dark chocolate flavours, fresh cedary oak and fine-grained tannins. Finishes long and sweet. A great Magill Estate year.

1997 NOW • • • 2012

Medium deep colour. Broodingly complex wine with wet coal/tar/blackberry aromas and earthy/wormwood/herb garden nuances. The palate is densely concentrated, packed with blackberry/wet bitumen/sweet-fruit/herbal flavours, underlying vanilla oak and dense, slinky, dry tannins. Finishes long and sweet. Has plenty of volume and richness. Drink soon.

1998 ★ NOW • • • 2025

Deep red–purple. Intense blueberry/raspberry/vanillin/herb garden aromas and some bitumen/smoked meat nuances. A very rich, soft, open-knit wine with plenty of blueberry/blackberry/plum flavours and plentiful fine-grained, slightly gritty tannins. It has more extract and power than 1996 but not quite the same finesse. Still a very fine year.

1999 NOW • • • 2020

Deep red. Intense, fresh, juicy blackberry/cedar/menthol aromas with touches of liquorice. Deep-set, powerfully concentrated wines with blackberry/sweet plum fruit, plenty of cedar/savoury oak and chocolaty, dry, firm, integrated tannins.

2000 NOW • • • 2024

Medium deep red. A lighter style but very fresh fruit dominant wine with redcurrant pastille/vanilla/cracked pepper aromas. The palate is buoyant and fleshy rather than concentrated with raspberry/redcurrant flavours and fine, chalky, dry, savoury tannins. An early drinking style.

2001 ★ NOW • • • 2020

Deep red–purple. Bright, fresh violet/camomile/blackberry/liquorice aromas and graphite/cedar nuances. Sweet blackberry/vanilla/cedar/herb flavours and fine, dense, slightly leafy tannins. Builds up firm but long and flavourful. Potent and intense.

2002 ★ NOW • • • 2025

Deep red–purple. An elegantly proportioned wine with brambly/blackcurrant/nutmeg/spice aromas and flavours; some smoky notes. Rich, succulent fruit, fine-grained tannins and underlying cedar oak. Finishes firm with plenty of flavour length. Delicious wine.

2003 2010 • • • 2028

Deep red. Fresh elderberry/mulberry aromas with some brambly/herb garden notes. Elderberry/blackberry/sweet-fruit flavours with some thyme/aniseed notes. The wine is still very elemental and fresh with assertive/sinewy tannins and plenty of fruit richness. Finishes long and sweet.

2004 ★ 2012 • • • 2030

Deep red–purple. Beautiful wine with intense, ethereal blueberry/nutmeg/spice aromas. The palate is smooth, round, concentrated and velvety with ripe blueberry/blackberry fruit, lovely new malt/savoury oak and ripe, chocolaty, dense tannins. Outstanding vintage.

2005 2010 • • • 2025

Deep red–purple. Very intense and elemental with fresh camomile/redcurrant/red cherry/herb garden aromas. The palate is buoyant and fresh with red cherry/cedar/dried spice/sandalwood flavours and fine, savoury, firm tannins.

2006 ★ 2012 • • • 2030

Deep ink purple. A plush, extravagant wine with rich, dark chocolate/dark berry aromas and savoury/toasted malt aromas. The palate is densely packed with abundant blackcurrant/mocha/espresso flavours, fine slinky tannins and plenty of new malt oak. Finishes firm and tight, long and sweet. A fabulous vintage.

DISCUSSION

The commentary for this tasting is fragmented because the panel only tasted vintage highlights rather than an entire vertical. (Andrew Caillard completed the tasting to allow a full review of tasting notes 1990–2006.)

1995 is travelling well with soft mulberry aromas, fine tannin and some toasty/mint notes. (CM) It has a distinctive leafy, eucalypt nose, but the palate is refined, sweetly fruited and elegantly proportioned with rich, soft, juicy flavours and slightly puckering tannins at the end. (NB)

1996 is more developed than 1995 and yet it is lovely, long and tangy with earthy/leather/plummy flavours and beautiful flow to the finish. It's a touch rustic which may account for looking so advanced. (CM) It was deeper and earthier with savoury tobacco fruit, dense silken structure but grippy and fleshy at the finish. (NB) 1996 was beautifully poised with bright, fresh plum, black cherry fruit and fine tannins. (JH)

1998 has more strident oak but so too is the glorious fruit flavours; minted plums, bitter herbs and olive. This wine has a very high yum factor. (CM) It was authentic and characterful with deep tobacco aromas and great syrupy richness, sweet plum fruit and supple tannins. (NB) 1998—with its rich blackberry/plum fruit—had more tannins, extract and power than 1996, but it didn't necessarily have the finesse or the length. (JH)

2001 looks really good. It's fleshy, fruity, ferrous, long and tannic. This is a super 2001; where has it been hiding? (CM) It was similar in colour to the 1998 with superb elegance, flesh and richness;

intense black fruits, slippery tannins and mid-palate length. (NB) 2001 was quite potent but it was without the silky textures of the previous wines. (JH)

2002 is interesting, with tobacco/mint/plum/dark cherry aromas and cedar/smoke nuances. It all works beautifully although it only has medium length. (CM) It was evocative with some peppery/savoury aromas and impressive smoothness on the palate. This is a very well-made, seductive wine. (NB) 2002 was very savoury and spicy; almost lemony. I am not sure about the staying power of this wine. (JH)

2004 has bangs of musky oak and lashings of juicy plum flavours. The wine is still very exuberant; I would like to see this wine once the oak has shuffled back to allow the fruit to bare its velvety skin. (CM) It had a fabulous nose with blueberry/peppery fruit and refined supple tannins. It's faintly bitter at the finish. (NB) I found the wine was totally beguiling and seductive with a lusciousness and depth none of the other Magills possessed. This was a round, velvety wine with great balance and length. (JH)

2005 is rich, tight, musky and luxurious in its design. It looks very impressive for a wine so young. I love the perfumed softness of these wines. Even the tannins have an appealing smoothness. It makes Magill Estate different to other Penfolds wines. (CM) This is a dense, rich and embryonic wine with tremendous fruit intensity and savoury characters. It's still very young but it should evolve well. Magill Estate is a wonderful addition to the Penfolds range. It has a very strong authentic character reflecting the vagaries of vintage and a unique vineyard site. (NB) 2005 had a mix of sweet fruit and herbal characters. At this stage it's not quite in the same league as 2004. I preferred the 2004 followed by 1996 and 2005. The latest vintages have great potential. (JH)

I particularly liked the last four vintages. They have a distinct style reminiscent of the Northern Rhône, with medium-bodied fruit and tannins. My standouts included 2001 with its scented raspberry/floral nose, persistent soft fruit, supple tannins and round freshness. 2004 was a richer vintage with an equal measure of tannins albeit slightly edgy. 2005 is very harmonious and elegant, the climax of the style, with floral/raspberry fruit and soft tannins. Magill Estate Shiraz is medium-powered, yet elegant and supple. This is a lovely, food-friendly wine style. (CPT)

I found the tannin structures completely different to other Penfolds wines. There was a ferrous quality that flowed across the palate—the tannins sometimes have a cast-iron skillet character. Yet the fruit is powerfully layered with generous blueberry/plum fruits and saturated flavours. I could see a crushed-ant character in 2002 that immediately made me wonder back to how the early Granges might have looked like. These wines have softness of fruit, but I found the tannins quite muscular, especially at the finish. (JG)

The Magill Estate style has come a long way since it was first released. The wines have lovely balance and the weight and texture to go with food. They are elegantly proportioned, intense and approachable with fine-grained tannins and ample sweet fruit. It's an atypical Penfolds style. In many respects it seems to row its own boat. (HH)

Penfolds St Henri

First Vintage:	1953 to 1956 experimental, 1957 commercial (not tasted).
Variety:	Shiraz and cabernet sauvignon.
Origin:	Multi-district blend, South Australia. Significant contributions of shiraz from Barossa Valley, Eden Valley, Clare Valley, McLaren Vale, Langhorne Creek and Bordertown; cabernet sauvignon from Coonawarra and Barossa Valley. Increasing percentage of Adelaide Hills fruit in recent vintages.
Fermentation:	Stainless steel tanks and open fermenters with wax-lined/wooden header boards.
Maturation:	18 months in large (minimum 1460-litre) old oak vats.
Comments:	Labelled Claret until 1989 vintage. Cabernet sauvignon plays a secondary role. Packaged in laser-etched bottles since the 1996 vintage. Released under screw cap in some markets since the 2005 vintage.

'Over the last decade St Henri has been completely refined in faithful guise to John Davoren's original wine.'

—HUON HOOKE, PANELLIST

Penfolds St Henri is one of Australia's greatest red wines, with a compelling history and heritage. The original Auldana Cellars, neighbouring Magill Estate, was established in 1853 by Patrick Auld (1811–86), an early South Australian settler who migrated from Scotland in 1842. Soon after arrival he purchased the land in two sections of 230 acres (93 hectares) at the usual price charged by the Crown of £1 an acre. Auld initially started as a publican and then became a wine and spirits merchant in Hindley Street, Adelaide. He planted a small vineyard at first, but, impressed by the quality of the fruit on return from a brief stint in England, he started commercial winegrowing in 1853. In 1861 he floated the South Auldana Vineyard Association with a market capitalisation of £12,000. The association's first vintage in 1862 produced 3000 gallons (13,650 litres) of white and red wine.

At one stage Auldana was one of the largest wine producers in the colony. *The Australian Dictionary of Biography* says: 'In the earlier years he [Auld] concentrated on producing a limited number of distinctively local wines without imitating European types. Meticulous and in some ways conservative, he nevertheless learnt from experience the most suitable vines for his area, and experimented with a method of maintaining a uniform quality throughout the vintage. A promising trade with Melbourne was hampered by heavy import duty, but Auld began promoting sales in London. There and in America and on the Continent he entered his produce with some success in exhibitions. In 1871 he opened an office in London to sell his wines. However, financial difficulties led to the mortgaging of Auldana and its transfer to the mortgagee, Josiah Symon, in 1888.'

Josiah Symon, a prominent Adelaide identity, was a vocal advocate of Federation. The fledgling South Australian wine industry had much to benefit from the colony becoming a part of the new Australian nation. Until 1901, trade tariffs between the colonies had created artificial trade barriers, resulting in localised wine markets. After Federation, South Australia experienced a substantial increase in vineyard plantings. The Auld family continued to be involved with the South Australian wine industry and pressed for legislation to prevent the introduction into the colony of *Phylloxera vastatrix*, which had caused widespread damage in New South Wales and Victoria. William Patrick Auld (1840–1912) became the first secretary of the Provisional Phylloxera Board after the introduction of the *South Australian Phylloxera Act 1899*.

The Auldana vineyard was one of the most important and well-known vineyards in South Australia. In *The Vineyards and Orchards of South Australia* (1862) Ebenezer Ward wrote: 'Entering the south vineyard on its northernmost side, the visitor finds himself at the foot of what is known as Verdeilho Hill [sic]. This hill and those beyond it to the south are admirably situated for the growth of the vine, inasmuch as they form a perfect natural basin and the slopes on which the vines are planted shelter each other from all winds, especially from the destructive wind which blows periodically from the south-west.'

The vineyard was planted to a fruit salad of varieties, including 'Tokay, Muscat of Alexandria, Grenache, Verdelho, Carbonet [sic]—grafted on Carignan, Mataro, Malbec and Shiraz'. The high price of labour and shortages of manpower restricted vineyard expansion. However, Auldana wines were highly regarded in the South Australian colony. In 1892, the Victorian, New South Wales and South Australian governments 'held court' at the famous Bordeaux Exhibition of 1892. The winemaker of the time was a Frenchman, Leon Edmund Mazure (1860–1939), who is credited as the creator of the famous and unique style of Australian Sparkling Burgundy!

The Australian Dictionary of Biography says: 'Leon Edmund Mazure was among the first vignerons in South Australia to make champagne on a large scale (in 1896), to preserve olives and to introduce levures (selected yeasts) into the making of wine. Between 1887 and 1912, while at Auldana, he was awarded 83 first prizes, 71 seconds and 12 thirds by the Royal Agricultural and Horticultural Society at the Adelaide wine shows. For three years in succession Auldana hock, chablis and sherry gained the champion ten-guinea cup against all Australia. A councillor of the South Australian Vignerons' Association, Mazure became a wine and pruning judge, initiated a pruning competition for boys under eighteen, and took out several patents for ideas, including the Mazure corkscrew, a corking machine and a windmill bird-scarer. He was a member of the Adelaide Stock Exchange and was appointed a justice of the peace in 1901.'

Mazure was also responsible for the creation of the St Henri label; the original name probably derives from the name of his son Henri and wife Henrietta. The first vintage under this label was around 1890. Curiously few bottles from this era have survived. A bottle of 1896 Auldana Cellars St Henri Claret, found in the cellar of a Tasmanian collector, surfaced in the late 1980s. A bottle of 1911 appeared at a Penfolds Red Wine Re-corking Clinic in Hobart in 1996. Mazure left Auldana around 1914, purchasing the Auld family's Home Park Vineyard.

The Auldana vineyard was acquired by Penfolds in 1943. The St Henri label was revived by John Davoren (1915–91), a brilliant Penfolds winemaker, in the early 1950s. Davoren had a strong family background in wine; both his father and grandfather worked at Dalwood, a famous Hunter Valley vineyard. Originally owned by the Wyndham family, it was subsequently split in half, with one portion of 52 hectares sold to Penfolds in 1904. John Davoren's father, Harold, a legendary Hunter winemaker, became manager. By the 1930s John Davoren was making wine at Penfolds Dalwood, soon becoming manager of the now defunct Penfolds Minchinbury Vineyards at Rooty Hill in Sydney. After serving in the Royal Australian Air Force in the South Pacific he returned to Australia. After a brief stint managing the newly purchased Kalimna Vineyard in the Barossa Valley he was appointed manager of Penfolds Auldana Cellars in 1947.

The revival and development of St Henri mirrored the story of Grange except that Davoren deliberately looked at the heritage of Auldana Cellars and his own family winemaking traditions for inspiration. John Davoren was keen to establish a wine based on the original work of Leon Edmund Mazure. Through his work at Auldana, he established a reputation as one of Australia's great winemakers. Both St Henri and Grange were regarded as classic Penfolds red wines within a decade of first release. In 1966 Dan Murphy, a respected Melbourne wine merchant, described them both as 'the best firm styles Australia makes'. Indeed, both wines were referred to by wine critics as 'special bottlings of Claret'.

The success of Grange was very much enhanced by the contrasting St Henri style. The two wines began life together in a climate of intense excitement, experimentation and research. John Bird, retired Penfolds winemaker who worked alongside both Max Schubert and John Davoren, said, 'Much has been spoken about the intense competitive relationship between the two men. The strong personal rivalry made good copy, but in fact Davoren reported to Schubert. Penfolds worked under a veil of secrecy throughout the 1950s and '60s; winemakers were not allowed to talk about their work to outsiders. Robust arguments and strongly held views were aired between the two men, but always within the framework of a common purpose. They were friends. You can see by the comparative styles that St Henri and Grange come from the same stable. The wines can look remarkably similar to each other—especially between ten and fifteen years of age.' In fact, without Max Schubert's support St Henri may not have been released.

Sandie Coff, Max Schubert's daughter, reflects, 'Dad and I were very close. He travelled a lot when I was a child in the 1950s and '60s, particularly to the Barossa, Riverland, Coonawarra, Griffith and Sydney. When he was in Adelaide I would be with him no matter what he was doing. This included visits to Penfolds and colleagues before and after school, weekends and holidays. I knew all of Dad's colleagues and the cellarhands, gardener, secretaries and management. Each person I referred to as Mr, Mrs or Miss—except one, Uncle John Davoren. Dad would take me to Auldana with him, and Uncle John would always greet us with a beaming smile. I have a photo of Dad pinning a long service pin on him and the look of pure affection on John's face explains the relationship they had.'

Initially St Henri achieved greater commercial success than Grange. It was a more elegant, approachable style whereas the revolutionary Grange was something of a blockbuster with a richness and fullness that few people cared for. Reports from the critics of the 1960s refer to St Henri as 'one of the only true claret [sic] styles in Australia'. Don Ditter says, 'There was a strong following for St Henri from the very outset. Initially both Grange and St Henri were priced at the same level. The demand for each of the wines, however, was soon quite similar, some preferring the lightly wooded maturation style of St Henri over the more strongly flavoured, barrel fermented and new oak-matured style of Grange.'

John Davoren's work with St Henri is not as well documented as Grange. This is perhaps because the wine was never planned. The first experimental vintage, made from Auldana and Paracombe district fruit, was made in 1953. While the 1957 vintage is officially recognised as the first release, John Davoren was still calling them trials until 1960.

Davoren replicated the original St Henri label used by Leon Edmund Mazure. Subsequent early vintages sourced fruit from Auldana, Magill, Morphett Vale, Modbury, Paracombe and Adelaide Hills. Kalimna cabernet sauvignon was also used extensively. Anecdotal evidence suggests that early vintages were not entirely shiraz–cabernet blends; John Davoren used mataro (mourvèdre) as a third component. In fact records prove the very early experimental wines were cabernet–mataro blends.

Urban encroachment and the subsequent wholesale clearance of prime vineyards within the Adelaide city boundary led to the eventual pulling-up of the Quarry Paddock, a highly prized mataro vineyard on the boundary of Auldana and Magill. Its loss was greatly felt by Penfolds. It now lies under a housing estate. Sadly, a number of great old Adelaide vineyards met the same fate.

The Auldana Vineyards ceased production in 1975. The Modbury Vineyard and most of Magill Estate, except for the front blocks, followed suit in 1983. Nowadays St Henri is a multi-district blend drawing shiraz from the Barossa Valley, Eden Valley, McLaren Vale, Clare Valley and Langhorne Creek. The Adelaide foothills, once a primary source of St Henri, is once again making significant contributions to the blend; Penfolds now draws an increasing percentage of fruit from Waterfall Gully, Wilton and Williamstown. Cabernet sauvignon, which adds both firmness and structure to the St Henri style, is sourced from the Barossa Valley, Coonawarra and Bordertown.

The first experimental vintages were foot-stomped in open-ended hogsheads. A relatively high percentage of stalks was also retained in the vinification. Davoren once explained this practice: 'We add stalks deliberately to keep the skins apart for the plunging cap, and to get colour as quickly as possible.' The St Henri style to this day is a highly perfumed, elegantly structured wine based on fruit clarity and maturation in older oak. For many years St Henri was partially aged in two-year-old American oak hogsheads—used first for Grange. Sandie Coff says, 'I remember Dad giving me my first taste of St Henri. He introduced it by saying it was a very special wine—the number two wine the company made. He had great respect for St Henri and for John Davoren. If anyone ever asked Dad to sign a bottle of St Henri he would always refuse. All credit for this wine should go to John Davoren, he would say.'

While the overall philosophy of wine style has not altered, vinification and maturation practices have changed over the years. Fruit selection, tannin management and maturation in large 1460-litre old oak casks have all contributed to an evolution of style. But some practices have remained the same. Winemakers will often use concentrated drainings and tannin-rich pressings as components to the blend.

The inclusion of stalks—a practice which in theory adds perfume and structure to the wine—is minimal; these attributes have already been achieved through vineyard management and selection. The sheer standard of fruit quality has improved substantially over the last decade. Peter Gago says, 'We can identify the desired aromatics, concentration and structure of potential St Henri fruit in the vineyard. The best parcels are typified by strong praline/chocolate characters, obvious fruit sweetness, intense flavour development and supple tannins.'

The red winemaking team is particularly focused on vintage character. While St Henri is made to a particular style, there is no standard winemaking recipe. Every year the wine is vinified along similar lines, but always in respect to the integrity of the fruit. Every parcel is batch fermented in headed-down stainless steel tanks at Nuriootpa and open fermenters at Magill. Each component is classified according to fruit profile and structure. The young wines which make 'the cut' are then matured for between fifteen and eighteen months in large 1460-litre old oak casks. Over this period the fruit builds up further complexity and richness while the tannins soften and develop. St Henri has a lacy, firm-grained palate texture that distinguishes it from other Penfolds shirazes.

This complete vertical tasting of St Henri showed the evolutionary and unfolding progression of style across the decades. Despite the enormous changes in vineyard resources and winemaking capability, the tasting revealed a remarkable sequence of vintages without compromising John Davoren's original intent. First released as Penfolds St Henri Special Vintage Claret (with a famous reputation for a label with fourteen different typefaces), the wines immediately enjoyed universal acclaim; they were compelling, interesting, authentic in style and delicious to drink.

St Henri is still greatly admired by wine collectors; like Grange it is universally cellared for further ageing. It also has a strong secondary wine market presence and trading history. Vintages from the 1950s and '60s still regularly appear at auction. While Grange has soared in value over the last 50 years, St Henri has remained an auction staple, attracting solid, reliable demand at comparatively affordable prices. At a retrospective St Henri tasting held at Taillevent restaurant in Paris, European journalists lionised the 1971 St Henri, many giving the wine the perfect score. This perhaps emphasises an Old World recognition of the original 'claret' monicker.

Market perception and previous Rewards of Patience tastings have regarded St Henri as a traditional or old-fashioned maturation style. However, this Rewards of Patience tasting revealed that St Henri is not locked in a time warp; the style is classical yet modern with seductive fruit quality and composed structure. Huon Hooke noted, 'Over the last decade St Henri has been completely refined in faithful guise to John Davoren's original wine. The St Henri style, however, is generally richer and more full-bodied.'

St Henri is typified by fresh mulberry/blueberry/dark chocolate/liquorice aromas and flavours, mid-palate richness, fruit sweetness and fine chocolaty tannin structure. Cabernet sauvignon provides aromatic top notes of violets/cassis and firmness at the finish. Maturation in older oak brings these components together into a 'harmonious whole'. With age these wines further develop, gaining more complexity, generosity, velvety texture and weight. Both the 1996 and 1998 are unfolding examples of the modern St Henri genre.

This extraordinary tasting shows that Penfolds St Henri is a great cellaring wine. The best vintages—usually the most delicious, powerful and concentrated—will evolve for up to 30 years and sometimes even further. But generally these wines are best consumed after ten years of age. St Henri has had a very strong and devoted following among collectors and wine enthusiasts for several generations. Today it is considered as an Australian classic, with a wonderful heritage and story of its own.

TASTING NOTES ~ ST HENRI

1953–1955

Since the fifth edition of *Penfolds: The Rewards of Patience*, the Penfolds Red Wine Re-corking Clinics have unearthed older vintages of St Henri in Adelaide. Inevitably this has questioned the first vintage of St Henri (under the Penfolds label). Unlike the experimental postage stamp labels of Grange, these bottles are labelled St Henri—the design harking back to the original nineteenth-century label. These authentic bottles suggest that John Davoren experimented and released small batches of St Henri, mostly to friends and acquaintances. The wines were often half-bottlings, further suggesting non-commercial releases.

1956   NOW • • • PAST

Brick red. Fresh herb garden/panforte/mocha aromas with some demi-glace/cedar/wood spice notes. The wine is still fresh with complex soy/panforte/sandalwood/herb garden/meaty flavours but fading fruit sweetness. The tannins are beginning to jut out and dominate the palate. This is really an old, interesting curio, just holding together. It will hold but the wine is really past its drinking window. Once thought to be the first experimental release.

1958   NOW • • • PAST

Brick red. Intense herb/leafy/cedar/roasted aromas reminiscent of old Pauillac. Well-balanced, minerally wine with herb/leafy/cedar/toffee flavours and chalky, firm, loose-knit tannins. Finishes long and minerally. The fruit is beginning to fade, but this is a much better bottle than previous Rewards of Patience tastings. However, drink up.

1959   NOW • • • PAST

Medium brick red. Intense, evolved roasted coffee/earthy/leafy/graphite aromas. The palate is mature with complex mocha/espresso/graphite flavours and slinky, dry, loose-knit tannins. Finishes cedary and long.

1961　　　　　　　　　　　　　　　　　　　　　　　　　　**PAST**

Medium deep brick red. Lifted herb tobacco/bitter chocolate/tobacco/animal aromas. The palate is drying out with herb/tobacco/meaty/vegetal flavours and brittle, dry tannins. Pronounced, chalky, firm finish. Definitely past its best.

1962　★　　　　　　　　　　　　　　　　　　　　　　　**NOW**

Deep brick red. A brilliant wine with classical mature cedar/roasted coffee/sweet-fruit aromas, complex, fresh earthy/cedar/dark chocolate flavours and ripe, loose-knit tannins. Finishes firm and long. A very good bottle, illustrating the sheer class of the 1962 vintage.

1963　★　　　　　　　　　　　　　　　　　　　　　　　**NOW**

Deep brick red. Bitter chocolate/redcurrant/demi-glace/roasted aromas. Crème brûlée, dark bitter chocolate/prune/leather flavours and ripe, chocolaty tannins. Finishes chalky firm and generously long. A really lovely old wine, but drink now.

1964　　　　　　　　　　　　　　　　　　　　**NOW • • • PAST**

Deep brick red. Fresh, complex ground coffee/honeycomb/tobacco/vellum aromas. Fully mature palate with lovely, sweet-fruit/mocha-berry/tobacco flavours and loose-knit, savoury, dry tannins. Like an old parchment. However, it's fading. Drink now.

1965　　　　　　　　　　　　　　　　　　　　**NOW • • • PAST**

Medium deep brick red. Dark chocolate/meaty/demi-glace/herb aromas. A richly concentrated palate with earthy/chocolate/meaty flavours and grainy-dry/savoury tannins. Finishes long and minerally. Almost over-mature. Just hanging on.

1966　★　　　　　　　　　　　　　　　　　　　　　　　**NOW**

Deep brick red in colour with cedar/blackcurrant/mocha/leather aromas. Sweet liquorice/polished leather/mocha/espresso flavours with mouth-filling, chocolaty tannins. Kicks up chalky firm at the finish. Delicious, well-balanced wine. Drink very soon. A great old St Henri.

1967　　　　　　　　　　　　　　　　　　　　**NOW • • • PAST**

Medium brick red. Intense floral/apricot/roasted meat aromas with some earthy notes. Well-concentrated roasted meats/mocha/soupy flavours and loose-knit, fine, grainy/drying tannins. It still has fruit sweetness and good flavour length, but the wine is over-mature and fading.

1968　　　　　　　　　　　　　　　　　　　　　　　　　**PAST**

Medium brick red. Old leather/raisin/crème brûlée/vegetal aromas. The wine is well past its prime with savoury/wood spice/mocha flavours and fine, lacy, dry tannins. The wine finishes sinewy and dried out.

1969　　　　　　　　　　　　　　　　　　　　　　　　　**PAST**

Medium brick red. An overdeveloped wine with fading orange marmalade/spicy aromas and grippy, dry tannins.

1970   NOW • • • PAST

Medium deep brick red. Complex, fresh, evolved cedarwood/roasted meat/demi-glace/herb garden aromas. A well-concentrated palate with rich, ripe cedar/fig/meaty flavours balanced by a strong swagger of tannins. Finishes long and sweet with a tannin slick. Holding but drink very soon.

1971 ★   NOW • • • 2015

Medium deep brick red. Beautiful wine showing classic St Henri form with intense mocha/dark chocolate/smoky/cigar aromas with touches of liquorice/panforte. A smooth, richly concentrated wine with saturated mocha/dark chocolate/gamy/liquorice flavours intertwined with chalky, fine, loose-knit tannins. Finishes firm, incredibly long and flavourful. A great vintage with remarkable complexity, buoyancy and persistency. Very consistent to last Rewards Of Patience tasting; in suspended animation.

1972   NOW • • • PAST

Medium deep brick red. Fragrant but evolved chocolate/herb garden/cedar aromas with some smoked oyster notes. The palate is starting to dry out, but it still has some sweet fruit and fine, lacy, dry tannins. Kicks up leafy/sappy dry at the finish.

1973   NOW • • • PAST

Medium deep brick red. Sweet fig jam/stewed plum/leather/vegetal/silage aromas. Complex, sweet meaty/stewed plum/earthy/vegetal—slight wet bitumen—flavours. The tannins are lacy dry, but finish firm. A touch overdeveloped. Holding by a thread.

1974   NOW • • • PAST

Deep brick red. Intense dark chocolate/espresso/molasses aromas. The palate is richly flavoured with mocha/panforte/demi-glace/molasses characters and chocolaty tannins. Finishes grippy and leathery dry at the finish. Sound but the structure is beginning to weaken. Drink up.

1975   NOW • • • PAST

Medium brick red. Bitumen/ground coffee/mocha aromas with some camomile notes. A rich, ripe fully evolved palate with ground coffee/mocha/earthy flavours and slinky, chalky, dry tannins. Tannins are muscling in. Drink up.

1976 ★   NOW • • • 2016

Deep brick crimson red. Dark bitter chocolate/herb garden aromas with some violet/liquorice notes. Sweet chocolate/herb garden flavours and plentiful fine, loose-knit, dry tannins. A well-concentrated and beautifully balanced wine with lovely mid-palate richness and wonderful persistency. Holding up really well. Will probably keep for quite a while, but best to drink soon.

1977   NOW

Deep brick red. Fragrant ground coffee/dried apricot/roasted aromas. Richly layered wine with dense mocha/leather/meaty flavours and fine grainy tannins. Finishes dry and grippy firm. Further cellaring possible but best enjoyed now.

1978 NOW • • • PAST

Medium deep brick red. Fresh redcurrant/mocha/leather aromas. The palate is quite wiry with redcurrant/leather/capsicum flavours and sinewy/drying tannins. Finishes firm and tight. Probably past its best now. Drink up.

1979 NOW • • • PAST

Medium brick red. Intense herb garden/rose petal/earthy aromas with touches of demi-glace/wet bitumen characters. Sweet, earthy damson plum/mocha/demi-glace flavours and loose-knit slinky, dry tannins. Becomes bittersweet and lean at the finish. Drink up.

1980 PAST

Deep brick red. Mushroom/polished leather/prune aromas with some musty/damp-earth notes. The palate is astringent with old polished leather/mushroom/raisin flavours underlying musty characters and firm, dry tannins. Not in the best of shape.

1981 NOW • • • PAST

Medium brick red. Very muscular/sinewy wine with smoky/graphite/leather/herbal aromas. The palate is well concentrated with smoky/leather/graphite flavours and some remnants of sweet fruit, but the tannins are pronounced and leafy dry. A touch metallic at the finish. This is not going to improve.

1982 NOW

Light brick red. Floral/camomile/rosehip/red cherry/mocha. A soft, smooth, fruit-sweet wine with rosehip/red cherry/herbal/beef stock/mocha flavours and ripe, loose-knit, plentiful tannins. A very elegant minerally wine. It won't improve, but it has held on really well. Drink soon.

1983 NOW • • • 2015

Medium brick red. A robust style with fresh, complex roasted/earthy/liquorice/dried herb/prune aromas. The palate is well concentrated with plenty of roasted/earthy/liquorice flavours, mid-palate richness and fine, grainy, dry tannins. Finishes firm and long.

1984 ★ NOW • • • 2012

Medium brick red. Leafy/mocha/graphite/sweet-fruit aromas. Fully developed, richly concentrated wine with earthy/leafy/sweet-fruit flavours and chocolaty dry tannins. The fruit drops off, leaving a stemmy/grippy finish. A thread of under-ripeness pervades the palate. It's not getting better.

1985 NOW • • • 2012

Medium brick red. Complex mellow leather/earthy/sweet redcurrant/minty aromas and flavours. The palate is smooth and fresh with very fine, gentle/supple tannins. The fruit fades towards the finish. Finishes bitter-sweet. Drink soon.

1986 NOW • • • 2015

Deep crimson. Roasted/meaty/prune aromas with some leather/prune notes. The palate is generous and powerful with dark chocolate/prune/fig flavours, ripe tannins and plenty of fruit

sweetness. Finishes chalky firm but long. It's definitely past its classic prime, but the wine still has volume and richness. Will hold. Regarded by collectors as a classic year.

1987   NOW • • • 2012

Medium deep brick red. Herb garden/roses/leatherwood/spicy aromas. The wine is elegantly proportioned with herb garden/redcurrant fruit, some richness and strong, firm tannin spine. Finishes leathery dry. A cool vintage. Holding well.

1988   NOW

Deep crimson. Intense mocha/redcurrant/dark berry/spicy aromas with some leafy/minty characters. A slightly underpowered wine with fresh redcurrant/herb/minty flavours and sweet lacy tannins. Finishes minerally and dry. Fruit is beginning to fade.

1989   NOW

Deep crimson. *Garrigue*/redcurrant/earthy/smoky aromas. Juicy fruit/jammy/herb garden/earthy flavours and supple, fine tannins. Builds up chalky dry/hard at the finish. Characterful and balanced considering the difficult vintage.

1990 ★   NOW • • • 2030

Deep crimson. Powerful, sweet blackcurrant/plum/dark chocolate aromas with leafy/violet notes. The palate is fleshy and rich with cassis/plum/dark chocolate flavours and slinky dry loose-knit tannins. Finishes long and sweet. Delicious, classic St Henri with plenty of cellaring life.

1991 ★   NOW • • • 2020

Deep crimson. Evolved cassis/earthy/mint aromas. The palate is well concentrated with plenty of blackcurrant/earthy/meaty flavours and sinewy/muscular tannins. The wine has become quite minty and stern, but it still has generosity and good flavour length. It will hold for quite a while.

1992   NOW • • • 2014

Deep crimson. Dark chocolate/prune/violet aromas with leafy/briary notes. Densely packed wine with deep-set plum/blackberry/leafy/leather flavours and silky tannins. A fruit-driven, but robust, almost hard, finish.

1993   NOW • • • 2012

Deep crimson. Prune/chocolate/red berry/silage aromas. Vegetal/herb/redcurrant/soupy flavours and leafy, firm tannins. Builds up stalky green at the finish. Acidity pokes out. Sweet and sour wine. Not a beauty. Drink soon.

1994   NOW • • • 2020

Deep crimson. Evolving but tannic wine with blackberry/mocha/prune/black olive aromas. The palate is richly concentrated with blackberry confit/black olive/briary flavours and dense, gravelly tannins. It finishes very firm. A robust, solid wine with plenty of volume and flavour length.

1995   **NOW • • • 2012**

Medium deep crimson. Lifted redcurrant/liquorice/violet aromas with a hint of leather. Fresh ground coffee/plummy/herb garden fruit and firm, dry—a touch sappy—tannins. Under-powered and short at the finish.

1996 ★   **NOW • • • 2025**

Deep crimson. Fragrant liquorice/plum/blackberry/rose petal/musky/spice aromas. Deep-set, richly concentrated wine with saturated plum/blackberry/liquorice flavours and fine, velvety tannins. Kicks up chalky firm at the finish. Puissance, harmony and poise. A great St Henri vintage.

1997   **NOW • • • 2015**

Deep crimson. Liquorice/dark chocolate/cinnamon/dried herb aromas. Sweet jammy/dark chocolate/dried herb flavours and fine, lacy tannins. Finishes leafy dry.

1998 ★   **NOW • • • 2025**

Deep crimson. Fresh, primary fig/redcurrant/cassis/blueberry aromas with some liquorice/spice notes. Lovely, buoyant, sweet redcurrant/plum/cassis/dark-chocolate flavours and slinky, loose-knit tannins. Finishes minerally and fruit sweet. An utterly delicious wine. A classic St Henri vintage.

1999 ★   **NOW • • • 2025**

Deep crimson. Lovely blackberry/redcurrant/cranberry aromas with some nutmeg/aniseed characters. A fruit-driven wine with plump blackberry/redcurrant/aniseed flavours and fine, slinky dry, a touch hard, tannins. Finishes long and sweet. Lovely weight and flavour length.

2000   **NOW • • • 2012**

Medium crimson. Early drinking style with cranberry/cassis/tomato leaf/faint leather aromas. The palate is fresh and squashy with plenty of redcurrant/raspberry/cranberry fruits and chalky, loose-knit tannins. A fruity, elegant wine. Ready to drink.

2001   **NOW • • • 2030**

Deep crimson–purple. Youthful, powerful blackcurrant pastille/juicy fruit/cinnamon/aniseed aromas. A grippy, generously flavoured wine with richly concentrated, powerful cassis/juicy sweet-fruit/liquorice flavours and fine, dense, chocolaty tannins. Finishes long and sweet with a slick of tannins. A big ripe St Henri with impressive structure.

2002 ★   **2010 • • • 2030**

Deep crimson–purple. Fresh mulberry/blueberry/dark chocolate/liquorice aromas. Beautifully balanced wine with succulent mulberry/dark chocolate/liquorice flavours and long, gravelly tannins. Plenty of fruit sweetness and flavour length. A lovely, modern, classic St Henri.

2003   **2012 • • • 2030**

Deep crimson–purple. Intense, fragrant elderberry/blackberry/liquorice/earthy/mint aromas. A plush, elemental palate with deep-set, generous elderberry/blackberry/sweet-fruit flavours and grippy/cedar tannins. Finishes sappy dry. A substantial wine which will need plenty of time to evolve.

2004 ★   **2015** • • • **2035**

Inky, deep crimson–purple. Beautiful camomile/pure blackcurrant/mulberry/aniseed aromas with hints of herb and violets. A lovely, buoyant wine with plenty of fruit volume, fresh elderberry/cassis flavours and dense, chalky tannins. Finishes firm with excellent flavour length. A top vintage.

2005 ★   **2015** • • • **2030**

Inky, deep crimson–purple. Very elemental, exuberant wine with fresh, pure blackcurrant/mulberry/cranberry fruit and hints of liquorice. The palate is well concentrated and mouth-filling with plenty of fruit sweetness, mulberry/blackberry flavours and sinewy, long tannins. A rich, ripe style packed with fruit and tannins.

DISCUSSION

This was a remarkable tasting showing the evolution of winemaking practice and the St Henri style. The first half dozen wines (1956–63) were quite different to the rest. They were all quite stalky, often showing smoky characters and developed leather notes. Some vintages were more fragile than others. The **1956** showed strong soy/leather/woodspice aromas and smoky, meaty flavours. Considering its age it was remarkably punchy and well defined. (CM) 1956 had a lovely bouquet, but the moment the wine entered the mouth the tannins came as a nasty shock and don't really go away. (JH) 1956 had a lovely old nose with vibrant cedar composure. The palate was refined and supple with saturated flavours and cashmere softness to the tannins; beautiful integrating flavours; no bitterness, no toughness and a gentle crescendo at the finish. (NB)

The **1958** was in delicious shape with lots of milk-chocolate/toffee aromas and some leather/tar notes. It still has excellent tannin structure and purity of flavours. (CM) 1958 showed an interesting combination of leafy, sweet and sour flavours. It was far from being unpleasant, with good flavour length. (JH) 1958 had lovely balance, poise, energy and vibrancy. There was softness at the heart of the wine and a fresh finish. (NB)

1959 was fully evolved with blackcurrant/mint aromas. The palate was bright and sustained with fresh tannins and a touch of crispness at the end. (CPT) It has an earthy, dusty, old-wine nose. It was still drinkable, but it's really a curio now. The wine is leanish; lacking both middle and fruit sweetness. (HH) It's very mature, graceful and rich with spicy, dark fig, date aromas and a luscious texture that gives pleasure. (JG)

> *'Penfolds were old when your Grandparents were young.'*
> —ADVERTISING SLOGAN, 1950s

1961 was rabidly characterful. The more I looked at it the more I came round to it; the palate structure was quite something. It had strange sour–sweet aromas reminiscent of fresh sausages and a good frame of tannins. I loved the wonderful palate structure but when I went back to it, I hated the nose. (CM) It had less elegance and finesse than 1959. The wine was a little dusty with tighter, grippier tannins, but impressive intensity of flavour. (NB) I found the wine a bit dried out and thinning off. It had some off-putting, animal-like aromas. It's barely drinking now. (HH)

1962 was delicious and well balanced with leather/cassis/mint/pepper aromas. The wine is still sweet and juicy with round tannins and lift on the finish. (CPT) The wine is on its way out; the tannins last more than the fruit. It's like a fading rose. (JG) I found it magnificent. It was tangy, perhaps citric, with signs of asparagus, stalks and subtle smoke. And then wow! What a palate! It was fleshy, interesting, tremendously long, perfectly composed, structured and complete! (CM) 1962 St Henri is a Penfolds classic. Even half-bottle formats recently tasted show remarkable freshness and complexity. (PG)

1963 had elements of sweet fruit and quite good line but it's just hanging in. I marked it quite high because it's old. (JH) I found it a touch reductive. It was lovely on the palate though with wood-spice, coffee and evolved blackcurrant fruit. (CPT) This was a very sound and superb drink with lovely roasted-meat/cedarwood nose and deep, firm palate. (HH)

'St Henri Claret—An Australian red to make the French turn green.'
—ADVERTISING SLOGAN, 1980s

1964 was a relic. (JH) It's nearing the end of its run but it's an effortless wine with exquisite drink-ability. (CM) The nose was glorious, harmonious and richly spicy but there was a touch of volatility. It was very dense and richly layered; almost soupy rather than complex. It dried out at the finish. (NB)

1965 was over-mature but rich, full and gentle. Even though it's well past its prime it still has some appeal. (JG) It's earthy and dusty with some meaty, gamy notes and a savoury, drying palate. It's getting a little tired now even though it's still a nice drink. (HH)

1966 was cedary with a whiff of blackcurrant. It was juicy and ripe with persistent fruit and supported by delicious, round acidity. This was a very balanced and very youthful wine; just like its pedigree, 1966 being the Year of the Horse. (CPT) It was significantly deeper in colour than the preceding vintages. There were some meaty notes and ripe fruit in a black range and touches of mocha/chocolate. (JH) This was unbelievably good with structure plus. Everything about this wine is great. It's beefy, leathery, twiggy, sizeable and mouth-filling with great reaches of tannin. (CM)

1967 had a dried cranberry, meaty, savoury nose. It was elegant and silken with flowing texture. This was a refined thoroughbred. (NB) It's fully mature now with fig, date, prune fruit and a supple, soft, generous palate. (JG) It's okay to drink, but it's very old now with a very aged honeyed/molasses nose and lots of drying tannin. (HH)

1968 was quite cedary with a gentle, honeyed richness. It buzzes with a quiet energy and fills the mouth with fig and dried fruit flavours. (JG) It smells great, of old leather, but the palate doesn't have a lot left. It's fading out. (AC)

The **1969** was not available for this tasting, but we have seen some of these bottles at the various Penfolds Red Wine Re-corking Clinics over the last few years. The wine is becoming over-developed now with fading marmalade, spicy aromas and grippy, dry tannins. It was never a great vintage and should be drunk now. (AC)

1970 has a mass of leathery, spicy fragrances and a swagger of tannin, but the wine carries it. The wine's really good. It's medium-class, but what class it is. (CM) It's very robust with old leather/roasted meat and strong tannins. It is still a good drink but the tannins are winning. There was a strong correlation between recognised Penfolds vintages and overall quality. The 1958, 1962 and 1963 were sensational wines. The 1966 was an equal high but had a very slight crushed-ant character. (HH) Winemaking was different in those days; grape stalks were added back into the ferments to add complexity of flavour. Combined with the use of continuous presses, the wines would have been more obviously tannic and grippy than the contemporary styles of St Henri. (SL)

1971 is arresting, with remarkably deep red, tawny colour and dark intensely fruited nose. The palate is compact and dense with saturated flavours and an abundance of supportive tannin. It's a little grippy and heavy, but overall it's impressive. (NB) This is a hugely interesting and persistent wine; it has the whole bag of game, leather, spice, smoke and cigars—and even some ferrous notes. But it's characterised by its length and exquisite, flavoursome tannin. (CM) It's the first wine in the line-up to show true form and character. It has plenty of structure holding the spectrum of spicy/sweet to savoury fruit. (JH)

1972 was not tasted. However, examples seen at the Penfolds Red Wine Re-corking Clinics are fragrant and evolved with chocolate/herb garden/cedar aromas and complex smoked-oyster notes. The palate, however, is starting to dry out, but it still has some sweet fruit and fine, lacy, dry tannins. It kicks up leafy/sappy dry at the finish. (AC)

1973 is mature and showing signs of maderisation. It has some chocolate, pepper notes and the tannins are thick. It lacks the grace of the wines from the 1960s. (JG) It has creamy mushroom, wood-spice aromas and flavours, and plenty of freshness. It's just a bit short at the finish. (CPT)

1974—considering the vintage—has surprisingly good sweet-fruit notes and no mouldy notes. The structure is weakening now. (JH) It had complex sandalwood/mint/blackcurrant aromas with juicy, ripe, succulent Christmas cake, liquorice, blackcurrant flavours. It has impressive intensity buoyed by long freshness. (CPT)

1975 has thinned out a bit. It shows some earthy/celery notes and slight maderisation. The palate is rather ordinary and falls away short. (HH) It has some chocolaty, salty flavours but not enough to support the strong tannins. (CM)

1976 is a richly silken and powerfully structured wine with some potent underlying stemmy notes. It's beautifully balanced with full appetising fresh acidity and great length of flavour. It's not fully tamed. (NB) This is a substantial wine with honeyed, leathery, briary aromas and some farmyard notes. Its big, beefy heart is ticking away loudly. (CM)

1977 is a fragrant, elegant wine, but not particularly powerful (like the 1976) but it does have fluid length. Further cellaring is possible but it's best enjoyed now. (JH) It smells of stewed capsicum and liquorice with espresso coffee/liquorice flavours and a fresh, long finish. (CPT)

1978 is very heady. Layered and complex fig, date, spice aromas and dense satisfying richness. The flavours trail off towards the finish. (JG) The wine smells of molasses and jammy fruit, but the palate is thin and fading. It just lacks flavour and weight; finishes short. (HH)

1979 is a leaner, earthier and greener wine with unappealing sour and sweet characters. (JH) I found the wine lovely and elegant with refined, satin texture and great depth of fruit. It's fresh and well sustained but the wine does not have the flavour spectrum or the finesse of the best vintages. It's a shade bitter at the finish. (NB)

> *'St Henri Claret. It's not cheap, it's not easy to find.*
> *But it is one of the finest red wines in Australia.'*
> —ADVERTISING SLOGAN, c. 1980

1980 is raisiny and short. It's just not in good shape. (CM)

1981 is a masculine wine in all respects, with robust, burly, ripe black fruits and substantial tannins. (JH) It's mellow and fully developed. It still has lots of fruit sweetness on the mid-palate, but it's not that powerful, intense or great. It's just good. (HH)

1982 is gentle and mature with ground coffee, earthy, smoky aromas and plenty of sweet fruit. (JG) It's much lighter than the other wines with some minty notes, but the fruit is engaging, round and fresh. This is an easy-drinking, delicious wine. (CPT)

1983 had an exciting nose with lightly stewed plum aromas and silky/syrupy texture. It is a richly satisfying, irresistible wine with well-sustained clarity and transparency of fruit across the palate. It will last and even improve. (NB) It's a big tannic wine which doesn't quite carry the style. (CM) The wine harks back to the classical St Henri style of the 1960s. It's firm, juicy, rich and savoury, and very long. There are some stemmy notes, but it just brings further complexity and interest. (JG)

1984 is fully developed and pristine with plummy, sweetly ripe aromas. The palate is medium- to full-bodied with lovely richness and fruit sweetness. It's not that complex and still has some ageing to do, but it's very good. I did see a thread of greenness but it came down. (HH) I didn't find it that successful. The aromas were quite balsamic, almost sour, but the palate had sweet raspberry characters; almost grenache-like. (CM) The wine was deep and satisfying with generous black fig, sweetly ripe flavours and lacy texture. It finished cedary and complete. (JG)

1985 showed plenty of light plums and soft blackcurrants. The palate is light with lively fruit and balanced by an overall freshness. It finishes a touch short. (CPT) It was more gently sweet than preceding vintages with ripe fruit and balanced tannins.

1986 was very meaty, mellow and developed with robust tannins and richness of flavour. It's very full-bodied for St Henri and not the most elegant, but it's very good. (HH) It was potently smoky, richly silken and very brisk with plenty of grip. (NB)

1987 had lots of oomph but not a huge amount of charm. It was powerful and tarry with some leather notes and a mass of tannins. For a twenty-year-old wine, this was in great shape. (CM). It has some substance but the sweet and sour characters are intensified by the vintage. (JH)

1988 has nice structure with some eucalypt and musky elegance but it finishes slightly metallic. (CM) It has some cola and vegetal scents with even, savoury flavours. (JG)

The **1989** had a slightly wild nose, but it's dense and harmonious with good depth of flavour. (NB) It had lovely balance with juicy blackcurrant, raspberry fruit matched by round tannins and acidity. (CPT) The St Henri style really steps up here. There's plenty of herbal, sweet and sour aromas and some plummy, smoky notes. It's very flavoursome and interesting. (CM)

1990 is the first older St Henri I would like to cellar. It had supple black fruits and harmonious tannins. (JH) It was medium deep and inky with a rich tomato-plum nose. It's plush, richly textured and densely woven. (NB) It will be great drinking for years to come. It had meaty/dusty/earthy aromas and plenty of richness and flesh. It's lively, fresh, clean and vibrant with satisfying length. (HH)

I loved the composition of **1991**—and the fact it was slightly edgy. It has a sweaty, sweet and sour personality and a meaty, long finish. (CM). It has riper fruit than 1990 with touches of prune and plenty of overall richness, but it's not quite in the same class. (JH) It was just a trifle tough with a cabernet-like sternness. (HH)

1992 had a freshness and surprising youthfulness with blueberry soft fruit and gentle tannins. (JG) It was greenish on the nose, but the palate was much better. (CPT) I found it slightly monolithic with unsettled acidity towards the finish. It had density and richness but it just seems to be closed in. (NB)

1993 is good, too, with violets, plum fruits and lots of tannin, freshness and structure. It's exceptionally youthful as well. These early 1990s are very good. (CM) It did have sweet fruit, but I found it slightly lolly-ish (compared with 1992) with minimal tannin impact. (JH)

> *'A new vintage release with a pedigree as long as your arm.'*
> —ADVERTISING SLOGAN, c. 1985

1994 is minty, leafy and red berried. It had good flavour but tasted a bit pinched. The palate is firm; very tannic, robust and solid. But it has plenty of depth, richness and body. This will go on for another twenty years or so. (HH) It showed powerful black fruits, liquorice and bitter dark chocolate with built-in tannins through the length of the palate. (JH)

1995 is flushed with black fruits and smoky, slightly medicinal nuances. It's massively tannic but has ample, smooth, swamping fruit and impressive clarity and intensity. (NB) It hits your mouth and runs! The dusty, briary, leafy characters work well. There are signs of creamy oak married into curranty fruit and the first signs of secondary leather characters are emerging. (CM)

1996 was strong in colour, rich but supple and showing no porty 'dead-fruit' characters. It has plenty of blackberry, blackcurrant, liquorice flavours and fine tannins. (JH) This was a rich, provocative wine with fresh nut-skin, blackberry aromas and bold intensity for St Henri. It's a fiercer, powerful style. I love the way the old oak doesn't tame the energy of the fruit. (JG)

1997 smelled of raspberries, bacon fat and crushed leaves, but the palate was a bit lean and pinched. (HH) The tannins are quite extracted and quickly overwhelm the soft fruit characters. (CPT)

1998 was a blockbuster-type wine with composed, ripe, sweet-fruit characters and a plump, well-rounded palate. (NB) This was a powerful, robust wine initially showing pure black fruits before a slight tweak of green emerges, but there was enough fruit power and energy to carry it. (JH)

1999 was a classy wine in a medium-weighted way. It would be beautiful with food—which is what it really needs. It's a bit minty and tannic but it's lovely, easygoing drinking. (CM) It's fully developed with fragrant raspberry/cassis aromas and hints of nutmeg and cranberry. It's elegant but ripe, clean and focused. It still needs time and will cellar for quite a while; up to 25 years. (HH)

'Penfolds: All you need to know about Red Wine.'
—ADVERTISING SLOGAN, c. 1990

2000 smells of shoe polish and cosmetics; strange bedfellows! (JH) It's quite jammy with tomato leaf, plummy notes. The wine is a touch dilute, and there's a minty burst at the finish. (CM)

2001 is very deep in colour, almost opaque, with blackberry/blueberry aromas and slippery, lacy tannins. It hasn't got the greatest concentration or the longest length, but it does have a thoroughbred quality. (NB) It's dark and very ripe with black fruits, panforte, star anise, Asian spice aromas and flavours. The palate is meaty with grippy tannins. (HH)

2002 had expected dense colour with luscious, deep-black fruits, great texture and structure despite the cool vintage. (JH) It has plenty of cola-like characters, coconut, mint, liquorice and malt, all hanging off a core of delicious ripe, pure fruit. Perhaps there is a touch too much eucalypt, but nonetheless it is an exceptionally pure, fruit-blessed St Henri. (CM)

2003 has the perfume of a young vintage port or a fragrant Côte Rôtie with violets/ripe raspberries and shimmering, silky fruit. This was my favourite of the entire tasting. It had a feminine quality and effortless structure. (CPT) It's very distinctive, stern and forbidding with nutmeg/spicy aromas and a very tight, almost pinched, palate. It's hard to imagine this wine ever softening. (HH) It's a wine of two parts. It starts with a sweet, slightly cosmetic fruit entry, then there's silence, and then savoury/green tannins on the finish. (JH)

2004 is a gorgeous wine with super-violet, pure sweet-fruit aromas and flavours. The tannins are excellent without being excessive. It has a perfume to die for. This is a long-term stunner! (CM) This is a really interesting wine. It's true to the St Henri style even with all on offer from the vintage; for a fleeting moment I thought it could be the best ever under this label, but the finish said otherwise. (JH) The wine is still coming together. The tannins are very grippy, which lend structure and support to very intense concentrated blackberry/raspberry fruit. (NB)

2005 is again floral with violet notes, but it's rich and ripe with elegant fruit and equal measures of tannins and acidity. It's a lovely wine. After seeing the last five vintages, St Henri seems to have reached a very high level of quality. (CPT) It was very raw and perfumed with a nice framework of tannin and fruit. There is a wave of mouth-filling deliciousness that washes across the palate. (CM)

I am a great fan of St Henri. Here is a wine that doesn't rely on oak; rather on sheer quality of fruit. There was a real trough during the 1970s and most of the '80s with only occasional highlights. They just aren't of the same consistency and interest of the 1950s and '60s. However, once you get to 1990 and 1991 there is a clear transitional phase. The fruit profile becomes chocolaty with pure, black-fruit characters. By 1994 the style has geared into a modern contemporary classic. (JG)

The overall fruit and vineyard selection is more focused than it was in the 1980s. In recent times we are trying to get more Adelaide fruit into the wine in an effort to give more perfume and elegance. In some respects the wheel has turned as we are now sourcing fruit from around all the old areas—although of course some of the original St Henri vineyards have disappeared. The wine is now roughly 10 to 15 per cent Adelaide Hills fruit, drawing material from Waterfall Gully, Wilton and Williamstown. (PG)

We still source plenty of fruit from around the Barossa, particularly from Kalimna, including our vitally important independent growers, and the Clare Valley. In cooler years we will go as far as McLarenVale. We seek fruit with distinct praline characters and solid tannin structure. The elegance is not achieved through early picking. After vinification in the original 1460-litre, 50-year-old oak vats at Nuriootpa, we often add pressings back into the wine. It's rare not to have pressings added. (PG)

In the old days Max Schubert would always have pressings sent down to him at Magill. He saw it as a useful blending option. He would often use drainings as well. This concentrated slurry of wine, still captured in the mass of skins, would be allowed to sit for a time. It can be compared to a cow letting down milk. After a while this lovely, richly concentrated material with wonderful astringency and without a trace of bitterness would be released from the skins. Max Schubert and John Davoren would capture this wine specially for blending. (RB) We still use these techniques today for making St Henri. (SL) The last decade of vintages shows that St Henri has been refined in faithful guise to John Davoren's original wine style. It will be very interesting to see how these wines age. (HH) St Henri has a very special place in the Penfolds story. Over the last decade, we have fine-tuned every aspect of winemaking philosophy to elevate the absolute quality of the wine. This has been achieved through selective fruit sourcing, improved classification of components and a real desire to further enhance St Henri's reputation as the alter ego of Grange. (PG)

WHITES

Reserve Bin A Chardonnay

First Vintage:	1994.
Variety:	Chardonnay.
Origin:	Adelaide Hills extending from the Piccadilly Valley to Birdwood.
Fermentation:	100% barrel fermented/100% malolactic fermentation.
Maturation:	Matured for 11 months in specially selected, tightly grained French oak barriques.
Comments:	The early vintages comprise some Tumbarumba fruit. 2002 not made. Vintages prior to 2001—drink now/past. Released entirely under screw cap since the 2003 vintage.

> *'An impressive flight of wines showing surprising limpidity and well-sustained flavour development.'*
> —NEIL BECKETT, PANELLIST

The Reserve Bin A Series Chardonnay has established a strong following since it was first released in 1994. During the early 1990s, Penfolds winemakers were asked to trial and develop a white winemaking philosophy that would mirror the success of Penfolds' red wines in the mainstream markets. With access to an incredible range of fruit in almost all major and minor Australian wine regions, it was felt that Penfolds should work towards making something that would have the intrinsic qualities of a great Australian white wine.

Initially the Penfolds white winemaking team worked on various trials based on three main varietals: semillon, sauvignon blanc and chardonnay. At a very early stage it was believed that the wine should be a relatively taut and linear with plenty of ageing potential. The old Hunter Valley semillons with low alcohol and fine lean acidities had plenty of history, but having sold one of the finest semillon vineyards in the Hunter Valley during the late 1970s, it was felt that Penfolds should not return to this style as a flagship wine. Further, it would have limited appeal. Sauvignon blanc was always an option. Plenty of barrel fermentation trials showed that complexity could be achieved, but the overall structure did not allow for long-term ageing.

Cool-climate chardonnay was seen as the best variety as it has beautiful perfume and pristine fruit when young, yet can develop richness and complexity with age. Much of the project centered on the Adelaide Hills and Tumbarumba—a relatively new cool-climate wine region in New South Wales. Initially it was thought that a component of Tumbarumba sauvignon blanc fruit would add lift and freshness to the wine. Early indications from the wine show circuit showed that this was possibly the way to go, as the 1994 vintage attracted plenty of plaudits in its early career. The wine developed too quickly and before too long it was realised that the Reserve Bin A style was best developed as a 100 per cent Adelaide Hills chardonnay.

Penfolds Reserve Bin A is sourced from vineyards mostly located around Birdwood, Balhannah, Morialta and Gumeracha—a fairly long stretch of varied cool-climate micro-climates along higher elevations of the Adelaide Hills. The wine centres specifically on ten key vineyards, all owned by loyal independent growers. Yields are kept low at around 3–4 tonnes per hectare to maximise flavour development and balance. Initially winemakers wanted a style that sat 'out of the square'. In some respects that was achieved during the early years at the expense of cellaring potential. More recent vintages are classically proportioned rather than worked styles with strong regional definition and vintage characters.

Penfolds is seeking to achieve as much flavour and ripeness as possible but at moderate alcohol levels and naturally balanced acidities. This has been achieved through vineyard management, better micro-site selection and refinement in vinification practices. The wine is naturally fermented in new tightly grained French barriques and then allowed to go through 100 per cent malolactic fermentation to achieve further integration of fruit and oak. Some parcels are purposely sulphide-influenced or fermented on solids with wild yeasts. Once considered as extreme winemaking practices, these techniques are considered as quite standard in achieving heightened complexity, flavours and texture. At the end of fermentation the wines are regularly stirred on their lees to bring more richness and depth of flavour.

Oliver Crawford says, 'Our aim is to make something extra special. The growers have got right behind it and are doing some amazing things to deliver the type of fruit we need. The Reserve Bin A is increasingly more refined and interesting. A better understanding of vineyard resources and blending options has taken the wine to a new level of complexity, volume and flavour, yet without compromising the inherent elegance and minerality of Adelaide Hills fruit.'

The Reserve Bin A Series Chardonnay embraces a tradition of experimentation and development at Penfolds. Each vintage reflects an evolution of winemaking philosophy and individual winemaking skills. The wine is only made in years with ideal growing conditions.

TASTING NOTES ~ RESERVE BIN A CHARDONNAY

2003 Bin 03A   NOW

Medium pale yellow. Classical, evolved wine with intense peach/grilled-nut aromas, butterscotch/nougat notes and savoury oak. A creamy, complex but forward palate with deep-set grapefruit/peach flavours and fine minerally acidity. Finishes a touch chalky but dry and long. 88% new oak. A sumptuous wine which is at its peak of development.

2004 Bin 04A ★   NOW • • • 2010

Pale yellow. Fresh, complex wine with pear skin/nectarine/lanolin/matchstick aromas and underlying savoury oak. The palate is smooth and creamy with nectarine/pear skin/white peach flavours and long mineral mouth-watering acidity. 85% new oak. A lovely vintage.

2005   Bin 05A   NOW • • • 2012

Pale yellow. Very restrained, elegant wine with white peach/nectarine/cashew nut aromas and some gunflint/savoury oak complexity. The wine is clean and fresh with nectarine/white peach flavours, some yeasty richness and high-pitched, slatey acidity. Finishes long and minerally. Oak is nicely understated. 85% new oak.

2006   Bin 06A   NOW • • • 2010

Pale yellow. Intense peach/pear/apricot/herb garden aromas. A mouth-filling wine with ripe peach/pear/apricot flavours, some grilled-nut complexity and underlying vanilla oak. Finishes minerally and long. Surprisingly soft and forward compared with 2005.

Most vintages prior to 2001 will have reached or passed their peak. These are generally medium-term cellaring wines which are best enjoyed early. They have a very attractive fruit complexity, creaminess and minerality when young, but develop more richness and weight with age. Realistically the wines will reach a peak around three to four years after vintage and then plateau for another three to four years. The 2002 vintage was not made. Indeed the wine is only released if the vintage reflects a decent growing season. If the fruit has struggled to achieve ripeness, it will not be used for the Reserve Bin A Chardonnay.

DISCUSSION

I found this an impressive flight of wines, showing surprising limpidity and well-sustained flavour development. (NB)

2003 was unexpectedly very developed in colour and palate. This is a wine which was festooned with medals. (JH) It had a very pale orange colour, it perhaps lacked a degree of focus, but it had a certain clarity of flavour: limes and minerals, and good acid balance. (NB) It was certainly developed in colour with rich toasty/roasted hazelnut aromas. However the palate was rich, fleshy and sumptuous with good flavour and length. (HH)

2004 was medium-bodied with light flint/vanilla notes and soft palate. (CPT) It was evocative of walking through an apple orchard! The wine had an apple freshness with golden delicious/pear aromas and subtle oak complexity. This wine is still taut and refined and should age well. (JG) I thought it was a major shift in winemaking style. The fruit profile is far fresher on both bouquet and palate. (JH) The fruit is reserved and the oak slightly bears down. However it's tight and complex with plenty of autolytic character and toasted butter notes. It's not at all blowsy and needs time for the fruit to come through. (JG) It was more restrained, soft but tight and less evolved. The palate was smooth and clean with lovely refinement and subtlety. The wine is ageing gracefully and slowly. This is a very long and satisfying wine. (HH)

2005 was clean, fresh and youthful with cashew nut notes and plenty of underlying malolactic and lees complexity. The oak is nicely understated but the wine really needs time. (HH) It had a lot of buttery/toasty oak freshness, an impressive density and ripeness and flourishing flavour length. (NB) It had very good texture and flavour complexity. The oak and acidity were neatly balanced around a seamless flow of creamy nectarine/white peach flavours. This was my top wine in the bracket, narrowly edging ahead of the 2004! (JH)

2006 was more intense than the above, with medium-bodied fruit and freshness on the finish.(CPT) The 2006 is more svelte, elegant and restrained with well-integrated acidity and flavours. It's a very good wine with a shade of warmth at the finish. (NB) There is a lot going on in this adolescent wine. It has plenty of floral/apricot notes and yeasty complexity derived from *bâtonnage*. The wine seems to be going in all sorts of directions at the moment. I can only assume that it will be ready to drink on release! (JG) Despite the lower alcohol (13.1%) this is a really mouth-filling wine which will perhaps develop more quickly than the 2004 and 2005 vintage. (JH) It's still hard to judge at this stage. It seems less tight and more rounded but it's too early to call. (HH)

Aged Release Riesling

First Vintage:	1992.
Variety:	Riesling.
Origin:	Clare Valley (including independently grown fruit), Woodbury and High Eden Valley vineyards. Regional source depends on vintage conditions.
Fermentation:	Stainless steel tanks.
Maturation:	Maturation in bottle for a period of 5 years before release. Only released when suitable parcels of fruit have been identified at vintage.
Comments:	Previously labelled Reserve Bin Riesling. Released entirely under screw cap from the 2005 vintage on.

'The Penfolds Aged Release Riesling highlights the compelling ageing process of highly defined and perfectly balanced riesling fruit.'
— OLIVER CRAWFORD, WINEMAKER

The Penfolds Aged Release Riesling is either an Eden Valley or Clare Valley wine, depending on vintage conditions. Winemakers are looking for fruit of exceptional acid balance and flavour concentration. Such strict fruit selection means that the wine can only be made in special vintages. The Penfolds Clare Estate, Woodbury and High Eden vineyards are the principal sources of fruit—although a small percentage of independently grown fruit is used in the Clare Valley vintages.

The Penfolds Aged Release Riesling is a wine which must have structure for medium- to long-term ageing. It highlights the compelling ageing process of highly defined and perfectly balanced riesling fruit. The youthful floral/citrus characters will gradually develop rich, toasty, honeyed aromas and flavours balanced by the variety's naturally high acidity. Regional differences do emerge with age. The Clare rieslings show plenty of toastiness, volume and fine-cutting acidity. The Eden Valley

rieslings are classically structured styles which, with development, show honeyed/oilskin/lime characters and fine, crisp acidity.

The Aged Release Riesling is released purposely after five years to highlight the exquisite maturation characters of aged riesling. When young, these wines are very aromatic but lean in structure. The wines are bottled soon after fermentation to preserve both freshness of fruit and the complex characters of mature riesling. As the wine ages it becomes more complex and develops very generous flavours on the palate. James Halliday was impressed by the 2005 vintage. 'It's a lovely tight wine and you can see easily why it should be kept for five years before release.' Huon Hooke found the wine 'still young, delicate and slow-ageing with great subtlety and balance'.

All vintages from first release 1992 to 2000 are sealed with corks. The bottles are actually quite variable because of cork ageing, but the best bottles of 1993, 1997 and 2000 showed excellent complexity and minerality. The 2005 and future vintages are sealed with screw caps. Oliver Crawford says, 'This form of closure will allow the wine to retain freshness for a longer period. After so many years of trialling screw caps, we are convinced this is the way to go, particularly with delicate, aromatic wine styles such as riesling.'

TASTING NOTES ~ AGED RELEASE RIESLING

1992   Eden Valley   NOW

Medium deep yellow. Intense honey/wet stone/oilskin aromas. A well-concentrated, fresh, but very developed style with honey/toasty flavours and long minerally/indelible acidity. Still holding but best to drink soon.

1993   Clare Valley   NOW • • • PAST

Medium deep yellow. Fragrant camomile/honey/hazelnut aromas with touches of herb. The palate is dry and flinty with gentle honey/lemon/camomile/hazelnut flavours and fresh crisp acidity. At full maturity. Drink up.

1995   Eden Valley   PAST

Medium deep yellow. Very evolved butterscotch/hazelnut/toasty aromas with some lime/oilskin nuances. The palate is dry with citrus peel/butterscotch/oilskin flavours and fine acidity. It finishes long and sweet but it has lost freshness and vitality. Past its best now.

1997   Clare Valley   NOW

Medium yellow. Intense lemon curd/grapefruit/pear aromas with toasty/oilskin/marmalade complexity. A remarkably fresh bottle with lemon curd/toasty/marmalade flavours and bright high-pitched spangling acidity. Finishes crisp and dry. Beware bottle variation.

1998   Clare Valley   NOW

Medium deep gold. Lemon curd/honey/crème-brûlée aromas with touches of apricot. The palate is well concentrated with lemony/crème brûlée/apricot flavours, plenty of richness and mineral acidity. The wine has lost its freshness.

1999   Eden Valley   **NOW**

Pale medium yellow. Lemon/grapefruit/oilskin aromas. The wine is slightly sweet with grape-fruit/lemon/lime essence flavours and crisp, a touch hard, acidity. It still has freshness and excellent flavour length.

2000   Eden Valley   **NOW • • • 2015**

Medium yellow. Bright lemon curd/grapefruit/pear aromas with some toasty/oilskin complexity. Sweet-fruited lemon curd/pear/herb/toast flavours and crunchy/quartz-like acidity. Finishes bone dry but long and minerally. Still has plenty of vitality.

2005   Eden Valley   **2010 • • • 2020**

Pale yellow. Intense, scented, pristine grapefruit/lemon aromas with a hint of fresh toast/lanolin. The palate is beautifully concentrated with plenty of lemon curd/grapefruit flavours and fine, minerally acidity. Finishes long and flavourful. A lovely, tightly balanced wine. Released in 2010.

CHAPTER EIGHT

Special Bin Wines

Penfolds Special Bin wines have a special significance and place among generations of Australian and international wine collectors. Deeply connected to Australian wine culture, each release or bottling has in some way represented a waypoint in the progress of the modern Australian wine industry. Some of these wines were preliminary sketches for masterpieces such as Grange or Bin 707. Others explored the landscape canvas of South Australian and New South Wales vineyards or the mixing of nature's colour for the sake of inquiry and knowledge. The wines became important conversation pieces among Penfolds winemakers, at wine shows and in the dining rooms of friends, rivals and wine collectors.

Penfolds Special Bin red wines were first released in the early 1950s during a momentous time of research and experimentation. When Max Schubert began his Grange project he used a control wine to compare the results of his work with barrel fermentation and maturation in American oak. While the control wine—several hundred dozen were bottled—showed 'all the characteristics of a good well-made wine in the orthodox mould' the wine did not reach the standard of the first experimental Grange. But, Max Schubert noted, 'It did, however, set the guidelines for production and marketing of a whole range of special red wines which have been sought after, vintage by vintage, to this day.'

*'True excellence is a constant
and endless journey—it's not a destination.'*
— MAX SCHUBERT

Penfolds Bin 1 Grange Hermitage and other experimental wines—often of exceptional quality or interest—were sometimes released or given away to friends and collectors. Indeed, some of these wines—including 1962 Penfolds Bin 60A Kalimna Shiraz, Coonawarra Cabernet, 1966 Bin 620 Coonawarra Cabernet Sauvignon Shiraz and 1967 Bin 7 Coonawarra Cabernet Sauvignon Kalimna Shiraz— enjoyed exceptional Australian wine show careers and extraordinary fame. The vineyards in and around Adelaide, Kalimna Vineyard and Coonawarra also became renowned as some of the very finest in South Australia.

During the 1950s and '60s, winemakers were allowed to experiment. Auldana-based winemaker John Davoren, for instance, was not a great fan of the Grange style, leading to unresolved and speculative controversy regarding his relationship with Schubert. Davoren's St Henri was a different style of wine yet, interestingly, there is a common thread—especially revealing with age. Observers within the Penfolds winemaking team suggest that both winemakers enjoyed a very fruitful and candid friendship.

The early St Henri vintages were experimental wines; the first vintage was completely unplanned as a commercial release. However, there were also one-off Special Bin wines made by other members of the Penfolds winemaking team and released for the sake of interest. These include the 1956 Bin 136 Magill Burgundy—originally sent up from Magill as blending material for a special Qantas bottling of shiraz–mataro. Don Ditter was so impressed by the wine that he decided to bottle it separately. Penfolds Bin S56 was a sister wine made from a similar parcel but bottled at Magill.

Block 42 Cabernet Sauvignon

First Vintage:	Only ever released in 1953, 1961, 1963, 1964, 1996 and 2004.
Variety:	Cabernet sauvignon.
Origin:	Block 42—Kalimna Vineyard (Barossa Valley).
Fermentation:	Stainless steel tanks with wooden header boards to submerge cap. Temperature maintained at less than 22° C. Daily rack and returns.
Maturation:	Fermentation completed in new American oak hogsheads. Approximately 13–18 months' maturation in oak (300 litres).
Comments:	Block 42 played a critical role in the development of Grange and particularly Bin 707. There are probably no examples left of the 1948 Kalimna Cabernet Sauvignon. Released under screw cap in some markets since the 2004 vintage.

'Mindblowing.'
—CAMPBELL MATTINSON, PANELLIST

Planted around 1888, Block 42 is located at the edge of the Kalimna Vineyard in the Moppa sub-region of the Barossa Valley and comprises cabernet sauvignon vines of ancient genetic origins. It belongs to a national heritage of great, old, nineteenth-century, pre-phylloxera Australian vineyards including Henschke's Hill of Grace, located in the Eden Valley sub-region of the Barossa, and the astonishingly small central Victorian shiraz vineyards planted in the nineteenth century by the famous wine families the Bests and the Tahbilks.

The 10-acre Block 42 was planted only 30 years after the great 1855 Bordeaux Classification, and comprises the oldest plantings of continuously producing cabernet sauvignon in the world. These original, very old, low-yielding, contorted, knotted and serpentine vines have deep, penetrating roots which extend through alluvial sands, rich brown soils and into the fissures and cracks of bedrock. For over 120 vintages the vines, planted on their own roots, have produced flavour-intense, mineral-rich fruit with exceptional concentration and balance.

Max Schubert experimented with parcels of Block 42 cabernet during the development phase of Penfolds Grange. He recognised the extraordinary potential of this vineyard site through the special bottlings of the late 1940s. Those early but very limited wines, made from pressings and matured in old oak puncheons, were deeply concentrated with immense flavour and classical, fine-grained tannins.

A few bottles of 1948 Kalimna Cabernet Sauvignon made from Block 42 surfaced in 1987. These wines emanated from the cellar of Max Lake who once described it in his seminal book *Classic Wines of Australia* (1966) as, 'becoming magnificent and can only be compared to the big cabernet wines of Europe'. One of the bottles was opened up at a Sydney Wine Show dinner in 1994. Despite the remarkable strides in winemaking science and practice, this utterly extraordinary wine—rarer than hen's teeth—was still distinctly Penfolds in character. Huon Hooke described the wine as 'powerful, rich, concentrated and fleshy. It brimmed with the trademark aged Penfolds bouquet of crushed ants, leather, chocolate and mint.'

Impressed and inspired by the wines of Bordeaux, Max Schubert had initially hoped that his 'different and lasting' Grange would be cabernet-based. On closer scrutiny he realised that the variable supply and overall quality of South Australian cabernet would compromise Penfolds' commercial objectives for a consistent, 'high-grade wine'. While Max Schubert struggled with this grape variety at first, improved viticulture and the acquired wisdom of succeeding vintages resulted in the release of Bin 707—a wine that was born from Block 42 but which eventually (after a stop–start history) found its core fruit source in Coonawarra.

Block 42 cabernet was never far from Max Schubert's mind during the early development of Grange. While the story of Grange is inextricably linked to shiraz, a 1953 Penfolds Grange Cabernet, entirely sourced from Block 42, was in fact commercially produced. The complex and fully mature 1953 Grange Cabernet is still a magnificent testimony to the perfume and staying power of exceptional Block 42 vintages. Neil Beckett described the wine as showing 'dried blackcurrant aromas and rich sweet flavours. The wine is so magnificently balanced with ravishing complexity and seamlessly woven, silken-like tannins. It begins a series of wines which have a wonderful, unforced, naturally expressive, floating quality.'

The low-yielding Block 42 neither provided enough fruit nor the required consistency every vintage. Max Schubert had a very clear idea of what constituted ideal cabernet fruit; it had to have deep colour, concentration, power, pure fruit definition and chocolaty ripe tannins. Block 42 has always provided high-quality fruit, but has rarely fulfilled the texture and weight required for the full Penfolds treatment, particularly the critical element of barrel fermentation. Notwithstanding its limitations, Penfolds released a 1961 Bin 58 Cabernet Sauvignon—a wine that is now beginning to fade. While it still has 'nice structure, cigars and leather', the tannins and fruit have dried out.

The 1963 Bin 64 Cabernet Sauvignon, a 100 per cent Block 42 wine, was entered into the 1964 Royal Melbourne Wine Show and won the prestigious Jimmy Watson Memorial Trophy for a young one-year-old dry red. The members of the Rewards of Patience tasting panel were greatly impressed by the wine. Joshua Greene said, 'It's not possible the wine is 44 years old. It has such fresh, damson plum aromas, curranty flavours and satin smooth tannins. While it's delicate and mature, it has plenty of life.' Campbell Mattinson said, 'It's incredible really. Despite the age it's solid and exceptionally composed.'

Providing 'lift and structure', Block 42 cabernet sauvignon was blended into many early bottlings of Penfolds Grange. The remarkably perfumed and beautifully structured 1964 Bin 707 Cabernet Sauvignon, entirely sourced from Block 42, remains one of the classic wines of the 1960s. This first vintage marked the beginning of a famous Penfolds wine. It was described by Huon Hooke as 'a very old and mellow wine with complex meaty stock flavours, great structure and length'. Campbell Mattinson said, 'It's seriously good; aromatic, varietal, intact, beautiful through the mouth, long through the finish and sliced with tannins.'

The valuable and historic Block 42 vineyard continues to be an important component of Bin 707, providing backbone and substance to the overall style. This partially explains why Penfolds has rarely released a single-vineyard wine in the past from Block 42. Nowadays neither Grange nor Bin 707 are entirely dependent on Block 42—especially in exceptional vintages. Improved vineyard management, access to exquisitely proportioned cabernet and better technology generally means that Penfolds can and will make another Block 42 when vintage conditions allow.

Although no Block 42 Kalimna Cabernet Sauvignon was made during the 1970s and '80s, it is quite possible that a special bottling could have been produced. However, the focus of Special Bins during these times was very much on honouring the famous 1962 Bin 60A and 1966 Bin 620. During the 1990s, a new generation of Penfolds winemakers have rediscovered the history and heritage of the Barossa Valley. The release of the 1996 Block 42 was the beginning of a new era at Penfolds and a renewed focus on trial winemaking, new styles, individual vineyard character and new varietals.

Since 1964, Penfolds has only released two single-vineyard Barossa wines; the 1996 and 2004 Block 42 Cabernet Sauvignon. Both of these vintages were exceptional in the Barossa. After a mild winter, the 1996 growing season started early with below-average rainfall and almost perfect cool-to-mild, dry, growing conditions. After vinification in stainless steel, the 1996 Block 42 was 100 per cent barrel fermented and then matured in American oak hogsheads for a period of about eighteen months.

James Halliday described the 1996 as 'a massive leap in style and substance. The wine is flooded with fine cassis blackcurrant fruit and superbly managed tannins. The wine is so beautifully balanced and so exquisitely textured and structured, it would be no crime to drink the wine now, although it will last for at least another twenty years.'

The 2004 season was generally warm and dry. Mild conditions and cool nights prevailed after hot mid-summer weather. The wine was vinified in the classical Penfolds technique but was matured in American oak hogsheads for fifteen months. This ethereal and perfumed 2004 Block 42 is evocative of its origins, yet shows all the hallmarks of Penfolds' winemaking philosophy. The dense colour, intense blackcurrant, dark chocolate, liquorice aromas, fine, slinky tannins and richly concentrated flavours are in perfect harmony. The sheer volume and weight of fruit explodes across the palate giving tremendous depth and flavour length.

The 2004 Block 42 is a complex palimpsest of flavours and textures which will evolve and intertwine over time. Peter Gago says, 'There is something really magical about the 2004 Block 42. It has an ethereal dimension and a saturated blackness on the palate that reveal the true class of this vineyard site. The wine is extraordinarily perfumed with layer upon layer of flavour. The wine will last for decades in the cellar.'

The intriguing mystery and rarity which surrounds the unforgettable 1948 Kalimna Cabernet Sauvignon and its link with 1953 Grange Cabernet may also explain the renewed winemaker curiosity and interest in Block 42. The 1996 and 2004 Block 42 Cabernet Sauvignons are great Penfolds wines. With a bit of luck, ideal weather conditions and the right parcels of fruit, Block 42 will continue to be periodically released.

Block 42 is only made when vintage conditions permit and when the fruit is not needed for Bin 707. In theory, however, it is possible that this wine can be made more than once in a decade.

TASTING NOTES ~ BLOCK 42 CABERNET SAUVIGNON

1953   Bin 9 Grange Cabernet ★   NOW

Medium deep brick red. Intense evolved leather/panforte/blackcurrant/herb garden aromas with touches of cedar/liquorice. Beautifully fresh, complex wine with concentrated and developed panforte/demi-glace/tobacco flavours and lacy, fine, grainy tannins. An endlessly long finish. A great Penfolds wine that seems to have reached a plateau of evolution. It's drinking brilliantly now but could go on for quite a while.

1961   Bin 58 Cabernet   PAST

Medium deep brick red. Cedarwood/mushroom/tobacco aromas. The palate is cedary and firm with some chocolaty fruit beginning to dry up. A twist of VA [volatile acidity] on the finish. Some good bottles will be hanging in, but generally over the yard-arm. Drink up.

1963   Bin 64 Cabernet ★   NOW

Medium deep brick red. An exceptionally well-composed wine. Complex chocolate/dark berry/sandalwood/leather/*sous bois* aromas. A rich, chocolaty, evolved palate with plenty of fruit sweetness/damson plum/mocha flavours and dense, loose-knit, sweet tannins. Finishes long and sweet. Utterly ethereal.

1964 Bin 707 Cabernet Sauvignon ★   NOW

Brick red. Mature cedar/meaty/mushroom/leather aromas with some old mint/sandalwood notes. The palate is still fresh, with sweet meaty/cedar/earthy/minty flavours and slinky, fine tannins. Finishes chalky firm but long and sweet. Almost entirely sourced from the Kalimna Vineyard's Block 42, established around 1888.

1996 Block 42 Cabernet Sauvignon ★   NOW • • • 2035

Medium deep crimson–purple. Cassis/cedar/mocha aromas spangled with rose petals/herb garden. Beautifully focused wine with dense cassis/plum/cedar/mocha flavours, underlying savoury oak and ripe, loose-knit, velvet tannins. A remarkable vintage with incredible fruit richness, energy and flavour length.

2004 Block 42 Cabernet Sauvignon ★   2015 • • • 2055

Opaque purple black. Plush inky/blackcurrant/cedar/aniseed/liquorice aromas. An immensely concentrated, densely packed wine with long, sweet blackcurrant pastille/cedary flavours, integrated malty new oak and sweet, ripe tannins. Finishes firm and long. This is a great vintage. All power, density, structure, fleshiness and balance. A 50-year wine.

> *'Glorious and lasting First Growth quality wines.'*
> —JOSHUA GREENE, PANELLIST

DISCUSSION

1953 Grange Cabernet was extremely refined and subtle with dried blackcurrant aromas and rich sweet flavours. The wine is so magnificently balanced with ravishing complexity and seamlessly woven, silken-like tannins. It begins a series of wines which have a wonderful unforced, naturally expressive, floating quality. A magnificent wine. (NB) It had a very healthy brick-red colour with fragrant, cedar spice aromas and a gorgeous, silky, textured palate. The tannins are totally resolved and the flavours just go on and on. (JH) It's a delicious old curio. (HH) This is a really ethereal wine. It's toffeed, but not excessively so, with old herbs, leather and elements of saltbush. It's not extraordinarily long at first but long enough to be impressive. Then it has this lovely tannin structure with cigars, coffee and decayed leaves; everything seems totally resolved. This is an emotional wine. You just don't want to leave it; just sit on it. (CM)

> *'Max Schubert is, quite simply, a winemaking genius who had*
> *the courage and imagination to ignore completely the conventional*
> *winemaking philosophies and techniques of his day.'*
> —JAMES HALLIDAY, PANELLIST

1961 Bin 58 Cabernet has lost its charm. The wine is very dry and very, very austere. (CPT) You can just about drink this wine, but it's faded and hollow. It has some traces of mushroom, but the flavours have dried out and it's past its drinking age. (HH)

It's almost impossible to believe the **1963** Bin 64 Cabernet is 45 years old. It still tastes of primary fresh damson plum fruit. The satin, soft, cushioned texture and sweet, remarkably long flavour suggest greater maturity. This must be one of the youngest oldest wines I have ever tasted. This could last another decade or two. (JG) It's still fresh with liquorice, leather, tobacco leaves and sweet, smooth, wood spiced liquorice fruit. It's best to drink up now. (CPT) After the initial fusty notes blew off, it revealed rich blackcurrant, dark chocolate characters and substantial but not assertive tannins. (JH)

1964 Bin 707 Cabernet Sauvignon was more potent than 1963 with ravishing, refined silken texture. It still has flesh and plenty of supportive structure. It's sweetly flushed and far from fading. The wine finishes clear and fresh. (NB) I really loved this wine. It's a seriously good wine; aromatic, varietal, intact and beautiful through the mouth, long through the finish and sliced with tannin. (CM)

'*Kalimna is and always will be the backbone of Grange Hermitage.*
To Max Schubert, it is the best red wine vineyard in Australia.
End of discussion.'
—HUON HOOKE, *MAX SCHUBERT—WINEMAKER*

1996 Block 42 Cabernet Sauvignon is still showing a tinge of purple. However, it's already showing some old floral/rose petal/cabernet aromas. The palate is mellow and getting fairly mature now but it still has a firm tannin spine. It has great intensity, yet softness, great line and length. It's lovely now but I can imagine this improving further. (HH) This was pure Barossa muscle with pure cassis aromas with some powerful tobacco notes and complex coffee/mocha oak. Those saturated curranty flavours extend across the palate forever. It's barely showing any maturity. This could last for as long as the 1963 or the 1953. (JG)

2004 Block 42 Cabernet Sauvignon is very impressive with intense cassis and a whiff of herbaceousness. The fruit is juicy and fresh with silky Rolls-Royce tannins. The fruit and tannins are sealed by round acidity. It's just richly balanced and very elegant in style. (CPT) This was a very opulent wine with blackberry, blueberry, incense aromas and gloriously refined texture. The flavours were saturated without being heavy. There was a grace and lightness on the palate. The wine was astonishing. (NB) It was as inky and deep in the mouth as the bouquet suggested. This is really a *Vin de Garde* in every respect. The fruit and oak tannins are in a titanic struggle, simply because they are in balance.

The Block 42 Cabernet Sauvignon is a true monopole-type wine that resonates a unique terroir. There are no walls or grand entrance gate to this historic property, but the wine is absolutely pure and derives solely from a single distinguished vineyard. (PG) Clearly this is a very special site; there is a beauty and energy of fruit, richness and floating quality to all the wines. There was something naturally expressive and wonderful about them all. (NB) These are great cabernets in every sense but they have nothing to do with Bordeaux. (CPT) But they are in every respect glorious and lasting First Growth quality wines. (JG)

Bin 60A Cabernet Sauvignon Shiraz

First Vintage:	Only ever released in 1962 and 2004.
Variety:	Cabernet sauvignon and shiraz.
Origin:	1962:
	Coonawarra cabernet sauvignon—Sharam's Block and Block 20.
	Shiraz—Kalimna Vineyards' original shiraz blocks.
	2004:
	56% cabernet sauvignon—Block 20, Coonawarra; 44% shiraz—
	Kalimna Blocks 4 & 14; Koonunga Hill Block 53G, Barossa Valley
Fermentation 1962 Bin 60A:	Wax-lined concrete fermenters with wooden header boards to submerge cap at Magill.
Fermentation 2004 Bin 60A:	Vinification took place at Magill and Nuriootpa. 10-tonne stainless steel static fermenters with inbuilt header boards at Nuriootpa. Wax-lined concrete fermenters with wooden header boards at Magill. Temperature maintained at less than 22° C. Daily rack and returns.
Maturation:	Fermentation completed in new oak. Approximately 12–15 months' maturation in American oak hogsheads (300 litres).
Comments:	1962 Bin 60A is arguably the most famous wine ever produced by Penfolds. Released under screw cap in some markets since the 2004 vintage.

'Bin 60A is regarded as one of the greatest
Australian wines made in living memory.'

—HUON HOOKE, PANELLIST

1962 Penfolds Bin 60A is one of the greatest Australian wines ever made. In a world where egos readily clashed, the 1962 Penfolds Bin 60A Kalimna Shiraz Coonawarra Cabernet unified wine critics and show judges. It is Penfolds' most successful show wine, winning nineteen trophies and 33 gold medals. A confluence of oenological, physical and philosophical achievement, 1962 Bin 60A was a cross-regional blend which exemplified the emerging Penfolds house wine style and highlighted the extraordinary synthesis of aromas and flavours derived from blending cabernet and shiraz. The seductive plum, dark chocolate aromas, fruit intensity, flavour richness, immense structure and ageing potential are hallmarks of Kalimna shiraz. In seeking his 'ethereal' wine, Max Schubert identified that such warm climate characteristics could complement the perfumed cassis/violet aromas, elegant flavours and fine-grained tannins of cool-climate Coonawarra cabernet sauvignon.

Experimental Special Bin bottlings of two-thirds Kalimna shiraz/one-third Coonawarra cabernet sauvignon and an 'on-blend' of two-thirds Coonawarra cabernet sauvignon/one-third Kalimna shiraz were entered onto the Australian wine show circuit, generating plenty of debate among wine judges and winemakers.

The 'on-blend', 1962 Bin 60A, significantly outperformed its sibling rival 1962 Bin 60. Its brilliant show career and success challenged the traditional views of the day and showed a way forward for both Penfolds and the fledgling modern Australian wine industry. Bin 60, the 'off-blend', is largely forgotten; the wine was not widely released. Max Schubert once said, 'It was never up to the Bin 60A, but a bloody good wine.'

According to Peter Gago, the Bin 60A was fermented in the last Magill open fermenter closest to the Magill reception door. Old-timers say that the grapes were foot-crushed. Max Schubert fermented the wine in the classical Penfolds winemaking style using header boards and rack and returns. Towards completion of fermentation the wine was basket pressed and barrel fermented.

The fame of Bin 60A has reached all corners of the globe. Max Schubert's direct contemporary Andre Tchelistcheff (1901–94), the founding father of the modern Californian wine industry, once told a room of startled Napa Valley vignerons, 'Gentlemen you will all stand in the presence of this wine!' Australian winemakers generally acknowledge the wine as a modern classic of profound and enduring academic importance. Leading critic Len Evans (1930–2006), who apparently took that bottle to California, once described the wine as 'one of the great reds I cut my palate on, and proved forever that the two varieties can blend beautifully together'.

Harvey Steiman, editor-at-large for the influential American wine magazine *The Wine Spectator*, said: 'The first attempts at blending shiraz with cabernet hit the jackpot early. One of the most highly prized wines in Australia's history is Penfolds Bin 60A, a 1962 vintage blend of Barossa shiraz and Coonawarra cabernet. More than 30 years later, it remains a heady, rich, incredibly profound wine, one of the greatest wines I have tasted anywhere.'

In 2004, the 1962 Penfolds Bin 60A Coonawarra Cabernet Sauvignon Kalimna Shiraz was the only Australian wine to reach the Top 10 ranking of 'Wines to try before you die' in the UK's authoritative *Decanter Magazine*'s 100 Greatest Wines of all Time'. This list was compiled by a Who's Who of eminent wine critics and identities from around the world.

James Halliday, Australia's leading wine author and tasting panel member, described it as 'an utterly superb wine, a glorious freak of nature and man … The 100-point dry red? Why not!'

The success of 1962 Bin 60A and the launch of Bin 389 Cabernet Shiraz paved the way for a generation of new cabernet–shiraz styles and coincided with a substantial investment in Coonawarra. Ray Beckwith said in his memoirs, 'Max's blends of Dry Red were among the first Australian wines to show the influence of prolonged new oak storage (hogsheads of about 65 gallons). This procedure was adopted readily by other winemakers—and in some instances to such a degree that some of their wines showed excess oak, thereby masking the varietal aromas.'

The 2004 Penfolds Bin 60A Coonawarra Cabernet Sauvignon Barossa Shiraz, which was first offered to the public as a futures release (*en primeur*), is Peter Gago's gesture to the great 1962 Bin 60A. Exquisite parcels of Block 20 Coonawarra cabernet sauvignon, Koonunga Hill and Kalimna Vineyard Barossa shiraz were identified and separately vinified at Nuriootpa and Magill in open and closed headed-down fermenters. Towards dryness, the wine was racked into 100 per cent new oak barriques where the wine completed fermentation. After malolactic fermentation, individual components were classified and then selected for inclusion in the 2004 Bin 60A blend.

Peter Gago said, 'The 2004 Bin 60A is destined to become one of Penfolds' great Special Bin releases. The restraint, pure fruit and elegance of 2004 Block 20 Coonawarra Cabernet Sauvignon is complemented by the power and richness of the 2004 Kalimna and Koonunga Hill Barossa Shiraz. Barrel fermentation in oak has woven all the fruit and oak elements into a wine of immense generosity, depth and complexity. This classically structured, beautifully balanced wine has all the finesse and integrity to develop and evolve in the cellar for many decades.'

John Bird, former Penfolds Senior Winemaker and consultant who worked with Max Schubert on the original experimental wines, said, 'The 2004 Bin 60A has looked very close to the mark at all stages of its development so far. I think this will be seen as one of Penfolds' top wines of the last twenty years.' James Halliday said, 'This is a huge, complex, deep and intense wine; wrapped in a starless night sky. There are so many layers that it is impossible to unravel them yet.'

The Special Bins represent a revolution in Australian red winemaking and a testament to Max Schubert's genius and foresight. The *en primeur* releases of the superb 2004 Block 42 Cabernet Sauvignon and 2004 Bin 60A Coonawarra Cabernet Barossa Shiraz continue a Penfolds great winemaking tradition of making Special Bin wines for the enjoyment and interest of Penfolds wine collectors and wine enthusiasts.

TASTING NOTES ~ BIN 60A CABERNET SAUVIGNON SHIRAZ

1962   Bin 60A Coonawarra Cabernet Sauvignon Kalimna Shiraz   ★   NOW

Deep brick red. Lovely classical and ethereal Penfolds wine with beautiful cigar box/polished leather/sandalwood/apricot aromas with touches of herb garden. Remarkably buoyant, soft and supple wine with meaty/cedar wood/sweet-fruit flavours and fine, lacy/silky tannins. The finish is endless; almost without vanishing point. Utterly superb. Arguably the greatest Australian wine of the era.

2004

Bin 60A Coonawarra Cabernet Sauvignon Barossa Valley Shiraz   ★ 2015 • • • 2050

Deep crimson/purple. Magnificently perfumed, intense, fathomless wine with striking plum/blackcurrant/aniseed aromas and ginger/vanillin/smoky nuances. The palate is sumptuous and velvet-textured with beautiful juicy plum/blackcurrant/liquorice/roasted coffee flavours, underlying savoury oak and chocolaty smooth tannins. It finishes brambly and endlessly deep and long. A spectacular, infinitely complex and generous wine. Truly exceptional.

DISCUSSION

1962 Bin 60A Coonawarra Cabernet Sauvignon Kalimna Shiraz

An utterly superb wine, a glorious freak of nature and man; ethereal and beguiling, yet the palate is virtually endless, with a peacock's tail stolen from the greatest of Burgundies; the fruit sweetness perfectly offset by acidity rather than voltaic acidity. The 100-point dry red? Why not! This is possibly the greatest red wine tasted in our times in Australia. It won't go on forever; it's probably at the tail end of its plateau. (JH) An ethereal wine. It has a presence in the glass beyond most of its brethren. It has lovely, bright red berry, grilled fig, sandalwood, cedar characters and extreme length of flavour. Seems it will last forever. (JG)

2004 Bin 60A Coonawarra Cabernet Sauvignon Barossa Valley Shiraz

This is a perfectly constructed wine. The tannin is significant but laced right through the fruit, working to soften the impact, but not its function. It's powerful, high in finesse with dark, juicy, lively fruit. This is a magnificently perfumed, great cabernet–shiraz. (CM) This is a huge, complex, deep and intense wine; wrapped in a starless night sky. There are so many layers that it is impossible to unravel them yet. (JH) It was composed and harmonious but almost luridly vivid with black glossy fruit; exotic and incense like. The palate was dense, plush and richly fruited. It has still to settle down on the finish. (NB)

Others

First Vintage:	1948 Kalimna Cabernet Sauvignon is the first known Special Bin-type wine. There are an astonishing number of 'one-off' releases, often limited to a single barrel or micro-blend.
Variety:	Generally based on shiraz and cabernet sauvignon. Mataro (mourvèdre) occasionally used.
Origin:	Multi-regional sourcing. Block 20, Coonawarra cabernet sauvignon, Kalimna and Koonunga Hill shiraz feature regularly.
Fermentation:	Stainless steel tanks with wooden header boards to submerge cap at Nuriootpa. Wax-lined concrete open fermenters at Magill. Fermentation completed in new oak.
Maturation:	Approximately 15 months in new American oak hogsheads (300 litres).
Comments:	Special Bins are exceptional parcels of limited-release wines especially made to highlight winemaking advances, experiments of interest or vintages of significant importance.

'The positive advances in the practice and technology of winemaking over a period of a working lifetime illustrate the old adage that succeeding generations are able to stand on the shoulders of their predecessors.'
— RAY BECKWITH,
PENFOLDS RESEARCH CHEMIST

The sheer output of Special Bins produced during the 1950s and '60s is simply extraordinary. Most releases were works in progress reflecting the ideas, convictions and

vineyard resources of the time. While Penfolds is famous for its house style winemaking philosophy and multi-regional blending, it is important to note that the nuances of vineyard site have always been the tangible yet enigmatic wildcard. Max Schubert's most successful Special Bins were based on the relatively new Penfolds vineyard acquisitions at Kalimna, Barossa Valley, and Sharam's Block in Coonawarra.

The rare 1957 Bin 14 Minchinbury Dry Red, made by veteran winemaker Ivan Combet, was a special bin to commemorate the last red wine vintage at the historic Minchinbury Estate. The property, on the soon-to-be-urbanised western plains of Sydney, was originally granted to Captain Minchin—a veteran of Wellington's Peninsular War—in 1821 by Governor Macquarie. Penfolds purchased the estate in 1912. Leo Buring, one of the great pioneer winemakers of the early twentieth century, was instrumental in establishing the reputation of the Minchinbury vineyard.

During the 1950s, Penfolds Minchinbury Champagne and Minchinbury Trameah were the leading sparkling and white table wines produced in Australia. The Minchinbury brand still exists but it is no longer a Penfolds wine. The vineyard was also planted to gamay, shiraz, pinot noir and cabernet. The 1957 Minchinbury Bin 14 Dry Red was described by Max Lake in 1966 as 'developing now into a superb true Claret; complex perfume, austere flavour and austere grip on the finish'. Remarkably this old relic was 'still very much alive' in 2007!

Not much is known about the limited release 1962 Bin 434 Coonawarra Cabernet Shiraz except that it was bottled at Auldana. It is quite possible that it belonged to the same trials as Bin 60 and Bin 60A. Coonawarra, long resisted by Max Schubert as a source of premium fruit, was in some respects a fait accompli; during the early 1960s, Penfolds was increasingly under pressure to sell off its vineyard holdings in and around Adelaide. It simply needed to plan for continuity of supply.

When Penfolds purchased Bill Redman's Sharam's Block vineyard, Schubert was initially quite concerned about the reliability and vintage consistency of this cool-climate, maritime-influenced region. Cabernet sauvignon, with its thick skins and small berries, can be quite sinewy in texture, particularly after a cool growing season. Indeed, up to this period, Coonawarra was more famous for its shiraz-based wines. While the vineyard characteristics of Kalimna were generally appreciated, many of the early trials were attempts to understand the nuances of both Coonawarra cabernet and shiraz fruit.

1966 Bin 620 Cabernet Sauvignon—a single varietal Coonawarra wine—was almost as famous as Bin 60A. It enjoyed plenty of success at Australia's major capital wine shows. As a younger wine it was almost always talked about whenever Bin 60A was mentioned. The wine was considered a classical 'Claret'-style wine. Wine judges of the day would have been impressed by the overall volume of fruit, concentration and substantial extract, elements that would have suggested long-term ageing potential. The wine has indeed lasted, but it does not have the shivering wraith-like quality of Bin 60A; the fruit is tiring now and the tannins are incredibly muscular.

1967 Bin 7—also a two-thirds Coonawarra cabernet sauvignon one-third Kalimna shiraz blend—was a famous show wine of its day, but it never reached the legendary status of Bin 60A. All the same, it still commands plenty of interest in the secondary market; it remains a compelling and enduring follow-up to its older sibling.

1973 Bin 169 and Bin 170, which were both released as single-region wines, were originally earmarked as blending companions—a 1970s version of Bin 60A. While 1973 was not considered a particularly good vintage, John Bird said that each component was 'pretty good'. Each component comprised roughly 750 gallons (3412.5 litres): 'Chris Hancock and I were told not to blend the wine. We were both a bit disappointed because the wine wasn't far off the Bin 60A or Bin 7 mark!' Considering these wines were never made for drinking in the 21st century, they have both held on remarkably well and are evidence of Penfolds' technical advantage of the time. Don Ditter, who took over from Max Schubert in 1973 as National Production Manager, said, 'maintaining freshness at bottling was considered of paramount importance. Winemakers talk about ripeness of fruit, blending options and maturation period. All decisions are based on timing; when to pick, length of fermentation, etc. Picking the right time to bottle is a skill in itself.' Both of the 1973s reached their full maturity many years ago, but the wines remain remarkably fresh considering the vintage and overall age.

The release of Bin 80A, Bin 820, Bin 90A and Bin 920 was—as their names suggest—a homage to Max Schubert and his two most famous experimental vintages. Using special parcels of fruit, these wines were largely vinified, matured and blended to Max Schubert's original specifications.

1980 Bin 80A and 1982 Bin 820 caused a sensation when they were released during the mid-1980s. This was a period of great excitement. Cool-climate wines, particularly from Margaret River, Coonawarra and Victoria, were gathering momentum. Despite its reputation for its big ripe chocolaty reds, Penfolds was more popular than ever. While Max Schubert had retired in 1976, he became a heroic figure in Australian 'wine lore' during the 1980s. Grange was on a stellar trajectory. The release of Bin 80A and Bin 820 gave the opportunity for collectors and critics to compare, contrast and appreciate the remarkable contribution of Max Schubert. While Don Ditter was responsible for this release, Schubert, who maintained an office at Magill, continued to mentor the red winemaking team. The wines would never have been released without his blessing; both vintages are indelibly marked with Schubert's fingerprints. These are fresh, buoyant wines with tremendous fruit volume, richness and understated power.

The remarkably fresh and youthful 1980 Bin 80A is based on parcels of Coonawarra cabernet sauvignon and Kalimna shiraz. With similar characteristics to the great 1962 Bin 60A, the wine is still yet to reach a peak of maturity. 1982 Bin 820—a Coonawarra cabernet sauvignon shiraz—derives from a controversial but interesting vintage. At one point the 1982 Coonawarra vintage was hailed as one of the greatest years ever. The growing season had been warm and hot with some good top-up rains in late spring. At release the wine—considered a *Vin de Garde*—showed outstanding pure blackcurrant/cassis aromas, beautiful fine-grained tannins and underlying savoury oak. Vintage personality pervades the wine. The exaggerated cherry/cassis fruit characters are typical of this Coonawarra vintage.

The 1990 Bin 90A and 1990 Bin 920 are John Duval's reprise of Schubert's famous experimental opus. These are both magnificent wines with the puissance and generosity of a very great Australian vintage. They capture the essence of

Penfolds' winemaking philosophy and style. Peter Gago says, 'these wines are some of the greatest Penfolds vintages of the modern era'.

The Penfolds Special Bins have been described as a remarkable body of work comprising the good, the great, the avant-garde, the postmodern and the curious. The most recent releases continue Max Schubert's vision of finding something new and interesting for avid Penfolds collectors. These wines also recognise the significant importance and sublime quality of Penfolds' classic Barossa and Coonawarra vineyards.

TASTING NOTES ~ SPECIAL RED BINS

1956   Bin 136 Magill Burgundy   PAST

Medium deep brick red. Overdeveloped wine with molasses/treacle/dark chocolate/herb garden aromas. Deep-set meaty/molasses/toffee flavours and fine-grained, slinky, dry tannins. Finishes bittersweet. It's just holding but it's definitely past its best. Also released as Bin S56 Magill Burgundy.

1957   Bin 14 Minchinbury Dry Red   PAST

Medium deep colour. Very old and complex wine with prune/crème brûlée/farmyardy aromas. The palate is still showing some fruit sweetness with leathery flavours and rusty firm tannins. It's well past its prime now but is still an interesting curio. Bottled and matured before release at Penfolds Tempe, New South Wales.

1962   Bin 60 Kalimna Shiraz Coonawarra Cabernet Sauvignon   NOW • • • PAST

Increasingly rare wine. At previous tastings this wine has shown fully mature aromas and flavours, plenty of sweet fruit and leafy, dry tannins. Some bottles are now fading.

1962   Bin 434 Coonawarra Cabernet Shiraz   PAST

Deep brick red. Very evolved wine with earthy/red cherry/dark chocolate/leather/treacle aromas. The palate is a touch maderised with dark chocolate/earthy flavours and firm, chalky dry tannins. Bottled at Auldana. Some bottles holding.

1966   Bin 620 Coonawarra Cabernet Sauvignon Shiraz   PAST

Brick red. Complex liquorice/mulberry/leafy/menthol/brine/boot polish aromas and flavours. The palate is still substantial and muscular with plenty of rich, evolved mulberry/bitumen/sweet-fruit flavours and dominatingly strong, firm tannins.

1967   Bin 7 Coonawarra Cabernet Sauvignon Kalimna Shiraz   ★   NOW

Brick red. Intense blackcurrant/mushroom/autumnal *sous bois* aromas with some leather/sandalwood notes. The palate is mellow, but rich and full with liquorice, mocha, blackcurrant/mushroom flavours and loose-knit leafy tannins. In remarkably good shape. Drink soon.

1973   Bin 169 Coonawarra Claret   ★   NOW

Brick red. Mature mulberry/cassis/cedar/mocha/graphite aromas. Sweet mocha/blackcurrant/herb flavours and fine, dry, hard tannins. Believed to be 100% cabernet sauvignon. Also bottled as Bin CC (Coonawarra Cabernet). Drink up.

1973   Bin 170 Kalimna Shiraz ★   NOW

Brick red. Fresh raspberry/cassis/earthy/tomato leaf aromas. Sweet meaty/earthy/blackcurrant pastille/mint flavours and supple tannins. Builds up cedary firm at the finish. Smells and tastes like cabernet sauvignon! Still holding.

1980

Bin 80A Coonawarra Cabernet Sauvignon Kalimna Shiraz ★   NOW • • • 2025

Brick red. Complex smoky/sweet cassis/cedar/shellac aromas with touch of mint. Fresh, smooth, sweet, smoky/cassis/cedar/leather flavours and abundant chocolaty dry tannins. Finishes grippy firm but long and sweet. A well-concentrated, solid wine with attractive mature fruit and strong tannin structure. Considered a classic Penfolds vintage. Will still benefit from further cellaring.

1982   Bin 820 Coonawarra Cabernet Sauvignon Shiraz   NOW

Brick red. Intense but exaggerated cassis/sour cherry/raspberry essence aromas. Medium concentrated wine with sweet and sour but soft cherry/cassis/earthy flavours and chalky, firm, loose-knit tannins. Elegantly proportioned wine. Drink now.

1990

Bin 90A Coonawarra Cabernet Sauvignon Kalimna Shiraz ★   NOW • • • 2030

Liquorice/pure blackcurrant/malty aromas with some cedar/herb garden notes. The palate is beautifully balanced and seductive with deep-set pure blackberry/mocha/herb garden flavours, underlying malty oak and plentiful, ripe, loose-knit tannins. It finishes savoury, firm and gorgeously long. A great Penfolds wine. You can drink it now but best to keep.

1990   Bin 920 Coonawarra Cabernet Sauvignon Shiraz ★   2010 • • • 2030

Deep crimson. Intense ethereal blackberry/bramble/herb garden/graphite aromas. A very concentrated, rich, luscious wine with ripe blackberry/bramble/sweet-fruit flavours and lashings of fine, grainy tannins. It finishes firm, but long, penetrating and sweet. An immaculately composed evocative wine with decades of cellaring potential. You can drink it now but best to keep.

DISCUSSION

1956 Penfolds Bin 136 Magill Burgundy

This had a beautiful nose with rich mocha/mint/toffee aromas with stemmy/spicy aromas. Elegantly rich, gloriously silken, round and rolling, it still had freshness, harmony and balance. (NB) The wine has plenty of honey, molasses, chocolate, honeycomb, meaty characters. It's very old now and a bit frail with some bitterness. (HH) Sandalwood and prunes on the nose. The palate is sweet spiced/leather/prune fruit that is supple and juicy. This 51 year old is still reasonably fresh, always a good yardstick for measuring a great wine. (CPT)

1957 Bin 14 Minchinbury Dry Red

The wine was very much alive with quite powerful black fruits and evident tannins. Spicy, earthy, savoury characters surround sweet fruit on the mid palate. (JH) It looks pretty good. Clearly it's a rustic style with farmyard, toasty, coffee aromas and rusty tannins. It's past its prime but it's still remarkably drinkable. (CM)

1962 Bin 434 Coonawarra Cabernet Shiraz

The wine is a bit tired and fading with cedar, bittersweet chocolate aromas and oxidised/maderised flavours. (JG) I liked this wine. It smelled of warm pudding, toast and leather. I loved the interplay between the old, leathery flavours and sponge-like tannins. It's hard and taut on the finish, but it puts on an enchanting show in getting there. (CM)

1966 Bin 620 Coonawarra Cabernet Sauvignon Shiraz

It is still in good shape with treacle, leather, toast, beef stock, bitter salty characters and firm palate structure. (CM) It has elegance and an ethereal quality with mocha, sandalwood aromas and refined silken entry. It becomes a little syrupy on the mid-palate. It doesn't have the finesse of other Special Bins but it still has very good length of flavour. (NB)

1967 Bin 7 Coonawarra Cabernet Sauvignon Kalimna Shiraz

A wine that has waxed and waned over the last 30 years; as soon as you think it's fading, it bounces back. It had an entrancing mix of blackberry and blackcurrant in a vibrant silky/glossy palate. The tannins were just sufficient for the structure. (JH) This was a very old and mellow wine but in sound condition with liquorice, mocha, coffee fruit and pronounced rustic tannins. It's quite robust really. (HH)

1973 Bin 169 Coonawarra Claret

It has a very aged, amber, tawny colour. It is still recognisably a Coonawarra wine, with mulberry, cassis, cedar aromas. It's quite intense and concentrated with mouth-coating, grippy tannins. It's hard work tasting this wine. (HH) It lacks grace now. While it has black fruit, cedar characters, it's very stemmy and tannic. It's well past its prime. (JG)

1973 Bin 170 Kalimna Shiraz

This wine had an opaque brick red colour. It had some cool mint characters on entering the mouth, filling out to plum, spice and blackberry. The tannins are soft and the oak is unobtrusive. (JH) I found the tannins were quite coarse and astringent. This is definitely a shiraz but there was a rustic quality to the wine. (HH) I found it a touch oxidised. The palate was rich and soupy but it dried on the finish. (NB)

1980 Bin 80A Coonawarra Cabernet Sauvignon Kalimna Shiraz

This was a luminous wine with fresh, sweet leather and good mint characters and a sound finish. (CM) I loved this wine. It had a very clear, bright and healthy colour with some signs of brick. It had lovely, bell-clear cassis and blackberry fruits juxtaposed against silky, smooth tannins and very good oak. It is at the peak of development but it will hold. (JH)

1982 Bin 820 Coonawarra Cabernet Sauvignon

This is developing deliciously, with soft leather, mint, mulberries and plum fruits. This is terrific Penfolds drinking. (CM) It had an exaggerated raspberry cordial nose. It is a lighter bodied eccentric style that lacks depth, concentration and power. The tannins are unbalanced. (HH) This is something of a love it or hate it wine. The jury is ordinarily split 50/50 whenever Bin 820 is shown to experts. (PG)

1990 Bin 90A Coonawarra Cabernet Sauvignon Kalimna Shiraz

This wine had astonishing cassis, incense-like intensity. The palate was amply cushioned, rich and thick. (NB) This was a very big, solid, firm and tight wine. While it has massive tannins, it is structured superbly. It's very powerful, deep and long. This is a whopper that needs further time; it's barely drinking yet. (HH) This was a beautiful wine—I prefer it to the 1990 Grange. It was bright and red-fruited with lush, delicious ripe flavours and savoury tannins. (JG)

1990 Bin 920 Coonawarra Cabernet Sauvignon Shiraz

This wine is still in its infancy, with amazing, intense, long and penetrating cassis, blackcurrant fruit. It's a truly beautiful wine which will change but not diminish for three decades. (JH) It had plenty of sweet berry, slightly exaggerated cassis aromas zooming through the nose. It's very concentrated, rich, luscious and powerful with lashings of tannins. It needs years yet. (HH)

CHAPTER NINE

Cellar Reserve Wines

The Cellar Reserve label—established by Peter Gago as an ongoing project— harks back to the experimental bins of the 1950s and '60s when Penfolds released special limited bottlings of works in progress for collectors and visitors to the cellar door. Originally these limited release wines were earmarked for cellar door (Magill and Nuriootpa) and premium restaurants, however, they have quickly established a strong following among collectors and wine enthusiasts across the globe. The wines have been developed without the normal constraints of the mainstream wine market. Penfolds is known for its strong and clearly articulated winemaking philosophy based on techniques developed by Max Schubert and his team. These wines are not widely available but always worth seeking out.

The Cellar Reserve label—based on special vineyards and micro-sites, new varietals, innovative vinification practices and trial and error—substantially reflects a more personal winemaking approach. These are essentially handcrafted boutique wines made in the spirit of creating something different and interesting. Often sold by hand and personal experience rather than conventional marketing, the Cellar Reserves are truly 'conversation wines', giving collectors and enthusiasts the opportunity to engage with winemakers and sommeliers at a more personal level, and are not beholden to a chronological vintage order. The Cellar Reserve range is a project in progress—a zinfandel, tempranillo, chardonnay and pinot gris are planned for release in the future.

REDS

Cellar Reserve Sangiovese

First Vintage:	1997 experimental, 1998 commercial.
Variety:	Sangiovese.
Origin:	Barossa Valley.
Fermentation:	Vinified in open fermenters. Natural yeasts.
Maturation:	11 months in up to 6-year-old French oak barriques— 'as old as you can get them!'

'The wines were a revelation; the integrity and purity of fruit sings through with lovely transparency of flavours and tannin structures.'
— NEIL BECKETT, PANELLIST

The early Cellar Reserve Sangiovese vintages were trial wines made from eight rows of vines planted at Kalimna in 1982 in conjunction with the South Australian Department of Agriculture. During the early 1990s, Penfolds' red winemaking team made several unreleased experimental wines to establish a clear direction of style. Encouraged by the results, a few Barossa growers including Paul Georgiadis, Penfolds Grower Liaison Manager, planted their own blocks of sangiovese during the mid-1990s. This Italian variety has adapted extremely well to Australian conditions. Indeed, the flaxen Barossa landscape punctuated with fields of yellow canola and purple Salvation Jane is reminiscent of the rolling Tuscan countryside. The fruit is particularly intense, with small berries, strong colours, deep flavours and slinky, dry tannin structures. Since the first commercial vintage in 1998, the wines have steadily improved in both definition and character. A chance exchange visit by Stefano di Blasi from the Italian wine house Antinori—who suggested a number of vinification techniques, including longer maceration on skins—had a profound effect on the style.

Peter Gago, Penfolds Chief Winemaker, said, 'The Cellar Reserve Sangiovese has evolved impressively over the last ten years. The wines are unmistakably Penfolds in style, yet articulate the essence of sangiovese. The wines are very deep in colour, incredibly perfumed and seductive with fresh black cherry aromas and velvety textured tannins. The wines are the "purest" made by Penfolds. By that I mean no added yeast, no pH correction, no new oak, no addition of any other variety, no fining, no filtration. Literally the only thing in the bottle other than crushed and fermented sangiovese grapes is a small addition of SO_2—an anti-oxidant and antimicrobial agent used in winemaking since Roman times.' The wines are vinified in open headed-down fermenters at Nuriootpa and then allowed to macerate for five weeks on skins before being basket pressed.

Ch'ng Poh Tiong observed that 'when the tannins are right, the flavours follow through beautifully. The most recent vintages are very modern with freshness and balance.' James Halliday said, 'The Cellar Reserve Sangiovese tasting was the biggest and most pleasant surprise of all. Since 2001 the wines are seriously impressive, with excellent varietal definition and character.' Neil Beckett agreed: 'The wines are a revelation; the integrity and purity of fruit sings through with lovely transparency of flavours and tannin structures.'

TASTING NOTES ~ CELLAR RESERVE SANGIOVESE

1998   NOW • • • 2012

Medium crimson. Red cherry/crushed raspberries/tobacco/meaty aromas with some earthy notes. The palate is evolved with earthy/red cherry flavours and slinky, dry, loose-knit tannins. Finishes chalky firm with some cherry essence notes.

1999   NOW • • • 2012

Medium deep crimson. Fresh red cherry/dark chocolate/iodine aromas with hints of herb garden. A gravelly, firm wine with red cherry/inky/dark chocolate flavours and dense, pronounced tannins. Finishes firm and tight.

2000   NOW

Medium deep crimson. Dark cherry/raspberry aromas with some herb garden/sea breezy notes. Sweet buoyant concentrated wine with dark cherry/prune flavours and loose-knit chalky tannins. The wine finishes slinky and long. Needs to be drunk soon.

2001   NOW • • • 2012

Medium deep crimson. Complex dark chocolate/bitumen/graphite aromas with some cherry stone notes. The palate is solid and strongly flavoured with dark chocolate/cherry/graphite flavours and hard, long tannins. Finishes sinewy and dry but the wine has plenty of fruit sweetness.

2002 ★   NOW • • • 2016

Deep crimson. Deep dark cherry/dark chocolate/tobacco aromas with touches of wet bitumen. The palate is deep-set and concentrated with roasted/dark cherry/dark chocolate flavours and dry, powdery, savoury tannins. Builds up firm and tight at the finish. Has lovely balance and flavour length.

2003   NOW • • • 2018

Medium deep colour. Fresh classical wine with dark cherry/redcurrant/raspberry/musky aromas and dark chocolate/herb garden nuances. Well-concentrated, fruit-sweet palate with plum/redcurrant flavours and fine, slinky, dry tannins. Finishes very firm and chalky.

2004 ★   NOW • • • 2018

Medium colour. A lovely, fragrant wine with red cherry/savoury/aromas and some scented camomile/herb garden notes. The palate is really well balanced with fresh, minerally, red cherry/savoury/tobacco flavours and chalky, loose-knit tannins. The wine finishes supple and long.

Medium deep colour. Fresh briary/rose petal/plum/red cherry/violet aromas. Plenty of fruit volume on the palate with briary/plum/dark chocolate/tobacco flavours, and sweet, textured, fine-grained tannins. Finishes chalky and firm, savoury and sweet.

2006 ★   2008 • • • 2020

Deep colour. Fresh juicy blackberry/briary/red cherry/bay leaf aromas. A very fruit-driven wine with plummy/juicy fruit/red cherry/redcurrant flavours, some savoury notes and chalky firm tannins. The fruit is really dense and sweet. A very seductive, velvety wine.

DISCUSSION

This has to be one of the biggest and most pleasant surprises of all the Rewards of Patience tastings. I have never shared an enthusiasm for Italian varietals but this was a seriously impressive tasting. (JH)

1998 had a lovely immediacy with supple tannins and correctly dry finish. (NB)

1999 was inky and smooth with some charcuterie notes, well-saturated flavours and plush tannins. (NB)

2000 is salty and savoury with a dry finish. It is distinctly odd in this company. (NB)

2001 had excellent varietal definition and lovely filigreed and lingering tannins. (JH) It was very impressive with a deep, layered, textured quality. (NB)

2002 had greater intensity and colour retention with more precise fruit and savoury tannins, perhaps reflecting a cooler vintage. (JH) The wine was parched with puckering savoury tannins. (NB)

2003 shows an obvious shift towards Marananga fruit. The tannins are finer and a cedar/tobacco fruit profile starts appearing. (JH) I really enjoyed the exotic zinfandel-like quality and silken texture of the 2003. (NB)

2004 was beguiling and harmonious with tremendous flavour length. (NB) The last three vintages (2004, 2005 and 2006) were the best wines, with beautiful fruit definition and natural balance. (JH)

2005 was surprisingly earthier with good density and considerable flavour. (NB) 2004, 2005 and 2006 were a significant step up from the rest. When the tannins are right the flavours will follow through. (CPT) 2005 is probably a bit shy so we are going to leave it in bottle for an extra year. 2006 will be released earlier. (PG)

2006 is an exciting wine with freshness, richness and excellent tannin structure. (NB) This particular wine has vast volume of fruit and velvety texture. (JH)

Cellar Reserve Pinot Noir

First Vintage:	1995 experimental, 1997 commercial.
Variety:	Pinot noir.
Origin:	Adelaide Hills and sometimes a small amount from Eden Valley.
Fermentation:	Cold soaked for up to 7 days and batch vinified (up to 30% whole bunch) in open fermenters. No pressings included. Natural yeasts.
Maturation:	11 months in 1-year-old and up to 70% new French oak.

'A fascinating evolution of style which ultimately triumphs with freshness of fruit, strengthening richness and overall stature.'
—JOSHUA GREENE, PANELLIST

The 1997 Cellar Reserve Pinot Noir was first released after a series of winemaking trials by Peter Gago at Magill Estate. The fruit has always been sourced from various cool-climate vineyard sites along the spine of the Adelaide Hills. The overall style is a work in progress. It simply takes years to understand the nuances and character of individual vineyard sites. The idea of optimum quality is ever changing against the backdrop of vintage conditions, pinot noir clone, vine maturity, new vineyards and ongoing winemaking experimentation in the cellars.

Penfolds and independent growers work closely to achieve the best results. Generally winemakers are looking for a variation of a specific fruit profile theme. No parcel of fruit is ever exactly the same. However, the required standards are achieved through intuitive tasting and basic field-testing of grapes in the vineyards. Once the fruit arrives in the winery, it is cold soaked for up to seven days in open fermenters to maximise colour and flavour extraction. The wine is then vinified (30 per cent whole bunch) using natural yeasts. A percentage (roughly 40 per cent) of stalks is allowed to remain in the ferment to achieve more complexity, tannin structure and vinosity.

Small batch winemaking practice is central to the overall style of the Cellar Reserve Pinot Noir. Around the clock hand plunging (pigeage) to further optimise flavours takes place until the wine approaches dryness. After completion of fermentation, the wine is run off into a proportion of mainly new and one-year-old French Dargaud and Jaegle, Seguin Moreau, Demptos, Nadalie and Sirugue oak barriques for maturation of around eleven months. Peter Gago says it is essentially a boutique wine using small batch winemaking philosophy: 'We use no pressings and we never add any sulphur dioxide until we have racked the wine off its gross lees immediately prior to bottling. It then goes through a natural malolactic fermentation.'

After ten years the Cellar Reserve Pinot Noir is showing a clear stamp of origin. Joshua Greene observed, 'a fascinating evolution of style which ultimately triumphs with freshness of fruit, strengthening richness and overall stature'. Penfolds will continue to experiment and refine the Cellar Reserve Pinot Noir. Presently the wine is best to drink when fresh and young. The best vintages can age and gain further complexity and richness with a few years in the cellar. The wine is bottled unfiltered.

1997   PAST

Medium deep crimson. Fragrant earthy/strawberry/sandalwood aromas with some herb garden notes. Well-concentrated palate with mature strawberry/earthy/sappy flavours and savoury, loose-knit tannins.

1998   NOW

Deep crimson. Dried plum/silage aromas with some herbal/animal notes. The palate is sappy and sweet with plum/chocolate/leafy flavours and fine, loose-knit, chalky tannins. Finishes quite grippy.

1999 ★   NOW • • • 2010

Medium deep crimson. Intense black cherry/strawberry aromas with black olive/barnyard notes. Soft, fleshy palate with nice texture, suppleness and slinky, dry tannins. Finishes bone dry but good flavour length.

2000   NOW

Medium deep crimson. Very fragrant violet/stalky/spearmint aromas with some dry straw/mulch notes. Powerfully structured and concentrated wine with red cherry/sappy flavours and harsh tannins.

2001   NOW

Mature deep crimson. Intense silage/chocolate/polished-leather aromas. The palate is rich and concentrated with raisiny flavours, dry, chocolaty tannins and some stemmy notes. It finishes harsh and astringent.

2002 ★   NOW

Medium crimson. Intense spearmint/redcurrant/raspberry aromas. Redcurrant/plum/minty flavours and fine, chalky, loose-knit tannins. Long finish. Bottled in claret-style bottle by mistake.

2003   NOW

Medium crimson. Evolved chocolaty/red berry aromas and some sappy notes. Developed earthy/redcurrant flavours with savoury, dry tannins. Finishes long and sweet.

2004 ★   NOW • • • 2012

Medium crimson. Fresh strawberry/dark cherry aromas with some toasty, new oak characters. Well-concentrated sweet strawberry/raspberry flavours with savoury, loose-knit, dry tannins and underlying oak. Finishes long and sweet. Lovely freshness and volume with potential to improve.

2005   NOW • • • 2010

Medium crimson. Rich, dense, tannic wine with strawberry/cherry/sappy aromas and flavours. The palate is fleshy and concentrated with grainy tannins and plenty of flavour length. Builds up slinky dry at the finish. Probably best to drink soon.

Medium deep crimson. Fresh strawberry/plum/mint aromas with some cherry stone notes. A fleshy rich palate with dense tannins and plenty of sweet plum/black fruit flavours. Finishes firm and long.

DISCUSSION

The more recent vintages are quite frankly better than many Italians. At first I was quite suspicious of the depth of colour. I was afraid the wines would be over-extracted. The wines, however, are a revelation; the integrity and purity of fruit sings through with lovely transparency of flavours and tannin structures. It was a wholly impressive flight. (NB)

This tasting illustrated a fascinating evolution of style, which ultimately triumphs with freshness of fruit, strengthening richness and overall stature. (JG)

1997, **1998** and **1999** showed plenty of stem characters but as vintages progressed the wines show better balance with more fruit generosity, silken textures and high-toned freshness. I was surprised by the level of stemminess, but it seems to pay off in some vintages such as the 1998. (NB)

2003 was a textural pleasure with roundness and warmth. (JG) **2004** is one of the best on the table with depth of fruit and tannin refinement. (JG) **2005** has plenty of flesh and bone and is a major step forward. (JG)

2006 has a richness and complexity reminiscent of Pommard. (JG) I found the wine bizarre, with its mint chocolate nuances, but the tannins are impressively plush. It will certainly develop but it's not a mainstream Pinot style. (NB)

There were a few ups and downs but many of the wines had classic slipperiness across the palate. I particularly enjoyed 1997, 1999 and 2004. (NB) I found many of the older vintages quite leathery/earthy with plenty of structure but without much flesh. Some of the tannins were quite harsh. The best vintages were 2004, 2005 and 2006, which all had fragrance, density, power and length. (HH)

Cellar Reserve Cabernets

First Vintage:	1993.
Variety:	Cabernet sauvignon and/or shiraz.
Origin:	One-off cuvées based on parcels of selected fruit. Coonawarra, Barossa, Clare Valley and Padthaway.
Fermentation:	Open, headed-down fermenters.
Maturation:	All matured in new and old oak for a period of up to 16 months.
Comment:	Released entirely under screw cap since the 2005 vintage.

Penfolds Cellar Reserve Cabernets do not necessarily fit to any particular genre. In many respects the whole winemaking process is a voyage of discovery. Without the expectations of making a wine to a house style, winemakers are allowed to play with the fruit and make something that is different. These are all effectively experimental wines, so vinification and maturation practices vary.

The 1993 Penfolds Cabernet Shiraz was the first of the Cellar Reserve line and is perhaps the most Penfolds in style. Primarily drawn from Coonawarra cabernet sauvignon and Clare Valley shiraz, this wine was described by Huon Hooke as 'a triumph of the year'. Joshua Greene was 'blown away by the standard of the wines. The 1993 is an ultra-typical Penfolds—built on tannin and oak—with really appealing, up-front maturity with real depth of flavour.' James Halliday described the 2005 Cellar Reserve Coonawarra Cabernet Kalimna Shiraz as 'a voluptuous and seductive near-Special Bin wine with cascades of cassis/blackberry fruit and high-quality tannin and oak'. Huon Hooke enjoyed the 2005 Cellar Reserve Barossa Cabernet Sauvignon: 'It's a cracker with wonderful fragrance. It has a strong, chocolate, vanilla oak-marked nose. The palate is deep and firm, young and vigorous, with great depth, fleshiness, concentration and drive.' The 2005 and 2006 comprise Block 42 and Block 41 material—often used for Penfolds Bin 707 Cabernet Sauvignon.

TASTING NOTES ~ CELLAR RESERVE CABERNETS

1993
Cellar Reserve Coonawarra Cabernet Clare/Padthaway Shiraz ★ NOW • • • 2012

Deep crimson. Intense mocha/dark cherry/chocolate/herb aromas with some toasty nuances. Well-concentrated wine with dark chocolate/black cherry flavours, ripe, sweet tannins and savoury oak characters. Finishes chalky dry. Classic Penfolds wine.

2005 Cellar Reserve Coonawarra Cabernet Kalimna Shiraz ★ 2010 • • • 2025

Deep crimson/purple. Very stylish elegant wine with fresh blackcurrant pastille/rose petal aromas and malty new oak nuances. The palate is beautifully concentrated with cassis/brambly/earthy flavours and fine chalky, dry, slinky tannins. Finishes savoury and sweet. 100% American oak.

2005 Cellar Reserve Barossa Cabernet Sauvignon ★ 2010 • • • 2025

Deep crimson/purple. Fragrant dark chocolate/espresso coffee aromas with floral/damson plum notes. Richly proportioned chocolaty cabernet with deep-set mocha/dark berry flavours, ripe tannins and spicy/ginger oak characters. Great depth, fleshiness and drive.

2006 Cellar Reserve Barossa Cabernet Sauvignon ★ 2012 • • • 2030

Deep purple red. A very classical *Grand Vin*-type wine with pure cassis/black plum aromas and fresh savoury/vanillin/spice new oak. Generous cassis/dark chocolate/liquorice fruit perfectly balanced with savoury/vanillin oak and fine-grained tannins. Finishes firm with plenty of flavour length. Lovely volume, fruit sweetness, poise and structure. Will age beautifully.

DISCUSSION

These Cellar Reserve cabernets progress you from one side of the universe to another. **1993** Cellar Reserve Coonawarra Cabernet Clare/Padthaway Shiraz is an ultra-typical, richly textured Penfolds red with classic blackberry/dark chocolate/vanillin characters, built-in tannins and oak. (JH) This is a triumph of a difficult year. It's earthy and varietal with dusty aged cabernet/herbal-notes. It has good depth and concentration and persuasive tannins galore. This is an impressively balanced wine which still has a future. (HH).

2005 Cellar Reserve Coonawarra Cabernet Kalimna Shiraz is an explosively complex wine with fragrant blueberry/floral aromas and a powerful, dark chocolate richness. There's an earthy/minerally quality to the wine that gives a certain transparency and evocation of soil. (JG) It's beautifully succulent wine with glowing refinement to the tannins. It almost floats in the mouth. This wine has tremendous harmony and integrity. (NB)

2005 Cellar Reserve Barossa Cabernet Sauvignon is lean and succulent with exotic red/purple fruits, coffee/espresso flavours and beautifully mature tannins. (JG) It has potent varietal character with rich blackcurrant fruit, quality oak and ripe, balanced tannins. (JH)

Cellar Reserve Grenache

First Vintage:	2002.
Variety:	Grenache.
Origin:	Mature bush vines, Seppeltsfield, Barossa Valley.
Fermentation:	Open, headed down fermenters.
Maturation:	11 months in older French hogsheads.

The 2002 Cellar Reserve Grenache is a unique, ultra-concentrated wine that evokes the heat and richness of the Barossa Valley landscape. Peter Gago describes it as a sublime freak of nature, 'the type of wine that can only be made once or twice in a decade'. The wine derives from low-yielding, contour-planted, mature bush vines at Marananga, Barossa Valley. The wine was traditionally vinified in open headed-down fermenters and racked into older French oak hogsheads for further maturation. No new oak was used to preserve the pure musky/floral fruit characters and natural exuberance on the palate. The wine has aged really well and still shows freshness and vitality.

TASTING NOTES ~ CELLAR RESERVE GRENACHE

2002 ★   **NOW • • • 2015**

Deep crimson. Very complex musky/plum/raspberry/dark chocolate aromas with some violet/earthy nuances. The palate is fresh and buoyant with concentrated musky/raspberry flavours and ripe, dense, open-knit tannins. Finishes chalky/savoury dry at the finish.

WHITES

Cellar Reserve Gewurztraminer

First Vintage:	2005.
Variety:	Gewurztraminer.
Origin:	Penfolds Woodbury Vineyard, Eden Valley—a sub-region of the Barossa.
Fermentation:	Stainless steel tanks.
Maturation:	10–14 months.
Comments:	Released entirely under screw cap since the 2006 vintage.

'It's truly expressive of Gewurztraminer, with lovely, intense ginger/spice aromatics, richness and fine minerally acidity.'

—OLIVER CRAWFORD, WINEMAKER

The Cellar Reserve Gewurztraminer is sourced from the Woodbury vineyard's Bay F1 Block in the Eden Valley. The vines were planted during the 1960s and have been yielding fruit of exquisite quality for many years now. Gewurztraminer, however, is not a mainstream grape variety in Australia. Indeed this Alsatian variety has been relatively unsuccessful until recent times. Penfolds, however, believes that this variety is now benefiting from older vines, better vineyard management and more intuitive winemaking. Oliver Crawford is especially enthusiastic about the fruit: 'It's truly expressive of gewurztraminer with lovely intense ginger/spice aromatics, richness and fine minerally acidity.' James Halliday noted that in the context of Australia, this was a 'particularly successful gewurztraminer style'. He preferred the 2006 with its 'rose petal/lychee fruit and citrus acidity' while Joshua Greene was impressed by 'the complex and exuberant 2007'. Overall, the Cellar Reserve Eden Valley Gewurztraminer is an early drinking wine that should be consumed soon after release.

TASTING NOTES ~ CELLAR RESERVE GEWURZTRAMINER

2005 ★   NOW

Medium pale gold. Ginger/lychee/clove aromas. Well-concentrated, sweet ginger/lime/tangerine flavours with light, minerally acidity. Chalky, dry finish but lovely flavour length. Quite soft and smooth. Drink now.

2006 ★   NOW

Pale yellow. Fresh rose petal/lime blossom/jasmine aromas with touches of ginger. The palate is clean and tight with plenty of sweet-fruit/lime/ginger/spice flavours and pronounced citrus acidity. Harmonious and balanced.

Medium pale yellow. Lime/spicy/lychee/violet aromas. Very classical lime/spicy/lychee flavours, soft mineral acidity and loose-knit, chalky texture. A potent, rich, mouth-filling but early drinking wine.

Cellar Reserve Sauvignon Blanc

First Vintage:	2006.
Variety:	Sauvignon blanc.
Origin:	Adelaide Hills—extending from Birdwood in the south to Gumeracha in the north.
Fermentation:	100% barrel fermented in old oak.
Maturation:	3 months' maturation on yeast lees with regular stirring to achieve further flavour complexity.
Comment:	Released entirely under screw cap since the 2006 vintage.

'Full-bodied, rich and weighty with a long, reverberating finish.'
— NEIL BECKETT, PANELLIST

The Cellar Reserve Sauvignon Blanc is an emerging style. After fermentation, the wine is matured for three months in older oak barrels. Some elements are stirred on its lees to add further complexity. Oliver Crawford said, 'This wine generally gets the very best of our Adelaide Hills fruit. In 2007 the vintage conditions were not quite good enough to justify releasing a wine.' Neil Beckett described the 2006 as a 'good food wine with more barrel-ferment and wild-ferment characters. The palate was full-bodied, rich and weighty with a long, reverberating finish.' Ch'ng Poh Tiong also liked the wine, enjoying 'the complex green melon/lanolin aromas and softly viscous mouth-feel'.

TASTING NOTES ~ CELLAR RESERVE SAUVIGNON BLANC

Pale yellow. Complex grassy/green melon/lanolin/lime aromas and flavours. The palate is well concentrated with mid-palate richness, plenty of fruit sweetness and some leesy complexity. Finishes long and minerally.

CHAPTER TEN

Bin Wines

*'Penfolds is a cornerstone of Australia's wine heritage,
the Australian secondary wine market and the great Australian
wine cellar. The Penfolds bin range—released at almost every
conceivable price point—is made for everyone who enjoys wine.
It is just this wondrous diversity and ageless appeal that sets Penfolds
apart as the most democratic and egalitarian of all wines.'*
—ANDREW CAILLARD, PANELLIST

REDS

Bin 389 Cabernet Shiraz

First Vintage:	1960.
Variety:	Cabernet sauvignon and shiraz.
Origin:	A multi-district blend, South Australia. Barossa Valley, Coonawarra, Padthaway, Robe, Bordertown, McLaren Vale, Langhorne Creek and Clare Valley.
Fermentation:	Stainless steel tanks with wax-lined/wooden header boards. Some components complete fermentation in barrel. 18 months in American oak hogsheads (300 litres); 20–30% new, 70–80% 1- and 2-year-old oak, including barrels used for the previous vintage of Grange.
Comments:	Released under screw cap in some markets since the 2005 vintage.

'The quintessential Penfolds red: dependable, still affordable, good to drink young, but with a terrific track record in the cellar.'
— HUON HOOKE, PANELLIST

Penfolds Bin 389 Cabernet Shiraz is the classic South Australian red wine with a reputation and universal appeal that transcends the ordinary. It best represents the ambitions and hopes of succeeding generations of Penfolds winemakers; this is a much-loved, beautifully consistent and utterly Australian style that shows all the hallmarks and benefits of cross-varietal/multi-regional blending, continuity of winemaking philosophy and brilliant teamwork. This is an Australian *Grand Vin*; a selection and interpretation of the best parcels from the best vineyard sites by a winemaking team steeped in the ethos and tradition of a great Australian wine style.

Huon Hooke describes Bin 389 as, 'The quintessential Penfolds red: dependable, still affordable, good to drink young but with a terrific track record in the cellar.' It is known affectionately as 'poor man's Grange' or by the Americans as 'Baby Grange'; the wine is the beneficiary of second-use Grange barrels and has a similar ethereal and lasting quality—at a fraction of the price! Almost half a century after first release, Bin 389, with all its ripe fruit, richness, volume and generosity, has become a sentimental and enduring favourite among wine consumers and collectors. It has featured consistently in the benchmark *Langton's Classification of Australian Wine* since the listing was first published in 1991. In 2007, it was Australia's most popular auction wine; not by value, but by volume of supply and demand. In the context of the world wine market, Bin 389 is a 'super-second' Australian wine with a wonderful track record of fulfilling its ageing potential.

The first Bin 389—named after its original 'binning' compartment at Penfolds' Magill cellars—was released during a time of intense but secret activity at Penfolds. A decade of technical advances, experimental winemaking and planning during the 1950s had provided a genuine competitive and commercial edge; a fine red wine boom was just around the corner. In his memoirs Ray Beckwith said, 'Following Max Schubert's observations in France, he set about producing the definitive standard in Australian premium red winemaking by selecting suitable grape material (by variety and location) and finishing the fermentation in oak hogsheads and storing the wine therein for a protracted period of one to two years.'

> 'Our early winemakers included many perfectionists always
> aiming at the perfect wine; always aiming to do a little better
> next vintage. The perception of what is a good wine, what is a good style
> has changed over the years, so that now we look for varietal or
> fruit characters in place of the "matured" style.'
> —RAY BECKWITH, PENFOLDS RESEARCH CHEMIST

Several red winemaking trials based on cabernet and shiraz were made during the 1950s. There had been early cabernet-based vintages of Grange and one-off special bins or blends. The very early St Henri wines were cabernet–mataro blends, so the successive releases of a single-vineyard 1960 and 1961 Bin 389 Auldana Cabernet Shiraz—both vinified at nearby Magill—complemented Penfolds' emerging fine wine portfolio.

No controversy accompanied Bin 389. Doug Crittenden, a Melbourne wine merchant, was an early supporter and used to transport the wine over from Adelaide by barrel. The pressures of a growing market and urban encroachment resulted in the wine gradually becoming a multi-district blend. In many respects it is Bin 389 that set in train the tradition of Penfolds house style and winemaking philosophy. It is also a compelling advertisement for the cabernet–shiraz blend. At first the early vintages were made from vineyards around the Adelaide foothills, including Magill. Gradually and then almost entirely they used Barossa Valley fruit. Over the last twenty years they were sourced from distinguished vineyards around South Australia including the Barossa Valley, Coonawarra, Padthaway, McLaren Vale, Langhorne Creek, Clare Valley, Robe and Bordertown.

From the very start, Max Schubert favoured warm- and hot-climate fruit as a source for Bin 389—reflecting his strong preference for richly concentrated 'buoyant' fruit. He wasn't really looking for varietal character as we articulate it today; rather he was looking for maturity and complexity of aromas, flavour development and structure. Nonetheless, Schubert fully understood the potential of cabernet and shiraz as blending companions. He believed that each component could bring something extra and different. The philosophy holds true today. Cabernet sauvignon is highly perfumed, elegantly structured and intensely flavoured with chocolaty, firm tannins. Shiraz is more opulent and fleshy, with power and generosity of fruit. Combined, the wine can show extraordinary volume of fruit, mid-palate richness and finesse. The style has evolved with the times, never stepping backwards. James Halliday once observed that Bin 389 'just can't work with cool-climate fruit'.

Ray Beckwith described the Penfolds winemaking process in 1967:

> The reds are commonly fermented at a maximum of about 85° Fahrenheit [29.5° C], allowing good colour extraction. Excessive temperatures result in loss of flavour and spoilage by bacteria. As fermentation proceeds, the winemaker watches the development of colour and, when he judges that it is sufficient, the fermenting juice is removed from the skins and the process completed in other tanks, with a constant check being made on temperature. For certain special red wines (including batches of Bin 389), fermentation is completed in new oak hogsheads of about 65-gallon capacity to allow extraction of the oak tannin.

Although Bin 389 is an intricate, cross-regional blend, it is ultimately the personality and the structure of the fruit that really matters. Penfolds Bin 389 was a major beneficiary of technical advances and evolution of winemaking practice during the 1970s and '80s. The introduction of refrigeration and stainless steel saw major progress made in style and control—the wine was fermented at lower temperatures, resulting in intense, clear fruit aromas and palate freshness. A quantum leap in vineyard management, improved seasoning of new American oak and barrel selection have also contributed to further refinement in style. The overall winemaking practices have not changed. The classical heading-down in open fermenters remains a key Penfolds technique. Further, some components of the blend still complete fermentation in the barrel to enhance complexity, richness and integration of new American oak.

Bin 389 is matured in a combination of new (20–30 per cent), one- and two-year-old (70–80 per cent) American oak hogsheads for eighteen months prior to bottling. The Rewards of Patience tasting records 'an army of lovely old wines' and a steady almost unbroken progress of quality and style. In previous editions the panel has noted 'an impressive discipline in fruit selection and winemaking'.

Neil Beckett said, 'Bin 389 is an overwhelmingly successful cabernet–shiraz blend. While each variety has different ageing potential, the wine benefits from the architecture of cabernet sauvignon and the furnishings of shiraz. The progression of style is noticeable over the decades; the wines fill out with beautifully extracted flavours and compact, fine-grained tannins. This is unmistakably Penfolds.'

Penfolds Bin 389 epitomises Penfolds' winemaking philosophy and the art of multi-district blending. For almost 50 years it has developed a strong identity for its consistency, reliability and value. Ordinary wine consumers buy it because it's delicious to drink—even when first released. Collectors appreciate it because the wine, especially in top vintages, has an enduring and memorable quality. It is this remarkable winemaking heritage and wide appeal that distinguishes Bin 389 from the rest of its field.

1961 ★   NOW • • • PAST

Deep brick red. A lovely old wine with mature mocha/coffee/dried nuts/panforte aromas. The palate is supple and elegant with mocha/meaty/panforte/leather flavours and fine, silky tannins. Finishes long and sweet. A really good bottle but some examples may have passed.

1964   NOW • • • PAST

Brick red. Intense bitumen/herb garden/meaty aromas with some earthy notes. Sweet, concentrated palate with meaty, sweet-fruit flavours and ripe, loose-knit tannins. Finishes slinky dry. A classical old Penfolds wine—just holding together.

1966 ★   NOW

Deep brick red. Beautiful old wine with fresh intense mocha-berry/sandalwood aromas. It's still holding up really well, showing plenty of richness, fruit sweetness, mocha/roasted coffee/herb garden flavours and fine chalky/savoury tannins. It finishes brambly, long and sweet. A delicious old wine.

1967   NOW

Brick red. Farmyard/leather/burnt chocolate/mint aromas. The wine has overdeveloped now. The palate is sinewy dry and firm with menthol/chocolate/tar/smoked meat flavours. Loses energy at the finish. It is fading now. Drink up.

1970   NOW • • • PAST

Brick red. Roasted coffee/dusty/earthy aromas with some meaty/bitumen/barnyard notes. Sweet dark chocolate/mocha/bitumen/earthy flavours and slinky, dry, loose-knit tannins. Finishes cedar dry. Beginning to dry out.

1971   NOW

Brick red. Infinitely complex wine with dark bitter-chocolate/prune/espresso/leather/herb garden aromas. Rich, ripe dark chocolate/roasted coffee/earthy/dried fruit flavours and fine, loose-knit, grainy tannins. Finishes lacy and chalky dry but long and savoury. Still holding but best to drink now.

1975   NOW

Brick red. Mature redcurrant/earthy/herb garden aromas with some malty/sandalwood notes. The palate is fully mature with brambly/chocolate/redcurrant/cedar flavours and chalky, dry, slightly grainy, firm tannins. It still has flow, flavour and balance. A beautiful marriage of cabernet and shiraz.

1976 ★   NOW • • • 2015

Brick red. Intense, powerful, dark chocolate/blackberry/plum/sweet-fruit/mint aromas, dense, sweet dark chocolate/dark cherry/leather flavours, underlying savoury oak notes and firm, slinky, fine-balanced tannins. Finishes grippy dry at the finish. A very structured wine with plenty of fruit volume and richness. A classic year.

1977 NOW

Medium brick. Roasted coffee/sweet-fruit/earthy/savoury/herbal aromas. Roasted coffee/dried plum/smoky/wood spiced/leather flavours and firm, strong, cedary tannins. Finishes sinewy dry. Drink up.

1978 NOW

Medium brick. Cedar/tobacco/leather/wet bitumen/herb garden/violet aromas. The palate is well concentrated with earthy/fruit pastille/farmyard characters and fine, sinewy dry—touch leafy—tannins. There's still some fruit sweetness and good flavour length, but the wine is beginning to fade now.

1979 NOW

Brick red. Smoky/meaty/demi-glace aromas with touches of apricot/dried fruits. Lovely richness and complexity on the palate with deep-set meaty/mocha/demi-glace/soy flavours, fine grainy tannins. Finishes chalky dry. Layered and firm.

1980 NOW • • • PAST

Brick red. Earthy/cedar/mint/gunflint aromas with a hint of redcurrant. Sweet cedar wood/redcurrant/herbal flavours and fine, long, dry, hard tannins. A grippy/leafy finish. The palate has length and movement but it is near its end.

1981 NOW • • • PAST

Brick red. Fresh spicy/red berry/sappy/Moroccan leather aromas with some minty notes. The palate is well developed, richly flavoured and firmly structured with sweet dark chocolate/dark berry/mint/spicy/leather flavours and leafy firm tannins. Tough but flavourful.

1982 NOW

Brick red. Tea leaf/rosehip/redcurrant/coffee aromas with some green herbal notes. The palate is medium-bodied with soft, supple redcurrant/mocha flavours and fine chalky—touch leafy—tannins. A sweet and sour wine. Drink up.

1983 NOW • • • 2015

Brick red. Expansive, generous wine with intense dark chocolate/molasses/liquorice/cinnamon/sweet-fruit aromas and flavours, fine, dense, chalky tannins and underlying savoury nuances. Finishes long and sweet. Still has plenty of life.

1984 NOW • • • 2016

Medium deep brick red. Rich chocolaty/gamy/malty/dried herb aromas. A fleshy, sweet-fruited palate with chocolate/meaty/aniseed flavours, underlying malty oak characters and fine, slinky, dry tannins. Finishes firm and savoury.

1985 NOW • • • 2015

Brick red. Highly aromatic wine with fresh black cherry/cigar box/mint aromas. The palate is grainy textured with cedar/black cherry/herb garden flavours and fine, granular tannins. Not a blockbuster but very enjoyable.

1986 ★ NOW • • • 2016

Medium deep red. Fresh smoky/cassis/dried plum/herbaceous aromas with some menthol/gum leaf notes. Sweet, deep-set liquorice/smoky/meaty/minty flavours and sinewy dry tannins. Builds up brambly and dry at the finish. A powerful, old-fashioned style harking back to the early 1960s.

1987 NOW

Medium deep red. Redcurrant/crème brûlée/herb garden aromas. The palate has plenty of juicy redcurrant/mocha/herb garden flavours, but the tannins are sinewy and dry. It builds up very leafy and firm. The tannins are unbalanced. Drink up.

1988 NOW • • • 2013

Deep red. Intense chocolate/mocha/redcurrant aromas with some soy/herb garden notes. A long, sustained, richly concentrated palate with chocolate/mocha/redcurrant/spicy flavours and chalky, dry, firm tannins. Fresh and substantial.

1989 NOW • • • 2012

Deep red. Classic choco-berry/liquorice/herb garden aromas with some leathery notes. Lovely, sweet, generous wine with plenty of chocolate/dark berry/leather flavours and fine, balanced tannins. Finishes savoury and long. Acidity pokes out towards the end. A very successful wine for vintage.

1990 ★ NOW • • • 2025

Deep red. Sweet plummy/mocha/chocolate/earthy/violet aromas. Very rich and complex palate with fresh mocha/dark chocolate/meaty flavours, plenty of fruit sweetness and dense, strong, chalky, firm tannins. A very powerful, intense wine. A classic year.

1991 ★ NOW • • • 2020

Deep red. Lovely, rich, complex wine with musky/savoury/dark chocolate/espresso aromas and malty, new oak characters. The palate is rich, ripe and multi-layered with deep-set dark berry/chocolate/musky plum/roasted coffee flavours, underlying savoury/malty oak and fine, granular tannins. Plush and lavish.

1992 NOW • • • 2012

Medium deep red. Well-concentrated wine with blackberry/vanilla/herb garden/earthy/tar. The palate is solid and mouth-filling with deep blackberry/earthy/leafy flavours and chunky, dry, mouth-coating tannins. There's plenty of sweet fruit, but the tannins are bitter dry at the finish.

1993 NOW • • • 2012

Deep red. Smoky/plummy/cedar/polished leather/mint aromas. Sweet redcurrant/dried plum/dark chocolate/leathery flavours and dry, grainy, loose-knit tannins. Finishes firm and minty.

1994 ★ NOW • • • 2025

Deep red. Dark chocolate/plummy/loamy aromas with some demi-glace/mint notes. The palate is well focused with lovely strength and density of fruit. There are still some primary blackberry

characters intertwined with evolved chocolaty/meaty demi-glace fruit and savoury, malty oak. It finishes with pronounced sappy firmness. Very strong, muscular wine with plenty of fruit volume.

1995   NOW • • • 2015

Medium deep red. Intense blueberry/blackberry/cassis/dried herb/leather aromas with some musky/minty nuances. Plenty of cherry/blueberry/dried herb flavours, underlying tobacco/earthy notes and fine, grainy, textured tannins. Builds up quite brambly and dry at the finish.

1996 ★   NOW • • • 2025

Deep red. Fresh, expressive wine with all the hallmarks of a 'Baby Grange'; lovely inky blackberry/meaty/cedar/graphite aromas, dense, rich, generous, sweet-fruit flavours, underlying malt oak and slinky/chocolaty tannins. This is a very great vintage with incredible fruit power and energy.

1997   NOW

Medium deep red. Soft cassis minty/cedar/herb garden aromas with some saddle leather notes. The wine is ready to drink with soft gentle cassis/coffee/herb flavours and grainy dry tannins. Finishes quite grippy but there's plenty of length. Probably at its best now.

1998 ★   NOW • • • 2030

Deep red. Intense inky/liquorice/plummy/roasted meat/chocolaty aromas with hints of menthol/briar. A remarkably concentrated, richly flavoured wine with deep-set roasted/plummy/mocha fruit, underlying malty oak and plentiful ripe, chocolaty tannins. Some complex leathery/demi-glace notes beginning to appear. This is still very youthful and elemental for its age. It's drinking well, but the best is yet to come. Outstanding vintage.

1999   NOW • • • 2020

Deep red. Evolving more quickly than 1998. Ripe red- and blackcurrant/chocolaty/liquorice aromas with a strong element of mocha/malt oak. A flowing, supple palate with plenty of ripe, developing black fruit/chocolaty flavours, fresh new oak and savoury tannins. It finishes firm and gritty but there is plenty of fruit that follows through. This could turn out to be a great Bin 389, however it needs more time.

2000   NOW • • • 2015

Medium deep red. Red cherry/cassis/herb garden aromas. The palate is juicy and fresh with cassis/red cherry/leafy flavours, underlying savoury oak and slightly green, grippy tannins. It will hold but it won't improve.

2001   NOW • • • 2020

Deep colour. Very concentrated, super-ripe wine with blackcurrant pastille/mulberry/liquorice/aniseed aromas. The palate is rich and fleshy with plenty of sweet-fruit, mocha oak and generous blackcurrant/mulberry/liquorice flavours. This is a fairly robust style; the dense, velvety tannins build up very sinewy and grippy at the finish.

2002 ★ NOW • • • 2030

Deep red. Lovely, elegant style with intense, pure cassis minty/*garrigue* aromas and hints of vanilla oak. A rich, beautifully balanced wine with opulent, clear blackcurrant/sweet-fruit flavours underlying new oak and fine-grained tannins. Finishes chocolaty firm. Perfectly balanced wine with a great future.

2003 NOW • • • 2015

Deep red–purple. Cherry/herb garden/dried plum/chocolaty/nutmeg aromas. It's big, rich, dense and tightly packed with plenty of sweet-fruit/plum/herb/nutmeg characters and fresh but solid tannins. It finishes grippy firm but there's plenty of flavour length. An early drinking style.

2004 ★ 2012 • • • 2030

Deep purple red. Superb, beautifully focused wine with fresh elderberry/mulberry/liquorice aromas and savoury oak nuances. The palate is densely packed with pure blackcurrant/elderberry/liquorice flavours, plenty of cedar/malty oak and mouth-filling, slinky, ripe tannins. Finishes long and sweet. A great Penfolds vintage. Wait.

2005 2010 • • • 2025

Deep purple red. Sumptuous and voluptuous with seductive ripe, intense, musky plum/blackcurrant/elderberry fruit and vanilla/malty new oak. It's richly concentrated, smooth, fleshy and incredibly sweet-fruited with great youthful exuberant flavours, mid-palate depth and structure. It finishes firm and profoundly long. It's very elemental, showing a riot of aromas and flavours. It could be another great Bin 389.

2006 ★ 2012 • • • 2035

Deep purple red. Gorgeous rich chocolate/plum aromas with fresh nutmeg/malt oak. Concentrated, full-bodied dark chocolate/plum flavours, fine savoury/grainy tannins and beautifully balanced malt/spicy oak. Finishes firm but long and sweet. The palate is still elemental but the wine is brimming with fruit sweetness and flavour richness. A spectacular Bin 389.

> *'The wines show plenty of fruit, richness and structure. Bin 389 must be the best-value wine in Penfolds' extensive portfolio. These are beautiful cellaring-type styles.'*
> —HUON HOOKE, PANELLIST

DISCUSSION

[Vintages 1962–63, 1965, 1968–69 and 1972–74 were not tasted. Most considered past.] Bin 389 is a distinctive house style which highlights the art of blending rather than distinguishing varietal characters or reflecting regional style. If cellared well, these wines have the concentration and overall balance to last 30 to 40 years. I really enjoyed the older wines. **1961** had a lovely, tawny, brick-red colour with old leathery, meat-stock, pan-scraping nose. The palate is a bit lean now, but it's still elegant and balanced. It starts falling apart in the glass; drink up. (HH) It's on its last legs—and probably past it—but it's pretty impressive all the same. It smells beautiful, with a lovely mix of dried herbs, honey and old leather; lovely tannins too. (CM)

1964 is starting to dry out although it still retains a fair volume of flavour and gentle leather concentration. (JH) It's fully mature—if not overdeveloped—with soft, luxurious texture and cocoa/woody/leathery flavours. (JG)

1966 smelled of pencil shavings and flint. It's quite persistent with juicy, leather, wood spice flavours. (CPT) It was fresher than the previous wine with a more meaty, savoury edge. The tannins were refined and supple, but still supportive of the fruit. It's still drinking really well. (NB)

1967 showed evolved sweet, wood spice, coffee fruit with a whiff of mint. It's lighter, more delicate and perhaps more balanced than 1966. (CPT) It was a supple, smooth old wine with leather, chocolate, earth, dried fruit flavours. (JH) I found the wine a touch farmyardy with bunched-up tannins; it's starting to dry out at the finish. (CM)

1970 has a drying, leathery, dusty nose with some meaty/celery notes. The palate is extremely tannic; it must have been a whopper in its time. However, it still has richness and flavour length. (HH) It had a savoury, cedar complexity, full, sweet entry and clinging, tenacious tannin structure. There's not much pleasure to be had with this wine now. (NB)

1971 smells of sweet cassis. It's almost liqueur-like. The fruit is soft and fading now, but the tannins are fully resolved and don't get in the way. (JG) It's the first wine to show a whiff of cassis. There's plenty of freshness, dried fruits, wood spice and persistency. This has been a very impressive and consistent start. (CPT) It had all the richness of 1963, 1966 and 1967, but there was more emphasis and weight. It showed gentler, riper fruit in a mocha, vanilla, sweet leather, spice spectrum. The tannins are just holding. (JH) (1972, 1973 and 1974 not tasted.)

1975 is a beautiful marriage of cabernet and shiraz. It has a fleshiness that you don't expect of a wine of this age. It was a really nice wine with flow, flavour and balance. (CM) It's not that complex or nuanced but it was big and chocolaty, fleshy and deep, rich and plush. It still has fruit sweetness and tastes of very ripe fruit, perhaps reflecting a high shiraz component. (HH)

1976 was still dense and tight but the tannins overwhelmed the fruit. The architecture of cabernet was more notable than the furnishings of shiraz. (NB) I thought it was the full kit. It was structured yet powerful, leathery and seductive. The cabernet and shiraz both pulled together in perfect harmony. (CM)

1977 showed quite savoury, earthy, brambly overtones to a sweet prune, dried fruit core. It had good tannin structure. (JH) It has subtle black olive/chocolate notes. The cabernet component doesn't taste fully mature. The palate is silky but there are some green characters in the wine. (JG)

1978 is the most impressive wine so far. It has mint, cassis, pepper, herbaceous aromas and very composed fruit and tannins. This is a very fresh, fine, elegant wine. (CPT) I thought it was just a touch mono-dimensional. It had some meaty, green herbal notes but the tannins were very drying, making the palate too harsh. (HH)

1979 was surprisingly good but probably at the end of its run. It had plenty of soy, leather, salty flavours all framed by a ribcage of tannins. (CM)

1980 was a pleasing classical wine showing the sweet spice of shiraz and the soft, herbal characters of cabernet. Dusty tannins hold the wine together. (JG) It had cool, minty overtones to a core of sweet fruit. The palate has length and movement. (JH)

1981 had a Moroccan leather/sandalwood nose. It's still pleasant to drink with fruit, sweet succulence and fine-grained tannins. (NB)

1982 was light and soft with blackcurrant aromas, soft, supple fruit flavours and balancing freshness. (CPT)

1983 was gorgeous with plenty of vanilla, mocha, mint, plums and leather, terrific tannins and plenty of flavour length. (CM) It's drinking now with honey, molasses and minty fruit but the tannins are beginning to dry out. (HH)

1984 was a bit closed at first, but it showed wafts of blackcurrants, sweet, juicy, dark cherry fruits and crisp tannins. (CPT) I liked this wine. It's all arms and legs but it had plenty of honey, soy, dried herb flavours, a touch of aniseed and good tannin structure. (CM)

1985 had a chocolate, savoury nose with some rum-like sweetness of fruit. The palate was ample and soft with a sink-into-the-sofa feel. It was a real comfort wine. (NB) It was a very mellow and mature wine with complex, stylish, cigar box aromas and rich, smooth flavours and texture. This was a delicious wine. (HH)

1986 was fragrant, soft, round and smooth with rose petal and almost grapey freshness to the fruit. It had a very long commanding finish. (JG) This is a very important and interesting wine. It is a direct descendant of the 1961 and 1966; twenty years has all but disappeared in a 'Dr Who' time box. (JH) It had a lovely fresh mint, herbaceous, cassis, cabernet-dominant palate profile paralleling the success of the 1986 Bordeaux vintage. It's a remarkably youthful and vivacious 21-year-old wine. (CPT) It had very sweet, ripe fruit on the palate but the gum leaf, mint aromas and flavours were surprisingly prominent. It will kick on for another decade plus. (HH)

1987 was very rich, slightly over-ripe and soupy. It had a seductive softness and granular tannins. It was perhaps less well-knit overall, but this is a convincing wine for the vintage. (NB) It's big and gutsy with mocha/chocolate fruit and chunky, chewy tannins. It's very grippy and unbalanced. (HH)

1988 is actually very good. It has strong beef stock/soy/dark fruit aromatics and more of that all-pervading mint. However, there's a lot here with good tannin structure and juicy length. Get into it now. (CM)

1989 is soft and fully mature with sweet, soft, round, very smooth and generous fruit. The alcohol and acidity are slightly noticeable, but the wine is still holding well. (JG)

1990 is a very powerful, intense wine. The tannins are a major component of this classic Penfolds vintage. However the blackcurrant, blackberry fruit does carry those tannins very well. (JH) It has a superb nose, with youthful plummy/charred meat/spicy aromas and very rich, complex flavours. It's a delicious wine at the peak of its life. (HH) It has a lively cabernet DNA with lovely crisp blackcurrant, mint aromas and fresh tannins. It ranks up with the 1978 and 1986. (CPT)

1991 is a good example of blending working well; the wine has a good, firm, savoury cabernet base and is richly spiced up by shiraz. The palate is concentrated and dense with more granular tannins than 1990. It has great freshness, harmony and length. (NB) I love the tannin structure here but there could be an argument that the palate isn't fleshy or powerful enough. (CM) I thought it was superb. It had another excellent nose with strong blackberry, plum, charred meat aromas and barely noticeable oak. The palate is fleshy and plush with grainy tannins galore. (HH)

1992 was a thoroughly enjoyable but serious wine with slinky glossy fruit—typical of the vintage—and fine tannins. It's very different to 1990 and 1991. (JH) It was firm and dark with bitter chocolate, savoury fruit and dense, taut tannins. (NB)

1993 is showing plenty of mint, boot polish, cedar, mocha and plum characters. It shows signs of leather but it's still essentially primary. I found it a touch rustic and didn't really like the minty aftertaste. (CM) It just doesn't have that lasting structure of previous vintages. I found it edgy with green tannins. It's not one to keep. (JG)

1994 is very firm and grippy. It smells of crushed leaves and the tannins are a bit too green and tough. (HH) I reckon it's one of the best Australian 1994s. It has lovely strength and depth of fruit with dark chocolate, mint, plum, loam, herb flavours. The fruit is tugged by tannin and polished up with mocha oak. (CM)

1995 is soft and plump. The shiraz tannin and spice is prominent with some cabernet tobacco bass notes. (JG) It's a very well-made, stylish wine with rich chocolate, cherry aromas and dense, very fine texture. (NB)

1996 was fresh, expressive and alive with cedar, currant, mint power. This was an absolutely gorgeous wine reminiscent of Grange. (CM) The wine was clean and fresh, pristine, tight and firm. It was packed tight and had really good concentration with lovely richness, body, weight and extract. (HH) This is a great Penfolds vintage. I can see it continuing to evolve for decades to come. (PG)

1997 was slightly grippy with some savoury—fractionally green—tannins and minty cabernet notes. (JH) It was not as ripe as the 1996 but had lots of freshness. (CPT)

1998 was plump, rich and smoky with plenty of spicy shiraz characters. It's a very sophisticated blend; not as powerful as some but sleek and generous. It has a tremendous fruit presence with a stronger overlay of bright, red spice shiraz fruit rather than the darker tones of cabernet. (JG) This was a very good wine with attractive, balanced, elegant, black fruit aromas and menthol top notes. The palate was ample, plush and expansive with firm, fine-grained tannins. There was a bitter chocolate gravitas to the finish. (NB)

1999 had nice structure and flow with slightly assertive mocha oak but excellent currant, vanilla, toast and coffee flavours. It might take ten years, but this wine could well turn into quite something. (CM) It was supple and sweet with a cascade of redcurrant, blackcurrant, blackberry, plum fruit and noticeably soft tannins. (JH)

2000 was juicy with ripe, cassis aromas and underlying oak. The oak worked much better in this wine. Still, there's dryness on its heels. (CPT) I found the aromas a touch fusty. It's quite unyielding with stern, grippy tannins. The palate is dry and savoury rather than bright and fruity. It could hold on for a few years, but it's not for the long haul. (HH)

2001 smells almost tannic. There's plenty of plummy fruit to balance out that awkwardness in structure. (JG) It was a rich, ripe, strongly structured wine with abundant blackcurrant, blackberry, plum fruit, good oak and ripe tannins. (JH) It was a big, rich, generous, sweet-fruited wine with masses of supple tannins. (HH)

2002 is deep, dense and richly powerful. It doesn't feel like it's come tighter yet. It has a lot of fruit and tannin, but not much complexity. It has the stuffing and the vague hints of dried ashen herbs to go to big places. (CM) It's a compact, well-formed wine that should evolve really well. It smells of dried cherries, cranberries, cinnamon and spice. The palate is round and supple but it carries an underlying firmness in structure. There's no bitterness whatsoever. (NB)

2003 is big, rich and dense with nutmeg, spice, shiraz aromas and some new oak peeping through. It's fleshy and loaded with ripe lovely fruit. It's remarkably smart for the year. (HH)

2004 was at once luscious yet restrained with layers of cassis, blackberry fruits all in harmony. The tannins are supple and the oak is very good. (JH) It's powerful and underdeveloped with full, plump, round black and red fruits, spicy richness and mellow oak tannins. It finishes chocolaty and long. This needs quite a few years to improve. (JG)

2005 was a riot of structured power. It had loads of musky, plum, currants, new vanillin oak and integrated mint. (CM) This is classic Pennies. It's rich and fleshy, sweet-fruited and concentrated. The mid-palate is incredibly deep and the flavours are very long. This is terrific stuff! I was particularly impressed by the final bracket (1996–2005). The wines show plenty of fruit, richness and structure. Bin 389 must be the best-value wine in Penfolds' extensive portfolio. These are beautiful, cellaring-type styles. However it is important to avoid lesser years if there are plans to age the wine. (HH)

There were very few disappointing wines in the entire tasting. The style illustrates the compelling synergies of cabernet and shiraz, the oak and Penfolds tannins. (JH) Many of the vintages were beautifully extracted, tight and compact with long, fine-grained tannins. The wines have great potential for ageing. (NB) There's a magical consistency across all vintages. Bin 389 is a remarkable wine style. (JG)

Bin 407 Cabernet Sauvignon

First Vintage:	1990.
Variety:	Cabernet sauvignon.
Origin:	Multi-district blend, South Australia/Western Australia, including Bordertown, Padthaway, Coonawarra, Robe, McLaren Vale, Clare Valley and Barossa Valley.
Fermentation:	Stainless steel tanks with wooden header boards. Some components complete fermentation in barrel.
Maturation:	12 months in new French and American (30%) oak. Also 1- and 2-year-old hogsheads—some of which were used for previous vintages of Bin 707.
Comments:	Released under screw cap in some markets since the 2004 vintage.

'It is easy to be seduced by their freshness, but with further cellaring they could end up in the top echelon.'
—JAMES HALLIDAY, PANELLIST

Bin 407 Cabernet Sauvignon, as its bin number suggests, is a more affordable cousin to the rich and opulent Bin 707 Cabernet Sauvignon. The wine was developed by John Duval, former Penfolds Chief Winemaker, in response to the increasing availability of high-quality cabernet sauvignon fruit and mounting pressure from the market for a versatile wine that could be enjoyed for immediate drinking or could develop well in the cellar. A cabernet sauvignon equivalent of Bin 389 was an obvious and glaring gap in Penfolds' red wine portfolio.

Bin 407 has always been a very consistent and enjoyable wine from the very first vintage. Most of the fruit has been sourced from south-east Australia, especially the Limestone Coast, including Coonawarra, Robe and Bordertown. Depending on vintage, winemakers have also selected parcels from Margaret River in Western Australia and from the warmer wine districts of the Clare Valley, Barossa Valley and McLaren Vale. The overall winemaking philosophy follows similar lines to Bin 389 down to the maturation of Bin 407 in second-use Bin 707 barrels (rather than Grange barrels). However it has never been called a poor man's Bin 707!

The wine is vinified in open stainless steel tanks with wax-lined wooden header boards, a traditional Penfolds technique. Some components are barrel fermented in new French and American oak to increase complexity and blending options. After fermentation the wine is matured for twelve months in a combination of new French (16 per cent) and American (14 per cent) oak—the remainder is aged in one- and two-year-old French and American oak.

Bin 407 is a restrained, elegant cabernet sauvignon style with clear, varietal blackcurrant/cassis aromas, fine-grained firm tannins and underlying cedary/savoury oak. The wine greatly benefits from both new oak and the maturation effect. However, Bin 407 still remains a strongly varietal wine with plenty of delicious up-front fruit, freshness and energy for immediate consumption. Further cellaring will allow the wine to develop further richness, volume and bottle complexity.

Steve Lienert, Penfolds veteran Senior Red Winemaker, says, 'Bin 407 has made huge leaps and bounds over the last decade. The early vintages had great fruit, but the tannins were often quite sinewy and hard—particularly in difficult vintages. We have greatly improved the overall balance and style of the wine. This has been achieved through better vineyard management and particular attention to tannin ripeness and oak maturation. The 2000s are lovely wines with pure cassis aromas, juicy flavours and chocolaty tannins.'

James Halliday said, 'This is a wine that shows the benefits of multi-regional blending. Bin 407 is all about the variety rather than place. The best wines seem to follow recognised Penfolds vintages. I particularly enjoyed the strong varietal fruit expression of 1996 and the rounded, smooth, silky 1998. The 2000s seem more layered and powerful. 2002, 2004 and 2005 are some the best wines; it is easy to be seduced by their freshness, but with further cellaring they could end up in the top echelon.'

Ch'ng Poh Tiong said, 'I was particularly impressed by this line-up of wines, particularly the 2002, 2003, 2004 and 2005. There is no reason not to drink these when young, but why not wait? Although some of the wines of the early 1990s were woody and dried out, the wines post-1996 are really well balanced and consistent with plenty of varietal fruit and decent ripe or close-to-ripe tannins.'

Bin 407 Cabernet Sauvignon is recognised for being affordable, classical, versatile and reliable. It is regarded as 'useful' or a 'safe bet' by sommeliers and wine experts across the globe because it is both an archetypal Australian cabernet style and punches well above its weight vis-a-vis its price category. In blind tastings Bin 407 can outperform wines with greater provenance, including renowned single-vineyard Australian cabernets and classed growth Bordeaux. Certainly the wine is a lovely contrast to the more opulent, more powerfully structured Bin 707.

TASTING NOTES ~ BIN 407 CABERNET SAUVIGNON

1990 ★   NOW • • • 2015

Medium deep red. Earthy/mocha/blackcurrant/mint aromas. Fully mature, mellow, elegant wine with well-concentrated roasted coffee/mocha/cedar flavours, mid-palate richness and fine, grainy tannins. Finishes chalky firm but minerally long. Still holding very well, but drink soon.

1991   NOW

Medium deep red. Black olive/roasted coffee/chocolaty aromas with some menthol/bitumen notes. The palate is savoury and dry with cedar/dark fruit/chocolaty/raisin flavours and leafy firm tannins. Drink now.

1992   NOW

Medium deep red. Classical cedar/cigar box/cassis/mint aromas. A muscular wine with cedar/blackcurrant flavours and sinewy, dry tannins. It still has some fruit sweetness but it finishes sappy firm. This is not going to get better. Drink soon.

1993 NOW

Medium deep red. Fresh, sweet blackcurrant/mocha/herb garden/violet aromas. Stewed plum/
blackberry flavours and fine brambly/sappy dry tannins. A bittersweet finish. Mature and ready
to drink.

1994 ★ NOW • • • 2015

Medium deep red. Intense cassis/chocolate/mint/brambly aromas. The palate is dense and chocolaty with blackcurrant/leafy flavours, abundant, loose-knit, chalky tannins and underlying oak.
Finishes long and sweet.

1995 NOW

Medium deep red. Roasted coffee/mocha/black olive/minty aromas. Well-concentrated palate
with roasted coffee/mocha/black olive/spearmint/earthy flavours and gritty dry tannins. The
palate is beginning to dry out.

1996 NOW • • • 2016

Deep red. Intense blackberry/mulberry/menthol aromas. Strong mint/mulberry/bitter chocolate
characters pervade the wine. It has plenty of fruit richness, ripe plush tannins and flavour length.
The wine is well balanced.

1997 NOW • • • PAST

Deep red. The wine has not aged well. It has developed earthy/silage/blackberry/tar/peppermint
aromas. The palate is overdeveloped and flat with earthy/silage/leafy/mint flavours and tough,
grippy tannins. It's not worth keeping.

1998 ★ NOW • • • 2018

Deep red. Beautifully intense cassis/dark chocolate/mocha/mint aromas. The palate is dense, rich
and fleshy with saturated, sustained cassis/choco-berry/mint flavours and fine, slinky tannins. It
finishes firm and has lovely generosity of fruit and plenty of length. A classic Bin 407.

1999 NOW • • • 2015

Medium deep red. Perfumed herb garden/black olive/cassis aromas. A well-concentrated wine
with blackcurrant/black olive/tobacco/spearmint flavours and chocolaty, fine tannins. The tannins are currently too strong for the fruit. Best to hold.

2000 NOW • • • 2012

Deep red. Lovely fresh cassis/raspberry/herb garden aromas. The palate is well concentrated
with plenty of blackcurrant/juicy red fruit/herb flavours and loose-knit, leafy, dry tannins. It's
not a very powerful wine, but it's fresh and juicy. Drink soon.

2001 NOW • • • 2016

Medium deep red–purple. Opulent black olive/tea leaf/cassis/plum aromas. Richly concentrated
wine with black olive/brambly/blackcurrant flavours and chunky dry tannins. It finishes grippy/
woolly dry. Has plenty of volume but lacks finesse. Best to drink while the fruit is dominant.

2002 ★ NOW • • • 2025

Deep red–purple. Intense blackcurrant, dark chocolate aromas with touches of aniseed/herb leaf. Generously proportioned, elegant palate with sweet, pure cassis/mocha characters and lovely dense, smooth, chocolaty ripe tannins. Finishes firm and minerally with plenty of flavour length. An exceptional vintage, with impressive weight and power.

2003 NOW • • • 2015

Deep red–purple. Deep-set mocha/raisin/prune/menthol/violet aromas. The palate is rich and densely packed with solid mocha/raisin/prune/liquorice fruit underlying smoky/toasty oak and substantial, sappy, dry tannins. Quite firm and tough. Cellar for a few more years but best to drink before tannins overwhelm the fruit.

2004 ★ NOW • • • 2020

Deep purple red. Fresh blueberry/elderberry/dark chocolate aromas with some nutmeg notes. A luxuriant palate with juicy blueberry/black cherry/raspberry fruit and slinky/chocolaty tannins. Finishes firm and dry with plenty of flavour length.

2005 ★ 2009 • • • 2020

Deep purple red. Intense elderberry/ginger/spicy/musky aromas with underlying savoury nuances. A very elemental wine packed with exuberant youthful fruit, dense chalky tannins and vanillin oak. Impressive now, but it will gain more richness, weight and volume with further bottle development.

2006 ★ 2010 • • • 2025

Deep purple red. Intense blueberry/sweet cassis/herb aromas with underlying savoury oak. Well-concentrated, richly flavoured wine with blueberry/cassis/aniseed flavours and fine, abundant tannins. Finishes savoury and fruit sweet. Still exuberant and youthful but fruit and oak in lovely balance. Another top vintage.

DISCUSSION

This tasting shows that Bin 407 is all about variety rather than regional definition or place. It does show the benefits of multi-district blending. There were few knockout wines but there was evenness across vintages and a distinct house style of cassis, mint, and pronounced firm tannin support.

The **1990** is definitely at the end of its plateau now. It's medium-bodied rather than full-bodied with an elegant structure that sets the overall standard and scene. (JH) It shows complex cassis/mint/stewed capsicum aromas and rich, ripe, yet very fresh, lively fruit. It has impressive intensity and wonderful balance. It's testament to how seductive Bin 407 can evolve. (CPT)

1991 has a well-woven, velvet mouth-feel but less weight than the 1990. It was gently elegant and well composed, perhaps drying a touch at the finish. (NB) It had better flavour and palate weight with some flesh and style. It's only medium-bodied with good balance although it finishes tough. (HH)

1992 has good leathery, minty, loamy appeal. It has surprisingly good tannin structure but it's not as charming as other vintages. (CM) It has less substance with some minty notes and abrasive tannins. Best to drink soon. (JH)

1993 was like a soft herbal claret but it's mature and ready to drink. (JG) It was quite a structured wine with luxurious mouth-feel, good purity and vibrancy. It finished herbaceous. (NB)

1994 was simple but good. It has big, mint-coated, curranty fruit and loads of tannin. (CM) It was a classic multi-regional cabernet with strong varietal expression. The tannins and oak are in sympathetic support of the fruit. (JH)

1995 showed the dreaded wine combination of spearmint and chocolate. It smells like confectionary. The palate attacks and then slides steadily away and then dries out a touch. It has a soft drinkability—if you are into this kind of drag—but the spearmint characters are too dominating. (CM) It's simple in structure and lacks a degree of concentration, definition and direction on the mid-palate. It has an almost tangy finish. (NB)

1996 was a bit green and stemmy with some rhubarb, tomato bush aromas, and a minty, raw palate. It's very firm and tight, needing more time to come around. (HH) It's a big wine with a black richness and edgy—almost gruff—tannins. The sweet cassis flavours are very lasting. (JG) I found this wine very enjoyable. It showed plenty of cassis, minty aromas and the palate was juicy and fresh. (CPT)

1997 was looking dull—almost as if the pH was a touch too high. However, it had some pleasant savoury, earthy *sous bois* characters. (JH) What an absolute contrast to the 1996! Drink up soon. (CPT)

1998 was somewhat majestic with polished blackcurrant aromas and fresh menthol, mint characters. It has a big frame of tannins, appropriate to the breadth of the palate. The mint characters lift the curranty flavours up out of the glass. (CM)

1999 was rich, black and smoky with some pipe tobacco characters. The palate was very juicy with lasting blackcurrant flavours and really well-integrated tannins. (JG) It had a classic blackcurrant cabernet nose. The palate was layered and fleshy; quite sumptuous and textural. This is a very good serious wine with grainy but fine tannins aplenty. (HH)

2000 had an easy appeal. It was rich and ripe with dense, plush, smooth tannins and decent length. (NB) It's hardly electrifying but it's in lovely form. It's settled and pure with blackcurrant, integrated mint and balanced tannins. It's not a blockbuster, but it's an even-tempered wine; an authentic presentation of Australian cabernet. (CM)

2001 is intense, long and still quite impressive. It has plenty of eucalypt, mint, cassis aromas, rich, ripe fruit and equally rich but not as ripe tannins. (CPT) It was more opulently ripe than the previous vintages, with plenty of tannin support. (JH)

2002 performs well beyond its place in the Penfolds line-up. It has a bright, rich berry scent and lovely generosity and structure. (JG) It's an outstanding bargain when you think about it. Purity is the thing here. It has gorgeous blackcurrant fruit and fine, integrated tannins. (CM)

2003 has a good, ripe cabernet nose with smoky, toasty, barrel-ferment type oak. It's sweet and earthy with black-olive, savoury notes, not just blackcurrants. The palate is tight and firm with abundant grip, but it's tight and tidy, if not on the firm and tough side. This is a very good wine for the year. (HH)

2004 was spectacular with glass-staining purple-black colour, lovely crème de cassis aromas and luxuriant silky/slinky texture. (NB) If you buy any of the Penfolds 2004s you can't go wrong. This is a lovely juicy wine with delicious black fruit flavours and silken, round tannins. (JG)

2005 has bangs of fleshy tannins with pretty floral, currant fruit and cedar, vanillin oak. (CM) It's even better than the 2004 with blueberry/floral fruit and rich, ripe, fine tannins. It has decades ahead of it. (CPT) It has greater texture and depth. If it's cellared for a while, it could land up in the top echelon of the 2005 vintage. (JH)

Bin 28 Kalimna Shiraz

First Vintage:	1959.
Variety:	Shiraz.
Origin:	Multi-district blend, South Australia. Significant contributions from Barossa Valley, McLaren Vale, Clare Valley and Langhorne Creek.
Fermentation:	Stainless steel tanks with wooden header boards.
Maturation:	15 months in older American hogsheads.
Comments:	Unearthed bottles of Bin 28 show that first vintage is probably 1959. Released under screw cap in some markets since the 2004 vintage.

'Bin 28 Shiraz is regarded as an Australian classic, valued for its integrity as a maturation-style fine wine and suitability as a fresh early drinking style for many different occasions.'

Penfolds Kalimna Bin 28 Shiraz is one of the most enduring and popular of Penfolds bin wines. It has universal appeal because of its intense fruit definition, ripe fleshy palate structure and generosity of flavour. The earliest releases were single-vineyard wines made from the renowned Kalimna Vineyard, acquired by Penfolds in 1945. A few years ago Penfolds unearthed bottles of the previously unrecorded 1959 vintage complete with Penfolds postage stamp-type label. The existence of

these bottles suggests that development of Penfolds bin wines started at around the same time as Max Schubert was asked to stop making Grange. It makes Bin 28 the earliest bin-range wine within Penfolds' portfolio. During the early 1960s, Bin 28 quickly established a strong reputation as an 'authentic Barossa-type red' which would develop 'additional character' with further cellaring. Today it is regarded as an Australian classic, valued for its integrity as a maturation-style fine wine and suitability as a fresh, early drinking style for many different occasions. It is probably the most reliable and consistent of wines within its class. Hence Bin 28 Kalimna Shiraz can be found in the swishest restaurants in London, New York or Moscow and dusty outback pubs in the Northern Territory. The wine has received numerous awards at various international wine shows around the world, including the International Wine Challenge in London.

The early Bin 28s were entirely single-vineyard Kalimna shirazes. The Kalimna Vineyard is, by European standards, large. Within its boundaries lie several individual blocks—overlying various soil types—each carrying its own particular nuances of place. Many of the vinification techniques originated from the development of Grange, including the use of open, headed-down fermenters and barrel fermentation. It is understood the very first vintages were matured in a proportion of new oak. However, the style has evolved where fruit complexity and natural tannin structure are essential elements. Today the wine is matured in one- and two-year-old American and French oak barrels.

During the late 1970s, Bin 28 Shiraz became a multi-district blend. The fruit is sourced from the Barossa Valley and McLaren Vale (including independent growers), Clare Valley, Langhorne Creek and even as far as Padthaway. Penfolds adheres to a very strict level of fruit selection, and while Bin 28 has moved from a single-vineyard wine to a multi-district blend, the overall winemaking philosophy remains the same. It is a showcase for warm-climate shiraz and a lead-in to the Penfolds house style of winemaking.

Campbell Mattinson said, 'Many of the older vintages are really lovely with plenty of sweet fruit, leather nuances and fine tannin structures. There was an overall deliciousness about the wines.'

During the 1980s the quality of pressing improved with the introduction of membrane presses. This has translated to better tannin structures, further improved by advances in tannin management during the 1990s. Penfolds also moved winemaking from Magill to Nuriootpa which meant that it could receive more fruit and make it into wine more efficiently. With so much good-quality shiraz grown in the Barossa and elsewhere, Penfolds has been able to increase the volume of production and improve the overall quality. This has been achieved through precision viticulture, earmarking of grapes prior to vintage, analysis and tasting when the fruit comes into the winery and detailed classification of individual wine parcels after fermentation. Peter Gago said, 'Bin 28 Shiraz provides momentum within the Penfolds portfolio. If we can keep making a wine at this quality and pricing, it means we must further add value and something extra to our other bin wines.'

Huon Hooke enjoyed the tasting: 'The wines more than supported their reputation. You don't immediately think of Bin 28 as a cellaring wine but they do hang on remarkably well. I enjoyed the overall freshness of the style.'

Steve Lienert said, 'The tasting really does show an evolution and improvement of style. The real point of difference between today and the past—aside from better presses and overall technology—is the relationship between the winemaker and the grower. Winemakers and grower liaison viticulturalists are spending more time in the field explaining exactly what their needs are. Most growers, including our own vineyard managers, have a real interest in the final destination of their fruit. This goes beyond the quality incentives provided by fruit grading and price premiums. Penfolds growers are second-to-none when it comes to attention to detail and teamwork.'

Bin 28 has very clear, ripe fruit definition, with plenty of fruit volume, ripe tannin structure and no new oak. It's a richer style than Bin 128 and Koonunga Hill. The wine has a reputation for improving with medium-term cellaring although it is an early drinking style. In exceptional vintages these wines can age for the long term. Penfolds believes this particular style, which relies so much on fruit complexity and freshness, will benefit greatly from screw cap closure.

TASTING NOTES ~ BIN 28 KALIMNA SHIRAZ

1959   PAST

Brick red. Very evolved wine which fades quickly in the glass. It first showed delicate plum/tangerine/mocha/mint aromas and flavours and lacy, fine tannins but amontillado characters developed in the glass. Thinning and tired but interesting curio all the same.

1962   PAST

Brick red. Earthy/leather/meaty/demi-glace aromas. A fully evolved wine with tea-leafy tannins and a lovely retention of fruit. Finishes long and sweet. Good bottles still holding.

1963 ★   NOW • • • PAST

Brick red. Lovely sweet-fruit/earthy/chocolaty aromas with touches of aniseed/leather. The palate is classically proportioned with earthy/chocolate/quince flavours, plenty of mid-palate richness and smooth ripe tannins. It finishes chalky dry but long. It's not going anywhere but it's a really lovely old wine.

1964 ★   NOW

Brick red. Fresh but evolved cedar/seaweed/mocha/vellum/demi-glace aromas. The palate is smooth and rich with demi-glace/dark chocolate/earthy flavours and fine, lacy tannins. Savoury dry finish. Still has life and 'deliciousness'! Drink now.

1967   NOW • • • PAST

Brick red. Intense dark chocolate/bitumen/tangerine/orange clove aromas. A generously flavoured palate with dark chocolate/dried plum/toffee/tangerine flavours and loose-knit, brittle, dry—a touch bitter—tannins. Finishes powdery and long. At the cusp of age. Drink it now.

1970 ★   NOW

Brick red. Very complex, ethereal wine with beautiful meaty/demi-glace/choco-berry fruit and dried herb notes. The quintessential old Penfolds wine with ripe choco-berry/roasted coffee/meaty flavours and slinky, long, dry tannins. Finishes grainy firm with excellent flavour length.

1971 ★   NOW

Brick red. Intense leather/demi-glace/cedar aromas with honeycomb/apricot notes. Fresh, soft, smooth wine with sweet leather/tobacco/chocolaty/liquorice flavours and satin tannins. Finishes long and sweet. Needs drinking soon.

1975   NOW

Brick red. Dark cherry/mocha/sweet-fruit aromas and flavours. The palate is tight and linear with fading earthy/mocha/prune/herb garden/lanolin flavours and lacy, dry, bitter tannins. At the very tail end of its life but still holding. Drink very soon.

1976   PAST

Brick red. Brambly/dark chocolate/driftwood/vellum aromas. Deeply concentrated wine with dark chocolate/bitumen/earthy flavours and granular grippy tannins. Finishes rusty and dry. Once again neither bottle lived up to vintage expectations. Drink up.

1977   NOW

Brick red. A savoury, well-developed wine with earthy/dark chocolate/graphite/wet bitumen aromas. The palate is sweet and concentrated with bitter dark chocolate/earthy sweet-fruit flavours and fine gravelly tannins. Bitumen-dry at the finish. Just holding on.

1978   NOW

Brick red. Dark chocolate/herb garden/graphite aromas with some leather/smoky notes. Sweet, complex, dark chocolate/walnut/amontillado flavours and fine, slinky, firm tannins. Finishes grippy and tight. More power than charm, but still impressive for its age.

1979   NOW • • • 2012

Brick red. Earthy/dark chocolate/cedar/herb aromas with some old leather notes. A loose-knit, cedary palate with some dark chocolate/earthy/bitumen flavours and rolling tannins. Finishes chalky dry but there's still plenty of sweet fruit following through.

1980   NOW • • • 2010

Brick red. Fully mature wine with chocolate/leather/demi-glace aromas and some slight maderised notes. The palate is still fresh with plenty of mocha/chocolate/leather/herb-mint flavours and slinky, firm, long, savoury tannins.

1981   NOW

Deep brick red. Fresh choco-berry/mocha/farmyard aromas. The wine is completely evolved with complex dark chocolate/meaty/lanolin/farmyard characters and dense, savoury dry/woolly tannins. Very robust wine. Ready to drink but will hold.

1982　　　　　　　　　　　　　　　　　　　　　　　　　PAST • • • NOW

Brick red. Red cherry/dried herb/dark chocolate/tobacco aromas with some old leather notes. A lighter-bodied wine with red cherry/rhubarb/mocha flavours and loose-knit, ripe tannins. Has softness and balance. Probably a touch past its prime. Drink now.

1983　　　　　　　　　　　　　　　　　　　　　　　　NOW • • • 2011

Brick red. Fragrant dark chocolate/panforte/tobacco/mint aromas. The palate is deeply concentrated and powerful with dark chocolate/panforte/demi-glace flavours and strong, thick, chocolaty tannins. Finishes grippy, tight and firm. Still has life but this is no beauty.

1984　　　　　　　　　　　　　　　　　　　　　　　　NOW • • • PAST

Medium brick red. Fresh mocha/beef stock/dark cherry aromas with some liquorice/cedar/sandalwood notes. The wine is mellow and mature with dark cherry/mocha/prune flavours and loose-knit, savoury tannins. Finishes long and minerally. Slightly overdeveloped. Drink now.

1985　　　　　　　　　　　　　　　　　　　　　　　　NOW • • • PAST

Deep red. Fragrant redcurrant/herb-mint/mocha aromas with some earthy/leather notes. Redcurrant/mocha/herb garden/mint flavours and silken/satin textures. The palate is a touch disjointed. The tannins rough up at the finish.

1986　★　　　　　　　　　　　　　　　　　　　　　　NOW • • • 2020

Deep red. Beautiful wine with intense choco-berry/earthy/leafy/tobacco/liquorice aromas. Classic Penfolds wine with plenty of dark chocolate/meaty/earthy/tobacco/aniseed flavours and ripe, sweet, supple tannins. Finishes long and flavourful. A very satisfying wine.

1987　　　　　　　　　　　　　　　　　　　　　　　　NOW • • • 2011

Medium red. Fresh earthy/mocha/mushroom/leafy/herb garden aromas. The palate is restrained with sweet earthy/dried cherry/herbal flavours and leafy/sinewy tannins. Fruit fades towards the finish leaving a dry tannin slick. Cool-vintage wine. Will hold but drink soon.

1988　★　　　　　　　　　　　　　　　　　　　　　　NOW • • • 2012

Medium deep red. Fragrant mocha/camomile/rose petal/sandalwood/dried plum aromas. The wine is still fresh and richly textured with attractive blackberry/redcurrant/dark mocha flavours and supple savoury tannins. Finishes firm and leafy dry. In good shape.

1989　　　　　　　　　　　　　　　　　　　　　　　　　　　NOW

Medium deep red. Fresh black cherry/chocolate/apricot/dried fig/herbal aromas with touches of camphor. Palate is sweet and well concentrated with blackberry/bitumen/raspberry/herb flavours and fine, chewy, firm tannins. Long lingering finish.

1990　★　　　　　　　　　　　　　　　　　　　　　　NOW • • • 2020

Deep red. Intense and powerful choco-berry/cedar/liquorice aromas. Well-concentrated choco-berry/redcurrant/meaty/liquorice flavours and ripe, dense, velvety tannins. Some demi-glace notes. Finishes long and sweet. A classic Penfolds vintage; living up to expectations.

1991 ★ NOW • • • 2020

Deep red. Ripe blackcurrant/dried plum/mocha/meaty aromas with some herb notes. A beautifully aged and balanced Penfolds wine with blackcurrant pastille/dried plum/mocha/liquorice flavours and supple, fine, grainy tannins. At its prime of life.

1992 NOW • • • 2012

Medium deep red. Dark cherry/musky/chocolate aromas with splashes of liquorice and spice. Fresh, juicy, dark cherry/raspberry/mocha flavours, some polished leather notes and cedary dry tannins. Will further develop for the medium to long term, however, probably best to drink soon rather than wait.

1993 NOW • • • 2010

Deep red. Fragrant panforte/espresso/blackberry/mint aromas. Rich, meaty wine with panforte/ herb garden/mint flavours and loose-knit, chalky, firm tannins. Builds up sappy firm at the finish. A fairly tough and robust wine. Not a wine to keep but will hold.

1994 NOW • • • 2015

Deep red. Well-developed cedar/blackberry/mint aromas. Fresh, fleshy wine with well-concentrated sweet redcurrant/blackberry/mint flavours and fine, loose-knit dry chalky tannins. Finishes long and sweet. Still has decent fruit sweetness and power with some background leathery/rustic notes. It could improve but something of an each-way bet.

1995 NOW

Medium deep red. Intense dark berry/chocolate/earthy/polished leather/liquorice aromas with some cedar notes. Concentrated earthy/dark berry/liquorice flavours and slinky, dry tannins. Finishes long and sweet but tannins are beginning to dominate. An average wine.

1996 ★ NOW • • • 2025

Medium deep red. Scented plum/blackberry/dark cherry/graphite/cedar aromas. A richly concentrated and gorgeously seductive wine with mocha/plum/graphite flavours, underlying spicy notes and supple sweet tannins. Finishes firm with plenty of flavour length. A great Bin 28. Still has a good cellaring future.

1997 NOW • • • 2015

Deep red. Dark choco-berry/liquorice/panforte/earthy/herb aromas. The palate is fresh and well concentrated with plenty of fruit sweetness, choco-berry/panforte/spice flavours and sappy dry tannins. The wine is drinking really well, but tannins are a touch under-ripe. Drink sooner rather than later!

1998 ★ NOW • • • 2025

Deep red. Abundant rich dark cherry/chocolate/liquorice/herb garden aromas. A richly concentrated, beautifully focused wine with deep-set dark cherry/blackberry/chocolate/cedar flavours and sweet, supple tannins. A very fresh, evolved wine with balance, length and movement. Will continue to develop. Fabulous wine.

1999   NOW • • • 2018

Deep red. Fresh black cherry/dried plum/mocha/liquorice aromas with touches of cedar. The palate has good richness and depth with medium-bodied plum/blackberry/cedar/espresso coffee flavours and ripe, fresh tannins. Finishes gravelly and long. More elegant and muscular than 1998 but evolving really well. Should keep and improve.

2000   NOW • • • 2010

Medium deep red. Intense musky/violet/red cherry/mulberry/slightly silage/mint aromas. Rich, fleshy palate with mulberry/red cherry/jammy flavours and chalky, loose-knit tannins. Not a bad wine but not one for the long haul. Drink very soon.

2001   NOW • • • 2018

Deep red. Ripe blackberry/dried plum/redcurrant/liquorice aromas. A very buoyant wine with redcurrant/plummy flavours and dense, chalky, firm tannins. The wine has plenty of volume and richness. It will hold but it won't necessarily improve. At its best now.

2002 ★   NOW • • • 2025

Medium deep red. A lovely vintage. The wine is fresh and primary with blackberry/liquorice/camomile/spice aromas, sweet plump blackberry/liquorice flavours and dense, ripe, generous, chocolaty tannins. Delicious to drink now but will steadily improve for another ten years.

2003   NOW • • • 2012

Medium deep red. Dark mocha/plum/raisin aromas with some aniseed/black pepper notes. Well-concentrated, dense but robust wine with dark mocha/dried plum flavours and chalky dry—a touch grippy—tannins. More muscle than charm. Best to drink soon before the tannins take over.

2004 ★   NOW • • • 2018

Medium deep red. Very fresh, vibrant wine with red cherry/aniseed/plummy aromas with some nutmeg/spicy/mint notes. Generous chocolaty/blackberry/red cherry flavours and slinky, dry tannins. Finishes long and bittersweet. A very well-balanced wine that should improve with further ageing.

2005 ★   2009 • • • 2020

Medium deep red/purple. Musky plum/black cherry/liquorice/dried spice aromas. The palate is fresh with black cherry/plum/liquorice flavours and fresh, ripe tannins. Finishes long and sweet. Abundant flavour, depth and structure. Delicious wine.

2006 ★   2010 • • • 2030

Deep red/purple. Lovely fresh blackberry/dark chocolate/liquorice/cedar aromas. The palate is ripe and densely packed with blackberry/plum/liquorice flavours and rich, smooth, chocolaty tannins. A great Bin 28 vintage. This is a wine that you can drink now, but it will also cellar for decades.

DISCUSSION

[Vintages 1960–61, 1965–66, 1968–69 and 1972–74 were not tasted. Most considered past.] Many of the older vintages are really lovely with plenty of sweet fruit, leather nuances and fine tannin structures. There was an overall deliciousness about the wines. (CM) The older wines are charming, with most vintages holding up very well. The wines are different to Koonunga Hill. They have more finesse, volume of flavour and mouth-feel. There was a wonderful, limpid clarity. I really liked that visual come-on. Most vintages are still fresh with beautiful depth of colour, richness, texture and fruit integrity. (NB) Overall the older wines more than supported their reputation. You don't immediately think of Bin 28 as a cellaring wine but they do hang on remarkably well. I enjoyed the overall freshness of the style. The best wines followed the pattern of acknowledged Penfolds vintages. (HH)

1963 is exciting to drink. It has a generosity of fruit and an appetising, flourishing finish. (NB)

1967 was ethereal with balloons of secondary aromas. The wine is extraordinarily generous—the type of wine you'd love as a grandparent! (CM)

1971 was probably not the best bottle but it still has the extra dimension of flavour expected from this great vintage. (JH)

1975 is a substantial wine with attractive, smoky, blackcurrant vanillin and firm but ripe tannins. It's still holding together top to bottom. (NB)

1976 is a blockbuster wine and swingingly tannic and astonishing brooding richness. It's a fairly monolithic wine and not really that well balanced. (NB) It smelled of animal hides and the palate is beginning to dry out. The tannins are winning the fight now. (HH).

1977 is always a surprise vintage with very good structure, balance and length. (JH)

1978 is just effortless with life, poise and balance. (CM)

The wines of the **1980s** are quite rustic and many are fully mature. Most are best to drink now and not worth keeping. (JG)

1983 was a whopper with meat stock, blond tobacco aromas and a big, firm tannic structure. It's a very robust vintage but I liked the overall concentration and power. (HH)

1984 is a funky old wine but has a lot of appeal. **1985** is fragrant but the palate is disjointed. (JG)

1986 has very good focus with deep and satisfying flavours. 1988 is still fresh and richly textured. Both 1987 and 1989 won't get any better. Best to drink now. (HH)

1990 has true complexity with elegance, weight and structure. (HH) I enjoyed this fresh, broadly textured wine. The fruit seemed to be so well back-lighted and vivid. (JG)

1991 was a really nice wine with serious structure and length. It just had layers of flavour and tannin. (HH)

1994 has intensity and punch with rich silky tannins. (JG) **1996** has extra power and elegance. It's robust and firm in the mouth but it's starting to drink really well. (HH)

1998 had lovely plummy aromas and rich, ripe fruit galore. (HH) The more recent vintages from 1999 to the present are really consistent with strength of tannins and buoyancy of fruit. The price point belies the ageing potential of Bin 28. (JG)

1999 is an excellent wine with plenty of plums, fresh supple tannins and balancing acidity. I tended to enjoy the younger, more floral, aromatic wines with their ripeness and smooth silky tannins. (CPT)

2000 is a surprise packet. I like this. It doesn't have the finish of a really good wine but it's much better than I expected of the vintage. It has plenty of mint, blackcurrant, plums, coffee and fresh acidity and still drinking youthfully well but I wouldn't keep it for too long now. (CM)

2001 is a big wine. It's a fraction grippy but has ripe fruit and prune/liquorice notes. It might show some improvement with time. (JH)

2002 has a very good deep colour. It has intensity but is somewhat introverted, with black fruit aromas and firm tannins. It's perfectly well balanced and patience will surely reward. (JH) The wine was wonderfully harmonious, ripe and very inviting. The palate is dense, focused and impressively taut. It is a wine of lovely balance and complexity. (NB)

2003 is very primary—almost grapey. The tannins have a slight green spicy/herbal edge. (JG) It has very full-bodied fruit with prominent tannins and chocolate/plum fruit. (CPT) It lacks the freshness and fruit vitality of the top years but is okay to drink now. (HH)

2004 is on the other hand a very robust and fresh, lively all-round wine with fully developed red fruit/raw nut/nutmeg/spice aromas, refined texture and lovely flavour. If cellared well it will go on for another twenty years. (HH) It is a feminine wine with floral/violet aromas, soft elegant fruit and silky tannins. (CPT)

2005 is a really super wine—much to my surprise like the 2004. It has musk-shot plum aromas and flavours and lovely tannin framework. (CM)

2006 has gorgeous perfume. It's on a roll with super-lifted chocolate, plums, musk, cedar characters. It's a profoundly good Bin 28 and the best for a while even though the last few were really good. Back up the ute, we need some cases of this in the cellar. (CM) It's still very youthful, of course, but it has abundant fruit; the tannins are there but still encased in puppy fat. It has excellent potential. (JH) It has impressive depth and richness of flavour. There is an overall harmony that bodes well. (NB)

Penfolds is paying its growers premium quality prices for Bin 28 fruit. The overall investment and attention given to the wine reflects a strong fine winemaking tradition. In the whole scheme of things Bin 28 lies in the middle of the Penfolds hierarchy. The younger wines, while showing abundant flavours and good tannin structure, are not necessarily long-term wines. The whole point about Bin 28 is that it is an early drinking style. However, the better Bin 28s—the ones that have aged well—have followed the overall pattern of acknowledged Penfolds vintages. (JH)

Bin 128 Shiraz

First Vintage:	1962.
Variety:	Shiraz.
Origin:	100% Coonawarra—mostly from Penfolds vineyards.
Fermentation:	Stainless steel tanks with wooden header boards.
Maturation:	12 months in new (20%) and aged (80%) French hogsheads. The changeover from American to French oak was progressive; it began in 1979 and was completed by the 1983 vintage.
Comments:	In 1981 the wine changed from Bin 128 Claret to Bin 128 Shiraz. Released under screw cap in some markets since the 2005 vintage.

'An impressive sequence of vintages,
showing freshness, liveliness and balance.'
—CH'NG POH TIONG, PANELLIST

Bin 128 Coonawarra Shiraz is an important and lasting regional wine that was first produced in 1962. The fruit is almost entirely sourced from extensive, mature, company-owned vineyards in Coonawarra. The wine, together with Bin 28, is renowned for its consistency and reliability as both a current-drinking and cellaring-type red. The Coonawarra fruit colony was first established in 1890. Winemaking followed, but it was not a commercial success. Bill Redman, one of the early pioneers, once said, 'from 1890 to 1945 you can write failure across the face of Coonawarra'. The problem was simply isolation. The region was beset by acute labour shortages, no electricity grid and poor access to market.

By the 1950s, renewed enthusiasm and wine successes, typified by the release of the now famed Woodley's Treasure Chest Series and 1955 Wynns Coonawarra Estate Michael Shiraz, attracted more investment capital. Penfolds was a later entrant, largely because of Max Schubert's preference for strongly flavoured and concentrated fruit. In 1960 he was persuaded by Bill Redman to purchase a parcel of Redman's vineyard called Sharam's Block. The release of the 1962 Bin 128 marked the beginning of a long and important period of Penfolds winemaking in Coonawarra.

Throughout the 1960s and early '70s, Max Schubert experimented with Coonawarra fruit, culminating in the release of both multi-district and single-region cabernet–shiraz blends, including the famous 1962 Bin 60A, 1967 Bin 7 and 1966 Bin 620. A whole string of successful wines during the 1960s, mostly based on cabernet sauvignon, attracted significant interest in the cool maritime climes and the terra rossa soils of Coonawarra. These were exciting times of extensive new plantings and new entrants. Shiraz, however, was the bridesmaid.

Despite the increasing hegemony of Coonawarra cabernet, Penfolds Bin 128 Shiraz was gathering its own momentum as one of the most reliable and interesting wines on the domestic Australian market. One critic who was particularly impressed with this emerging line was the late Len Evans, authoritative wine writer and wine industry leader, who described the 1966 as 'one of the top young reds of the last couple of years; the nose is very full and quite extraordinary for the straight shiraz that it is. The fruit is so very big, yet full of that delightfully austere Coonawarra character. There is evidence of small oak maturation; this is probably being with American oak. There is little doubt that Penfolds are really masters of this kind of treatment. Unlike many reds being made today for the demanding market, there is no suggestion of thinness before the finish asserts. I feel this wine will go on for many years. It could be eight to ten years before it shows its best.' This same wine, reviewed almost 40 years later at this 2007 Rewards of Patience tasting, was still drinking reasonably well with relative freshness and bittersweet tannins.

Penfolds now possesses over 100 hectares of prime Coonawarra vineyard and also draws fruit from independent growers in the region. During the 1960s and early '70s, the fruit used to be crushed with the aid of an old car engine in a tin shed and the wine pumps were operated with steam. The must was then tankered up to Magill and later Nuriootpa for vinification. Investment in processing facilities followed during the late 1970s.

The original release of Penfolds Bin 128 reflected the perceived view of the day that shiraz was a more reliable performer. Certainly the wine has been made every year—regardless of vintage conditions. While winemaking practice and philosophy is essentially no different to the first vintage releases, Penfolds gradually adjusted its barrel maturation program to enhance regional and varietal definition. A gradual changeover from American to French oak between 1979 and 1983 saw a marked improvement in fruit and regional definition. This same period of transition also saw striking advances in viticulture. During the 1970s viticulturalists employed a system of mechanisation and minimal pruning in the vineyard.

By the early 1980s, Penfolds invested heavily in reconfiguring its vineyards, initiating better canopy and block management and adopting new data-gathering technologies. The Bin 128 wines have benefited enormously from this focused approach. The combination of riper fruit, mature tannin structure and refined French oak maturation has resulted in more consistent and better wines. The aromas are buoyant and expressive, while the flavours are more saturated and sustained.

Bin 128 is an authentic Coonawarra shiraz style. Vinification follows a traditional Penfolds winemaking philosophy. Towards dryness the wine is transferred into new and used French oak hogsheads to complete fermentation. The wine is matured in approximately 20 per cent new, one- and two-year-old tightly grained French oak for a period of about twelve months prior to bottling.

Neil Beckett observed, 'The Bin 128s showed very strong regional characters with black fruit aromas and mint/marine characters. The wines tasted very savoury, showing glorious refinement and texture. Even if the fruit had faded, the textural quality could still be enjoyed. The early vintages, while mostly past, are still interesting to look at; they show a steady progression of style and increasing attention to tannin ripeness and oak management.'

Peter Gago said, 'There has always been a philosophy of difference between Bin 128 and Bin 28. The Coonawarra shiraz has always shown more transparent and restrained regional fruit characters—further enhanced by better viticultural management and intuitive contemporary winemaking. In 2007 a decision was made by Penfolds to release the 2006 Bin 128 Shiraz a year earlier to better capture the spice/floral/pepper characters and to offer a further point of difference to Bin 28 Kalimna Shiraz.'

TASTING NOTES ~ BIN 128 SHIRAZ

The 1969, 1977 and 1979 vintages were not tasted. These wines are considered past. Other vintages that were not tasted by the panel have been tasted by Andrew Caillard (text in italics).

1962   PAST

Brick red. Completely evolved wine with/mocha/leather/mushroom aromas and flavours. The palate is still showing some sweet fruit, but the palate has become sinewy and dried out.

1963   PAST

Brick red. Fully mature wine with mocha/dark chocolate/earthy/dried fruit aromas. The wine has faded with earthy/walnut, slightly maderised/toffee flavours and sinewy, dry, savoury tannins.

1964   PAST

Brick red. Very developed wine with meaty/gamy/mushroom/leathery aromas. The palate has faded with some savoury chocolate/mushroom notes and leafy tannins.

1965   PAST

Brick red. A mature old wine with coffee/chocolate/mushroom aromas and flavours. Plenty of freshness and sweet fruit on the palate, but it is beginning to dry out.

1966   PAST

Brick red. Fresh wet bitumen/leather saddle/cedar/leafy aromas. Earthy/mocha/leather flavours and fine grippy—almost stalky—tannins. Finishes astringent and hard. Has lost its charm.

1967   PAST

Deep red brick. An earthy/savoury wine with some smoky/sweet spicy nuances. The palate is rich and earthy with chocolaty, loose-knit tannins. Fine, old mellow wine.

1968   PAST

Brick red. Aged, slightly tired old wine with mushroom/fig-jam/caramel aromas and flavours. A mature/ evolved palate with some savoury notes and richness.

1970   PAST

Brick red. Classical meaty/prune/espresso/apricot aromas and flavours with fine, chalky, firm, loose-knit tannins. Finishes long and sweet, but quite grippy. The fruit is dropping out now. Drink up.

1971   NOW • • • PAST

Brick red. Lovely old wine bouquet with sweet mocha/strawberry/honeyed/herb/leather aromas. The palate is quite fragile now with mocha/strawberry/herb/walnut/leather fruit and delicate and supple, lacy tannins. Still a good drink.

1975   NOW

Brick red. Intense, bitter dark chocolate/menthol/brine/sandalwood aromas. A complex mouth-filling wine with bitter dark chocolate/prune/herb garden/tobacco/mint flavours and gravelly firm tannins. Finishes grippy and tight. The palate is very structured with little promise of softening but drink soon.

1976 ★   NOW

Deep brick red. Complex liquorice/redcurrant/mocha/mint aromas with some savoury notes. Richly concentrated redcurrant/sweet-fruit/demi-glace/slightly raisined flavours and slinky, fine tannins. Finishes chalky firm, long and sweet. A powerful rustic wine. It's drinking beautifully now, but it will probably hold for a while.

1978   NOW

Medium deep brick red. Lovely complex earthy/liquorice/cassis aromas with a hint of cedar. Earthy/liquorice/leather/sweet-fruit flavours and ripe, supple, fine, lacy tannins. Finishes minerally and long. A touch underpowered, with fruit beginning to fade.

1980   NOW

Brick red. Smoky/graphite/cedar/prune aromas with faint tomato leaf notes. The palate is savoury dry with some prune/mocha/red fruit flavours and fine, slinky, firm tannins. Finishes chewy and long. Best to drink up.

1981   PAST

Brick red. Complex mocha/toffee/earthy aromas with hints of herb/mint. Mocha/chocolaty flavours on the palate with pronounced gritty tannins finishing a touch green.

1982   NOW • • • PAST

Medium brick red. Meaty/dried red cherry/rose petal/chocolate aromas with touches of crème brûlée. Sweet kirsch/choco-berry/crème brûlée/herb flavours and fine supple tannins. Finishes a touch minty/leafy.

1983 NOW

Medium brick red. Earthy/plum/minty/leafy aromas. The palate is medium concentrated with generous earthy/leafy/red berry flavours and fine, dense, loose-knit, chalky tannins.

1984 PAST

Light brick red. Earthy overdeveloped aromas with some aromatic notes. A lean, under-powered wine with a tough tannic finish.

1985 NOW

Medium light brick red. Perfumed camomile/dark choco-berry aromas with hints of leather/herb garden. A sweet, deep-set wine with choco-berry/camomile/vanillin flavours and fine gritty tannins. Finishes grippy dry but long and minerally.

1986 ★ NOW

Medium brick red. Beautiful wine with smoky/graphite/rose petal/plum aromas with hints of cedar. The palate is chocolaty with plenty of blackberry/plum/mocha/cedar/tobacco flavours and fine, dense tannins. Finishes firm and chalky.

1987 PAST

Medium brick red. Tobacco/leafy aromas. The palate has some vegetal/minty/leafy flavours. Drink up.

1988 PAST

Medium brick red. Earthy/redcurrant/plummy aromas and flavours. The palate is austere with plenty of gritty tannins and fading fruit. Finishes lean.

1989 NOW

Medium brick red. Intense chocolate/prune/crème brûlée/herb garden/old honeyed aromas. Fresh, evolved lengthy wine with chocolaty/herbal/prune/meaty/leathery flavours and fine, leafy, dry tannins. Finishes woolly dry.

1990 ★ NOW • • • 2020

Medium deep crimson. Fragrant dark cherry/mocha/seaweedy aromas with touches of mint/leather. The palate is substantial and richly layered with rich dark cherry/choco-berry/earthy flavours and supple, dense, loose-knit tannins. Finishes firm, long and sweet. Classic Bin 128.

1991 NOW

Medium red. Earthy/plum/pepper aromas and flavours. A mouth-filling wine with plenty of mid-palate richness, sweetness of fruit and supple, fine, slinky tannins. A long, tangy aftertaste. Best to drink soon.

1992 NOW

Medium red. Fresh liquorice/rum/raisin/dark cherry aromas with some herb notes. A well-concentrated palate with dark cherry/kirsch/raisin flavours, underlying savoury notes and fine, grainy tannins. Finishes hard and leafy dry.

1993   NOW • • • 2018

Medium deep red. Complex earthy/red cherry/bitter chocolate/mocha aromas and flavours with some silage/minty notes. The palate is densely packed with plenty of sweet fruit but the flavours are submerged under substantial grippy tannins. A robust vintage.

1994   NOW

Medium red. Black fruit/earthy/walnut/meaty aromas with touches of graphite. A well-concentrated wine with plenty of blackberry/blueberry/leathery flavours and ripe, loose-knit tannins. Finishes chalky dry. Not particularly complex, but lovely buoyancy of fruit.

1995   NOW

Medium brick red. Fresh red fruits/blueberry aromas with mint/cedar nuances. The palate is soft with gentle red fruit flavours and lacy, savoury tannins. An early drinking wine at or slightly beyond its peak. Drink soon.

1996 ★   NOW • • • 2016

Medium deep red. Intense liquorice/dark chocolate/cedar aromas with hints of leather/spice. A dense, richly flavoured wine with plenty of smooth choco-berry/liquorice fruit, underlying cedary notes and strong, velvety tannins. It builds up leafy firm at the finish.

1997   NOW

Medium red. Red fruits/cassis/menthol/pepper aromas with developed gamy/polished leather notes. Medium-bodied meaty/spearmint/white pepper flavours and slinky, dry tannins. Finishes juicy, minerally and long. Drink soon.

1998 ★   NOW • • • 2018

Deep red–purple. Very fresh, lively, mouth-filling wine with intense chocolate/dark berry/meaty/minty aromas. The palate is richly layered with plenty of dark berry/mocha/sweet-fruit flavours, some smoky notes and dense, chocolaty, ripe tannins. Perfect to drink now but will age further.

1999 ★   NOW • • • 2018

Deep red. Lovely liquorice/blackberry essence aromas with some savoury notes. The wine is intensely concentrated and generous with blackberry/mocha fruit and plush, chocolaty, dry tannins. An excellent follow-up vintage.

2000   NOW

Medium red. Fresh raspberry/blueberry/vanillin aromas. The wine is lighter in style with plenty of raspberry/blueberry/minty fruit and loose-knit, supple, savoury tannins. The fruit tapers off, leaving a dry, chalky finish. It's not really a wine to cellar. Drink soon.

2001   NOW • • • 2020

Deep red–purple. Deep-set blackberry/plum/mint/menthol aromas with some cedar notes. Very juicy, concentrated palate with intense blackberry/mint flavours and strong gravelly tannins. Finishes a touch sappy green at the finish. Best to drink while still relatively primary.

2002 ★ NOW • • • 2020

Deep red–purple. Glossy blackberry/juicy fruit/black pepper/vanillin aromas. Long, focused palate with sweet, soft blackberry/black pepper/spice flavours, underlying vanillin nuances and plenty of sweet fruit. The tannins are smooth and silky. Finishes chalky firm. A top vintage.

2003 NOW • • • 2020

Deep red–purple. Blueberry/dark chocolate/briary/vanilla aromas with touches of mint/herb. Rich, ripe, concentrated wine with blueberry/dark choco-mint flavours and loose-knit tannins. Builds up leafy at the finish. You can drink it now but its best lies ahead.

2004 ★ NOW • • • 2020

Deep red–purple. Saturated elderberry/plum/spicy/nutmeg/*pain-grillé* aromas. The palate is beautifully exuberant and powerful with ripe elderberry/blackberry/plum fruit and chocolaty, firm tannins. Lovely weight, texture and tannin ripeness.

2005 2009 • • • 2025

Purple crimson. Raspberry/menthol plum aromas with some brambly notes. The wine is juicy and richly concentrated with plenty of raspberry/brambly flavours, underlying oak and fine, tight, leafy, firm tannins. It has good intensity, volume and balance.

2006 ★ 2010 • • • 2030

Deep crimson–purple. Beautiful crushed elderberry/mulberry/musky plum/blackstrap liquorice aromas. Rich, ripe, inky, deep, luscious wine with generous, elemental elderberry/mulberry/dark plum/aniseed flavours, and plush, dense, grainy tannins. Expansive and expressive. A brilliant wine. A great Bin 128.

DISCUSSION

The Bin 128s showed very strong regional characters with black fruit aromas and mint/marine characters. The wines tasted very savoury, showing glorious refinement and texture. Even if the fruit had faded, the textural quality could still be enjoyed. The early vintages—while mostly past—are still interesting to look at; they show a steady progression of style and increasing attention to tannin ripeness and oak management. 1963 was a very good start. The fruit was still intact on the nose while the palate was fully flavoured with waxy/velvety texture and plenty of richness. It is remarkable that it has survived so well. (NB)

1963 was once quite a famous wine. It's really past now though. It has an amalgam of soft aged leather, earth, dried fruit aromas and a nice, aged mouth-feel but the tannins have departed. 1966 was a better wine with more freshness and vitality. (JH) 1963 was a very fresh, enjoyable and engaging wine with plenty of sandalwood/sweet spice, dried Chinese sour prune characters. (CPT)

1966 was almost Bordeaux-like with its cedar/sandalwood aromas and ravishingly sumptuous structure and rich, seamless flavours. (NB) 1966 was more exotic with some medicinal characters. The palate was much better with chocolaty, coffee, wood spice fruit. (CPT)

Many of the wines during the 1970s and '80s showed leafy/herbal nuances. The best vintages of these decades have a lovely transparency of strawberry fruits. The wines are not complex but they are sound and pleasing. (JG) Those herbal characters are most likely derived from minimal pruning; the standard viticultural practice of the time. (SL) It was a strange period. Viticulturalists were coming up with techniques to please the bean counters. The practices were considered perfectly acceptable—even innovative at the time. A huge investment in vineyard rehabilitation was made during the 1980s and early 1990s. Completely different canopy and block management, new infrared technologies and a more sophisticated approach to growing top-quality fruit can be seen in the wines of the 1990s and 2000s. (JH)

1970 was a touch funky with some meaty characters and rather drying, firm, dry tannins. (HH) There are lots of old green and dry, leafy notes. The tannins are grippy firm. It's big and expressive, but it has become tired and disjointed. (CM)

1971 was a lovely, red-fruited, delicately structured wine with fragile structure and persistent flavour. (JG) It's still drinking marvellously well. It still had a lovely, sweet, honeyed, old wine bouquet with some minty notes. The palate is quite rich and deep; there's an extra dimension here. (HH)

1975 smells of sandalwood and mint. It has plenty of sweet fruit including tobacco/wood spice flavours. The finish is drying but there's some persistency of fruit. (CPT) It's in pretty good shape for a 32-year-old wine with fresh menthol/mint aromatics and flavours. (CM)

1976 is noticeably darker in colour. It's a powerfully rustic wine with strong earthy components and fractionally grippy tannins. (JH) Again, it has a minty freshness on the nose. It's beautifully lithe and supple with glove-leather notes. The palate is powerful, expansive and mouth-filling, with sweet, pruney fruit and good, strong flavour length. (NB)

1978 is like a good roll in the countryside with sweet leathery flavours giving the mid-palate the substance a lot of these early wines lack. (CM) It's very impressive for its age with cassis/dried cherry/white pepper/sandalwood/coffee fruit and lingering finish. (CPT)

1980 was not showing a lot of fruit. The palate was dry and savoury with chewy rustic tannins. (HH) The wine showed plenty of green herb/green pepper character. (JG)

1982 was beginning to thin out; it's a lighter-bodied wine with herbal, cassis, vegetal characters and fine, supple tannins. It's an unusual wine but I quite liked it. (HH)

1983 was drinking very well with a power of stalk and mint. There was a touch of farm floor but it was well structured, pure and generous. (CM) It's a charmer, with fragrant mint/cassis aromas and a light, fresh palate. (CPT)

1985 was quite light and delicate but it still has gentle sweet fruit and wisps of French oak in the background. (JH) It had a fresh cranberry, spice nose and a soft, supple palate. There was not much backbone or guiding spoke, but there was good flavour length. (NB)

1986 showed a healthy brick-red colour. It was the first wine to show real class. It had very good structure; sweet plum, mocha flavours, integrated oak and fine tannins. (JH) It was a fascinating wine; a *Médoc*-ian style with very lively cedary/spicy characters and capsicum/herbaceous notes. I found it more cabernet sauvignon-like than shiraz! (CPT)

1989 has some flavour and body, freshness and length. It was firm and rather astringent but it had redeeming meaty/leathery old flavours. (HH)

1990 was an attractive wine at the peak of its mature power. It had a mix of black cherry/plum fruit, fine, supple tannins and long finish. (JH) The wines from the 1990s were universally excellent. I found it difficult to find a wine I didn't like. I found it substantial with some mint, leather nuances and plenty of tannins. It was spotlessly clean and rather boring. 1991, however, was really nice with a spread of mint, fresh dark leather, pepper flavours through the mouth. (CM) There were some earthy aspects, but there was a core of black fruits and surprising length and aftertaste, courtesy of acidity. (JH)

1992 was still powering on with spicy richness and fresh, zesty acidity. (HH) It had an intense blackcurrant/incense nose and dense, woven texture palate. It was good in a robust way. (NB)

1993 was very balanced, fresh and appealing with cassis aromas, medium-bodied fruit and balanced, ripe, enveloping tannins. (CPT) The wine has some lovely ripe berry/peppery fruit but the alcohol, spice and strong tannin take over on the palate. (JG)

1994 was structured, fine, elegant and delicious with sweet honey/mint aromas and lots of nice leathery flavours. It's a lovely wine but ready to drink now. (CM)

1995 has nice spicy red fruits but it lacks the focus and intensity of the other wines in this bracket. (JH) It's simple and fragrant; perhaps in line with the older-style Bin 128s. However, it's still showing good fruit transparency and clean flavours. (JG)

1996 is drinking beautifully. It still had a good amount of primary fruit; lovely cherry, strawberry/peppery flavours and developed leather notes. It still has lots in it for further cellaring but it's great to drink now. (CM) It's got plenty of extract, breadth and richness. The palate is fleshy and deep with chewy, savoury tannins. (HH)

1997 was savoury and smoky. The fruit seems to be stressed by the oak. It perhaps needs more time for its real personality to show through. (NB) It is something of a surprise. The wine is unexpectedly supple and smooth with gentle fruit and no green tinges. But I don't think this is going to further improve in the cellar. (JH)

1998 has bitter chocolate/savoury aromas and the full spectrum of flavours. The palate is tightened up by wood. (NB) It's a bit clumsier than the 1996 but it has decent dark, chewy liquorice, redcurrant, blackberry fruit/roasted pepper aromas and good concentration without being heavy. It's a very good wine. (JG)

1999 is showing deep, dark berry, slightly minty aromas and clean firm tannic palate. There's lots of grip and cut. It needs ages. (HH) I liked the 1999 more than the 1998—which is regarded as a classic Penfolds year. I was attracted to the ripe fruit, pepper-spice characters and the intermingling of secondary and primary characters. This was an elegant, electrifying wine with balance, structure and complexity. This is highly drinkable but also has excellent cellaring potential. (CM)

2000 was distinctly minty with fine, savoury tannins. (JH) It had plenty of dark plum, juicy fruit aromas and equally ripe tannins and oak. I found the oak better managed than 1999. (CPT)

2001 is a hot-year wine with floral, liquorice, dried fruit aromas and touches of mint. The fruit is very ample and soft but the tannins are pronounced. It will need further cellaring to come around. (HH) I found the wine had a mixed ripeness although the green characters integrated well with the black fruits. (JG)

2002 was a beautiful wine with pepper, cherry, musky, rhythm and cool-year blues. Basically it was pure and delicious. (CM) The cool year manifests itself in the lashings of mint and spice. It had a long, focused, slinky, smooth palate. (JH) I really enjoyed the blackberry/blueberry, fresh fruit and crisp tannins. It was a very balanced, elegant wine; a *Vin de Garde*. (CPT)

2003 had a very vivid fruit quality to the nose with plenty of cherry, blackberry, raspberry aromas. The palate was rich and plush in texture, but still supple and long. (NB) It's not very giving at the moment but it's perfumed and neat with herbal/minty notes and a lean, narrow profile. (HH)

2004 was black, smoky and tense with plenty of primary purple fruit, some blueberry characters and lots of new oak. The palate showed lovely black ripeness and very long, chewy tannins. (JG) The Coonawarra yields in 2004 were huge with big bunches and big berries. (JH) It was even better than 2003 with elegant, silky florals, raspberry fruit and equally impressive tannins. (CPT)

2005 had a floral, minty, blueberry nose with some spicy, nutmeg notes. This was a classic ripe shiraz with subtle but good oak support and fine, tight tannins. It's marvellously intense and long, more fine and linear in structure than 2004. This is a long-term wine and will benefit from further cellaring. (HH) The wine is super fresh, very fruity and perfumed. The musky, peppery flavours only come through towards the end. (CM)

2006 is very elemental with bold primary juicy fruit and oak. It is a very potent, expressive wine that should come together well. (JG) It's very intense with blackstrap liquorice, sharply defined primary fruit. The palate is dense, rich and supple with saturated, sustained flavours and textured refinement. 2005 and 2006 are another step up. These are very successful wines. (NB) 2006 was a real highlight—the best wine of the 1990s and 2000s. (CPT) The Bin 128 style is an excellent contrast to the more chocolaty Barossa shirazes. There was nothing abrasive or rough about the wines. I was particularly seduced by the youthful buoyancy of the most recent vintages. When you look at the older wines from this perspective, they look comparatively skeletal. The 2000s are in a completely different league; they have excellent richness and suppleness of flavour. (HH)

Bin 138 Grenache Shiraz Mourvèdre

First Vintage:	1992.
Variety:	Grenache, shiraz and mourvèdre, in varying proportions depending on vintage conditions.
Origin:	Barossa Valley, South Australia.
Fermentation:	Stainless steel tanks with wooden header boards.
Maturation:	12 months in older (often 6+ years) oak hogsheads.
Comments:	Sourced from several vineyards—average vine age 35 to 100+ years. Elevated to bin range with 1998 vintage. Released entirely under screw cap since the 2005 vintage.

'The contribution of each variety is sotto voce *yet the wine evokes the richness and generosity of the Barossa landscape.'*
— PETER GAGO, CHIEF WINEMAKER

Penfolds Bin 138 Grenache Shiraz Mourvèdre is a traditional Barossa blend. This highly perfumed, slinky, textured style is based on selected parcels of fruit, including old vine material going as far back as 1895. Bin 138 is a relatively new addition to the Penfolds bin range. The first vintages (1992–97) were originally released as Penfolds Old Vine Grenache Shiraz Mourvèdre. The compelling musky fragrance, fruit generosity and seductive flavours of grenache are central to the style. However, these characters are tempered and balanced by the inky coloured, chocolaty smooth texture of shiraz and the spicy top notes and savoury tannin structure of mourvèdre.

Bin 138 was first released in response to an increasing international interest in regional wine styles and the resurgence in popularity of the Barossa. The Barossa Valley, settled by Silesian and English settlers in the 1830s, was planted extensively with shiraz, mataro and grenache from very early on. However, grenache was for a long time considered better suited to the production of fortified wine. During the 1950s Penfolds experimented with shiraz and the robust grape variety mataro (now referred to by its more lyrical French synonym mourvèdre). The 1954 Bin 158 Shiraz Mataro—an experimental bin—is now a curio and extremely rare.

The release of 1960 Bin 2—a precursor to Bin 138—was a culmination of extensive trials. The pale-coloured, aromatic but relatively under-flavoured grenache was discarded because it simply did not have the required fruit profile or power for the emerging Penfolds house style. Indeed, few producers in the region tried to emulate the perfumed, fleshy styles made famous by the wines of Chateauneuf-du-Pape. Grenache, if it was used at all, was conveniently blended into claret-, dry-red type wines. Today Barossa grenache is a highly fashionable variety. Improved viticulture, increased vine age of more recent plantings, advances in technology and a more worldly and contemporary winemaking perspective have made Barossa grenache–shiraz–mourvèdre one of the most compelling and exciting genres of wine style in the world.

Bin 138 fruit is sourced from low-yielding, often independently grown, grapes from the north-western sub-regions of the Barossa Valley around Greenock, Kalimna, Moppa, Ebenezer, Marananga and Stonewell. The average age of vines is around 35 to 100 years. This includes venerated dry-grown, low-yielding bush vine material. Blended together, grenache, shiraz and mourvèdre can make a sublime wine with great personality and structure.

Vintage conditions and the nature of the fruit determine the final mix of varietal components. In some vintages, shiraz can lead the blend. In others grenache can be the principal element. Grenache, for instance, comprised 70 per cent of the wine. Interestingly, Bin 138 is the only Penfolds wine that remains in component form during maturation. It is only assembled together after several rackings and just prior to bottling.

The original vintages from 1992 to 1997 represent an evolution of style and a steep learning curve. Peter Gago says, 'The contribution of each variety is *sotto voce* yet the wine evokes the richness and generosity of the Barossa landscape.' After vinification the wine is matured in old hogsheads to enhance fruit aromas, promote integration of flavours and soften tannin structure. Bin 138 is a relatively early to medium drinking style, which develops rich, complex, earthy nuances with age. Joshua Greene observed, 'Without a mass of new oak, the wines had a wonderful floral, perfumed edge and refinement of tannins. I enjoyed the unadorned nature of the fruit and the overall elegance of the style.'

TASTING NOTES ~ BIN 138 SHIRAZ GRENACHE SHIRAZ MOURVÈDRE

1992   NOW

Brick red. Very complex, fully mature wine with leather/demi-glace/prune/hazelnut aromas. The palate is generous but medium-bodied with plenty of juicy, sweet fruit, spicy/earthy notes and sinewy dry tannins. Mourvèdre, grenache, shiraz blend. Drink now.

1993   NOW

Brick red. Fresh, sweet, dried plum/musky/grilled nut aromas. Well-concentrated sweet plum/ panforte/grilled nut flavours and slinky dry/bony tannins. Still has buoyancy of fruit and good flavour length. Shiraz, grenache, mourvèdre blend. Best to drink now.

1994   NOW • • • 2012

Brick red. Developed meaty/musky plum/demi-glace/polished leather aromas. Full-flavoured wine with meaty/musky plum/leather/demi-glace/earthy flavours and firm chalky/grippy tannins. A lovely old red with ample tannin structure. Grenache, shiraz, mourvèdre blend. Drink this one soon.

1995   NOW

Red brick. Intense plum/dark cherry/wet bitumen/herb aromas. The palate is well concentrated with dark cherry/liquorice/tar/herbal flavours and dusty/savoury tannins. The fruit is beginning to dry out. Shiraz, mourvèdre, grenache blend. Drink now.

1996   NOW • • • 2012

Medium deep crimson. Intense, evolved, dark cherry/walnut/polished leather/liquorice aromas. A richly weighted wine with plum/liquorice/sandalwood flavours and dense, mouth-filling tannins. Still has volume and energy. Grenache, mourvèdre, shiraz blend. Drink soon.

1997   NOW

Medium deep crimson. Fresh musky plum/redcurrant aromas with some mint chocolate notes. The palate is well developed with plum/redcurrant flavours and fine, slinky, firm tannins. Finishes chalky dry but good flavour length. Shiraz, grenache, mourvèdre blend. Drink now.

1998 ★   NOW • • • 2015

Deep crimson. Fresh blackberry/plum/herb garden/violet aromas. Ample, expansive palate with beautifully concentrated choco-berry flavours, plenty of fruit sweetness and ripe, supple, loose-knit tannins. Some spice/leather notes at the finish. Wonderful volume and richness. Shiraz, grenache, mourvèdre blend. Drinking very well now but will hold.

1999   NOW • • • 2015

Deep crimson. Fresh damson plum/redcurrant/aniseed aromas with some leafy/herb nuances. A rich, savoury, multi-layered wine with bitter dark chocolate/plum/herb flavours and chalky, dry, loose-knit tannins. Builds up leafy firm, but long and flavourful. More structured than 1998. Shiraz, grenache, mourvèdre blend.

2001   NOW • • • 2012

Medium deep crimson. Rich chocolate/dried plum/raisin aromas with some musky/violet notes. Sweet, well-concentrated cassis/prune flavours and bittersweet tannins. Finishes grippy dry. Almost sweet and savoury in character. Will hold but tannins are overtaking fruit. Shiraz, grenache, mourvèdre blend. Drink soon.

2002 ★   NOW • • • 2020

Medium deep crimson. Fresh youthful blackberry/raspberry/aniseed/violet aromas. Plenty of richness and concentration on the palate with rolling redcurrant/blackberry flavours and chocolaty ripe tannins. Finishes firm and long. A beautifully balanced wine which will continue to evolve. Grenache, shiraz, mourvèdre blend.

2003   NOW • • • 2012

Medium crimson. A very fruit-driven, early drinking wine with juicy rhubarb/redcurrant/black cherry aromas and flavours. The palate is buoyant and fresh with plenty of fruit sweetness and fine, chalky, mouth-puckering tannins. Finishes grippy firm. Grenache, shiraz, mourvèdre blend.

2004 ★   NOW • • • 2020

Medium crimson. Very fresh, bright blackberry/musky plum/redcurrant/violet aromas. Supple, rich, dense wine with beautifully ripe blackberry/redcurrant/raspberry flavours and velvety smooth tannins. A very succulent and immaculately balanced wine. A great Barossa grenache year. A great Bin 138. Grenache, shiraz, mourvèdre blend.

Medium deep crimson. Fragrant violet/rose petal/musky plum/red berry aromas. The palate is sweet and concentrated with silky redcurrant/raspberry flavours and chalky, dry tannins. Finishes a touch grippy/chewy firm. An earlier-drinking style. It will hold, but best to drink over the next five years. Grenache, shiraz, mourvèdre blend.

Medium, deep crimson. Lovely musky/violet/dark chocolate/dark berry aromas. Rich musky/dark chocolate/blackberry flavours and dense, loose-knit tannins. Finishes long and savoury. A superb year.

> *'Bin 138 surprised us by being*
> *consistently good and ageing remarkably well.'*
> —HUON HOOKE, PANELLIST

DISCUSSION

Bin 138 was originally released as Old Vine Grenache. Over the first five vintages we were really on a steep learning curve. Initially we were concerned about the type of fruit used in the blend and how each component would relate to each other. The intensity and character of the three grape varieties varies each vintage. The wine just cannot be made to a recipe. In some years shiraz will lead the blend. At other times grenache will have the character and velocity of fruit to dominate the wine. Mourvèdre is very much a structural component. Maturation takes place in older oak to allow the wine to mellow and soften prior to release. We are very focused on maintaining Penfolds house style and regional definition. The contribution of each variety is *sotto voce* yet the wine evokes the richness and generosity of the Barossa landscape. (PG)

It was a real pleasure to see all of these wines together. I found the effects of older wood maturation quite fascinating. The best vintages are very exciting. Without a mass of new oak the fruit was fresh and buzzing with glorious generosity of flavour. (JG)

1992 was a very complex old wine; mellow and layered with plenty of meaty, earthy aromas and smooth but savoury, dry palate. It's still nice, but drink up. (HH) The best days are over for some of the older vintages. 1992 was a beautiful drink with plenty of juicy fruit and grapey tannins, but it's beginning to fade. (CM)

1993 has a touch of raisin/liquorice but it's rich and fleshy with a spine of drying tannin. Very good but drink up. (HH) The 1993 and 1994 broke what was a very consistent line. These vintages were quite grippy; the tannins appear likely to outlive the fruit. (JH)

1994 is a lovely old red with ample tannin structure. (CM) I enjoyed this wine. It was lush and heady with pronounced tannins but it was sweet and balanced. (JG)

1995 is full flavoured with plenty of developed characters, but the tannins are quite dusty. This is not going to get any better. (AC)

1996 is the perfect Bin 138 or Old Vine as it was then called. This is a beautiful wine in an effortless but structured style. (CM) It was complete and harmonious with satin-soft tannins. There was an old vine certainty about the vintage. It's coasting up to maturity; a graceful, relaxed wine with delicious freshness. (JG)

1997 is ready to drink now. The palate is well developed with some plum/redcurrant flavours and chalky, firm tannins. (AC)

1998 was quite spectacular with an expansive but smooth and supple palate structure. I enjoyed the younger wines. (NB) This is a very smart wine with loads of flavour, but it's big and tannic again. (HH)

1999 has lots of peppery/animal/mourvèdre characters. It's rich and deep with profound flavour and structure. There's lots happening but it does need a bit of time. (HH) This is a lovely food wine. The wine has plenty of red fruit/spice characters, ripe tannins and lots of freshness. (CPT)

2001 is too funky and feral for me! (HH) The aromas of this wine reminded me of a young exuberant ruby vintage port. (CPT) It smelled like a basket of blueberries, toffee, raspberries and violets. The tannins are beginning to dry out. But this is a really nice drink. (CM)

2002 is superb; a long-term wine with plenty of soft, sweet-fruit flavours and lovely balance. (HH) I particularly liked the juvenile red fruits/raspberry profile of both 2002 and 2004. The 2002 is a particularly great grenache vintage in the Barossa—as typified by the 2002 Cellar Reserve Grenache—but this wine, too, will also be very long-lived. (JH)

2003 is very dry and savoury. The tannins are very firm and puckering. I can't see this developing well. (HH) I think it is one of the better 2003s. It has a fair whack of juicy fruit and lots of tannin. I would punt on it. (CM)

2004 has a big future. It's smooth, soft and supple with plenty of florals, blackberry fruits and aniseed. It has a really good, long spine without being overtly firm. (HH) 2004 has a high deliciousness factor. It's big, fleshy and ripe with effortless swings of fruit and then rolls of silken tannin. Wonderful stuff! (CM) Both the 2002 and 2004 were stunning wines, reflecting top vintage conditions. But I also liked the grenache lift of the 2005. (JG)

2005 is tauter and narrower in profile to 2004, but it's a really well-balanced elegant wine. (HH) It had plenty of raspberry, floral, violet notes and succulent/silky tannins. There was a delicious freshness and vitality. (CPT) 2005 was all tar, roses and guns with great lift and great flavour. (CM) You will notice the alcohol levels are often less than 13.5%. We are making a deliberate effort to achieve concentration of fruit without driving up alcohols. (PG) The 2000s were generally quite impressive and a step up from the early vintages. (CM) I loved the unadorned nature of the fruit. The wines had a delightful florality rather than a meaty, dry red edge. I enjoyed the refinement of tannins and the seductive, flowing fruit. (NB) The main stars of this tasting were 1996, 1998, 2002 and 2004. Generally the overall tannin management in the wines is spot on. (JH)

Bin 2 Shiraz Mourvèdre

First Vintage:	1960.
Variety:	Shiraz and mourvèdre.
Origin:	Multi-district blend, South Australia. Barossa Valley, Clare Valley, McLaren Vale and Langhorne Creek.
Fermentation:	Stainless steel tanks.
Maturation:	12 months' maturation in 5–6-year-old oak hogsheads and larger vats.
Comments:	Originally labelled Shiraz Mataro.

Penfolds Bin 2 Shiraz Mourvèdre, originally labelled Shiraz Mataro, was one of the early Penfolds bin wines. First released in 1960, it was discontinued during the 1970s at the height of the white wine boom. It was reintroduced to the Australian wine market in the early 1980s but again failed to find favour. The remaining stocks of the 1980 and 1981 vintage were redirected to the United Kingdom market, where the wines attracted plenty of media attention and became an immediate commercial success.

During the 1950s, Penfolds experimented with shiraz and mataro quite extensively. It even produced a single varietal 1954 Bin 158 Mataro. This is one of Penfolds' first dry reds and the beginning of a series of one-off bottlings comprising shiraz and mourvèdre. The rare and famous 1956 Bin S56 Magill Burgundy Shiraz has a small component of mourvèdre. The thinking at the time was that shiraz—billowing with sweet fruit but softly structured—needed to be stiffened up by tannins. New oak was not considered an option in those days. Mataro, also known as mourvèdre, was introduced to Australia during the 1830s. While extensively planted in Châteauneuf-du-Pape and Bandol in France, it is believed to have originated from around Mataro in Catalonia or Murviedro near Valencia, Spain. In France it is sometimes referred to as *Estrangle-Chien* or dog strangler. This pretty well sums up the brawny nature of this variety. Mourvèdre is dark in colour, smells of Provençal herbs/spices and has plenty of tannin stuffing. It is a quality which has compelling potential. Penfolds has consistently returned to the mourvèdre component. The 1960 vintage seems to be the year when Penfolds made several different bins using fruit from Kalimna, Magill and other vineyards in the Adelaide Hills. 1960 Bin 51 Shiraz Mataro, 1960 Bin 56 Kalimna Mataro Shiraz, 1960 Bin 2 Shiraz Mataro and 1960 Bin 630 Cabernet Mataro all prove that mourvèdre was considered a very useful variety. The release of 1967 Bin 67D Burgundy Shiraz Mataro, a Barossa/Hunter Valley blend, illustrates the extent of the mourvèdre question and its use. Throughout the 1960s and early '70s the Bin 2 Shiraz Mataro blend increasingly comprised fruit from Penfolds' extensive and ill-fated Wybong vineyard in the Hunter Valley (sold off in 1977), Coonawarra and Barossa. The original Bin 2 was a traditional 'Australian Burgundy' style—typically a generous, medium-bodied wine based on shiraz—but shot with the aromatics and muscular strength of mourvèdre. This blend was one of the main precursors to the popular Rhône-style blends found in the market today.

Mourvèdre remains greatly valued by Penfolds winemakers for its blending attributes. It tones down the exuberant qualities of shiraz, adding overall complexity and palate grip. Says Peter Gag, 'Bin 2 is a fresh, juicy style with ripe blackberry fruit, plenty of buoyancy and richness on the palate and fine, long, dense, chalky tannins. You can see how shiraz and mourvèdre intertwine. We deliberately allow the earthy spice qualities of mourvèdre to flow through the palate. It brings extra energy and freshness.' The contemporary Bin 2 style is based on warmer vineyard sites such as the Barossa Valley—including the Kalimna Vineyard—Clare Valley, McLaren Vale and Langhorne Creek. The wine is vinified in stainless steel and aged in five- to six-year-old hogsheads and larger vats. This allows the maturation effect to further evolve and soften the wine.

A rare bottle of 1962 Bin 2 was tasted by the panel. This early vintage was based on Kalimna shiraz and Adelaide foothills mataro. Campbell Mattinson said, 'This is an old, good wine with lovely honeyed/spicy/leather/demi-glace characters and a nice stream of tannins through to the finish.' Neil Beckett said, 'It reminded me of a great old St Julien; a poignant reminder of past glory.' James Halliday said, 'It's past its best of course, but it's still drinkable; a very interesting wine.' The 2005 Bin 2, comprising 15 per cent mourvèdre, was on the other hand 'a supple, mouth-filling wine with plenty of red and black fruits and fine soft tannins'.

Ch'ng Poh Tiong observed: 'Bin 2 does benefit greatly from modern winemaking. It's a fresh, well-balanced style with fruity/floral/violet aromas, juicy succulent flavours and fine, round tannins. The bin style embraces the ripe blackberry aromas, fleshiness and fruit sweetness of shiraz and the lean earthy—even spicy—qualities of mourvèdre. The two varieties compliment each other well making an easy-drinking wine which is not overtly concentrated but has plenty of fruit and flavour length.'

TASTING NOTES ~ BIN 2 SHIRAZ MOURVÈDRE

1962 ★   NOW • • PAST

Brick red. A sample of an older vintage. Intense demi-glace/beef stock/toffee/leather/herb aromas. The palate still has sweetness of fruit with some demi-glace/soupy flavours and fine, lacy, dry tannins. It's beginning to dry out but the wine is still drinking well. Many lesser and experimental bins of this age—if cellared well—can offer tremendous drinking pleasure.

2005 ★   NOW • • • 2018

Medium deep crimson. Fresh, juicy blackcurrant/mulberry/plum aromas with touches of liquorice/aniseed. Plenty of sweetness of fruit and volume on the palate with blackcurrant/mulberry flavours and soft, ripe tannins. Finishes long, juicy and sweet. A smooth, buoyant style for immediate drinking but with the concentration and balance for medium-term ageing.

2006 ★   NOW • • • 2020

Deep crimson/purple. Intense and highly perfumed blueberry/plum/liquorice/herb garden aromas. Deep-set blueberry/plum/herb garden/juicy fruit flavours and ripe, plentiful tannins. Finishes firm, savoury and long. A classic Penfolds wine.

Bin 8 Cabernet Shiraz

First Vintage:	2003.
Variety:	Cabernet shiraz.
Origin:	A multi-district blend drawing fruit from vineyards throughout South Australia, including Coonawarra and Barossa Valley.
Fermentation:	Stainless steel tanks with wooden header boards.
Maturation:	12 months in a combination of 2- and 3-year-old French and American oak hogsheads.
Comments:	An early drinking style which will keep for a few years but best soon after release.

'Bin 8 Cabernet Shiraz has been crafted in the traditional Penfolds style. Ripe, sweet-fruit flavours are supported by softly integrated oak resulting in a silky, smooth red wine.'

Penfolds Bin 8 Cabernet Shiraz is a recent addition to Penfolds bin range. It was introduced in response to an interest in early drinking cabernet sauvignon–shiraz blend—a classic Australian wine style which has caught the attention of export markets.

Although Penfolds bin numbers were originally named after the original binning location after bottling, more recent additions have been numbered to suggest associations. Bin 8 was given its number because it is the common factor of Bin 389, Bin 128 and Bin 28; the wine is matured in older oak previously used for these bins. Eight is also one of the strongest numbers in the alphabet across several cultures. In science it is a 'magic' number. It is also a geometric shape of equal parts, perhaps reflecting the equity between cabernet sauvignon and shiraz. Notwithstanding the final blend of components, each variety contributes equally in terms of its character.

From the very start of Penfolds' fine winemaking, Max Schubert favoured warm- and hot-climate fruit as a source for Bin 389—reflecting his strong preference for richly concentrated, 'buoyant' fruit. Schubert fully understood the potential of cabernet and shiraz as blending companions. He believed that each component could bring something extra and different. While the Bin 8 style is not as powerful, the overall philosophy holds true today. The perfumed, elegantly structured cabernet sauvignon is a perfect partner to the more generous and richly flavoured shiraz. Together the wine represents more than the sum of its parts. Bin 8 is vinified in the traditional Penfolds technique in headed down, open stainless steel fermenters. After vinification the wine is aged for around twelve months in a combination of two- and three-year-old French and American oak hogsheads—previously used for Bins 389, 128 and 28.

Winemaker Peter Gago says, 'Bin 8 Cabernet Shiraz is typically fresh and vivacious with black cherry, dark chocolate aromas with some mint and toasty oak nuances. The palate is generous and smooth with plenty of ripe black cherry, cassis, spicy fruit cake flavours and velvety tannins. This is a very relaxed, easygoing wine built for immediate enjoyment rather than long-term cellaring.'

WHITES

Bin 311 Chardonnay

First Vintage:	2005.
Variety:	Chardonnay.
Origin:	2005 and 2006 Tumbarumba, 2007 Orange, New South Wales.
Fermentation:	100% barrel fermented in older oak.
Maturation:	10–14 months.
Comments:	Matured for around 11 months in older oak. Released entirely under screw cap since the first vintage.

*'These are pleasantly balanced, cool-climate wines with grapefruit/
blossom aromas, long sinuous palate structure and perfect oak balance.'*
—JAMES HALLIDAY, PANELLIST

Penfolds Bin 311 Chardonnay—first vintage 2005—is a house style based on the best cool-climate fruit available. This fresh, elegant wine based on fruit complexity and naturally balanced acidity was developed as a by-product from the longstanding White Grange project of the mid-1990s. Penfolds has had a long association with winemaking in New South Wales. In 1904 it acquired the famous Dalwood Vineyard in the Hunter Valley. In 1912 it purchased the Minchinbury vineyards at Rooty Hill (now a suburb of Sydney) and in the 1920s it further expanded its vineyard holdings at Sparkling Vale near Lovedale in the Lower Hunter Valley.

In 1958, Penfolds imported and planted the first cuttings of chardonnay at Dalwood. At the end of the 1970s Penfolds was solely producing white and sparkling wines in New South Wales. Consolidation and change of ownership led to the divestment of Penfolds vineyards in New South Wales. By the 1980s Penfolds was known as a red wine brand based on South Australian vineyards. It is a quirk of fate that the quest for a great long-lived Penfolds white wine led the Penfolds winemaking team back into New South Wales!

All of the Bin 311 Chardonnays are derived from highly elevated, cool-climate vineyards. The first few vintages came from Tumbarumba, a sleepy agricultural town located on the southern granitic soil slopes of the Snowy Mountains in New South Wales. Tumbarumba, meaning 'sounding ground' in the local Wiradjuri dialect, probably alludes to the way noise travels during the cold winter months. Initially the vineyards were earmarked for sparkling wine production. Penfolds winemakers were impressed by the pear skin/white peach aromas, lean structure and marked acidity of Tumbarumba fruit—particularly as a blending option for Yattarna.

The overall Bin 311 style is based on a clear, articulated fruit profile based on chardonnay with more richness and volume. In 2007 Oliver Crawford decided to

make a switch from Tumbarumba to Orange—located in the central west of New South Wales. Without the constraints of tradition or single-vineyard designation, Bin 311 is likely to develop in parallel to Penfolds' traditional winemaking philosophy where style takes precedence over vineyard site.

Orange shares a common thread with Tumbarumba, enjoying cold winters and mild summers. Both these centres, at a similar altitude of approximately 700 metres, came to prominence as a result of the gold rush of the 1850s. Significant capital investment in viticultural development has only occurred over the last twenty years. Orange, a major regional town, is dominated by Mount Canobolas, an extinct volcano, which rises to almost 1400 metres. Most of the vineyards—on rolling elevated flaxen landscape—are north and north-east facing and located at altitudes of around 600 to 800 metres. At higher elevations, the Orange vineyards are planted on predominantly red volcanic soils. At lower sites, the soils are mainly loess. Penfolds has wide access to various micro-climates and soil types within this important emerging region. Penfolds winemakers and many other observers believe that Orange is increasingly capable of producing intense chardonnay fruit of exceptional balance and quality.

The overall Bin 311 style is based on fruit character and complexity. Hence the wine is fermented and matured in older French oak barriques. *Bâtonnage*—or lees stirring—further adds to richness, mouth-feel and flavour length. Overall the wine is minimally handled to maintain purity of fruit and improve freshness. The wine is not made for long-term ageing but it can be cellared for a few years.

Oliver Crawford says, 'We are generally looking for stone fruit/nectarine type aromas, a touch of creaminess on the mid-palate and bright linear acidity. In 2007 the Orange Chardonnay was neatly balanced with beautiful concentration, richness and mineral acidity.'

Penfolds Bin 311 is definitely a work in progress. With only a handful of vintages, Penfolds winemakers are continuing to explore all options regarding vineyard origin and refinement of style. The development of cool vineyard sites throughout New South Wales has been an exciting feature of the contemporary Australian wine scene. Penfolds believes that Bin 311 can continue to evolve as a chardonnay, but always based on the best single-regional fruit available each vintage. Tumbarumba, Orange and other emerging wine regions may variously feature, depending on vintage conditions. Richard Neagle, Penfolds Grower Liaison Manager NSW and Murray Valley, says, 'We believe strongly in the potential of these regions. We have already committed the company to long-term relationships with our viticultural partners. We are convinced that both Orange and Tumbarumba have a great future for fine wine.'

Ch'ng Poh Tiong found the 2005 'impressive, with flint/mineral/vanilla aromas, intense steely fruit and delicious vivacity'. James Halliday also described the wine as 'an impressive, slowly ageing wine with grapefruit blossom aromas and great mouth-feel. The 2006 is richer and creamier with many similarities to the 2005. However, that extra touch of alcohol impacts on the finish.' Huon Hooke noted that the 2006 had 'plenty of appeal with yeasty/floral aromas, richness and depth of flavour'.

2005   NOW • • • 2012

Pale yellow. Intense grapefruit/lime blossom aromas with some pear skin/smoky notes. The palate is fresh and complex with sweet juicy pear/lanolin fruit, plenty of creaminess and bright clean acidity. Has structure to age, but best to drink early.

2006   NOW • • • 2012

Pale yellow. A richer and weightier wine with stone fruit/nectarine aromas and underlying savoury notes. Sweet nectarine/ripe peach flavours and some leesy/yeasty complexity.

2007   NOW • • • 2014

Pale yellow. Intense white peach/pear skin/lemon/camomile aromas. Very tight linear wine with pear skin/white peach flavours and minerally, long acidity. Will evolve richness and further complexity.

Bin 51 Eden Valley Riesling

First Vintage:	1999—originally labelled Eden Valley Reserve Riesling.
Variety:	Riesling.
Origin:	Woodbury and High Eden vineyards.
Fermentation:	Stainless steel tanks. Bottling in July.
Maturation:	Bottled early to retain freshness and released towards the end of vintage year.
Comments:	Released entirely under screw cap since the 2002 vintage.

'Bin 51 Riesling has both power and delicacy,
reflecting the pure unadulterated perfume of riesling
and mineral smell and flavours of vineyard site.'

The Bin 51 Eden Valley Riesling, with its pristine fruit quality, natural energy and fine acid backbone, is a classic Eden Valley riesling style with the structure and concentration to age for the medium to long term. The fruit is primarily sourced from the mature Woodbury and High Eden vineyards which were originally planted between 1940 and 1960. These highly prized vineyards, 450 metres above sea level, are located in the Eden Valley, a sub-region of the Barossa. The relatively high altitude means a cooler growing season—ideal for aromatic grape varieties, especially riesling.

Eden Valley soils are derived from schistic and sedimentary rock. They are mostly red clay soils and sandy, silty loams interspersed with schistic gravels. The Penfolds vineyards are located on particularly lean soil structures. Winemakers have long valued the intense floral/lime aromas and minerally complexity of Eden Valley

riesling. This is a definitive bone-dry style with 100 per cent natural acidity and clear fruit aromas and flavours. Peter Gago says, 'Since 2002 we have bottled the Eden Valley Riesling under screw cap to preserve the pure fruit aromas, overall intensity and freshness on the palate. We believe that this form of closure is ideal for riesling; the wine matures in the bottle more gracefully and offers compelling nuances of toast and lime while maintaining vibrancy and minerality.'

Huon Hooke noted that the 2001 suffered under cork ageing: 'While the wine showed buttery complexity and richness, the flavours faded towards the finish.' The 2002 had also evolved. Four years earlier it was showing 'very clear lime aromas and strong mineral tones'. Hooke commented that 'the wine was still vivacious with lovely intensity but had developed kerosene-like characters'.

Joshua Greene described the wine as having 'orange and lime marmalade characters with plenty of freshness and flavour length'. James Halliday made the point that this vertical tasting was a striking comment on how riesling develops under screw cap: 'There is a completely logical line from 2002 to 2007. At no point do the wines dip or recede into themselves. You can start at either end of the telescope and forecast how the wine looked like when it was young or how it develops with age. Here is an example where screw cap really makes a huge difference.'

Screw cap is gaining significant ground in Australia. Most producers of riesling are now bottling their wines under this form of closure. Screw cap is not new to Penfolds rieslings—1971 and 1972 Penfolds Autumn Rieslings and 1980 Penfolds Dalwood Riesling were, for example, sealed under screw cap. These wines are still fresh and minerally despite showing significant bottle age. The periodic move towards screw cap in the 1970s and '80s never really captured the imagination of the consumer. A consolidated effort led by Clare Valley riesling producers in the 1990s led to widespread fine-wine consumer acceptance. Seasoned observers of this aromatic style believe that screw cap is 'definitely the way to go'.

Oliver Crawford, former Penfolds Senior White Winemaker, said that the rebadging of the Eden Valley Riesling to Bin 51 Eden Valley Riesling in 2006 was acknowledgement that the style had reached a level of consistency and character to warrant inclusion in the bin range. 'Using the same vineyard resources, we have been working hard to take the wine to a new dimension where we can capture more floral and rose petal characters rather than citrus and lime. This has been achieved by walking through the vineyard and observing micro-site specific nuances. We have found that the rose petal characters derive from fruit grown on weaker soils—especially the yellow podsolic soils lying on a shallow bed of lime.'

At harvest the vineyards are triaged according to fruit profile, resulting in wines that are very floral with beautiful rose petal/camomile aromas, impressive concentration and mouth-watering natural acidity. There are nuances of lime—a regional characteristic. However, this is a wine that has both power and delicacy, reflecting the pure, unadulterated perfume of riesling and mineral smell and flavours of the vineyard site. The 2006 and 2007 Bin 51 Eden Valley Rieslings are a continuum of the Eden Valley Reserve bin range. The wines are delicious to drink young or can be cellared for several years.

2001   NOW

Chrysanthemum tea/pale straw colour. Intense lemon curd/lime/buttered toast aromas. The palate is well concentrated with broad lemon curd/toasty/marmalade/lime juice flavours and fine cutting acidity. Finishes long and minerally. Good bottles will keep for a while but the wine is probably at its peak. Eden Valley Reserve Bin.

2002 ★   NOW • • • 2012

Medium straw. Still remarkably fresh and intense wine with toasty lime aromas and classical oilskin/kerosene complexity. Beautifully concentrated and tangy palate with toasty/lime/wildflower honey flavours and vivacious/slatey acidity. Finishes bone dry but long and minerally. Has plenty of life, intensity and drive. Probably at its peak but will hold for at least another five years. Eden Valley Reserve Bin.

2003   NOW • • • 2010

Pale straw. Fresh, complex wine with restrained lemon/camomile/thyme aromas and flavours. The palate is lean in style but possesses fresh mineral acidity and plenty of tangy flavour length. It doesn't have the fruit richness and intensity of top years, but it's drinking well now. Eden Valley Reserve Bin.

2004 ★   NOW • • • 2015

Pale straw. Lovely clean, fragrant, flowery/lime/herb garden aromas. A very youthful, crisp and tight wine with strong mineral/green apple/lemon curd/lime flavours and mouth-watering acidity. An especially refined wine with lovely delicacy and poise. Has great cellaring potential. Eden Valley Reserve Bin.

2005 ★   NOW • • • 2015

Pale straw. A delicate, harmonious wine with lime blossom/camomile/slatey aromas with a hint of grapefruit. The palate is juicy and minerally with concentrated lime/lemon flavours and long, crisp acidity. This is an elegant vintage with lovely feel, line and flow. Eden Valley Reserve Bin.

2006   NOW • • • 2012

Pale gold. A powerfully intense wine with lime/rose water/oilskin/toasty aromas and flavours. A richly concentrated, weighty palate with deep lemon curd/camomile/apricot flavours and searing acidity. Finishes chalky dry and slightly grippy. A wine with plenty of volume and flavour. A forward, relatively early drinking style. However, with careful cellaring this wine could evolve. Bin 51 Eden Valley Riesling.

2007   NOW • • • 2012

Pale gold. Very classical lemon curd/floral/herb garden aromas with some spice/ginger notes. A very bright, unevolved wine with plenty of deep-set lemon curd/spicy/touch yeasty flavours and strong indelible acidity. Finishes long and sweet. Will not be especially long-lived but will always have charm. Bin 51 Eden Valley Riesling.

DISCUSSION

This was an impressive bracket showing an evolution of style and a strong stamp of place. **2001**, which was sealed under cork, shows exactly why an aromatic style like riesling benefits from screw cap. In the context of this tasting, 2001 really suffered under cork ageing. The wine showed buttered toast development and hints of mustiness. The fruit faded towards the finish. It's a pleasant drink but if it had been sealed under screw cap it would have had more freshness and vitality. (HH) It had attractive, evolved riesling character with plenty of honeyed/toasty characters. It is a lovely middle-weighted wine with impressive minerality of flavour. (NB) This was a delicious wine nearing or at its peak with buttered toast and lime juice flavours filling the mouth. It's not really going to get any better. (JH)

2002 had a light chrysanthemum colour with intense citrus/apple fruit and long, soft, medium-bodied palate. (CPT) The wine is showing mature fusel tones and plenty of toasty marmalade elements. It's a bit shorter on fruit than I would like but it has a smoothness and richness of flavour which is attractive. (JG) This is a wine with life, intensity and drive. It is showing maturity with a tinge of kerosene but it is fresh and tangy with lively, vivacious acidity and clean, lingering, dry but fruity finish. This wine definitely has a future. (HH)

2003 is more developed with some toast and kerosene characters. However, the palate heads off in a different and completely unexpected direction with far more fight and intensity. The wine is verging on schizophrenic but the palate wins the day. (JH) It had good clarity and length with classic Eden Valley flavours and a good fatness to it. (JG) It lacks the fruit richness and intensity of top years. (HH)

2004 does not have the colour density of the 2003 but it has well-sustained and pleasing mineral and lime flavours but a slightly sour finish. (NB) It's an elegant wine with some minerally notes. I like the delicacy and finesse on the palate. (CPT) This was a very youthful, crisp, tight wine with floral/blossom aromas, strong mineral/green apple flavours and a background regional note of lime. (JH) This was a superb wine with a lovely clean, fragrant, flowery nose. It's light-bodied, delicate, refined, subtle and very clean. It has lovely fresh varietal character and is true to style. That limey acidity will allow plenty of cellaring potential; up to twenty years. (HH)

2005 is a harmonious wine with lovely feel, line and flow. Its fruit profile is almost heading into grapefruit territory. (JH) The wine had fine balance. It's still very fragrant and young with lime pith and peel aromas and minerally dry flavours. There's a touch of toasty development. (JG) The wine is showing plenty of promise but it does need more time to settle down. It has plenty of substance, volume and acidity. (NB) The wine is almost colourless with very pure lemon/lime aromas and steely acidity. It is a very fresh and impressive wine. (CPT) The wine has a long and great future with delicate blossomy aromas and juicy, mouth-watering acidity. It's still very young and vivacious but refined and harmonious. (HH)

2006 is a serious food wine with powerful, full-flavoured richness, but some grippiness on the palate. (NB) I found the wine quite shy on the nose but clean and true. There is an apparent sweetness with some slight toasty straw notes and a warm alcoholic kick at the finish. It needs a bit of time, but at this stage it lacks a bit of delicacy. (HH) 2006 felt different in the mouth. This is not considered a great vintage, but it seems to have more volume of aromas and flavours. It's seemingly much riper than earlier vintages, but why? (JH) The wine is definitely a shift in style. It is only coincidental that the label changed also in this year. We want to take this riesling style to a new dimension reflecting the work we are doing in our vineyards and the evolution of our winemaking philosophy. We are seeking fruit with pronounced floral/rose petal aromas rather than the obvious lime/citrus characters that abound in the Eden Valley. Ultimately we are evolving the style to show micro-specific site characters, more volume of flavour and tautness in structure for medium- to long-term cellaring. The 2006 and 2007 vintages are clearly showing these results. (OC)

2007 was impressive, with ripe citrus, floral aromas, vivacious acidity and long flavours. It was one of the top wines in this bracket along with 2005 and possibly 2002. (CPT) The wine had an almost gewurztraminer character. The palate is fresh with plenty of grapefruit/spicy flavours and zingy bright acidity. (NB) The wine had a lovely, perfumed fruit character with some honeyed notes. It is surprisingly forward, a bit soft and sweet with undeveloped flavours, pronounced acidity and plenty of ripeness. This should develop well. It is interesting to note that 2004 and 2005 showed plenty of lime characters, whereas 2006 and 2007 were completely different. (JG) Yet we are sourcing the fruit from exactly the same vineyards. (OC)

CHAPTER ELEVEN

Organic Wines

There has been an increasing awareness of organic wine over the last ten years. While Penfolds has maintained a low-input viticulture and winemaking philosophy for several decades, it was one of the first major wine companies to make and release a widely commercially available organic wine into the mainstream markets. These wines are only made when favourable vintage conditions permit. While organic wine is becoming increasingly popular in today's market, Penfolds believes that it should also be interesting and worthwhile. Further, it should also possess freshness, clarity of fruit, strength of flavour and overall balance. Penfolds Organic wines are always made without compromise and further add to the myriad wine experiences within the Penfolds portfolio.

Organic wine is simply wine untainted by man-made fertilisers, herbicides and pesticides. For a long time Penfolds has applied a philosophy of low-input viticulture; achieving optimum fruit quality with minimal intervention is a priority. This is achieved through good vineyard management, including vineyard design and trellising systems, bunch and leaf thinning, and maintaining low yields. It also helps if the vineyard is planted in the right place, with good natural drainage and aspect.

'For a long time Penfolds has applied a philosophy of low-input viticulture; achieving optimum fruit quality with minimal intervention is a priority.'

Penfolds adheres to a strict classification system at vintage. The whole idea of fruit quality is ultimately based on the condition of the fruit, its concentration and flavour profile. In some wine areas it is not practical to run an organically certified vineyard—particularly in the more maritime-influenced regions where humidity can wreak havoc on developing grape bunches. In the past, Penfolds sourced its organic fruit from the Clare Valley, a region known for its warm, dry continental weather.

In the winery, Penfolds follows a strict organic winemaking approach. The wines are not fined and winemakers use separate hoses, pumps and tanks. While it is a natural product, organic wine must have minimal traces of sulphur dioxide, a compound used as a preservative since Roman times—just enough to ensure the wine remains fresh on the shelves for a while. To put this all into context, the amount of sulphur used in a normal bottle of wine is about ten times less than the sulphite level used in the commercial production of dried fruits such as raisins and apricots. In a bottle of organic wine the level is further reduced.

Peter Gago says, 'Penfolds Organic Wines are very much a work in progress. However, we have a very high regard for organic principles. We have already applied various organic techniques into our mainstream viticulture and believe strongly in a low-input philosophy across all of our wines. In years to come, the intention is to make further inroads through innovation and experimentation. If the wine can make the cut, there is no reason why we can't release a Cellar Reserve organic wine in the future.'

Clare Valley Organic Chardonnay

First Vintage:	1993.
Variety:	Chardonnay.
Origin:	Clare Valley, South Australia.
Fermentation:	Stainless steel tanks. Some components undergo malolactic fermentation.
Maturation:	No oak maturation, no fining agents, minimal filtration.
Comments:	Screw caps available in some markets.

'The Penfolds Organic Chardonnay showed impressive
intensity of flavour and flourishing harmony and ripeness.'
—NEIL BECKETT, PANELLIST

The Penfolds Organic Chardonnay aims to provide an organic equivalent to the classic Australian unoaked chardonnay style. The wines are fresh, elegant and lively with plenty of peach/melon aromas and flavours. This is an early drinking style, best drunk relatively soon after release. In recent vintages the wines have become more interesting and complex. The panel noted that the wines were 'promising, complex

and intriguing'. Neil Beckett was impressed by the intensity of aromas and flavours. Joshua Greene found the wine had citrus/lemon/lychee fruit and some yeasty richness. However, it was noted that the Organic Chardonnay, as stated in previous editions of *Penfolds: The Rewards of Patience*, is a 'drink now' wine.

Clare Valley Organic Cabernet Sauvignon

First Vintage:	1993.
Variety:	Cabernet sauvignon, sometimes including shiraz and merlot.
Origin:	Clare Valley.
Fermentation:	Stainless steel tanks.
Maturation:	No oak maturation, no fining agents, minimal filtration.
Comments:	Screw caps available in some markets.

Penfolds Organic Cabernet Sauvignon is an early drinking style but is a contemporary varietal blend with buoyant, ripe berry flavours, plenty of sweet-fruit concentration and fine savoury tannins. Penfolds recommends these wines be consumed within a couple of years of release to take advantage of primary fruit freshness.

CHAPTER TWELVE

Thomas Hyland Wines

T he Penfolds Thomas Hyland range is named after Thomas Francis Hyland, an officer of the Victorian Civil Service, who married Christopher Rawson and Mary Penfold's daughter, Georgina, in 1862. Their new son-in-law initially helped market Penfolds wines into the emerging Victorian wine market. On the death of his father-in-law, Thomas Hyland moved to South Australia to help run the family business. In 1870 Penfolds & Co. was formed—comprising the new partnership of Mary Penfold, her devoted son-in-law Thomas Hyland and cellar manager Joseph Gillard. Thomas Hyland's considerable administrative skills and stewardship resulted in a rapid rise in fortunes. By 1896 Penfolds accounted for one-third of South Australia's wine production—a remarkable achievement. The Thomas Hyland range is comprised of intensely varietal wines made for all seasons and all comers.

The Thomas Hyland range is inextricably linked to the Adelaide Geographical Indication Super-Zone. This is a significant greater-regional appellation which centres on Adelaide, the state capital of South Australia, and includes the Barossa, Mount Lofty Ranges and Fleurieu Peninsula. Peter Gago says, 'The Adelaide Super-Zone is a remarkably diverse region with a multitude of prestige micro-climes and communes—from the elevated vineyards in Adelaide Hills and Eden Valley, and the maritime-influenced McLaren Vale, to the classic warm climate of the Barossa and Clare valleys. The state political boundary, Schubert, named in honour of Max Schubert and which is centred in the Barossa, also falls within this super-zone. The Thomas Hyland range neatly follows the Penfolds philosophy of multi-regional blending, yet adheres to the idea of identity. Adelaide is a great wine city, like Bordeaux in France. Its immediate environs possess some of the finest vineyards in

South Australia. Winemakers draw from its wealth of vinous resources to make wines of freshness, intense fruit definition, richness of flavour and balance. These are serious wines which evoke the gentle landscape of Adelaide's 'home shires' and the art of blending. Peter Gago says, 'Penfolds' aim is to make a wine that delivers more than the sum of its parts. The Thomas Hyland range epitomises the strengths of Penfolds' winemaking philosophy, our remarkable grower and company vineyard resources and viticultural and winemaking teamwork. These wines punch well above their weight in the context of their price category. I think Mary and Dr Christopher Rawson Penfold—if alive today—would enjoy the idea that Magill Estate lies at the very heart of the Adelaide GI.'

REDS

The Penfolds Thomas Hyland red wines—comprising Shiraz and Cabernet—are house style wines based on multi-regional fruit. These are fresh, early drinking wines with plush, ripe fruit, plenty of richness and chocolaty tannins. The wines are a prelude to the bin range wines, offering plenty of style and classic Penfolds fruit sweetness. It is the sheer consistency of this style and the stamp of individuality that makes these useful, easy-drinking wines a favourite among wine experts, collectors and sommeliers.

Thomas Hyland Shiraz

First Vintage:	2000.
Variety:	Shiraz.
Origin:	Previously multi-district blend, South Australia: McLaren Vale, Coonawarra, Barossa Valley, Padthaway and Robe. As of 2006—Adelaide.
Fermentation:	Stainless steel tanks.
Maturation:	11 months in new (15%) and aged (85%) French and American hogsheads.
Comments:	Screw caps available in select markets.

'The Thomas Hyland Shirazes are beautifully bright, fruit-driven wines.'
—HUON HOOKE, PANELLIST

The Thomas Hyland Shiraz draws fruit from across the Adelaide area. The wine is a fruit-driven style underpinned by a touch of new oak to enhance overall complexity and freshness. The wine is matured for eleven months in a combination of new (15 per cent) and aged (85 per cent) French and American oak.

The Thomas Hyland Shiraz is a buoyant, fresh style with plenty of juicy blackberry fruit aromas and flavours with chocolaty, ripe tannins and some savoury oak nuances.

Penfolds Chief Winemaker Peter Gago said, 'The wine is made for early drinking, but there's no problem keeping the wine for a few years. The overall balance of fruit, concentration and structure is certainly there.' Both James Halliday and Campbell Mattinson suggested the 2004 and 2005 would hold on until around 2015.

Ch'ng Poh Tiong found the wines 'attractive with soft persistent fruit'. Neil Beckett described 2004 as 'appetisingly fresh and succulent'. Joshua Greene noted 2005 as 'juicy, clean and primary'. Huon Hooke said, 'The Thomas Hyland Shirazes are beautifully bright, fruit-driven wines; they are well-made, generous wines but overall lighter in weight than the Penfolds bin range.'

TASTING NOTES ~ THOMAS HYLAND SHIRAZ

2004   NOW • • • 2015

Medium red. Intense liquorice/blackberry/juicy fruit aromas. The palate is sweet and concentrated with succulent blackberry/plum/vanilla flavours, chocolaty ripe tannins and savoury notes. A friendly, easygoing style.

2005   NOW • • • 2016

Medium deep red. Fresh blackberry/plum aromas with some savoury notes. A bright, fleshy wine with smooth blackberry/liquorice flavours and sweet, supple/silken tannins. Finishes long and sweet.

2006 ★   NOW • • • 2018

Medium deep red. Intense blackberry/redcurrant/aniseed aromas with some herb garden nuances. The palate is well concentrated with pure blackberry/mocha flavours and ripe, loose-knit tannins. Finishes long and minerally. Lovely weight and balance.

Thomas Hyland Cabernet Sauvignon

First Vintage:	2001.
Variety:	Cabernet sauvignon.
Origin:	Previously multi-district blend, South Australia. Coonawarra, McLaren Vale and Robe. As of 2007—Adelaide.
Fermentation:	Stainless steel tanks.
Maturation:	11 months in new (15%) and aged (85%) French and American hogsheads.
Comments:	Screw caps available in select markets.

Penfolds Thomas Hyland Cabernet Sauvignon is a multi-regional wine based on Coonawarra, McLaren Vale and Robe fruit. It is a Penfolds house style which emphasises the classical elements of ripe blackcurrant/cedar aromas, a core of fruit sweetness and fine-grained but firm tannins.

The wine exemplifies the benefits of multi-regional blending. Coonawarra cabernet sauvignon features prominently, bringing perfume and generosity of flavour on the palate.

The addition of ripe, powerful McLaren Vale fruit and elegantly proportioned Robe cabernet enhance the overall style. Vinification takes place in headed-down, stainless-steel vats and rotary fermenters allowing a gentle extraction of colour, flavour and tannins. The wine is matured in a combination of new (15 per cent) and aged (85 per cent) French and American oak hogsheads for approximately a year before bottling.

> *'The Thomas Hyland Cabernet Sauvignon is a Penfolds house style which emphasises the classical elements of ripe blackcurrant/cedar aromas, a core of fruit sweetness and fine-grained but firm tannins.'*

James Halliday said these are 'solid and substantial wines which offer both richness of flavour and firmness in structure'. Campbell Mattinson observed 'the wines are very similar in style to the Shiraz but with lengthier tannins and juicier fruit flavours. These are impressive wines at this level and fully belong to the Penfolds family of wines.'

While Penfolds Thomas Hyland Cabernet Sauvignon is made for relatively early drinking, the overall fruit concentration and firm tannin structure will allow the wine to cellar for the medium term.

TASTING NOTES ~ THOMAS HYLAND CABERNET SAUVIGNON

2004　　　　　　　　　　　　　　　　　　　　　　　NOW • • • 2016

Medium deep red. Fresh chocolate/cassis/herb garden aromas. Solid, substantial palate with sweet, concentrated chocolate/juicy blackcurrant/brambly flavours and loose-knit, grainy tannins. Finishes long and flavourful.

2005　　　　　　　　　　　　　　　　　　　　　　　NOW • • • 2016

Medium deep red. Blackcurrant/dark cherry/mint aromas and flavours. The wine is buoyant and fresh with cassis/mocha/mint flavours and grippy, firm tannins. A muscular style that may benefit from further cellaring.

2006 ★　　　　　　　　　　　　　　　　　　　　　NOW • • • 2018

Medium deep red. Intense cassis/cedar aromas with a touch of black olive. Classically proportioned wine with pure cassis/black olive/cedar flavours and fine-grained tannins. Finishes firm, long and sweet. An outstanding year.

WHITES

The Penfolds Thomas Hyland white wine range, first introduced in 2001, comprises a riesling, a sauvignon blanc and a chardonnay. The fruit is now exclusively sourced from the Adelaide Geographical Indication Super-Zone, which includes the Mount Lofty Ranges, Fleurieu and the Barossa zones. Penfolds sources primarily from the Adelaide Hills, a region renowned for its cool-climate fruit; the Eden Valley, a higher-altitude sub-region of the Barossa; and the more continental and drier Clare Valley wine regions. The winemakers are seeking to make medium-bodied wines of pure, varietal fruit character, richness, liveliness and plenty of flavour length.

The Thomas Hyland wines are usually early drinking styles with plenty of fruit sweetness and volume. All vintages are sealed with screw cap to maintain freshness and shelf life. Winemakers have worked hard to makes something different and fun to drink in an increasingly crowded market. Joshua Greene observed that the Thomas Hyland Riesling had 'a complex fruit profile but maintained sweetness and balance'. Oliver Crawford made the comment, 'This is a completely new style for Australia with apple blossom fruit characters, naturally high acidity and beautiful fruit sweetness. We are trying to make a wine that has power and linear strength.'

James Halliday described the Thomas Hyland Sauvignon Blanc as being 'far from the mainstream, with big, opulent textures and minerality reminiscent of contemporary Loire winemakers such as Didier Dageneau'. Certainly Penfolds is attempting to make a wine that has 'more fruit lift and punch'. Joshua Greene described the 2007 as showing 'pure zing, softness and gentle balance'. Ch'ng Poh Tiong found it 'very aromatic and lively with guavas and grapefruit characters and soft, silky viscosity'.

The Thomas Hyland Chardonnay has also evolved since the first vintage in 2001. The wine has become increasingly refined, with stone fruit characters and minerally flavours reflecting a higher component of Adelaide Hills fruit. The wine is 100 per cent barrel fermented to increase complexity of aromas and flavours. After primary fermentation the wine is matured in new and one-year-old French oak barriques for a period of around seven to nine months. The wine is regularly stirred on lees to further enhance palate texture and flavours. One hundred per cent malolactic fermentation is also encouraged to add creaminess and weight. Winemakers have adjusted down the level of new oak over succeeding vintages to bring out the clear fruit definition of Adelaide Hills chardonnay. Minimal filtration is also employed to preserve the elegance of fruit flavours.

While Thomas Hyland Chardonnay is a modestly priced wine in Penfolds' portfolio, it includes relegated Yattarna fruit. Both Huon Hooke and Neil Beckett found the wines 'relatively understated', with restrained fruit and subtle oak. Indeed, these wines reflect a boutique, small batch, fine winemaking philosophy. Increasingly, vintage and regional character have become as important as house style. As a result these highly consistent wines have plenty of personality and difference across vintages. While the best years may have some cellaring potential, the Thomas Hyland wines are essentially fine wines for everyday drinking.

Thomas Hyland Chardonnay

First Vintage:	2001.
Variety:	Chardonnay.
Origin:	The fruit is now exclusively sourced from the Adelaide Geographical Indication Super-Zone, which comprises the Mount Lofty Ranges, Fleurieu and the Barossa zones. Primarily Adelaide Hills.
Fermentation:	100% barrel fermented.
Maturation:	Matured for 6 months in a combination of new (roughly 25%) and 1- and 2-year-old French oak.
Comments:	Comprises relegated Yattarna fruit. Bottled unfiltered. Early drinking style. Screw caps available in select markets.

'The Thomas Hyland Chardonnay style is on song—
it's what I like to drink.'

—JOSHUA GREENE, PANELLIST

TASTING NOTES ~ THOMAS HYLAND CHARDONNAY

2004   NOW

Pale yellow. Intense toasty/lime/pear skin aromas with some cashew nut/creamy complexity. A well-focused wine with lime/pear skin/toasty flavours, fine minerally acidity and off-dry but fresh, long finish. Moderately complex wine but at peak.

2005   NOW • • • 2010

Pale yellow. Fragrant, minerally, clear-fruited wine with toasty/white peach/nectarine aromas. The palate is fresh and tangy with sweet white peach/pear/nectarine flavours, steely acidity, lovely viscosity and flavour length. Has intensity, flavour and balance. However, drink soon.

2006   NOW • • • 2011

Pale yellow. Very tight minerally/quartz/lemon curd/juicy pear aromas with underlying savoury oak complexity. Well-concentrated wine with lemon curd/nutty/herb garden flavours, mid-palate richness and fresh acidity. Finishes a touch chalky, but has good line, length and balance.

2007   NOW • • • 2012

Pale yellow. Very youthful wine with intense Fuji apple/pear/nectarine aromas and flavours. The palate is fresh and crisp but lean and tight. A very well-balanced wine that will develop more richness with a few years of bottle age.

Thomas Hyland Sauvignon Blanc

First Vintage:	2006.
Variety:	Sauvignon blanc.
Origin:	The fruit is exclusively sourced from the Adelaide Geographical Indication Super-Zone, which comprises the Mount Lofty Ranges, Fleurieu and the Barossa zones. Primarily Adelaide Hills and McLaren Vale.
Fermentation:	Stainless steel tanks.
Maturation:	Bottled and released to market early.
Comments:	Early drinking style. Screw caps available in select markets.

TASTING NOTES ~ THOMAS HYLAND SAUVIGNON BLANC

2006   **NOW • • • 2010**

Pale gold. Very aromatic, lively wine with intense guava/grapefruit/melon aromas with hints of herb and grass. The palate is creamy and soft with yeasty richness and tangy acidity. Finishes clean and smooth. A big, opulent, textured, early drinking style.

Thomas Hyland Riesling

First Vintage:	2007.
Variety:	Riesling.
Origin:	The fruit is exclusively sourced from the Adelaide Geographical Indication Super-Zone, which comprises the Mount Lofty Ranges, Fleurieu and the Barossa zones. Primarily Adelaide Hills.
Fermentation:	Stainless steel tanks.
Maturation:	Maturation on yeast lees for 4 months to achieve more volume and complexity of flavour. Bottled early to retain freshness and youthful appeal. Screw caps available in select markets.

TASTING NOTES ~ THOMAS HYLAND RIESLING

2007   **NOW • • • 2011**

Pale gold. Intense fresh lemon curd/tropical fruit/camomile aromas. The palate is well concentrated with up-front lime/sweet-fruit/camomile flavours and plenty of lemony acidity. Drink now or keep for a few years.

CHAPTER THIRTEEN

Koonunga Hill Wines

Koonunga Hill is a Penfolds success story. Since the first vintage of Koonunga Hill Shiraz Cabernet in 1976, the brand has evolved to the point where it is almost a 'brand within a brand'. Don Ditter, retired Penfolds Chief Winemaker, counts this wine as one of his major achievements while in charge of production: 'I still regularly drink Koonunga Hill at home. It never disappoints and it's good value.' The very first vintages were based on the newly planted (1973) Koonunga Hill Vineyard located on the northern edge of the Barossa Valley. The wines have a reputation for over-delivering on quality. In great Penfolds years, such as 1996, 1998, 2002 or 2004, these wines can have remarkable cellaring potential.

'The Koonunga Hill reds are all about freshness, generosity of flavour, richness and vivacity of fruit. These are affordable and great everyday drinking styles that reflect Penfolds' remarkable vineyard resources and outstanding red winemaking skills.'

—PETER GAGO, CHIEF WINEMAKER

REDS

Koonunga Hill Shiraz Cabernet

First Vintage:	1976.
Variety:	Shiraz and cabernet. The proportions vary but shiraz is usually the dominant variety.
Origin:	Multi-district blend, South Australia. Barossa Valley, McLaren Vale, Clare Valley, Coonawarra, Padthaway, Langhorne Creek and Bordertown. May vary considerably depending on vintage conditions.
Fermentation:	Stainless steel tanks.
Maturation:	12 months' maturation in 3–4-year-old oak hogsheads.
Comments:	Released and labelled Koonunga Hill 'Claret' until 1991 vintage. This is a 'drink now' style. Only the very best vintages will benefit from age. Screw caps available in select markets.

*'Penfolds is making Koonunga Hill for early drinking.
The fact that it can age just emphasises the sheer work and
effort put into the overall style.'*
— ANDREW CAILLARD, PANELLIST

Koonunga Hill, first produced in 1976, is named after Penfolds' renowned Koonunga Hill vineyard in the Barossa Valley. Celebrating over 30 years of vintages, it has established a reputation far exceeding its price point and expectations as a commercial entry-point wine. It has been voted Great Value Red Wine of the Year and the 2002 was listed as one of the top 50 New World wines by *Decanter* magazine. For years, wine collectors have regarded it as something of a 'cellar-filler'. Don Ditter, creator of Koonunga Hill, once observed that 'there's never been such a thing as a crook Koonunga Hill. It's always a reliable drop, but in top years you can expect something out of the ordinary.' Older vintages—when they turn up for auction—are snapped up eagerly because they offer tremendous value and have a track record for ageing well.

Koonunga Hill is a multi-district shiraz–cabernet based largely on Barossa, McLaren Vale and Coonawarra fruit. It is a classic Penfolds maturation-style wine where fruit complexity and vivacity rather than oak is highlighted. The wine is vinified in open fermenters and then matured in three- to four-year-old oak hogsheads for a year to allow the fruit to mellow and the tannins to soften.

In theory, Koonunga Hill represents a confluence of varietal and regional character. The shiraz component generally brings ripeness, volume and sweetness of fruit. Fragrance, further complexity and a rigid tannin base are provided by cabernet. Through rigorous selection and myriad blending options, red wine-makers are able to maintain style, weight and concentration each year regardless of vintage conditions. Occasionally, relegated fruit destined for either Bin 128 or Bin 28 is included in the blend.

The original 1976 release of 20,000 cases is now regarded as a classic Penfolds vintage. The wine has become increasingly rare, but good bottles are still fresh and compelling. James Halliday observed that the wine, while fully mature, still 'has substance and has always been the very best of the early vintages'. This original wine was sold at under A$2 a bottle. At the time, the Australian wine industry was at the tail end of a red wine boom. The domestic Australian market was flush with stock, export opportunities were almost non-existent and marketers needed to find imaginative ways of moving excess volumes of Penfolds bin wines. Koonunga Hill was an instant hit and for many years was the entry point to Penfolds' portfolio of red wines.

While production levels have increased substantially over the last 30 years, Koonunga Hill has benefited from the increasing wealth of Penfolds vineyard resources, vine age, improvements in winemaking technology and accumulation of knowledge.

Koonunga Hill remains true to its origins of style. However, there has been a steady progression of refinement. Increased fragrancy and richness of fruit, buoyancy and weight make these wines immediately appealing. The wines 'punch well above their weight' and in recognised Penfolds vintages can benefit from laying down. Joshua Greene observed, 'The older vintages are charming wines slowly maturing into a sweet senility!' Campbell Mattinson was impressed by the 1990, describing it as 'a strong substantial and winsome wine with another fifteen years of cellaring potential'. Huon Hooke described the 1996 as a 'big generous wine with lots to give and a way to go yet'. Joshua Greene enjoyed the 1998: 'It's spot on for drinking and shows the best of both varieties.' James Halliday singled out the 2004, 2005 and both the 2006 (the Seventy Six and standard) vintages as modern Koonunga Hill styles with cellaring potential. However, he pointed out that 'the wines are so fresh and appealing when young that it does raise the question about whether cellaring is worthwhile'.

The 2006 Koonunga Hill Seventy Six Shiraz Cabernet is a 30th anniversary wine that pays homage to a remarkable long-lived style. It is a special selection bottling first released through cellar door restaurants. The wine is a refined version of its stablemate and shows 'extra dimension and complexity'. Seventy Six is made for current drinking but it will also benefit from a few years of extra bottle age.

Ch'ng Poh Tiong described it as a 'more intense and polished wine with a longer finish. Seventy Six also commemorates the Year of the Fire Dragon—a powerful force that promises happiness and good fortune.'

2006 Seventy Six has already enjoyed strong plaudits on the show circuit, winning the Wine Press Club of New South Wales trophy at the Sydney Royal Wine Show in 2008 for the Best Dry Red in Commercial Classes.

1976 ★   NOW

Medium deep tawny brick red. Intense mocha/dark chocolate/vanilla/wet bitumen aromas with some leather/herb garden notes. The palate is fully mature, complex and fresh with leather/plum/dark chocolate flavours and fine chalky, lacy, dry tannins. Starting to dry out now but still impressive for age.

1977   NOW

Deep brick red. Complex mocha/tobacco/dried herb/mint aromas with hints of liquorice. Complex older wine with tobacco/spice/dried herb/meaty flavours and loose-knit, dry tannins. Finishes astringently firm. Still fresh with plenty of fruit sweetness and flavour length. Just past its peak.

1978   NOW

Medium brick red. Developed earthy/choco-berry/briary/cedar aromas and flavours. Well-concentrated palate with earthy/choco-berry/redcurrant flavours and firm, gritty dry tannins. The wine is still drinking well, but beginning to fade.

1979   PAST

Brick red. Over-developed wine with sandalwood/leather/meaty/raisin aromas and flavours. The palate is drying out with pronounced leafy tannins. Definitely past its best now.

1980   PAST

Brick red. Leather/earthy/dried herb aromas. Lean austere palate. The fruit has dropped out leaving a long tannin slick and pronounced acidity.

1981   PAST • • • NOW

Brick red. Sandalwood/spearmint/tobacco aromas with some wet bitumen notes. Tobacco/dark cherry/bitumen flavours and bitter dry tannins. There is still plenty of volume, fruit sweetness and flavour length. Tannins kick up dry and grippy at the finish. Definitely on the final stretch.

1982   PAST • • • NOW

Brick red. Fully mature mocha/leather/sweet-fruit/honeycomb aromas. Sweet mocha/chocolate/panforte/clove flavours and silky dry—a touch leafy—tannins. Fruit is drying out. Drink up.

1983   NOW

Brick red. Classical choco-berry/meaty aromas with herb/graphite notes. The palate is rich and fruit sweet with choco-berry/espresso coffee flavours and slinky, loose-knit tannins. Finishes firm and chalky dry. Fully evolved and unlikely to improve.

1984   NOW

Brick red. Mature beef stock/dark chocolate with some toffee/panforte characters. Mellow palate with fully developed meaty/panforte flavours and dry, savoury tannins. Finishes grippy firm. Still holding but drink soon.

1985   NOW

Brick red. Dark chocolate/redcurrant/sweet vanilla aromas. Fresh, concentrated wine with dark chocolate/redcurrant flavours, plenty of fruit sweetness and ripe, fine, loose-knit tannins. Volume fades towards the finish.

1986   NOW

Brick red. Intense leather polish/rose petal/red cherry aromas with some autumnal, dried, leafy notes. The palate is rich and chocolaty with red cherry/bitumen/sandalwood characters and fine, powdery tannins. Finishes firm and dry. Will hold for a while but best to drink now.

1987   NOW

Brick red. Lovely dark chocolate/meaty aromas with leather/liquorice notes. The palate is sweet and solid with roasted coffee/leather/dark berry fruits and hard slightly green tannins. Finishes firm and oily. Drink soon.

1988   NOW • • • 2010

Brick red. Classic sweet-fruit/plum/redcurrant aromas with musky/rose petal nuances. A substantial wine with fresh complex redcurrant/panforte/demi-glace flavours, plenty of mid-palate richness and chocolaty tannins. Finishes earthy and firm. Excellent drive and weight. Still holding really well, but best to drink soon.

1989   PAST • • • NOW

Brick red. Fresh redcurrant/black cherry/bitumen/dried herb aromas and flavours. The wine has volume, richness, fruit sweetness and fine, lacy, dry tannins, but acidity is beginning to poke through at the finish. It's still lovely to drink now but not one to keep.

1990 ★   NOW • • • 2016

Brick red. Lovely earthy/panforte/demi-glace aromas with mint chocolate notes. Plush. smooth. deep-set palate with plenty of sweet-fruit, panforte/dark cherry flavours and rich ripe tannins. An impressive wine reflecting a classical Penfolds vintage. It's great to drink now but will hold.

1991 ★   NOW • • • 2012

Brick red. Dark chocolate/tobacco/leafy/dried herb aromas with touches of leather. Well-balanced wine with sweet, developed choco-berry/dried herb flavours and loose-knit, savoury firm tannins. Lovely old wine.

1992   NOW • • • 2012

Brick red. Interesting dark chocolate/dried plum/silage/mint aromas. Well-concentrated dried plum/tobacco/minty flavours and fine, chalky tannins. Finishes grippy firm. Drink soon.

1993   NOW

Brick red. Mocha/red cherry aromas with hints of mint and leather. The palate is fresh and minerally with mocha/red cherry/vanilla fudge flavours and chalky, loose-knit tannins. Finishes leafy and firm. Much better than expected for vintage.

1994   NOW • • • 2014

Medium crimson. Developed dried fruit/graphite/meaty aromas. Bitter dark chocolate/bitumen flavours and fine, firm, chalky, dry tannins. Finishes long and sweet. Ready to drink.

1995   NOW

Medium crimson. Fresh minty/tomato leaf/earthy aromas. The palate is well concentrated with red fruit/chocolaty/earthy/dried herb flavours, high-pitched acidity and dry, sinewy tannins. The fruit is just holding up.

1996 ★   NOW • • • 2015

Deep crimson. Lovely fresh blackberry/camomile/herb garden aromas. A rich, round, full-flavoured wine with plenty of fruit sweetness, blackberry/blueberry/mocha/liquorice characters and dense, ripe, chocolaty tannins. A big, generous wine.

1997   NOW

Medium crimson. Quite developed wine with earthy/sage/raspberry/capsicum aromas. A solid wine with dark cherry/capsicum/earthy flavours and hard, sinewy tannins. Finishes bittersweet. Drink now.

1998 ★   NOW • • • 2018

Medium deep crimson. Fresh panforte/dried plum/herb garden/liquorice aromas. A richly concentrated, full-bodied wine with deep-set panforte/dark chocolate flavours, balanced with dense savoury tannins. Finishes grippy dry. A substantial wine with plenty of weight and structure but oddly lacks finesse.

1999 ★   NOW • • • 2015

Deep crimson. Intense raspberry/blackcurrant/mocha/aniseed aromas. Rich and concentrated wine with deep-set raspberry/roasted coffee/dark chocolate flavours and lovely, fine-grained tannins. Finishes minerally and long. The tannins have really softened out. A beautifully aged complete wine with gorgeous freshness and complexity. Drink now or hold.

2000   NOW

Deep crimson. Red plum/mulch/herb garden aromas. The palate is medium concentrated with red plum/raspberry essence/herb flavours and slinky, loose-knit tannins. Under-powered. No point keeping. Drink now.

2001   NOW • • • 2012

Deep crimson. Fragrant blackberry/red cherry/aniseed aromas with a hint of ginger. Pure blackcurrant pastille/herb garden flavours, lovely mid-palate richness and sweet, supple tannins. Showing some aged leather/meaty nuances. Finishes savoury and long. Drinking very well.

2002 ★   NOW • • • 2014

Deep crimson. Highly aromatic, pure blackberry/red plum aromas with some herb/black olive notes. A fresh, richly concentrated, fruit-driven palate with blackberry essence flavours and gentle, ripe, slippery tannins. Finishes savoury and fruit sweet. An utterly seductive wine. Drink now or cellar for a while.

2003	NOW

Deep crimson purple. Intense mulberry/cassis aromas with some tropical fruit notes. Sweet, concentrated palate with blackcurrant/dried plum flavours and rich, ripe chunky tannins. Finishes long and sweet. Drinking well, but don't keep.

2004 ★	NOW • • • 2018

Deep crimson purple. Fresh raspberry/blackberry minty/aniseed aromas. Delicious, well-concentrated wine with fresh, deep-set raspberry/blackberry/aniseed flavours and supple tannins. Builds up chalky firm at the finish. Excellent weight and depth. Drink or keep.

2005	NOW • • • 2014

Deep crimson purple. Elegant, smooth wine with raspberry/blueberry/plummy/espresso coffee/aniseed aromas. Sweet and fleshy palate with blueberry/plummy/mocha flavours and supple, sweet, satin tannins. Finishes chalky and long. Drink or keep.

2006 ★	NOW • • • 2016

Medium deep crimson purple. Bright dark cherry/plum/liquorice aromas with some savoury/minty notes. Well-concentrated wine with liquorice/dark cherry/dried herb/mint flavours, chocolaty tannins and plenty of flavour length. Has good fruit and good potential, but this is a drink now style. Drink now without guilt or keep.

2006 Seventy Six ★	NOW • • • 2018

Medium deep crimson purple. Special blend to commemorate 30th anniversary. Classic, fruit-driven, shiraz-led wine with intense choco-berry/musky aromas. Rich, dense, plush palate with pure blackberry sweet fruit, dense chocolaty tannins and plenty of savoury complexity. Great length and balance. Lovely, current drinking wine although structure suggests excellent ageing potential.

DISCUSSION

The older Koonunga Hill wines, pre-1990, are either fading or have reached the end of their cellaring life. (HH) There is a sweetness *and* sweet-fruit character that pervades through many vintages. I can see a honeycomb note in many individual wines. Most older vintages were fully mature or past their prime. (JH) The older vintages are charming wines slowly maturing into a sweet senility! Certainly a few stood out; 1976 particularly. (JG)

1976 While impressive considering the objectives of the overall wine style, it is beginning to show frailty. (HH) It has always been the best of the early vintages and it still is. (JH) I really enjoyed this wine. It's still drinking very well. (CPT)

1977 is also showing signs of maderisation. Many of the wines showed chocolate-honeycomb, beef stock, raisin characters, but also a dry tannin astringency. The fruit has dried out in many of the vintages and the acidity is also poking out. (HH) But it still has integrity as an old wine. (JH)

1978 is a particularly good bottle but the structure is weakening. (JH) It's fresh, with developed earthy, chocolate/dark berry aromas and firm, gritty, dry tannins.

1979 and **1980** not tasted in this forum but deemed as past their best. (AC)

1981 is fading now. It has strong spearmint/tobacco aromas and bitter, dry tannins. (AC) I found it more vegetal than fruity. The palate was fresh with plenty of tannins but it is drying out now. (JG)

1982 was mellow and chocolaty. (HH) It has fragile remnants of elegance. (JH) However, it's still holding on and still has appeal. (JG)

1983 is still alive but obviously fully mature and at the end of the plateau. But its still has enough fruit to satisfy. (JH) It is completely evolved and not long for this world but it has a sweetness that lingers and maintains freshness and structure. (JG)

1984 is fractionally green with savoury tannins but the fruit is still holding. (JH) The aromas suggest some over-development, but the palate is much fresher. (AC)

1985 still had body weight but was mature and fading. (HH) The tannins have virtually disappeared now. (JH)

1986 has a feisty bouquet, but it has some real life with plenty of red and black fruits and fine tannins. (JH) It's quite developed, with some red cherry, leather, boot polish aromas, but the palate has lovely concentration and powdery tannins. (AC)

1987 is very mature and smells of blackberry jam and smoked meats. (JG) It possessed a mix of sweet and sour fruit characters and savoury/green tannins. (JH)

1988 was the highlight of the older vintages. It seemed to have extra richness and substance. (HH) 1988 is a gorgeous mature wine. (JG)

1989 is lighter bodied with some caramel fudge characters. (JH) I found it fresh and exuberant with redcurrant/black cherry/meaty aromas and plenty of richness and flavour length. The tannins are quite chalky at the finish. (AC)

1990 shows all the hallmarks of an excellent vintage with more body and weight. These older vintages are all wines to drink now. No point in further cellaring. (JH) I thought it was really impressive. It had fresh primary fruit and a touch of age. The more I tasted the more it floated on the palate with orange peel/cocoa/plum/toffee and mint characters. This is a strong substantial and winsome wine with another fifteen years of cellaring potential. (CM)

1991 to **2006** vintages reflected a modern pattern of winemaking. Recent vintages are more substantial and impressive with better overall balance and structure. The acidity takes over in some vintages, such as 1994, 1995, 1996 and 2003, but overall these wines are well balanced. (NB)

1991 possessed very high-pitched blackberry, dark chocolate aromas with a touch of leafy tobacco. I liked the developed sweet-fruit flavours and loose-knit but firm, leafy tannins.

1992 to 1995 vintages were a little disjointed but when I hit **1996** the wines started to over-deliver. (JG) **1992** was quite aromatic, with a polished entry, plenty of mid-palate richness and then tannins to support. I thought it was definitely still there. (JH)

1993 has a calm composure with a rosehip maturity. It's just on the edge of ripeness but it still has great definition. (NB)

1994 is a substantial wine with more structure and weight than any preceding wine with plenty of black fruits and bitter chocolate characters. (JH)

1995 showed plenty of dark, sweet-fruit characters but the tannins were a little harsh. I picked up a whiff of balsamic notes as well.

1996 had a lovely intensity of blackberries and liquorice. The palate was dense and smooth with an essential simplicity of fruit.

1997 was peppery with a refined, elegant and supple structure. (NB) It was a very solid wine with dark cherry, earthy herb aromas and sinewy tannins. (AC)

1998 was impressive with its deep, pruney richness, beautiful concentration and grippy/clingy tannins. (NB) By 1998 the Koonunga Hill Shiraz Cabernets show more depth and presence of fruit. (JG)

1999 had pristine blackcurrant aromas, good depth of fruit and mid-palate richness. (NB)

2000 has plenty of raspberry, red cherry fruit. The primary characters haven't really evolved and I am not certain that it has the structure to last. I would drink it now. (JG)

2001 had an abundance of blackberry fruit, a sapid acidity and compact, firm tannins. It's not fleshy, but a worthy food wine. (NB)

2002 is an enveloping and densely woven wine with overall succulence and vibrancy. It's a really pleasing drink. (NB) I enjoyed the lovely, round freshness of the 2002 and 2003. (CPT)

2003 is not really a keeper but it has plenty of sweet red- and blackberry fruit characters, a touch of prune and plenty of fruit sweetness on the palate. (JG)

2004 seems more cabernet in character with elegant, flowing, supple cassis flavours but there is a metallic note to the finish. (NB) There's another shift from 2004, perhaps reflecting youthfulness rather than a change in style. (JG) The marked shift upwards from 2004 is explained by three consecutive good vintages. (HH)

2005 is a deep brooding wine with nascent complexity but with the restraint to go with food. (NB)

2006 comprised the standard and special Seventy Six bottling. They are very appealing wines with plenty of freshness and supple tannins. The Seventy Six is perhaps more ample, with impressive saturation and vibrancy. This I feel will evolve extremely well. (NB)

The 2006s are very sophisticated wines. They share an elegant, fragrant black cherry aroma and richness on the palate. The Seventy Six has extra dimension and complexity. (JG) They are both lovely wines. The Seventy Six is a turbocharged version of the standard vintage. (HH) It's an interesting idea to have this commemorative *Grand Vin*. It might be an even better idea, at least for the Chinese-speaking market, to refer to it as Year of the Dragon Seventy Six! (CPT)

The earlier vintages I noticed have bigger tannins, but now the wines are more balanced with better fruit character. This is much to do with winemaking refinements, better fruit from the vineyard and winemaking technology. For instance, in the early days Penfolds used continuous presses which perhaps over extracted the fruit. (SL)

One of the generalisations and major points about Koonunga Hill is that these wines are made for immediate consumption. The wines will last in the cellar if you happen to forget them. The use of screw cap closures will add further cellaring life and freshness. (JH)

Koonunga Hill Shiraz

First Vintage:	2002.
Variety:	Shiraz.
Origin:	Multi-district blend, South Australia, with significant proportions from the Barossa Valley—also McLaren Vale, Padthaway, Langhorne Creek, Coonawarra and Riverland. May vary considerably depending on vintage conditions.
Fermentation:	Stainless steel tanks.
Maturation:	15 months in seasoned French and American oak.
Comments:	Screw caps available in select markets.

The Koonunga Hill reds are all full-flavoured but fruit-driven wines—in contrast to the maturation style of the Shiraz Cabernet. The wines are all multi-regional blends. The Cabernet Merlot is an early drinking style with clear, bright blackcurrant/plummy fruit, fine-grained tannins and plenty of flavour length. The Cabernet Sauvignon is aromatic with cassis/cedar/violet aromas, lacy dry tannins, plenty of fruit sweetness and trademark Penfolds integrated oak. The Shiraz is a plumper style with plush red-berried fruits, generosity of flavour and supple ripe tannins.

Koonunga Hill Cabernet Sauvignon

First Vintage:	2002.
Variety:	Cabernet sauvignon.
Origin:	Multi-district blend, South Australia, with significant proportions from the McLaren Vale and Langhorne Creek—also Barossa Valley, Padthaway, Coonawarra, Riverland. May vary considerably depending on vintage conditions.
Fermentation:	Stainless steel tanks.
Maturation:	A proportion of the blend is aged for 15 months in seasoned French and American oak.
Comments:	Screw caps available in select markets.

Koonunga Hill Cabernet Merlot

First Vintage:	2001.
Variety:	Cabernet sauvignon and merlot.
Origin:	Multi-district blend, South Australia. McLaren Vale, Barossa Valley, Padthaway, Langhorne Creek, Coonawarra, Riverland. May vary considerably depending on vintage conditions.
Fermentation:	Stainless steel tanks.
Maturation:	A proportion of the blend is aged in seasoned French and American oak.
Comments:	Screw caps available in select markets.

Koonunga Hill Merlot

First Vintage:	2005.
Variety:	Merlot.
Origin:	Multi-district blend, South Australia. McLaren Vale, Barossa Valley, Padthaway, Langhorne Creek, Coonawarra, Riverland. May vary considerably depending on vintage conditions.
Fermentation:	Stainless steel tanks.
Maturation:	A proportion of the blend is aged in seasoned French and American oak.
Comments:	Screw caps available in select markets.

WHITES

Koonunga Hill Chardonnay

First Vintage:	1991.
Variety:	Chardonnay.
Origin:	Multi-district blend, South Australia. Barossa Valley, McLaren Vale and Langhorne Creek, South Australia. May vary considerably depending on vintage conditions.
Fermentation:	Stainless steel tanks. Some components undergo malolactic fermentation.
Maturation:	Some components are barrel fermented and oak matured for 3–5 months in French oak barriques.
Comments:	Screw caps available in select markets.

Koonunga Hill Chardonnay was first released in 1991 to match a worldwide demand for a Penfolds white wine. While there are benefits from the huge economies of scale available to a large company, the wine needed to be highly consistent with Penfolds' red winemaking reputation. Both Koonunga Hill whites are well-proportioned wines with distinctive primary fruit characters and good levels of intensity. The Chardonnay, matured for several months in small French oak barriques, is a richly concentrated wine with plenty of varietal definition and creamy flavours.

Koonunga Hill Semillon Sauvignon Blanc

First Vintage:	1996.
Variety:	Semillon (70–80%), sauvignon blanc (20–30%).
Origin:	Multi-district South Australian blend. Predominantly Adelaide Hills with some parcels of Barossa Valley fruit.
Fermentation:	Stainless steel tanks.
Maturation:	4 months on lees without the influence of oak.
Comments:	Screw caps available in select markets.

The Semillon Sauvignon Blanc is a riper style with tropical fruit aromas, plenty of fruit sweetness and crisp acidity. Penfolds handles Koonunga Hill whites with the same attention to detail expected in an ultra-fine wine. These wines have been described as 'convincing, well-made wines that show what Australia is able to do well'.

CHAPTER FOURTEEN

Fortified Wines

Penfolds fortified wines are an Australian institution. These tawny styles continue a long tradition of fortified production at Penfolds. They are a link with yesteryear evoking memories of summers past, vast stacks of oak barrels filled with slowly maturing tawny fortified wines and a grand wine industry heritage. Many of these beautifully concentrated and complex tawnies are living history with material going back decades. These wines are the epitome of complexity, richness and utter indulgence.

'Open the port, steward. Penfolds of course, sir!'
—ADVERTISING SLOGAN, c. 1920

Penfolds has had a long tradition of fortified wine production going back to its origins in the mid-1800s. As elsewhere in the world, fortified wines were extremely fashionable; sherry, Madeira and Oporto (port) enjoyed considerable fame in the nineteenth century. The addition of grape spirit contributes significantly to wine stability. Yeasts and bacteria cannot live in solutions of more than around 18 per cent/ per volume alcohol. The practice of fortification, therefore, was a practical method of wine production in many wine-producing countries. Sherry and port-style wines were particularly suited to the climate and frontier culture of Australia in the 1800s. Indeed, by 1881 Penfolds was responsible for one-third of South Australia's wine production—almost all of it fortified wine.

Penfolds continues to have a remarkable share of the Australian fortified, specifically the tawny-style, wine market. Penfolds Club Tawny began its life in the 1940s as Penfolds Five Star Club Tawny Port, but the term 'port' is no longer used by

Penfolds in keeping with international standards and trade agreements. The Penfolds Tawny range comprises: Club, Club Reserve Tawny, Penfolds Bluestone Ten-Year-Old Tawny, Grandfather Liqueur Tawny and Penfolds Great Grandfather Liqueur Tawny. These tawny styles are all aged in small, old oak casks at Penfolds Kalimna Tawny Cellars located in the Barossa Valley. All of these tawnies are multi-regional wines, a key feature of Penfolds' house style.

Max Schubert's idea of being able to make an all-round table wine is partially a reflection of Penfolds' winemaking culture during the 1940s and '50s, when winemakers were able to source fruit of specific quality and character from several different vineyards and growers to maintain consistency of style across Penfolds' extensive fortified range. Classification, batch vinifying and barrel maturation play a very important part in contemporary Penfolds tawny production, as it does in its table wine production. Fruit richness, grape tannin balance, the 'maturation effect' derived from ageing in old oak hogshead casks and grape spirit/brandy character are essential elements of the Penfolds tawny style. Indeed, selection is the crucial factor.

The Riverland and the Barossa Valley are the principal sources of Penfolds tawny fruit. Club, Club Reserve and to a lesser extent Bluestone Ten-Year-Old Tawny (Club styles) have a significant Riverland component. Grandfather and Great Grandfather (Grandfather Tawnies) are largely Barossa Valley wines. They are all based on shiraz, mataro (mourvèdre) and smaller percentages of cabernet sauvignon and grenache— grape varieties introduced to Australia during the very early nineteenth century.

While each of the tawnies differ in concentration, richness and complexity, there is a continuity of house style based on rich, full-bodied fruit. Selection of fruit begins in the vineyard. Winemakers are looking for optimum ripeness; a combination of flavour composition, vitality and potential alcohol levels of 14 to 15 Baumé. The Club styles and Grandfather Tawnies are differentiated by overall structure and weight. The style of fruit used for the Grandfather Tawnies is similar to the requirement of St Henri and Bin 389 with their pristine fruit dimension.

Vinification takes place in small stainless steel fermenters; each style component is batched. During fermentation the wine is regularly pumped over to extract colour and flavour. Fortification takes place towards the middle stages of fermentation; fruit and sugar sweetness is an element of the Penfolds tawny style. The choice of fortification spirit is an important one. The style and quality of spirit, which add complexity and mouth-weight, can also have regional differences.

Penfolds uses two different spirit types which have a similar character: rich, full and oily, varying only in the level of intensity. The primary function of both spirits is to accentuate primary fruit qualities and add initial complexity. A richer, more intense spirit is used to complement the richer, more intensely concentrated, Grandfather style. The Club styles and Grandfather styles are further differentiated after fortification. Pressings of varying percentages are added to the early drinking Club styles to further add structure and balance. The Grandfathers are made from 100 per cent free-run wine. This maturation Grandfather style relies on the fuller spirit and the extended small old oak maturation to gain overall complexity and optimum balance.

Club, Club Reserve and Bluestone

The Penfolds tawnies are aged in 'Solera Systems' at Penfolds Kalimna Tawny Cellars. The wines are all aged in old 300-litre hogsheads (filled to 280 litres)—averaging between twenty and 60 years! The maturation process deliberately takes place under corrugated iron. At the height of summer the temperatures on the top stack can be as high as 55 degrees Celsius. In winter the temperatures can fall below 8 degrees Celsius. These cyclic swings in temperature are vital to the maturation process; evaporation, concentration and controlled oxidation are all a part of the complex nature of aromas and flavours.

The Solera is a fractional blending system which allows a continuity and consistency of style. The Club styles use a modified Solera System for early release with an average age of around three years. The Reserve and Bluestone spend a longer time achieving more complexity and richness.

TASTING NOTES

Club Tawny   NOW

Tawny colour. Sweet, fragrant orange/tangerine/musky/nutty aromas. The palate is rich and intensely concentrated with sweet toffee/orange/butterscotch flavours and a hint of rancio at the finish.

Club Reserve   NOW

Tawny colour. More concentrated butterscotch, menthol, rancio aromas and flavours. More refined in structure with some chalky texture and layered complexity. Finishes long and sweet.

Bluestone Ten-Year-Old Tawny   NOW

Tawny colour. Lovely intense aniseed, butterscotch, nutty, rancio aromas. Sweet butterscotch/nutty amontillado/aldehyde flavours with brandied warmth at the finish. A very long, lingering finish.

Grandfather and Great Grandfather

Penfolds Grandfather Tawny is batch-aged in old oak hogsheads for an average period of eight years before it enters the six-stack 'Grandfather Solera'. During this initial period, these batches comprise the components of a single vintage, grape variety and vineyard. At the end of this initial maturation period the components are classified and blended to achieve the style required to maintain consistency of the Solera. This is a very complex selection process as it comprises myriad parts; each of these components will age slightly differently. Shiraz, with its overall opulence and fruit density, ages more slowly. Mataro (mourvèdre) matures more rapidly—a characteristic which enhances complexity. Grenache, used to a lesser extent, contributes mouth-feel and another layer of fruit intensity.

Each year winemakers draw one-twelfth of each barrel from the lowest level of the Solera. The barrel is topped up from the barrel above and this process is completed when the top barrels are one-twelfth empty. The top barrels are then topped up with the blended eight-year-old Grandfather Tawny. Theoretically, the wine

drawn from the lowest level of the Solera is twenty years of age, having been in the fractional blending system for twelve years. During this entire maturation process, the wines become more concentrated and complex; opulence, weight and sweetness is intertwined and balanced by the alcohol, acidity, oak nuances and volatility. The highly evocative term 'rancio' is used by tasters to describe this character. The wine has a dense, tawny colour with a green patina, seductive, rich, spicy/nutty/panforte aromas and extraordinary intensity and viscosity on the palate.

Ray Beckwith said, 'My first contact with Grandfather Port was in 1935 when Alfred Scholz told me that it had its genesis in the 1915 vintage. The wine was matured in hogsheads and quarter casks of American oak and stored on top of the dome tanks in No. 2 Cellar, just underneath the iron saw-tooth roof, thereby being subjected to warm to hot conditions with a consequent high rate of evaporation. Initially Grandfather Port was not marketed—it was only given away—and in half-gallon (2.25-litre) flagons. As far as I know the wine was confined to Nuriootpa only and it certainly did not appear on stock sheets under the title Grandfather Port—as there was no such official designation.'

The Great Grandfather Port, first released in 1994, was introduced to celebrate Penfolds' 150th anniversary. The wine, blended from exceptional aged Solera material and 'other great stuff lying around the cellar', has an average age of more than 30 years. The wine is immensely complex and powerful. Great Grandfather Port is Penfolds' rarest wine; only 1000 bottles are available each release. The first release, in 1994, deliberately comprised 1994 bottles.

TASTING NOTES

Bin S6 Grandfather Aged Tawny Port
1945 Bottled 1969   NOW • • • PAST

Deep tawny colour. Old rancio/malmsey Madeira/raisin/panforte aromas. Dried herb/panforte/rancio flavours with cutting brandy spirit. Finishes nutty dry but rich and flavourful. Increasingly rare.

Grandfather Fine Old Liqueur Tawny
20–25-year-old Tawny   NOW

Deep tawny colour. Fresh, complex, powerful butterscotch/rancio/dried fruit aromas. Rich and flavoursome tawny with smooth butterscotch/dried fruit/panforte/walnut flavours and pronounced brandy cut. A very long finish.

Great Grandfather Rare Old Liqueur Tawny
40–45-year-old Tawny   NOW

Deep tawny colour. Intense complex rancio/walnut/praline aromas. Fresh, elegant, luscious tawny with concentrated rancio/butter menthol/chocolate flavours carried across the palate by a beautiful line of brandy spirit. Extraordinarily long sweet and savoury finish.

CHAPTER FIFTEEN

Reflections on the Penfolds Styles

NEIL BECKETT, UK

Born in 1964 to a Scottish father and an American mother, Neil Beckett began his professional life as an academic, ascending what he hoped might be an ivory tower in St Andrews with a first class honours degree in English and Medieval History (St Andrews), a doctorate in Medieval History (Magdalen College, Oxford) and a fellowship of the Royal Historical Society (University of London). Also taking with him a taste for wine, he soon wanted to spend more time down in the cellar than up in the tower, and between the two did an MBA, managing to wangle a dissertation on White Burgundy.

After working a vintage in Burgundy, Beckett started writing for fine wine shippers Richards Walford. During a year at Lay

& Wheeler wine merchants he graduated with distinction in the Wine & Spirit Education Trust Diploma and took the top prize, before going on to *Harpers Wine & Spirit Weekly*, on which he was contributing editor for several years and wrote a regular column on fine wine.

In 2004 Beckett became the first editor of *The World of Fine Wine*, an award-winning quarterly review on which he still works with Hugh Johnson and Andrew Jefford. He has judged at national and international wine competitions, has won prizes for his wine writing, and, along with Anthony Hanson, MW, is one of the two British tasters on the Grand Jury Européen.

What were your top five wines of the tasting?

In any Australian English dictionary, this could be the definition of invidious. There were so many outstanding wines over the course of these four days that to identify five is not even a question of trying to find the first among equals in each of the top flights. Even restricting myself to five different bins and five different vintages, I could give you a different and equally honest answer every day for a week. But today let it be this: 1962 Grange (tomorrow it could have been the 1952 or 1953, the day after the 1963, then the 1966, 1996, 1998 and 2004); 1966 St Henri (tomorrow the 1956, the day after the 1962, then the 1983, 1991, 1998 and 2005); 1996 Bin 707 (then the 1964, 1966, 1967, 1994, 2001 and 2004); 2004 Kalimna Block 42 Cabernet Sauvignon (then the 1996 ... not so many of these, so a short week); and the 2005 Cellar Reserve Coonawarra Cabernet/Kalimna Shiraz (ditto). I've already more than used up my five, but if I were allowed a white as well, it would be the 2004 Yattarna (tomorrow the 2006).

Were there any surprises?

Yes, and again so many that it's very difficult to know where to begin. Overall, I was amazed by the quality and longevity of some of the supposedly lesser wines, even though I had been expecting this on the basis of previous Rewards of Patience tastings. It's difficult to believe—and on taste terms alone, you wouldn't—that until 1991, Koonunga Hill was the 'entry level' wine: the 1976 and 1986 are still richly satisfying, and will remain so for a few years yet.

At the opposite end of the scale (and this is largely ignorance on my part), I hadn't expected the older vintages of Grange, from the 1950s and '60s, to have anything like the energy, harmony or integrity, nor the elegance, finesse or subtlety, that they did. I had expected them to be hugely impressive, but not in quite these ways. In a sense, the 1959—for me, as for others, the best of the 'hidden' Granges—was as surprising as any, in that it had to be made in secret and without any new wood. Among more recent vintages, I was perplexed, even startled, by the 1990 Grange which, a bit like some modern art, I found difficult to appreciate or understand, even though it is such a highly regarded vintage. To my surprise, given their respective reputations, I preferred the 1991 and the 1992.

Then there were all the surprises in between Koonunga Hill and Grange. Although it's a range I've always enjoyed, I was again forcefully struck by how undervalued St Henri is: after this flight, the most enjoyable of all for me after Grange, I found it all the more incredible that recent vintages of this wine are about £100 a bottle cheaper than for Grange (which is not to take anything away from it). There were also revelations in the shape of wines that (to my shame) I had barely even heard of, let alone tasted—not only older Special Bins, like the 1956 Magill Burgundy Bin 136 or the 1957 Minchinbury Bin 14, but also younger wines like the sangioveses. This is such a difficult variety to get right and yet, despite being what Peter Gago called 'the most natural wine in the whole group' (no added yeast, no new oak, no acid correction, unfined, unfiltered), it was the most persuasive sangiovese I've come across outside Italy, and would put many from Tuscany to shame.

Among the whites, I was not prepared for the quality and variety of the range as a whole, especially the more recent releases. The Cellar Reserve Sauvignon Blanc was challenging and daringly different, the gewurztraminers (another tricky variety) standing out for their race as well as their restrained spice. And it is remarkable how successful Oliver Crawford has already been in avowedly emulating a more 'Alsace' style: the 2006 and 2007 Bin 51 Eden Valley Rieslings, for example, impressed me with their combination of freshness and richness. It was revealing to see the difference that the higher proportion of Adelaide Hills chardonnay made to the 2004 Yattarna, and that the introduction of Tasmanian chardonnay made to the 2006—an exciting new departure. The most died-in-the-wool white Burgundy fan (and I suppose that still includes me, despite the problems they've been having over the past ten years or so) would have been amazed by how favourably the 2004 Yattarna showed alongside the Bonneau du Martray of the same vintage at the final Rewards of Patience dinner. I'm a great admirer of the Corton-Charlemagne domaine, and I prefer 2004 as a white Burgundy vintage to 2005 and 2006, but the Yattarna was not only drinking better on the night, it also seemed to have as much complexity, potency and potential.

On the human side of things, I was amazed, never having had the pleasure of meeting him previously, by how lucid, spry, and sprightly Ray Beckwith was at 95, after a lifetime in wine and by the way in which Peter Gago and his entire team not only managed to keep going, but to look as if they were actually enjoying the whole thing as much as we pampered tasters were!

Describe the evolution of winemaking philosophy and style across both white and red wines.

This is slightly more difficult for me, as I know the wines and vintages less well than most of the other tasters and I'm not a trained winemaker, so inevitably I'm influenced in part by what I've heard or read—though this certainly seemed to tally with what I tasted. I think that in the early days (1950s and '60s) it is easy to see that the dominant style at the time was fortified wine, even though these were deliberately setting out in a radically different direction. Although the three 'hidden' Granges were still interesting, particularly the 1959, it is clear that the circumstances of their production didn't allow them to shine as those before and after did.

The 1970s and '80s was the least exciting phase for me, relatively speaking. Peter Gago felt that the priority attached to Grange had led St Henri to suffer slightly in the 1970s, and that makes perfect sense. Looking back at my favourite wines in this flight, I have at least three vintages from every decade except the 1970s, where I have only one (the 1976). The results are similar, in fact, with respect to the other wines from the 1970s as well, including Grange. We were a little unlucky with both bottles of the 1971, which I've known to be magnificent on other occasions, and there was still plenty to admire in the 1972, 1974, 1976 and 1978. But a few of the other vintages were relatively disappointing for me, seeming dried out and leathery now, and even the best didn't hit the heights of the best from other decades. The 1980s seemed better overall, though Steve Lienert suggested that some of the winemakers might not have spent enough time in the vineyards, picking rather too early in an attempt to secure more elegance in the wines. This appeared to explain some of the rather tart and tannic wines, especially at the less exalted level of Koonunga Hill and Bin 128.

Standards across the range seem to have risen through the 1990s, especially in terms of fruit quality, though I would (without sparing Peter Gago's blushes) distinguish between the 1990s and the 2000s. Even at the top end, some the wines from the 1990s seemed rather more extracted, tannic, tight and woody—not only RWT with its new French oak, but also St Henri, which sometimes seemed to lack the very qualities that most seduced me in other years (though I still fell head over heels for the 1991 and the 1998). The integrity and purity of the fruit seem to shine most brightly in the most recent vintages, and the handling in the winery seems even more respectful and skilful. The wines have lost nothing in richness, but now have an elegance, smoothness and succulence to match. At every level the difference can be dramatic, but the upturn was most obvious for me in the following wines: Kalimna Bin 28 2000 and 2001; Bin 128 2005 and 2006; Bin 138 2004 and 2005; Bin 389 2001 and 2005; Bin 407 2004 and 2005; Bin 707 2004 and 2005; Magill Estate 2001, 2002 and 2004; and RWT 2002, 2004 and 2005. The 2004 Kalimna Block 42 and 2004 Grange were as special as anything we tasted all week and will be among the all-time greats.

As for the whites, I've discussed these elsewhere, but to reinforce the point, I think that these are going in exactly the right direction in terms of greater definition and tension.

What were the standout vertical tastings?

Grange. No surprise here. It was of course a particular pleasure and privilege to be part of the largest tasting ever held of Australia's most famous wine, and in such a setting too (even for somebody who barely knows the bat from the ball, the Adelaide Oval added to the sense of occasion). It was clear from the first two wines, the 1952 and 1953, onwards that its awesome reputation is richly deserved. Quite apart from the historic interest of tasting the earliest commercial releases, and that the wines had to be made in secret, it was fascinating to follow the stylistic ups and downs and the vintage variation of 54 wines over six decades. And yet, for all that, the impression of a unique individual remains, just as we all go through different life stages and mood swings with our essential personality still intact and recognisable. The best wines (for me the 1952, 1962, 1963, 1966, 1981, 1982, 1983, 1992, 1996, 1998 and 2004) were as miraculously and profoundly thrilling as any in the world.

St Henri. This was for me the most exciting flight after Grange with almost as many showing the added dimension of great wine (the 1956, 1958, 1959, 1962, 1966, 1976, 1983, 1991, 1998 and 2005). I loved the elegance, finesse, poise and silken refinement of these, and the effortless, naturally expressive, unforced quality. As with the Barolos, Barbarescos and Brunellos that are generally more to my taste, it seems as though the larger, older wood lets the fruit relax and sing with a clear, strong voice. These wines are well known to connoisseurs, of course, but still hugely undervalued by most.

Bin 707. I found this flight (and the RWT) heavier going than the St Henri, but it was still very interesting to taste a range spanning 40 years. Moreover, it began with a lovely, mature wine from my own vintage (1964), and the quality of the top wines was still extremely high: the 1996 is supremely stylish. About a decade ago I remember Michael Broadbent writing in *Decanter* that he thought it had the better of the '96 Lafite, and I'd be surprised if it's been overtaken since. Splendid stuff.

Cellar Reserve/Special Bins. These best demonstrated the endlessly innovative side of Penfolds. There were some pleasant surprises here—like the pinot noirs and the sangioveses—while the best wines, such as the 2005 Cellar Reserve Coonawarra Cabernet/Kalimna Shiraz and the 2004 Kalimna Block 42 Cabernet Sauvignon, were superlative.

Yattarna. Although there were several very enjoyable and interesting flights among the whites, I thought that this was the most exciting for the progress made in recent vintages and for the promise it showed for the future.

How do you think Penfolds stands in the wine industry?

Early on, Max Schubert and John Davoren were clearly ahead of their time and hugely influential in changing the course of Australian wine history, while the advances on the technical side by Ray Beckwith transformed the prospects for the new wine styles. Subsequent chief winemakers have continued to set a high standard for others to follow.

In a global context, Penfolds clearly helped to establish Australian wine as a staple worldwide, to the point where Australian wine now accounts for the biggest share of retail sales in the United Kingdom, more than any other country of origin. By contrast, in some European restaurants Penfolds is often the only flag-waver. At a good Swiss restaurant recently, lunching with colleagues from the Grand Jury Européen, including a Bordeaux chateau owner and a French world champion sommelier, we drank well: 1994 Laville Haut-Brion Blanc, 1997 Lafon Meursault Clos de la Barre, 1982 Pichon-Longueville Baron, 1990 Beauséjour Duffau-Lagarrosse—and 1982 Grange, the only Australian wine on the list, though present in several vintages. We all agreed it was magnificent and as splendid as any of the rest.

Equally importantly, Penfolds is a salutary reminder that the basis of production varies very widely and that it is possible for large companies to make superb wines that rank alongside any in the world. Old World producers with half an acre here and half an acre there, one barrel of this and one of that, often with incomprehensible, unpronounceable names, have no monopoly on personality or quality. More than ever before, Penfolds seems to be making Peter Gago's dream of 'the world's largest boutique winery' a reality.

What have you learned from the Rewards of Patience tasting experience?

Not a new lesson, but a forceful reminder of an old one, was the extent to which bottles and tastes vary. I discovered that the Chinaman and the Scotsman seemed to share similar tastes, though that made it all the more convincing when we all recognised some wines as outstanding. It was also highly instructive for me to taste with Andrew Caillard, James Halliday, Huon Hooke and Campbell Mattinson who were able to comment on the evolution and typicity of some of the wines that I was tasting for the first time, and equally revealing to hear the winemakers tell the story behind the wines: I didn't know, for example, that Bin 138 is the only wine that is assembled shortly before bottling, the rest being blended earlier, in what Peter Gago called a 'no guts, no glory' approach. Overall, I also learned that the quality of many of the wines is higher, and the range even wider, than I had realised, and that the stereotypical terms in which too many Brits and Europeans still think of Australian wines are often way wide of the mark.

Any other comments?

For its quality as well as for its stylistic variety, this was as impressive as any one producer's tasting I've ever attended, and I felt very privileged to be part of it. In Adelaide, with past and present winemakers tasting alongside us, it felt like the wine equivalent of seeing all Shakespeare's plays performed by the Royal Shakespeare Company in Stratford-upon-Avon on consecutive nights with the playwright in the front row.

I admired the bravery and honesty of these tastings where, for the sake of completeness and fuller understanding, Peter Gago and his team showed the ruined palaces as well as the cloud-capped towers. I also appreciated greatly the cheery efficiency of the entire Penfolds support staff who created and sustained an atmosphere in which we could taste properly and in the right spirit. You know you're with producers who are real wine lovers when they also serve wines that are not their own, partly to make a fair point, and partly for the sheer shared pleasure of them. At the final dinner we were treated to 1970 Latour, 1982 Latour and 1982 Mouton Rothschild—all irresistible, yet none more sublime than the 1962 Bin 60A Cabernet/ Shiraz served alongside them.

CH'NG POH TIONG, SINGAPORE

Ch'ng Poh Tiong is a lawyer by training. He is publisher of *The Wine Review*, the oldest wine publication in South-East Asia. Ch'ng also publishes the world's first *Guide to Bordeaux* in Chinese and the annual *Asian Sommelier Guide*, which contains the 'Aussie Rules' supplement. His articles and columns appear in other magazines, including *Sommelier India*, *Noblesse* (China Edition), *Decanter* (UK) and *Lianhe Zaobao*, Singapore's largest-circulation Chinese daily.

Ch'ng Poh Tiong is a Regional Chairman, for *Decanter*'s World Wine Awards and founder of Sommelier Seminars, the *Lianhe Zaobao Wine Review* Annual Wine Challenge, Singapore's first independent wine competition, and the International Congress of Chinese Cuisine and Wine.

Ch'ng is one of the most skilled, authoritative and influential English and Chinese language wine writers in Asia. As a publisher, he is a pioneering force in fine wine criticism and journalism for the growing South-East Asian and Chinese wine markets.

Based in Singapore, Ch'ng travels the length and breadth of the world, regularly reporting insightful stories, anecdotes and tasting notes with a rare and articulate wit and charm. He is an important figure and observer in the emerging Asian wine markets. He is a popular and forthright speaker at international seminars, especially for his philosophical essays on fine wine and interpretation of market sentiment and opportunities in Asia. Ch'ng Poh Tiong is well versed in the vintages and history of Penfolds and has regularly travelled to South Australia over the last twenty years. This is the second time he has been a Rewards of Patience panellist.

What were your top five wines of the tasting?
1. Grange 2002
2. Grange 1998
3. RWT Barossa Valley Shiraz 2001
4. St Henri 2003
5. Bin 389 Cabernet Shiraz 1986

Were there any surprises?
Bin 128 Coonawarra Shiraz 1986: this was, for me, very 'Medoc' in spite of the fact it is a shiraz. Then again, maybe because it is from Coonawarra (and most likely

of a cool-ish vintage), the aroma and palate profile are so cabernet sauvignon-like: capsicum/herbaceous/cedary/spicy and incredibly fresh and lively.

Describe the evolution of winemaking philosophy and style across both white and red wines.

I don't personally like to use the expression 'style' to describe wine, as it connotes, for me, something forcefully imposed by a person/s over a wine. Nevertheless, I accept that the human equation is crucial to growing grapes and making wine, from fundamental decisions such as where to plant to how long to macerate, whether to pigeage or pump over. As a broad statement, it seems to me that Penfolds is very concerned that its wines have continuity from the past into the present. And future. The winery, no doubt, also makes experiments and takes into account market trends, but the fact that it puts on the Rewards of Patience tastings and, more importantly, invites former winemakers to the tasting, demonstrates very clearly an ongoing effort to learn and benefit from the past even as it takes advantage of modern know-how, whether this be in the vineyard, winery or cellar. In the case of white wine, I see (and taste) a desire to produce wines that are more balanced between freshness and fruit, rather than making fruit the dominant sensual experience. As for the reds, rather than merely making big, blockbuster wines, I also taste great strides in producing wines with fuller phenolic ripeness, layered wines with more nuanced fruit and flavours.

What were the standout vertical tastings?

Other judges are more competent to speak about this point as they are more familiar with Australian wine generally, and Penfolds wine in particular. I do not, however, want to avoid the question but instead, wish to approach it differently. The thing that stands out for me in Penfolds' winemaking is its philosophy of producing the best possible wine from fruit sourced from different vineyards, even several regions. This is, of course, very different from the concept of single-vineyard wines. It is easier to make comparisons between different vintages of the same source of fruit, that one same piece of ground. Penfolds' philosophy (except for Magill Estate and Block 42) is akin to that of Champagne, where the concept of creating the best possible blend or cuvée is the goal. Krug, for example, with its flagship Champagne Grande Cuvée sourced from as many as 20–25 vineyards (and as many as 6–10 vintages). Both approaches, namely producing wines from single vineyards and from blending the fruit of different vineyards, have their merits and the wine world is richer for them.

How do you think Penfolds stands in the wine industry?

Penfolds, from the time of the original good doctor who inspired the wines, to the big company that now keeps the flag flying, is living proof of what can be achieved when you bring together devoted viticulturists and impassioned winemakers. The story—now part of wine lore and legend—of Max Schubert surreptitiously laying the foundation of what was to become Australia's defining star on the world stage and in wine culture, is the stuff of story books. It continues to inspire all of us, whether winemaker or wine writer, to have a vision.

What have you learned from the Rewards of Patience tasting experience?

That the best wines speak of their site/s, varietal/s, characteristics, personality as a blend, winemaker's aspirations, ageing potential and evolution from the exuberance of innocent youth into mature masterpieces.

Any other comments?

Bin 389 Cabernet Shiraz 1996, an eleven-year-old red, provided a very instructive eye-opener. Tasting the same wine blind, one sealed by a cork and the other held down by a screw cap, the latter wine was so much more fruit-alive and vivacious, relative to the other sealed by a cork, which was considerably more cedary and with drier tannins. This may have been just one example (and it may be that the cork was 'raw') but the screw cap wine was much more convincing and delicious. It was also interesting that even though less exposed to screw cap wines, most of the non-Australian judges guessed it right, over our Australian counterparts who are normally more exposed to such wines.

JOSHUA GREENE, USA

Editor and Publisher of the influential New York based *Wine & Spirits* magazine since 1986, Joshua Greene first began drinking wine with meals during a summer in Galicia, Spain, at age thirteen. Later, he worked in wine shops in western Massachusetts and spent a summer as the wine captain for Wheatleigh, a small inn in Lenox. After graduating from Princeton University in 1981, Greene pursued a career in magazines, starting in management of special-interest publications. His involvement with *Wine & Spirits* began on a consulting basis and eventually led to his purchase of the magazine in 1989.

In addition to his duties as editor and publisher, Greene serves as the wine critic for wines of California, Bordeaux, Burgundy, Champagne, Northern Italy, Portugal, Rioja, Australia, New Zealand and South Africa.

Greene has forged an impressive wine media career. He is a highly regarded international wine critic with a reputation for fair, independent and insightful opinion. His writing is thoughtful, constructive and expressive. His authoritative and philosophical voice is underscored by an eye for detail, wide tasting experience and worldwide perspective. The personalities and drama of the fine wine world are often interwoven in his commentary giving a rare, intuitive and often colourful perspective.

As both publisher and critic Greene is a popular speaker at wine forums and an occasional wine judge. He is widely travelled and regularly visits the numerous wine regions that fall within his bailiwick.

What were your top five wines of the tasting?

The 1953 Bin 9 Grange Cabernet. What a treat to taste this wine. Nothing less than astonishing. It manages to combine the aristocratic structure of great cabernet with a cheerful Barossa sweetness. I didn't want to taste anything after it. But as it turned out the entire flight of cabernets from Block 42 was a highlight of the week. The 1963 Bin 64 JWT still tastes of fresh damson plum; it seemed impossible that this wine could be 44 years old. The only thing mature about it was the texture: satin soft. It was one of the youngest old wines I've ever tasted. The 1996 Kalimna Block 42 hasn't begun to approach maturity: still Barossa muscle, taut blackcurrant fruit and complex notes of new oak. This and the 2004 are both 50-year wines. We tasted the 2004 twice during the week and it showed beautifully both times, vibrant and glorious cabernet, First Growth quality with a completely distinctive character. Like no other cabernet in Australia, or anywhere else.

The 1955 Grange, a wine that hinted at the tailored Penfolds style to come, is the kind of wine I'd like to spend a day and evening with as it evolves with air. Everything you could hope for in a mature shiraz, plus a lot more elegance that you might expect.

The 1971 St Henri, a pretty dramatic wine, particularly following the lovely maturity of several of the St Henri vintages of the 1960s—the heady and generous 1963 and the dark, sunny and beautifully preserved 1964. The 1971 has not yet reached its plateau, still driven by deep scents of shiraz, bold and expressive. Not a powerhouse, not buffed up by new oak, this has a natural firmness and the seamless weave of a great Penfolds wine.

The 1998 RWT, perhaps not as great as the 2004, but it's kind of a shocker how young and lithe this feels. It's a dark, muscular, powerful wine still surrounded by puppy fat. There's nothing ponderous or chocolaty about it, just the taste of the grape from great vines. Energised.

Were there any surprises?

1996 Bin 707, from a lovely cabernet year, though not at the level of the 1996 Block 42, this wine's blackcurrant flavour seems to have light shining through it. The silken texture and long fruit flavours hit the mark.

1996 Koonunga Hill, a wine that seemed to bring together a lot of the work of John Duval and his team in the 1990s, modern in the depth of its fruit and the power of its aroma—a spectrum of ripe fruit from red to black. It far outperformed its place in the Penfolds' hierarchy.

1991 Bin 389, an explosively fruity wine, remarkably young, fresh and bright. It has the depth of cabernet flavour and dimension from spicy shiraz, the two varieties moving in and out of the shadows in the blend.

2002 Bin 407, for its spot-on blackcurrant fruit character, the pure, bright berry scent, a generous wine with some tension to it; again, performing far beyond its place in the Penfolds line-up.

2004s in general, and the consistency through 2006.

Describe the evolution of winemaking philosophy and style across both white and red wines.

It would be hard to separate the winemaking philosophy at Penfolds from the corporate structure that has provided its sustenance. As a private company in the 1940s and '50s, there was enough support for the idiosyncratic winemaking Max Schubert brought to the table and enough backing for the scientific research of Ray Beckwith, that the two seem to have come together in a pragmatic form of creativity.

What were the standout vertical tastings?

Block 42. As noted above, these wines were all among the best of the tasting in my book. And I don't think of Barossa first and foremost for cabernet.

Grange. A chance of a lifetime to taste the complete range of one of the world's great red wines—within sight of where many of the vintages were grown and made.

St Henri. Truly the sleeper in the Penfolds line-up, a wine that shows its stamina with age.

How do you think Penfolds stands in the wine industry?

It's easier to describe what distinguishes Penfolds than what contribution the firm has made, as the concept of a winemaking team is employed here more effectively than at most other large wine producers. Certainly, the work that members of that team have undertaken over the years, such as Beckwith's work with monitoring pH or Schubert's work with old-vine shiraz matured in new oak, have both had an indelible influence on the quality of New World winemaking.

It was a window into the early days of table wines at Penfolds, the development of one of world's great winemaking teams. Remarkably, the legacy of those early wines is still intact and still has a strong influence on the Penfolds' team today. The best of the modern Penfolds wines have impeccable tailoring—more Savile Row than R.M. Williams. Schubert made seamless wines and set the standard for this masterful blending the team engages in today.

Any other comments?

Aside from the wines, the memory that stays with me was of lunch at Kalimna with Ray Beckwith. Neil Beckett and I were intent on getting him talking, a challenge since he can't hear particularly well. But once he got going, he could spin a yarn in all directions. 'Leslie Penfold Hyland drove a Hispano-Suiza from Murray Bridge to Nuriootpa every Monday,' he recalled. 'His son Jeffrey and he had some conflicts. At one point, Jeffrey told his father what to do with the chimney on top of the winery. His father sent him down to McLaren Vale.' He spoke with a scientist's candour about the challenges that winemakers faced in the 1940s and '50s, and with youthful enthusiasm about the flor sherries he'd made. There was something of the competitive schoolboy in him when he described an annual Penfolds company tasting and the results. 'This time it was at Griffith,' he said. 'Max used to produce the Amontillado and Montillo. I used to make the Royal Reserve and Golden Sherry.' In the end, they were all lined up and ranked: 'The Royal, number one. Golden, number two. Then three and four, Amontillado and Montillo. Max was not amused. The wines we were making [Royal and Golden] had an easy appeal ... but it was rather funny.' Don Ditter and John Bird were also part of the team with Schubert and tasting with them was a highlight of the proceedings. But talking with Beckwith—at 95, still energetic, articulate, a gentleman of the old school—there was a little bit of magic in that.

JAMES HALLIDAY, AUSTRALIA

James Halliday is Australia's most influential wine critic and wine writer and has written or contributed to more than 50 books on wine. He is the founder of Coldstream Hills Winery in the Yarra Valley and an original partner of Brokenwood in the Hunter Valley. For a period of time he was Group Winemaker, Regional Wines, for Southcorp.

Halliday is also a highly respected Australian Wine Show judge and chairman with over 30 years' experience.

Originally a lawyer, James Halliday has played an important role in the development of the Australian wine industry as observer, winemaker and participant in various industry initiatives. In 1995 he was the recipient of the Maurice O'Shea Award for Outstanding Contribution to the Australian Wine Industry. Previous winners have included Max Schubert, Len Evans and Ray Beckwith. Halliday has won numerous awards for his books. Many titles have been translated into foreign languages, including French, German, Japanese and Danish. He has also contributed to Jancis Robinson's *Oxford Companion to Wine* and the *Larousse Encyclopedia of Wine*.

James Halliday is Australia's best-travelled wine writer and a regular participant in international wine forums and wine shows. His sheer body of work is remarkable. With such a wealth of wine experience, James Halliday is Australia's unchallenged international wine authority. He continues to write a weekly column for *The Australian* newspaper. His *Australian Wine Companion* is the most successful annual wine book with a circulation of over 45,000 copies. In 2006 James Halliday was the recipient of the New South Wales Wine Press Club's Wine Communicator of the Year Award. Halliday has participated in four Penfolds Rewards of Patience tastings.

What were your top five wines of the tasting?

There seems no point in doing anything other than playing a straight bat to this question, however predictable the answer may be. The top of the list for me was the 1952 Grange, still a gloriously vibrant satin and velvet brocade with amazing length and harmony. Well-corked and cellared bottles will still give pleasure as the wine approaches 100 years of age. I place 1962 Bin 60A at the same level, a glorious freak of nature and man, ethereal and beguiling with a virtually endless palate. The 1953 Grange Bin 9 Cabernet Sauvignon (from the then 70-year-old vines on the Kalimna Block) is always a luminous example of what might have been had there been sufficient quantities of cabernet sauvignon to allow Max Schubert to more closely model Grange on the great classic vintages of Bordeaux he tasted a few years earlier. A wine of exquisite quality and, of course, great rarity.

In what I might term the 'modern era', any number of wines jostle for recognition. My choice ultimately falls on 1990 Bin 920 (although 1990 Bin 90A would have been an equally valid choice) because the wine is still in its infancy, with amazingly intense cassis and blackcurrant fruit with the promise of evolving serenely over another three decades at least.

Finally, 2004 Yattarna Chardonnay puts beyond doubt the proposition that Penfolds is not just a red winemaker and that Yattarna is now achieving the destiny sought for it when then Managing Director Ross Wilson gave the winemaking team carte blanche to come up with a white wine to sit alongside Grange.

Were there any surprises?

Absolutely. First and foremost, the exceptional quality and varietal character of the '04, '05 and '06 Cellar Reserve Sangiovese. These take this somewhat problematic variety to another level, appropriate given the direct input of Stefano di Blasi from Antinori. Next, I have to confess to being slow in recognising the vast strides made with the Hyland Chardonnay, and even during the Rewards of Patience tastings, not entirely giving the 2006 recognition that it deserves, and which was subsequently given at the National Wine Show.

The other surprise was the comparative tasting of the 1996 Bin 389 under cork and screw cap, which showed no statistically meaningful preference for one closure over the other, an outcome which I subsequently learnt had been the same for the senior Penfolds winemakers when doing the same tasting a few weeks earlier. The proponents of cork will argue that this proves cork is every bit as good as a screw cap in conserving fruit and style quality, while the proponents of screw caps will argue it shows that red wines under screw cap do develop over a ten-year period in a very similar fashion to that of cork. The fallacy, or the hidden agenda, is that the cork-closed bottles were deliberately selected as the best of a number opened at the same time, whereas all the screw-capped bottles were and are identical to each other. Bystanders will read the entrails as they wish.

Describe the evolution of winemaking philosophy and style across both white and red wines.

This barely arises with the white wines. Until the Yattarna challenge, the Penfolds-branded white wines were few and far between, the only one of ancient historical importance being Penfolds Trameah, a traminer from the western outskirts of Sydney. Through an *ex post facto* merging of brands during the 1990s, Penfolds inherited a veteran white winemaking team famous for making Eden Valley and Clare Valley riesling. The real development has been with Yattarna and Reserve Bin A Chardonnay where, over a period of ten years, the style has been consistently refined, with less oak and more subtle winemaker thumbprints. The introduction of the screw cap has also enormously aided the cause of these wines and their future development.

It is with the red wines that one sees more changes, although direct comparison of the Granges of the 1950s and '60s versus those of the 1990s and 2000s has obvious inherent problems. It is possible to say (without resort to chemical analysis, source vineyard blocks, yeasts and so forth) that in the glass there is an apparent evolution of style.

It may seem like wish fulfilment or a motherhood statement to say there has been no fundamental change in philosophy in the making of the bin wines up to the Special Bins and Icon wines. Nonetheless, I firmly and fundamentally believe this is the case. While greater quantities of some of the wines are made now, the architecture of the Penfolds red wines has been altered by adding to the base, rather than brand or large volume extension at the top. Thus, first Koonunga Hill, then Rawson's Retreat, then Thomas Hyland have been put in at the bottom, and the only high-quality wine added at the top of the pyramid has been RWT. (Magill Estate may seem an exception, but there was, for example, a Magill Estate Burgundy in 1956.) Moreover, the winemakers have always been allowed to make the decisions on the amount of wine available for any one bin label in any one vintage. Quantities have not been dictated by the marketing department nor the financial controllers, however much they might have wished to do so. There is a fierce commitment by the red winemakers to the bin wines and above, and the process of grading the innumerable parcels of wine, which are kept separate until a final call on blending is made, follows the same criteria and processes of the best small wineries.

What were the standout vertical tastings?

It is impossible not to single out Grange as by far the most inspiring vertical tasting, showing as it does the extraordinary ability these wines have to age, and a brand style every bit as consistent as that of a First Growth Bordeaux producer.

The other vertical of particular interest was that of the Bin 389, here for a number of reasons. First, it is the most important cabernet–shiraz blend made in Australia, a blend which may not be as unique to Australia as some have thought (witness the widespread use of wine from the Hill of Hermitage in the Rhône Valley with the great Bordeaux of the mid-nineteenth century), but is nonetheless a quint-essential Australian wine. Second, I found outstanding wines in every decade: 1961, 1966, 1971, 1986, 1988, 1990, 1991, 1996, 1998, 1999, 2001, 2002, 2004 and 2005. The greater number of outstanding wines since 1990 may in part be due to the fact that there has been an above-average number of excellent vintages, and in part to the fact that corks have not yet had a chance to significantly interfere with the wine, but it's hard to imagine that the wines of bygone vintages were better at an equivalent age to the best from the 1990s and onwards.

How do you think Penfolds stands in the wine industry?

This is something of a Dorothy Dix question; quite simply, there is no other Australian red winemaker (or red and white maker, for that matter), which can come close to the contribution of Penfolds and its wines. Grange and the Special Bins have been recog-nised in all corners of the globe as wines of supreme quality, variously listed as wines you must drink before you die, or in the top ten of the decade, the top ten of the year and so on and so forth. The one curiosity is that, outside of Grange, Penfolds is signifi-cantly under-represented in the restaurant lists of Australia. There are many reasons for this, and it is not relevant to go into them here. The fact remains, however.

What have you learned from the Rewards of Patience tasting experience?

As ever, one of the major lessons has been the frailty of corks as a closure. The mul-tiplicity of bottles opened to find one considered representative continues, even with some Penfolds clinic-screening in some instances. I have previously commented that in the earlier Rewards of Patience tastings I was concerned about the apparent inconsistency in my notes from one tasting to the next of a given wine. It may be there is some human error, for none of us are perfect, but I think a major factor in the inconsistencies has been the performance of the cork.

The other interesting aspect is to look back over the many years of the tastings, and see the outer limit of the drinking span of the wines, and finding that these are constantly exceeded, sometimes dramatically. This underlines the inherent quality of the majority of these wines, which have the ability to continue on a plateau of peak enjoyment for decades rather than years.

> 'It is impossible not to single out Grange as by far the most inspiring vertical tasting, showing as it does the extraordinary ability these wines have to age, and a brand style every bit as consistent as that of a First Growth Bordeaux producer.'
>
> —JAMES HALLIDAY, PANELLIST

HUON HOOKE, AUSTRALIA

Huon Hooke is one of Australia's leading and most popular independent wine writers, with a reputation for incisive, impartial and fair wine criticism and journalism. In 2008 he was the recipient of Wine Communicators of Australia's Wine Communicator of the Year Award for his outstanding contribution to the field of wine criticism.

Based in Sydney, Hooke makes his living entirely out of writing, judging and educating about wine. A journalist first and wine professional second, he has tertiary qualifications in both fields. He is a Roseworthy graduate in wine marketing and has been writing about wine for 25 years.

Huon Hooke is the regular wine correspondent for the *Sydney Morning Herald*. He also contributes to international wine magazines, including *Decanter* (UK), *The World of Fine Wine* magazine (UK), Tom Stevenson's annual *Wine Report* and *Slow Food Guide to Wines of the World* (Italy). He is the Contributing Editor of *Gourmet Traveller Wine* magazine and has published fifteen books, including *The Penguin Good Australian Wine Guide*, *Words on Wine* and *Max Schubert—Winemaker* (1994), a biography of the creator of Penfold's Grange.

Huon Hooke—a veteran of four Penfolds Rewards of Patience tastings—is widely travelled throughout the world of fine wine, and a regular speaker and guest wine show judge at international forums and wine shows. He is a distinguished Australian wine show judge with over twenty years' experience and is an eminent voice within the Australian wine community.

What were your top five wines of the tasting?

1. 1953 and 1963 Granges, the two most mesmerising wines of the tasting.
2. 1962 Bin 60A, 1990 Bin 90A and 2004 Bin 60A—country cousins separated by 28 years and fourteen years respectively, and all extraordinary.
3. 1990 and 1991 Bin 389s, an inseparable pair, both superb wines at their peak but with a lot of living still to do.
4. 2005 Yattarna Chardonnay—the best yet: the epitome of finesse.
5. 2005 Cellar Reserve Barossa Cabernet Sauvignon—an exciting and rare wine.

Were there any surprises?

The improvements in the pinot noirs, the high quality of the sangioveses, the way the Bin 138 GSMs had aged so well. The ongoing, perennial good value of Bin 389.

The 2005s and 2006s looked especially smart—lots to look forward to!

The refinement of RWT: the 2004, 2005 and 2006 are streets ahead of the earliest vintages.

St Henri has had its ups and downs, with only the top vintages really impressing and perhaps it has been starved of good fruit, because renewed effort showed in the 2004 and 2005, which showed a new level of depth and sophistication.

Bin 128 has also jumped into a higher gear with the 2004, 2005 and 2006. Most impressive.

Describe the evolution of winemaking philosophy and style across both white and red wines.

A few generalisations first: all the reds went through a lesser period during the 1970s and into the early '80s, as did most Australian wines, due to rapid growth in the market and a shortage of good grapes. The best wines of the 1950s and '60s were probably not rivalled in the 1970s and '80s (except for a few rare stand-out vintages like 1971 and 1986) but from the 1990s onwards, things are in very good order.

Penfolds' red wines conform to a very marked vintage pattern: in the best years, all the wines go up to a higher level. In these vintages—such as 1986, 1990, 1991, 1996 and 1998—the modestly priced reds become tremendous value buys.

The reds have become more polished, with softer tannins, rounded structures and higher alcohols—especially in the last decade or so—making them more voluptuous and better drinking earlier. Oak is more likely to be unobtrusive; it's not necessarily a simple matter of French being substituted for American in some places, but also a better quality of American oak being used. Bin 707 is notable for being a bit old-fashioned: American oak in cabernet is very unusual these days. It has, however, improved in style where the fruit and oak are better balanced.

With Grange, the style evolution parallels the Penfolds evolution, and the wines are less formidable when young. Their optimum drinking windows have widened as a result. Grange is softer, rounder, more opulent and friendly. In the young Grange, jarring American oak is less likely to stand out and tannins are less likely to be astringent as they sometimes were in the past. But perhaps the only question mark is whether the Granges and other Penfolds reds with 14.5 per cent alcohol will mature as gracefully, retaining their balance and turning out to be such lovely mature drinks as the best wines of the 1950s and '60s, when alcohols were significantly lower.

In whites: chardonnay has obviously become more refined and subtle. Oak has been progressively downplayed, there is less overt new oak, and the wines have finesse and age-worthiness. Even at the lower end, Penfolds chardonnay is much improved and is excellent value.

Less obvious changes are apparent in riesling but while many wines are superbly delicate in youth, their acidities are softer and they are less likely to be harsh or sharply astringent in their youth. Screw caps are having a very positive effect, but so is the increased attention to careful acid correction where it's needed, and gentler extraction of juices leading to softer, more seamless palates.

What were the standout vertical tastings?

Grange, because of the sheer quality and consistently high standard of the wines. Bin 389, for similar reasons: it's a very reliable wine that is still in the affordable price league. Bin 28, because it is always a good drink at a fair price, and Bin 138 GSM, again for value for money, consistency and a surprising ability to age.

How do you think Penfolds stands in the wine industry?

Penfolds has a reputation for ignoring fashion, no better example than refusing to pick under-ripe grapes during the late 1970s when many others fell into that trap. Penfolds has largely rowed its own canoe, sticking doggedly to such practices as blending across vineyards and regions to achieve consistency of style, using American oak, adding tannins, barrel fermenting and using oxidative practices. Its wines taste more and more distinctive as a result … more Penfolds-like. This is no bad thing. In some ways Penfolds is missing out on the terroir fad, the regionality craze, but there is more than one way to make interesting wine and it will always be thus. As the wine market becomes increasingly crowded, and more and more wines taste same-ish, distinctiveness will be rarer and distinctive wines more prized. Penfolds stands to profit by its individuality.

What have you learned from the Rewards of Patience tasting experience?

Penfolds continues to develop and grow in stature: nearly every wine showed some improvement over recent vintages. The white wine portfolio continues to expand, and thoughtful, if subtle, improvements continue to be made. Penfolds is certainly not standing still.

The perspectives of international tasters are often different from an Australian's, which is why their input is so important in this kind of tasting. It often caused me to question what I consider to be desirable in wine and even to question some of my assumptions about quality. This makes for a stimulating tasting.

Any other comments?

Nothing lasts forever, not even Penfolds red wines! This tasting showed that some of the earlier vintages of several styles are getting on and have seen better days, reminding us that it's always better to drink a wine a bit too young than too old. This is the purpose of this book: to help wine lovers enjoy wine at its best and hopefully prevent us keeping wine too long. 'Rejoice in the freshness of youth or the splendour of maturity, but do not await decrepitude!'

CAMPBELL MATTINSON, AUSTRALIA

Campbell Mattinson is the publisher and contributing editor of *The Wine Front* (www.winefront.com.au) a respected and engaging wine newsletter written with unusual passion and energy. His easy-going style, courageous opinion and enthusiasm have captivated a new generation of fine-wine drinkers, the Australian wine industry and wine media colleagues. His unstuffy, refreshing and joyful approach to wine has brought him a remarkable swag of plaudits and accolades. Mattinson is a writer of considerable breadth. He won the Australian Sports Writing Award in 1996 and since 1999 his fictional short stories have appeared in many publications, including the annual anthology *Best Australian Short Stories*.

Campbell Mattinson is a regular contributor to *Australian Gourmet Traveller Wine* magazine and other publications. He won the Independent Young Writer of the Year Award in 1995, and was the winner of the NSW Wine Press Club Wine Communicator Award in both 2004 and 2006. Mattinson is a prolific wine author. In 2006 he released the book *Wine Hunter: The Man Who Changed Australian Wine*, a biography of the Hunter Valley winemaking legend Maurice O'Shea. In 2007 he published the highly personal and provocatively titled book *Why The French Hate Us: The Real Story of Australian Wine* and in 2008 released Australia's only guide specifically devoted to red wines, the *Big Red Wine Book*. Mattinson has burst onto the Australian wine scene with considerable flair. This is his first Penfolds Rewards of Patience tasting.

What were your top five wines of the tasting?
1. 1996 Bin 389
2. 1964 Bin 28
3. 2005 RWT
4. 2005 Bin 389
5. 1996 Grange

Were there any real surprises?
I was surprised at just how good the wines of 2004 onwards looked. I expected to love St Henri, but ended up enjoying the Bin 389, Bin 28 and Grange flights the most; I walked away thinking Bin 389 is a great wine to have in the cellar.

Having tasted almost every important Penfolds wine, can you comment on the evolution of winemaking philosophy and style across both white and red wines?

Notwithstanding a number of lacklustre vintages from the 1970s, winemaking philosophy seemed consistent across most decades. The recent years, particularly post-2000, are very sophisticated, reflecting a more intuitive application of French and American oak. There were times when it was difficult to work out the character and identity of the oak. I thought a few of the recent bins had seen French oak—when they hadn't. Clearly there's American oak and there's Penfolds American oak. The latter is better quality than it once was. Overall, the Penfolds wines of the 1950s and '60s are balanced and, as old wines, ethereal; the wines of the 1970s a little murkier and less interesting; the wines of the 1980s and '90s strong, robust, textural and seductive; the wines of the last few years fresher, classier—perhaps modern versions of the wines of the early 1960s.

What were the standout verticals and why?

Grange was the standout vertical. As an old wine it can be tender and silken, haunting and kaleidoscopic. The emperor has lots of fine clothes. Bin 389 was very strong. I actually preferred this to the Bin 707 vertical.

Can you comment on the contribution and wines of Penfolds in the context of both the Australian and global wine industries?

Many wine producers, both in Australia and around the world, would ache for the balanced ripeness that Penfolds wines routinely deliver. It has shown the way for an entire category of wine. To have done this consistently and unswervingly through 50-plus years is remarkable.

What have you learned from the Rewards of Patience Tasting experience?

I was stunned at the freshness and longevity of many of the wines. There were a swag of wines that, corks permitting, seem capable of going on for decades. This was not just a lesson about Penfolds wines, but also a message on Australian reds: well-balanced wines can hold, develop and intrigue for long periods of time. I also learned that monolithic, fruit-saturated, young brutish wines—if balanced from the very start—can transform into something soft, ethereal, mesmerising and magical.

ABOUT THE AUTHOR

Andrew Caillard, MW, is a specialist wine auctioneer, co-founder of Langton's Fine Wine Auctions—Australia's leading wine auction house, and publisher of the highly influential *Langton's Classification of Australian Wine*. A recognised authority on ultra-fine Australian wine, he is the author of several *Langton's Wine Guides* and four editions of *Penfolds: The Rewards of Patience*. Caillard is also a regular columnist and tasting panellist for Australia's top wine collector's magazine *Gourmet Traveller Wine*. He is widely travelled and regularly visits Australian, New Zealand and European wine regions.

Caillard's career is inextricably linked to the development of the secondary ultra-fine wine market for Australian wine. Much of the research, analysis, communication and auction sales generated by Langton's have provided valuable data and information to fine-wine buyers, the wine trade, wine producers, the wine media and the Australian wine industry's various agencies. Langton's interactive internet auction format—www.langtons.com.au —provides instant access to a wide range of information on ultra-fine Australian wine, including historic auction price data back to 1987, vintage reports, tasting notes and secondary market reports. It is one of Australia's most frequented wine internet sites. The influential *Langton's Classification of Australian Wine*—which is headed up by Penfolds Grange—is regarded as an unofficial honour roll of Australia's finest wines. It has achieved an extraordinary worldwide profile over the last ten years.

Andrew Caillard has strong links with the Australian wine industry. His great (x4) grandfather was John Reynell who brought some of the first grape vines to South Australia. English-born and educated, he began his career in wine in Bordeaux, Germany and the United Kingdom. He is a Roseworthy graduate in wine marketing (1984) and a Master of Wine (1993). In 1993 he was recipient of the Madame Bollinger Foundation Medal for excellence in wine tasting. He is also the Chair of the Institute of Master of Wine (Australasia), a member of the Australian Wine Industry's 'Wine Australia's—Directions to 2025' Taskforce, an occasional freelance writer/critic to both Australian and United Kingdom publications, consultant wine expert, charity auctioneer and a landscape painter! Caillard lives in Sydney and is married with three sons.

His painting of Penfolds' Kalimna Block 42 Barossa Valley vineyard appears on the special edition cover of this book.

PENFOLDS ADDRESSES
AND CONTACT DETAILS

Penfolds Magill Estate Winery and Restaurant
78 Penfold Road, Magill SA 5073
Cellar Door telephone +61 (0)8 8301 5569
Restaurant telephone +61 (0)8 8301 5551

Penfolds Barossa Valley Winery
Tanunda Road, Nuriootpa SA 5355
Cellar Door telephone +61 (0)8 8565 9408

Penfolds Consumer Relations
Australia 1300 651 650
New Zealand 0800 651 650
United States 1800 255 9966
United Kingdom 020 8843 8400